CW01302116

LIBERALISM AS IDEOLOGY

Photograph by Keiko Ikeuchi

Liberalism as Ideology

Essays in Honour of Michael Freeden

Edited by

BEN JACKSON AND MARC STEARS

OXFORD
UNIVERSITY PRESS

OXFORD
UNIVERSITY PRESS

Great Clarendon Street, Oxford OX2 6DP

Oxford University Press is a department of the University of Oxford.
It furthers the University's objective of excellence in research, scholarship,
and education by publishing worldwide in

Oxford New York

Auckland Cape Town Dar es Salaam Hong Kong Karachi
Kuala Lumpur Madrid Melbourne Mexico City Nairobi
New Delhi Shanghai Taipei Toronto

With offices in

Argentina Austria Brazil Chile Czech Republic France Greece
Guatemala Hungary Italy Japan Poland Portugal Singapore
South Korea Switzerland Thailand Turkey Ukraine Vietnam

Oxford is a registered trade mark of Oxford University Press
in the UK and in certain other countries

Published in the United States
by Oxford University Press Inc., New York

© The several contributors, 2012

The moral rights of the author have been asserted
Database right Oxford University Press (maker)

First published 2012

All rights reserved. No part of this publication may be reproduced,
stored in a retrieval system, or transmitted, in any form or by any means,
without the prior permission in writing of Oxford University Press,
or as expressly permitted by law, or under terms agreed with the appropriate
reprographics rights organization. Enquiries concerning reproduction
outside the scope of the above should be sent to the Rights Department,
Oxford University Press, at the address above

You must not circulate this book in any other binding or cover
and you must impose the same condition on any acquirer

British Library Cataloguing in Publication Data
Data available

Library of Congress Cataloging in Publication Data
Data available

Typeset by SPI Publisher Services, Pondicherry, India
Printed in Great Britain
on acid-free paper by
MPG Books Group, Bodmin and King's Lynn

ISBN 978–0–19–960067–0

1 3 5 7 9 10 8 6 4 2

Contents

Acknowledgements	vii
List of Contributors	viii
Preface: Return of the Native	ix
David Marquand	
Introduction	1
Ben Jackson and Marc Stears	

Part I: Liberal Languages

1. A Cautious Embrace: Reflections on (Left) Liberalism and Utopia David Leopold	9
2. Socialism and the New Liberalism Ben Jackson	34
3. Liberalisms in India: A Sketch Rochana Bajpai	53
4. Liberalism and American Stories of Peoplehood Marc Stears	77
5. The Liberal Dilemma: The Economic and the Social, and the Need for a European Contextualization of a Concept with Universal Pretensions Bo Stråth	95
6. The Problem of Political Parties in Western Liberalism, 1868–1968 Paolo Pombeni	119

Part II: Ideologies and Political Theory

7. Liberalism and Analytical Political Philosophy David Weinstein	139
8. Political Ideology and Political Theory: Reflections on an Awkward Partnership Andrew Vincent	159

9. Ideology, Political Philosophy, and the Interpretive Enterprise:
   A View from the Other Side   178
   Gerald Gaus

10. Civil Society and the Reconstruction of the Public Sphere:
    Ideologies between Theory and Politics   199
    Gayil Talshir

11. In Defence of Political Understanding?   221
    Michael Kenny

12. Getting 'Real' About Political Ideas: Conceptual Morphology
    and the Realist Critique of Anglo-American Political Philosophy   241
    Mathew Humphrey

13. The Professional Responsibilities of the Political Theorist   259
    Michael Freeden

Michael Freeden: A Bibliography   278
Index   285

Acknowledgements

We have greatly enjoyed editing this work together, not least because everyone we have approached about it has wished to help the project along its way. We are very grateful to all of the contributors for the time, energy, and intellectual passion that they have invested in this book. We would also like to thank Dominic Byatt of OUP for his characteristically intelligent and generous-spirited editorial support; Abbie Jang for inspired production assistance; Lise Butler and Kit Kowol for their work on the index; Bonnie Honig, Desmond King, Lizzy Pellicano, and Zofia Stemplowska for their support and encouragement; and the Department of Politics and International Relations, the Faculty of History, Mansfield College, and University College, all of the University of Oxford, for their sponsorship of the conference in honour of Michael Freeden at which many of these chapters were first delivered. Thanks are also due to Andrew Gamble, Jose Harris, John Horton, Stuart White, and Laurence Whitehead for generously acting as chairs and discussants at that conference. We deeply regret the passing of one other contributor to the conference, Duncan Tanner, whose untimely death in 2010 was a blow to all who knew him and his scholarship. Duncan's paper on the cultural roots of the Liberal–Labour divide was a highlight of the conference, and he is greatly missed.

List of Contributors

Rochana Bajpai is Lecturer in Politics at the School of Oriental and African Studies, University of London.

Michael Freeden is Emeritus Professor of Politics at Oxford University and an Emeritus Fellow of Mansfield College.

Gerald Gaus is James E. Rogers Professor of Philosophy at Arizona University.

Mathew Humphrey is Reader in Political Philosophy at Nottingham University.

Ben Jackson is University Lecturer in Modern History at Oxford University and a Fellow of University College.

Michael Kenny is Professor of Politics at Queen Mary, University of London.

David Leopold is University Lecturer in Political Theory at Oxford University and a Fellow of Mansfield College.

David Marquand is a political writer and historian. He was Principal of Mansfield College, Oxford (1996–2002) and Professor of Politics at Sheffield University (1991–6).

Paolo Pombeni is Professor of Contemporary History at Bologna University.

Marc Stears is Professor of Political Theory at Oxford University and a Fellow of University College.

Bo Stråth is the Academy of Finland Distinguished Professor in Nordic, European, and World History at Helsinki University.

Gayil Talshir is Lecturer in Political Science at the Hebrew University of Jerusalem.

Andrew Vincent is Professor of Political Theory at Sheffield University.

David Weinstein is Professor of Political Science at Wake Forest University.

Preface: Return of the Native

David Marquand

I first met Michael Freeden at a seminar in Oxford around forty years ago, but our encounter was brief and unremarkable. Twenty years later, however, we and our respective wives all attended a marvellous conference at Trani, in the deep south of Italy, arranged by that consummate conference organizer and distinguished historian, Paolo Pombeni of the University of Bologna. The Freedens and Marquands spent a lot of time together, and parted firm friends. Four years later, I received a totally unexpected letter from Michael, telling me that the Principal of his Oxford college, Mansfield, was about to retire, and wondering if I would like to apply for the post. I did so; and to my astonishment I was elected. (Michael had been my brilliantly effective campaign manager.) Six happy years followed, during which Michael became one of my dearest friends as well as a marvellous, stimulating, and—just occasionally—obstreperous colleague. But none of this qualifies me to pronounce on his wide-ranging and path-breaking contribution to academic political theory. Instead, I shall try to describe his remarkable personal journey and speculate about its effects on his values and personality.

As this book bears witness, he is a distinguished scholar, one of the most distinguished scholars I know. It would be wrong to say that he invented the academic study of political ideology, but there is no doubt that he has transformed it from an appendage to the history of ideas into a rigorous and demanding subdiscipline in its own right. There is much more to him than that, however. He is a man of passion and fire, driven by a rare mixture of intellectual integrity and philosophical imagination. He is also a dyed-in-the-wool liberal. He has a passion for justice, in small things as well as big. Normally he is courteous and quietly spoken, but when he scents injustice he can be surprisingly belligerent. As that implies, there is nothing pale or namby-pamby about his liberalism. It is existential at least as much as intellectual: a matter of emotion and commitment rather than of dry-as-dust ratiocination—a liberalism of the heart.

And also of inheritance. Michael's parents were unobservant Jewish émigrés from Hitler's Germany (in his father's case) and Austria (in his mother's). His father came to Britain from Berlin, his mother from Vienna. Both escaped the Nazis in the nick of time in 1939, in other words after the state-sponsored German pogrom known as the *Kristallnacht*. The screws of Nazi persecution were tightening fast, and the Second World War was patently imminent.

Michael's parents met in Britain, and were married there in 1942—his father having been interned briefly in the Isle of Man as an 'enemy alien', along with many other anti-Nazi refugees, many but by no means all of them Jewish. (This was one of the least inspiring chapters in the history of Britain during the Second World War, and it should be better known than it is.) Both were naturalized as British citizens.

Michael himself was born in Swiss Cottage in 1944. He and his parents lived in West Hampstead from 1944 to 1950, when the family emigrated to Israel. (Intriguingly, his parents never acquired Israeli citizenship.) The family's culture was German rather than Jewish: Michael points out that, for German Jews, Goethe was 'our Goethe'. He was an only child; and like many only children a precocious one. In particular, he was an avid reader; by the age of seven he already owned 400 English books. Among his early political influences his father's social liberalism, or perhaps liberal socialism, stands out. Freeden père voted Labour in 1945; the family took the *News Chronicle*. The paper was owned by the Cadbury family and was still redolent of the high-minded Nonconformist Conscience that had saturated British Liberalism in the glory days that would provide the subject matter of Michael's first book. Notable contributors included Vernon Bartlett, who had been elected as a Popular Front MP in a famous by-election in 1938, and Ritchie Calder, one of the pioneers of popular science journalism. (Arthur Koestler had been a *News Chronicle* correspondent in Spain, during the Civil War.) Michael's first political memory is of following the Korean War in its pages.

A more unexpected influence was a once-famous best-seller by H. E. (Henrietta Elizabeth) Marshall, *Our Island Story*. It was a sixth birthday present, given to Michael when the family was still living in Hampstead, and it still has an honoured place in his sprawling library. Marshall was a Scot, educated at a girls' boarding school in Melrose, who earned her living by her prolific pen. *Our Island Story* was the most successful of her many books. It was originally published in 1905, quickly became a best-seller, and went through several editions before going out of print in the 1960s. (The think tank Civitas, in alliance with various national newspapers, has recently brought it back into print.) It is good, old-fashioned narrative history, with plenty of heroes and villains, of the sort children love and too many academic historians disdain.

All the good stories are there: indomitable Boadicea versus arrogant Romans; Arthur and the Knights of the Round Table, with Merlin in the background; King Alfred burning the cakes; Canute proving he could not hold back the waves; Pope Gregory exclaiming 'not Angles but angels'; the princes murdered in the Tower. The storyline is best described as populist Whig; the implicit moral is remarkably close to the ethos of the *News Chronicle*. Edward the Confessor is condemned for thinking more of 'building churches and buying relics than of trying to make the lives of his people peaceful and

Preface: Return of the Native xi

happy'. Hereward the Wake, resisting the Normans, is an unmitigated hero. But Richard I is not: he should have stayed at home looking after his people, instead of wandering off on a self-indulgent Crusade. The poll tax rebel, Wat Tyler is another hero: his rebellion 'was the beginning of freedom for the lower classes in England'. Henry VIII gets a poor press. His reign was 'a great one for England', but he was 'bad and selfish' and became 'a cruel tyrant'. Guy Fawkes was 'very brave, although he was wrong'. The verdict on Cromwell is revealingly mixed. He was 'stern and despotic', but unlike the Stuarts 'he really thought of the good of the country and the Stuarts thought only of themselves'. Predictably, William of Orange does much better: unlike William the Conqueror, he was 'no conqueror but a deliverer'. In good Whig fashion, Londonderry is dubbed 'Brave Londonderry'. As for the Great Reform Act of 1832, 'One more step towards liberty had been taken'.

An unapologetic patriotism runs through the book. In Marshall's own words, she tells the story of a 'little green island' whose people 'grew to be a great people'. When they grew so numerous that their island was too small for them 'they sailed away over the blue waves to far-distant countries'. Now they possessed lands all over the world—lands that formed 'the empire of Greater Britain. Many of these lands are far, far larger than the little island itself. Yet the people who live in them still look back lovingly to the little island from which they or their fathers came, and call it "Home"'. Michael might be reluctant to admit it, but I suspect there is more of Marshall's popular-whiggish British patriotism in him than meets the eye.

One reason is that the transition from West Hampstead to Jerusalem was painful, perhaps even traumatic. In England Michael had been a sociable, as well as an intellectually precocious, little boy. He was still precocious in Israel, but he was thrown onto his own resources and 'lost the sociability' he had had in London. He was known to his Israeli schoolmates as 'the Englishman'. Why? 'Because he was polite!' (A comment that will make total sense to anyone who has ever visited Israel.) He was also fiercely loyal to British culture and the English language: Marshall's history had left an enduring impress. When George VI died in February 1952, Michael produced a handwritten newspaper mourning the King's death. He was given special permission to go home early to listen to Elizabeth's Coronation in June 1953. He now feels that he was never truly at home in Israel—though, unlike his parents, he did acquire Israeli citizenship. (He gave it up in the 1980s, by now firmly installed in Britain, because he thought it would be wrong to retain the citizenship of a country he had no intention of living in again.)

Had he ever been a Zionist? 'No'. He had always disliked Israeli 'collectivism'; and the atmosphere and ideology of the Kibbutz repelled him. He thinks Israeli culture was, and still is, marked by the stifling—albeit at times warm and cosy—inheritance of the *shtetl*: the Yiddish word for the partially self-governing, but inward-looking, tradition-dominated, claustrophobic Jewish communities of the so-called Pale of Settlement that ran from near the Baltic to the Black Sea in Tsarist days. The *shtetl* offered security in exchange for conformity, community as a substitute for independence of mind. The outside world was full of dangers; non-conformity was the first step towards the ultimate treachery of apostasy.

As an example of the *shtetl*'s impact on the mentality of the Israel in which he grew up, Michael describes the way his Israeli school authorities reacted to the death of Chaim Weizmann, the great Zionist leader of pre-independence days, and Israel's first President. 'We've been orphaned!' exclaimed his teachers. I couldn't help noticing the parallel with Soviet reactions to the death of Stalin; and that led me to wonder if the conspiratorial, schism-prone, heresy-hunting socialism of Tsarist Russia might also have contributed to the political culture of Israel. Michael thought it probably had. But to understand him, the sources of Israeli collectivism matter less than his reaction to it. He has no doubt that his visceral distaste for it contributed heavily to his liberalism. West Hampstead, *Our Island Story*, and the *News Chronicle* proved stronger than the Zionist dream: the 'Englishman' trumped the Israeli, and in doing so became more English than before.

Michael was an undergraduate at the Hebrew University of Jerusalem from 1962 to 1965, and stayed on to do graduate work. But he did not prosper under an authoritarian supervisor, and in the end his supervisor's 'oppression' forced him to leave. The 'pull' of British culture was as strong as the 'push' of alienation from Israeli collectivism and illiberalism. In the course of a thirty-day stay in London during his Israeli years he went to thirty-one plays in London theatres. He was particularly impressed by Lawrence Olivier and Vanessa Redgrave, and struck by the contrast between everyday English 'repression' and the 'surrender to emotion' that English actors displayed on the stage. He had always dreamed of returning to Britain to study for a higher degree, and in the end he did so. He was a graduate student at St Antony's College, Oxford, from 1969 to 1972; and was awarded a D.Phil. for the dissertation that provided the basis for his first book, *The New Liberalism*. From Oxford, he returned to Israel, this time as a lecturer at Haifa University, but in 1978 he returned to Oxford as Politics Fellow at Mansfield College.

He had come home. His life's work could begin. *The New Liberalism* was followed by *Liberalism Divided*; by his masterpiece, *Ideologies and Political Theory*; and by a host of journal articles and shorter books. He founded (and still edits) the *Journal of Political Ideologies* and, much later, the Centre for Political Ideologies at the Oxford Politics Department. He has been a mainstay of Mansfield College, as well as a devoted undergraduate teacher and post-graduate supervisor. In principle, he might have done as much had he stayed in Israel, but in practice, he needed the freer air of England to flourish. At a seminar during a visit to Israel in the late Eighties he posed the question: 'Can Israel be both democratic and Jewish?' He was attacked as a 'lily-livered

Oxford liberal', and replied robustly that he had 'learned my liberalism in Jerusalem not Oxford'. But to the extent that this was true it was because Jerusalem had taught him that he did not belong there. Now he says, without equivocation, that he 'loves' living in Britain, which he sees as a 'haven of liberalism'. The ghosts of Henrietta Marshall and the *News Chronicle* writers of the 1940s would applaud.

Introduction

Ben Jackson and Marc Stears

Over the course of his academic career, Michael Freeden has done more than anyone else to help us understand liberalism as an ideology. Michael's work has shaped a range of disciplines and subdisciplines, including intellectual, social, and political history, political philosophy, interpretive political theory, and cultural studies. The scope of his influence is witnessed best, of course, through the impact of his major monographs. His two authored books on the British liberal movement of the early twentieth century, *The New Liberalism* and *Liberalism Divided*, were both instant classics, and have rightly found their place on history and politics reading lists across the world. No one can hope to have a proper understanding of the way in which liberal political thinkers and actors responded to the social and economic challenges of the early twentieth century without reading them. His study of the nature of ideology, *Ideologies and Political Theory: A Conceptual Approach*, had a similar reception. Since its publication in the late 1990s, it has restructured the way in which scholars approach the study of liberalism by changing the manner in which we think about political ideologies in general. Scholars now await his next large-scale study on the nature of political thinking with eager anticipation, certain that it too will alter the way in which we imagine liberal politics and study its arts.

Any academic who has generated this degree of intellectual excitement deserves the unique combination of scrutiny and celebration encompassed in a book of essays like this. But Michael Freeden's contribution to academic life goes far beyond that made by his published work. For over forty years, Freeden has also been a tutor, supervisor, colleague, and academic interlocutor. He has continuously improved the work of others through the power of his argument and engagement, and has always done so by deploying his unique brand of humane generosity and intellectual focus and ambition. This book, then, is not just the result of our contributors' deep engagement with his scholarly output. It is entirely the work of people who owe a personal debt to Michael Freeden. He was the undergraduate tutor of some of our essayists, or the graduate supervisor, or the colleague and collaborator of still others. Whatever the relationship, though, everyone in this volume owes Michael Freeden at least two things: intellectual inspiration and academic friendship. The resulting text is, in part, a thank you for that.

Our volume is more than a thank you, of course, vitally important though that is. It is also a broad and critical examination of the key themes in Freeden's work. As such, it covers the two general debates that are most associated with Michael Freeden today. The first involves the history of liberalism, especially in the late nineteenth and twentieth centuries. The second concerns the methods that should be deployed in our study of political theory, in general, and ideology, in particular.

The first Part of our book opens with David Leopold's reflections on the place of utopian theorizing in liberalism at both ends of the twentieth century. Leopold carefully compares and contrasts two figures who have featured prominently (for different reasons) in Freeden's work: the British new liberal thinker, J. A. Hobson, and the American philosopher, John Rawls. Leopold insists that despite the differences between these two liberals—differences that Michael Freeden has done much to highlight—they can both nonetheless be seen to grapple with questions of how we should consider the nature of an 'ideal' society while continuously addressing ourselves politically to the problems of the 'real'.

Leopold's examination of idealism in Hobson leads on to a more detailed engagement with the new liberalism in Ben Jackson's chapter. Jackson tackles a key theme in Freeden's early work: the relationship between socialism and new liberalism in early twentieth-century Britain. By analysing liberal attitudes to the public ownership of property, Jackson congratulates Freeden for drawing our attention towards the radicalism of new liberal thinking, but pushes his arguments still further by insisting on the many ways in which liberal ideology of this era was shaped by core socialist considerations. Our historical reflection on early twentieth-century liberalism, Jackson insists, should not hide temporarily unpopular perspectives from view. Instead, it should welcome them as an encouragement to our own times. If we can recall just how economically radical early twentieth-century liberalism really was, he concludes, it might free our own thinking and enable us to grapple with the desperate inequalities and injustices that blight our own economies today.

In the third chapter, Rochana Bajpai continues the historical examination of liberalism, but leaves British shores to take us to India. Like Jackson, Bajpai reminds us of the radicalism of many strands of early twentieth-century liberalism. She insists that many forms of thought, often dubbed socialist, nationalist, or anti-caste thinking, were actually forms of liberalism, and she deploys Michael Freeden's methodology as a means by which to develop her case. Intriguingly, though, she also argues that liberalism in the Indian setting often lost sight of one of the key elements of its ideological form elsewhere: the need to limit the state for the sake of individual freedom. It seems almost as if the radical infusion of liberalism in the distinctive context of Indian politics took the ideology away from its origins, resulting in an ideological form that can only be properly appreciated in a comparative context.

Marc Stears in our fourth chapter also examines the development of liberalism in a distinctive institutional and cultural environment, this time the United States. Opening with a comparison of Michael Freeden's approach to liberalism and that taken by Louis Hartz in his celebrated *Liberal Tradition in America*, Stears examines the status of liberal thinking in the US in the immediate aftermath of the Second World War. He reminds us that Hartz often presented liberalism as enjoying a dangerously hegemonic place in American theorizing. He then demonstrates, however, that many American public figures were deeply anxious about the erosion of popular liberal sentiment in post-war America, even producing mass civic festivals, such as the American Freedom Train, to try to inculcate liberal norms across American society. Stears demonstrates the different ways in which Hartz and Freeden might understand this phenomenon, before concluding that the internally flexible, adaptable, and open-ended nature of American liberalism has enabled it to prevail across time, in ways that neither Hartz nor Freeden might fully appreciate on their own.

In the fifth chapter, Bo Stråth continues this examination of liberalism in hard times. Taking a broad historical sweep, Stråth examines the ways in which European liberal political thinking has been reshaped by its interaction with economic and social crises. In one particularly insightful section, Stråth demonstrates how liberalism responded to the economic decline of advanced capitalist countries in the late twentieth century not by adapting successfully to new circumstances but by exaggerating aspects of its own ideological identity at the expense of others. In this way, he shows, liberalism became increasingly associated with a form of economic reductionism, and was rendered incapable of developing the subtle political responses to the situation that were required. Liberalism suffers in these moments of crisis, Stråth argues, when it turns away from non-liberal solutions and indulges in what he describes as an 'overdose of liberalism'.

Paolo Pombeni continues this theme in the sixth, and final, chapter of this Part. Returning to some of the issues raised by Leopold's opening chapter, Pombeni identifies another crucial crisis in liberal thinking at the outset of his own. Liberalism, he suggests, has often struggled as it decides whether to adopt a realist or an idealist assessment of political possibility and as it tries to relate its account of social change to its description of political processes. He illustrates these difficulties with particular reference to the place of political parties in a liberal constitutional order. Liberalism across Europe, Pombeni argues, has often struggled to develop a plausible account of parties, even though everyone has to admit their centrality to our political life. The result is an insistence on the need for a more realistic assessment of political parties, and of the other key elements in our political structure, in our political theory. Liberalism, Pombeni concludes, must not be squeamish about the necessary elements of democratic politics. If it is, then it is only to the benefit of its non-liberal, even totalitarian, rivals. It is a conclusion with which Michael Freeden would surely agree.

The relationship between ideal theorizing in politics and the interpretation and description of core elements of politics that emerges so powerfully in Pombeni's chapter moves us naturally into the second Part of our book. The next set of chapters, that is, examines Michael Freeden's methodology, in general, and, in particular, his reflections on the ways in which ideology and political theory should be studied. This Part begins in Chapter 7 with David Weinstein's call for contemporary political theorists to engage with a broader set of intellectual predecessors than they have had a tendency to discuss of late. Weinstein insists that if only contemporary political theorists studied the history of liberalism with the depth and careful consideration we associate with Michael Freeden, then they would free themselves of many of the restraints that currently shackle their thinking. The open-mindedness of many liberals of the past, Weinstein argues, stands in sharp contrast to the narrow outlook of many liberals today.

Chapters 8 and 9, by Andrew Vincent and Gerald Gaus respectively, continue this debate by contesting the nature of the relationship between the historically informed study of ideologies, on the one hand, and philosophical investigation of normative political theory, on the other. One of the highlights of the conference out of which this book emerged was a lively and intense dispute between Vincent and Gaus on these themes, and that dispute is now brought to a wider audience through these powerfully argued chapters. Having analysed what he takes to be the range of possible relationships between ideology and normative philosophy, Vincent calls for 'positive segregation' between the two, in which each is admitted to be of significant scholarly value but each of which is also said to demand very different scholarly skills. Gaus, on the other hand, suggests that such a distinction is hard to maintain, and argues that work presented as ideological interpretation can sometimes be better understood as a form of normative disputation. Michael Freeden's own analysis of John Rawls is deployed as an example here, with Freeden said to be a 'participant in the first-level philosophical dispute, not a student of political doctrines.'

In the next chapter, Gayil Talshir takes a less radical stance. She accepts the distinction between normative political theory and the study of ideology, but suggests that the study of ideology can often actually provide a bridge between the study of normative political theory and the empirical investigation of comparative politics. Ideology studies thus provide a supplement or complement to political theory, rather than either being a rival or collapsing into it. Talshir demonstrates her case by a careful analysis of the phenomena of partisan dealignment and realignment in modern liberal democracies. Neither political theory nor comparative politics alone, she contends, can fully understand the processes of dealignment and realignment, but when ideological approaches are added to the mix a new form of understanding becomes possible.

This insistence on the relationship between the study of ideology and the study of 'real politics' is deepened still further in the final two chapters of this Part by Michael Kenny and Mathew Humphrey. Both Kenny, in Chapter 11, and Humphrey, in Chapter 12, compare the way in which Michael Freeden studies and understands politics and ideology to other major efforts to do the same. Kenny contrasts Freeden's approach with that of Bernard Crick, while Humphrey draws Freeden into conversation with political realists such as Raymond Geuss. Both find these comparisons instructive as they enable us fully to appreciate the subtleties of Freeden's own understanding of the relationship between ideology, political theory, and real politics. They both indicate, too, the ways in which this understanding is likely to be deepened by Freeden's forthcoming work on the nature of politics and political thinking, and as such they make a fitting conclusion to our contributors' essays.

Our book does not end there, however. For as all of the contributors have long been interlocutors of Michael Freeden's, we thought it appropriate to continue that exchange here too. The final word in our volume thus goes to Michael Freeden himself, who with characteristic virtuosity critically engages with all of the themes described above and many more that are to be found in these pages. Although debates and disputes undoubtedly remain, this final chapter reveals that Michael Freeden found much of value in the essays that comprise this book. That is very pleasing. It means that we have achieved our first ambition in putting this book together. Our second ambition, though, remains outstanding. That ambition was to share that debate with others in the hope that they too would discover a lively conversation that continues the best traditions of liberal political thinking. Only you can decide if we have been successful in that. If we have, then it would be a fitting tribute to Michael Freeden's outstanding contribution to our collective intellectual life.

Part I
Liberal Languages

1

A Cautious Embrace: Reflections on (Left) Liberalism and Utopia

David Leopold

INTRODUCTION

When I was sixteen, going on seventeen, I had no idea of going to university, let alone the University of Oxford. I knew little about the latter, but that little made it clear that it was not for people like myself (or so I then thought). Barely eighteen months later—as the unlikely result of an unlikely series of events—I found myself an Oxford undergraduate 'reading', as I would learn to call it, 'PPE' (Philosophy, Politics, and Economics) under the direction of Michael Freeden. It was a wholly unexpected and astonishing privilege. For all that I was socially and culturally intimidated by my new surroundings, I found myself intellectually stimulated in ways, and to an extent, that I would previously have found unimaginable.

In a somewhat unconventional sense, I might be said to have received 'a liberal education' in those three undergraduate years. In its 'non-political' meaning, the idea of 'being liberal' has been said to evoke 'generosity, tolerance, compassion', and promise 'open, unbounded spaces' in which personality can be freely aired.[1] Those remarkable qualities were certainly exemplified by Michael in his role as my undergraduate tutor. He gave freely of his time and energy, certainly well beyond any call of duty; he treated my own wayward, and not always congenial, views with a respect which they did not always merit; and he showed a sympathetic understanding of my visceral estrangement from aspects of contemporary Oxford. Above all, he played a vital role in generating an atmosphere of intellectual seriousness and

---

[1] Michael Freeden, *Liberal Languages: Ideological Imaginations and Twentieth-Century Progressive Thought* (Princeton: Princeton University Press, 2005), 3.

opportunity in which I slowly began to feel more comfortable, and even to flourish a little.[2] I am greatly in his debt.

In the years since, I have come to know Michael much better. Although he was not my supervisor when I later returned to Oxford as a graduate student, he remained engaged with my work and well-being. The same intellectual and personal support was also evident when, more recently, I became one of his colleagues in the Department of Politics and International Relations. Yet it is that much earlier memory of Michael as an undergraduate tutor that is especially vivid as I write this.

I recall many serious and animated tutorial discussions, and I always left Michael's distinctive basement office in Mansfield College with new ideas and questions. We traversed a huge range of subjects over those three years, but returned most often to the character and merits of liberalism. And whilst we did not always agree, I always learnt from him.

I was initially puzzled as to why this distant set of recollections should have pushed out many more recent ones. I now think that the very process of writing this chapter is part of the most likely explanation. It was by re-reading some of Michael's work that my own thoughts about what I might discuss began to solidify. And it was that interaction with his ideas and arguments that rekindled my memories of Oxford 'back in the day'. Indeed, I now see it as especially pleasing to have been reminded of that formative educative process by its continuing (albeit a little less directly) into the present.

In what follows, I offer some reflections on a point at which some of Michael's longstanding intellectual concerns meet up with more recent interests of my own. More specifically, I am interested in certain aspects of the relation between liberalism and utopia.

FREEDEN AND LIBERALISM

An engagement with liberalism has always been central to Michael Freeden's work.[3] Yet that sustained engagement resists easy summary. Two particular obstacles loom large.

The first obstacle is the variety of topics that Freeden has covered. His work has ranged from systematic accounts of: major transformations marking the history of liberalism, especially in Britain in the period between the death of John Stuart Mill and publication of the Beveridge Report (not least,

---

[2] Michael's PPE colleagues at the time—David Owen (Philosophy) and Dieter Helm (Economics)—also made important contributions here.

[3] I mark the move to a less personal mode by referring to Freeden (rather than Michael) from this point.

book-length treatments of the new liberalism, and of the interwar division of British liberalism into left and centrist strands); through detailed accounts of individual liberal thinkers (such as T. H. Green and D. G. Ritchie) and groups (the 'Rainbow Circle'); to careful examinations of the liberal treatment of particular concepts (including community, poverty, and power).

The second obstacle is the variety of approaches that Freeden has adopted, and argued for, over the years. His work has evolved from historical studies which creatively combine questions of interest to political theorists with the serious archival work of historians; through accounts of ideological morphology, which examine the complex structures in which core and adjacent concepts are configured and 'decontested'; to more recent theoretical attempts to analyse 'actual political thinking', the various vocabularies, nuances, and arrangements, of ordinary manifestations of political thought.[4]

Rather than attempt an unwieldy summary, I pick out one thread from this large and varied body of work in order to contextualize and focus my own discussion. A persistent theme in Freeden's work concerns the historical development of liberalism. Those of a Whiggish disposition are liable to be disappointed by his reflections. Rather than a single reassuring story of all-conquering progress, he invokes the idea of multiple narratives in which advances in some areas are accompanied by significant deformations and distortions elsewhere. Nonetheless, the complex pattern that emerges does have some dominant threads.

One such thread concerns the character and respective merits of two emblematic movements from either end of the twentieth century, and with centres of gravity in different continents: the 'new liberalism' and 'philosophical liberalism'. The 'new liberalism' refers to the late Victorian and Edwardian development in British liberalism associated with Leonard Trelawny Hobhouse, John Atkinson Hobson, and others; whilst 'philosophical liberalism' is Freeden's label for the resurgence of liberalism, especially in the American academy in the last third of the twentieth century, associated with John Rawls, Ronald Dworkin, and others.

Freeden identifies a number of 'varying' and 'even irreconcilable' differences between these liberalisms.[5] Two comparisons can illustrate his account.

The first comparison runs between these two liberal variants and the ideological core of liberalism established in the nineteenth century (not least, by John Stuart Mill). That benchmark 'Millite' structure is seen to consist of a particular interpretation and configuration—carefully elaborated by

---

[4] One overall trend here is the increasing 'democratization' of Freeden's subject matter. See, in this context, Michael Freeden, 'Thinking Politically and Thinking about Politics: Language, Interpretation, and Ideology', in David Leopold and Marc Stears (eds.), *Political Theory: Methods and Approaches* (Oxford: Oxford University Press, 2008), 196–215.
[5] Freeden, *Liberal Languages*, 11.

Freeden—of the concepts of liberty, individuality, development, rationality, general interest, sociability, and rule-limited government. (Liberal toleration is not absent, but appears here as a dispositional flexibility in the interpretation and configuration of concepts, rather than as a substantive value.)

The new liberals brought changes to this 'Millite' structure. For example: the core concept of individualism was detached further from the pursuit of narrow self-interest (and reconciled with the general interest); the (already) peripheral right to private property was increasingly marginalized (subordinated to communal priorities); the state was brought adjacent to the liberal core (supporting individual flourishing); and the concept of liberty was brought into a more harmonious relation with sociability (broadening the notion of constraint).[6] That summary does scant justice to the details of Freeden's account, but perhaps the central claim is that in sympathetically transforming the intellectual tradition they inherited, the new liberals preserved its essential structure (teasing out features that were implicit, and underestimated, in that earlier incarnation).

In contrast, the changes to that 'Millite' structure wrought by philosophical liberalism are seen as less sympathetic. For example: individuality (at the heart of Mill's liberalism) is excluded from the liberal core (as a 'comprehensive' rather than 'political' ideal); liberty is elaborated in a restrictive manner (associated with rational self-determination); there is an attempt to promote equality to a (sometimes 'the') core concept; and sociability is demoted (reflecting a wider underestimation of the varieties of liberal community).[7] Again, much detail is missed in this kind of summary, but Freeden's central claim is perhaps that in borrowing a 'false horizon' from Kantianism, philosophical liberalism broke in significant respects with the 'Millite' core (and with its development by previous generations of American liberals).[8]

The second comparison runs between these two liberal variants and engagement with what is often called the real world of politics (the world of institutions, political power, and compromise). Again, Freeden draws a stark contrast between new and philosophical liberalisms.

Confronted by a changed intellectual environment and unprecedented social problems, the new liberals accomplished a distinctive modernization of liberalism. That modernization not only managed to preserve the intellectual tradition that they had inherited (unlocking its potential in a changed environment), but also succeeded in transforming the wider social and political world. In particular, Freeden sees the new liberalism as contributing decisively to the intellectual preconditions of the emergence of the modern

---

[6] See, for example, Michael Freeden, *Ideologies and Political Theory: A Conceptual Approach* (Oxford: Oxford University Press, 1996), 194–210.
[7] See, for example, Freeden, *Ideologies and Political Theory*, 226–75.
[8] See Freeden, *Ideologies and Political Theory*, 118; and Freeden, *Liberal Languages*, 13.

welfare state. Familiarity, he cautions, should not lead us to underestimate this accomplishment; the welfare state is perhaps the most important domestic achievement of Western political systems in the twentieth century.[9]

By comparison, the revival of liberalism accomplished by philosophical liberalism is doubly limited. Freeden does not deny the intellectual achievement here; the 'analytical insights, critical appraisals, and ethical sensitivities' of philosophical liberalism, he remarks, have undoubtedly been to the 'refinement of political thought'.[10] However, he sees these cerebral gains as accompanied by a loss of political and intellectual engagement. Philosophical liberalism is portrayed as out of touch, not only with the political and cultural constraints of the real world of policymaking, but also with academic disciplines other than philosophy (including political science, psychology, and sociology).[11]

In elaborating these contrasting liberal attitudes towards political practice, Freeden ventures a revealing analogy with the twentieth-century history of Marxism. The flourishing of philosophical liberalism is likened to the intellectual revival known as 'Western Marxism' (associated with Theodor Adorno, Herbert Marcuse, and others). Western Marxism is a complex phenomenon, but is often seen as having combined an increase in philosophical sophistication with a loss of practical contact with working-class struggles.[12] The intended parallel seems clear. The resurrection of a major ideology can sometimes take a one-sided and academic form, divorced from political practice and tending towards scholasticism.[13]

These two comparisons should give a sense of this thread in Freeden's controversial account of the development and transformation of liberalism. Here, the contrast between new and philosophical liberalisms is used to contextualize and focus the discussion that follows. It is a trivialization, but perhaps not an exaggeration, to say that Hobson emerges from Freeden's discussion as one of the (unsung) heroes of twentieth-century liberal thought, and Rawls as one of its (overpraised) villains. Consequently, it seems appropriate to use these two figures to structure my own reflections on the relation between liberalism and utopia.

I will suggest that, in this context, the differences between Hobson and Rawls are both less stark, and less obviously to the advantage of the former. However, my primary aim is not to nuance, or qualify, Freeden's narrative, but

---

[9] Freeden, *Liberal Languages*, 4. See also, Michael Freeden, 'The Coming of the Welfare State', in Terence Ball and Richard Bellamy (eds.), *The Cambridge History of Twentieth-Century Political Thought* (Cambridge: Cambridge University Press, 2003), 7–44.
[10] Freeden, *Liberal Languages*, 9.
[11] Freeden, *Liberal Languages*, 6, 8.
[12] See, for example, Perry Anderson, *Considerations on Western Marxism* (London: Verso, 1976), 92–4.
[13] See Freeden, *Ideologies and Political Theory*, 227.

rather to see how well these two figures can be accommodated by a familiar characterization of the liberal attitude towards utopia. That familiar, but questionable, characterization—which Freeden does not endorse—portrays liberals as having always 'strongly denigrated' the idea of utopia.[14]

This relentlessly hostile characterization gains plausibility, not least, from the view of utopia adopted by so-called 'cold-war liberals' (including Raymond Aron, Isaiah Berlin, and Karl Popper).[15] Berlin provides a clear and well-known example. In several essays he dissects the central intellectual and practical failings of the utopian attempt to identify, and progress towards, the ideal society. The intellectual failing of utopianism is seemingly its acceptance of the idea that all the supreme values are compatible with one another, an idea which Berlin views as 'incoherent' given the pluralism that is a permanent and unalterable feature of our moral universe.[16] The practical failing of utopianism is seemingly that, believing that perfection is a possibility, utopians are too quick to inflict great suffering on others in order to bring it about. After all, he asks rhetorically: What could be too high a price for making humankind 'just and happy and creative and harmonious for ever'?[17] Whatever we make of these lines of argument—and I do not mean to endorse either of them here—Berlin's hostility to utopianism looks to be quite thoroughgoing. The utopian project, on this account, is both incoherent and dangerous.[18]

Such thoroughgoing hostility is not typical of all liberalisms. Not least, as will become apparent, neither Hobson nor Rawls provides much support for such a characterization.

HOBSON AND UTOPIANISM

Hobson is not now a well-known figure. For much of the twentieth century, his reputation largely rested on the testimonials that he received from two more famous authors. His economic interpretation of imperialism was acknowledged as an important source by V. I. Lenin in *Imperialism, the Highest Stage of Capitalism* (1917); and his unconventional underconsumptionist view of economic crises was generously praised by John Maynard Keynes in *The*

---

[14] Barbara Goodwin, 'Utopia Defended Against the Liberals', *Political Studies*, 28 (1980), 384.
[15] See Jan-Werner Müller, 'Fear and Freedom: On "Cold War Liberalism"', *European Journal of Political Theory*, 7 (2008), 45–64.
[16] Isaiah Berlin, 'The Pursuit of the Ideal', in his *The Crooked Timber of Humanity: Chapters in the History of Ideas*, ed. Henry Hardy (New York: Alfred A. Knopf, 1991), 13.
[17] Berlin, 'The Pursuit of the Ideal', 15.
[18] Isaiah Berlin, 'The Decline of Utopian Ideas in the West', in *The Crooked Timber of Humanity*, 26.

General Theory of Employment, Interest, and Money (1936).[19] However, the scale and variety of Hobson's published output is scarcely captured by these compartmentalized, and potentially misleading, appreciations.[20] With Freeden in the vanguard, much recent scholarship has sought to extend Hobson's reputation beyond any role that he might have played in the prehistories of either Marxist theories of imperialism or Keynesian economic thought. A much fuller justification of Hobson's claim to be considered an important and innovative political thinker has emerged, generating a lively and largely constructive debate about whether, and to what extent, his distinctive combination of views—including his organic conception of society, positive account of the state, and evolutionary view of human nature—might have expanded or breached the traditional boundaries of liberalism.[21]

Confirming the range of Hobson's writings, my own discussion concerns a review of Edward Bellamy's *Looking Backward 2000-1887* (1888), written for the *Humanitarian* (in 1898).[22] Hobson began his working life teaching literature (amongst other subjects), first in schools (in Faversham and Exeter) and then in university Extension departments (primarily for the Oxford Committee for University Extension and the London Society for the Extension of University Teaching).[23] However, it would be a mistake to consider his reflections on Bellamy's novel to be of merely biographical interest. The use of unconventional sources is typical of Hobson's various attempts to grapple with what he saw as new and distinctive social problems. He sought to draw upon, and integrate, the insights of a wide variety of disciplines, including economics, ethics, sociology, politics, and biology. Literature also has a place

---

[19] For some of the complexities here, see Peter Cain, *Hobson and Imperialism: Radicalism, New Liberalism, and Finance 1887-1938* (Oxford: Oxford University Press, 2002), 230-2; and Peter Clarke, 'Hobson and Keynes as Economic Heretics', in Michael Freeden (ed.), *Reappraising J. A. Hobson: Humanism and Welfare* (London: Unwin Hyman, 1990), 100-15.

[20] There are over 700 items in the bibliography in John Pheby (ed.), *J. A. Hobson after Fifty Years* (London: Palgrave, 1994), 252-77.

[21] See Michael Freeden, *The New Liberalism: An Ideology of Social Reform* (Oxford: Oxford University Press, 1978); Michael Freeden, *Liberalism Divided* (Oxford: Oxford University Press, 1986); J. A. Hobson, *Confessions of an Economic Heretic: The Autobiography of John A. Hobson*, ed. Michael Freeden (Hassocks: Harvester Press, 1976); *J. A. Hobson: A Reader*, ed. Michael Freeden (London: Unwin Hyman, 1988); Michael Freeden (ed.), *Reappraising J. A. Hobson: Humanism and Welfare* (London: Unwin Hyman, 1990); and Michael Freeden, 'J. A. Hobson as a Political Theorist', in John Pheby (ed.), *J. A. Hobson after Fifty Years: Freethinker of the Social Sciences* (Basingstoke: Macmillan, 1994), 19-33. Other contributors to this debate include John Allett, Peter Cain, Peter F. Clarke, Alon Kadish, Alan J. Lee, and Jules Townshend.

[22] J. A. Hobson, 'Edward Bellamy and the Utopian Romance', *Humanitarian*, 13 (September 1898), 179-89. It has been said that Hobson's transformation into a new liberal thinker was 'largely complete' by 1896 (which is not to deny later developments in his thought, especially following the Great War. See Cain, *Hobson and Imperialism*, 30; and Hobson, *Confessions of an Economic Heretic*, 104, respectively.

[23] See Alon Kadish, 'Rewriting the *Confessions*: Hobson and the Extension Movement', in Freeden (ed.), *Reappraising J. A. Hobson*, 137-66.

in this attempted synthesis. In his Extension lecturing, Hobson seems to have thought of literature as providing an effective introduction to moral reflection and the study of society, but he does not view the role of literature as solely heuristic.[24] He notes that, on occasion, 'fiction is truer than history'; that is, human imagination can sometimes order the 'outward and inward events of life' in such a way that 'deep essential truths shine forth more clearly' in fiction than they do from the messy complexity of everyday life.[25]

Hobson's review of *Looking Backward* offers an appropriate vantage point from which to examine his view of utopia. I use the term 'utopia' here in a conventional (if unfashionable) manner, to refer to a detailed description of an ideal society. Those of a typological bent might be inclined to say that utopia is thereby identified with 'positive utopias' or 'eutopias'.[26] Utopias, in this sense, are typically concerned not only with moral and political values, but also with the institutions and ethos that might best embody those values. All such utopias might be called 'fictions', in that they concern a world which is not actual (save on the implausible Panglossian view that we already live in the ideal world). However, they are not required to—although particular examples may—take the characteristic narrative form of a literary utopia proper (in which a visitor from the world of the author encounters a superior civilization in a geographically or temporally distant location).

Looking Backward does, of course, adopt that familiar literary form. Bellamy's protagonist, Julian West, wakes from a lengthy cataleptic sleep (lasting some 113 years) to find himself in Boston, Massachusetts, in the year 2000. West is enchanted by the new society that he discovers, a society organized around state capitalism, scientific management, and shopping. The poverty and corruption of the nineteenth century have disappeared from everyday life, surviving only as the imaginative raw material of a powerful nightmare that West experiences towards the end of the novel.[27] (Those of a romantic—or perhaps psychoanalytic—disposition might also like to know that West finds personal happiness with Edith, the great-granddaughter of his long-deceased fiancée Edith.)

Looking Backward enjoyed an extraordinary degree of contemporary success. In Bellamy's native America it became the second best-selling novel of the century (after *Uncle Tom's Cabin*), and led to the so-called 'nationalist' movement propagating his ideas.[28] By 1891, Dutch, Italian, French, German,

---

[24] See Kadish, 'Rewriting the *Confessions*', 156.
[25] Hobson, 'Edward Bellamy', 179.
[26] See Lyman Tower Sargent, 'The Three Faces of Utopianism Revisited', *Utopian Studies*, 5 (1994), 9.
[27] See Edward Bellamy, *Looking Backward 2000-1887*, ed. Matthew Beaumont (Oxford: Oxford University Press, 2007), ch. XXVIII.
[28] See Everett W. MacNair, *Edward Bellamy and the Nationalist Movement, 1889-1894* (Milwaukee: Fitzgerald, 1957); Arthur Lipow, *Authoritarian Socialism in America: Edward Bellamy and the Nationalist Movement* (Berkeley: University of California Press, 1982); and

and Portuguese translations had appeared, and worldwide sales may have topped a million copies.[29] As late as 1935, three distinguished American public intellectuals (John Dewey, Charles A. Beard, and Edward Weeks), when asked to list the most influential books of the last fifty years, ranked *Looking Backward* in second place (after Marx's *Capital*).[30]

Hobson shares something of that enthusiasm. He does not hesitate to characterize the publication of *Looking Backward* as 'one of the most important literary events of the century', and more precisely as 'the most important contribution America has made to the education of the great British public'.[31] That contribution consists in having created sympathy and support for 'large projects of structural reform in industry and politics', using economic arguments adapted to 'the intelligence of the average man', and avoiding the association with revolutionary violence which had previously 'tainted' such projects.[32] Hobson was especially keen to insist on the merits of Bellamy's novel because he felt that its popular success had been accompanied by a certain amount of critical condescension. Not least, the 'superior academic person' and the 'professional agitator' had united against Bellamy's work; professors of political economy and sociology resented the author's lack of 'book-learning', whilst socialist propagandists of all stripes (Fabians as well as blood-red revolutionaries) resented his proselytizing success.[33] In response, Hobson maintains that the 'critical' and 'constructive' merits of Bellamy's work are more substantial than often thought.[34]

Whilst not uncritical of Bellamy, Hobson insists that *Looking Backward* has one overwhelming merit; namely, that it anticipates a new and superior approach to the ideal society. The problem with all previous utopias, he maintains, is their flawed relation to the existing world, they were simply 'opposed' to the existing society.[35] (Thomas More and William Morris are identified as representing this older and inferior approach.)[36] This objection

---

Franklin Rosemont, 'Bellamy's Radicalism Reclaimed', in Daphne Patai (ed.), *Looking Backward, 1988–1888: Essays on Edward Bellamy* (Amherst: University of Massachusetts Press, 1988), 147–209.

[29] On his extraordinary international impact, see Sylvia E. Bowman et al., *Edward Bellamy Abroad: An American Prophet's Influence* (New York: Twayne, 1962).

[30] A list of 'fifty influential books' was compiled from three separate lists of twenty-five works each. See *Publishers Weekly*, 127 (23 March 1935), 1227–9.

[31] Hobson, 'Edward Bellamy', 179, 180. Hobson acknowledged a supporting role for Henry George's *Progress and Poverty* (1879) in this regard. See also, J. A. Hobson, 'The Influence of Henry George in England', *Fortnightly Review*, 62 (1897), 835–44.

[32] Hobson, 'Edward Bellamy', 180.

[33] Hobson, 'Edward Bellamy', 180.

[34] Hobson, 'Edward Bellamy', 181.

[35] Hobson, 'Edward Bellamy', 179.

[36] (With great difficulty) I refrain from defending Morris against Hobson's criticism here. However, see the 'Introduction' to William Morris, *News From Nowhere*, ed. David Leopold, revised edition (Oxford: Oxford University Press, 2009), pp. xi–xxiii.

seems to concern both the *content* of, and *transition* to, the ideal society; that is, both its institutions and ethos, and the mechanism whereby it was reached. In contrast, Bellamy is said to have anticipated what can be called the 'realistic utopia', an account of the ideal society that stands in the right kind of 'organic' connection with the existing and non-ideal world.

Regarding transition, previous utopians are said to have failed to identify any mechanism in the non-ideal present that might bring about their ideal. Either they posited a 'cataclysm' between the present and the future, or they began *'de novo'*, discovering their ideal in a distant, unknown, and happily 'vacant' location.[37] In contrast, Bellamy's ideal slowly developed out of the dominant tendency of modern industrial life, namely 'the concentration of capital in business in large masses controlled by a few men'.[38] Bellamy saw this process of monopolization as inevitable, and identified good reasons (for consumers, workers, and government) to determine that 'a public monopoly is preferable to a private one'.[39] His ideal state emerged gradually from a two-stage historical process, whereby monopoly first extended across all industries, and then those monopolies passed into public ownership and control. Whilst Hobson does not wholly endorse the result of this narrative (see below), he does approve of its being evolved in an orderly manner out of the structural tendencies of the present. As far as the transition to the ideal society is concerned, the new institutions and ethos must 'grow naturally and consistently from known phenomena of present life'.[40]

Regarding content, Bellamy's achievement is said to have been to appreciate that the institutions and ethos of the ideal society must also 'express and develop what is permanent and sound in existing society'.[41] However, Hobson claims that, whilst Bellamy understands this requirement for a 'realistic utopia', the institutions and ethos that he actually proposes do not always comply with it. As a result, Hobson saw scope to improve Bellamy's own vision, bringing its content closer in line with this aspiration to 'realism'.

As far as the institutions of the ideal society are concerned, *Looking Backward* is criticized for failing to appreciate what Hobson sees as a 'natural' and 'impassable' divide between the sphere of 'machine' production and the sphere of what he (confusingly) calls 'artistic' production.[42] Hobson allows that 'a public monopoly is preferable to a private one', but is sceptical of Bellamy's claim that all industries have a tendency towards monopoly.[43] Mechanical production satisfies routine wants, which everybody shares, and does have a tendency to monopoly. Whereas artistic production serves consumers whose 'taste and fit' do not conform to 'some common type', and

---

[37] Hobson, 'Edward Bellamy', 182.
[38] Hobson, 'Edward Bellamy', 183.
[39] Hobson, 'Edward Bellamy', 183.
[40] Hobson, 'Edward Bellamy', 179.
[41] Hobson, 'Edward Bellamy', 179.
[42] Hobson, 'Edward Bellamy', 184.
[43] Hobson, 'Edward Bellamy', 183.

supplies 'arts, handicrafts, personal services and other non-routine activities' which are resistant to mechanical perfection and the consequent tendency to monopoly.[44] (Note that this distinction cuts across industries; thus, to use a later example, trams and buses running regular timetables are said to lend themselves to collective control, in a way that cabs responding to individual fares do not.)[45] Hobson allows that these 'finer kinds of work' could be forcibly regimented, but only at the cost of violence to their essential character and a consequent loss of attractiveness in the associated ideal.[46] In this context, Hobson suggests that Bellamy's metaphor of an 'industrial army' is revealing; society is portrayed in *Looking Backward* as an 'organisation' (in which the individual is simply a 'means to an end') rather than an 'organism' (in which the individual is also 'an end').[47] Two lines of criticism seem to converge here: empirically, Bellamy is mistaken in claiming that all productive activity can be reduced to mechanical routine; normatively, he is wrong to think that, were this reduction possible, it would be desirable. In this context, Hobson prefers an institutional structure, which embodies 'a carefully contrived combination of state-ownership and private enterprise'.[48] Of recent utopias, the closest approximation to this aspect of his own ideal is identified as Theodor Hertzka's *Freiland: Ein sociales Zukunftsbild* (1890).[49]

As far as the ethos of the ideal society is concerned, Bellamy is criticized for seeking to replace 'anti-social' motivations entirely with 'social sentiments' (not least, with 'genuine patriotism', namely, the desire to secure the good of the commonwealth).[50] Hobson commends Bellamy for his accurate diagnosis of the existing capitalist economy, as operating on the basis of the 'anti-social' sentiments of humankind (including 'greed and selfishness').[51] He also commends Bellamy for accepting the dictum of political economy that 'all useful work was essentially disagreeable and undesirable for its own sake', and for recognizing the problem that this creates for motivating its performance.[52]

---

[44] Hobson, 'Edward Bellamy', 184. See also J. A. Hobson, *The Crisis of Liberalism: New Issues of Democracy*, ed. P. F. Clarke (Hassocks: Harvester Press, 1974), 118–26.

[45] This example is taken from Hobson, *The Crisis of Liberalism*, 125.

[46] Hobson, 'Edward Bellamy', 185.

[47] Hobson, 'Edward Bellamy', 185. On Hobson's distinctive 'liberal organicism', see Freeden, *The New Liberalism*, 94–116; and Freeden, *Liberal Languages*, ch. 6.

[48] Hobson, 'Edward Bellamy', 189. For further discussion of this aspect of Hobson's thought, see Ben Jackson's chapter in this volume.

[49] An English translation, by Arthur Ransome, had appeared in 1891. On *Freiland*, see Paul Jackson, '*Freiland*: Theodor Hertzka's Liberal-Socialist Utopia', *German Life and Letters*, 33 (1980), 269–75; and P. Rosner, 'Theodor Hertzka and the Utopia of Freiland', *History of Economic Ideas*, 14 (2006), 113–38.

[50] Hobson, 'Edward Bellamy', 187. That Bellamy combines 'genuine patriotism' with the desire for personal distinction and the good opinion of others appears to blunt some of Hobson's criticism here. See, for example, Bellamy, *Looking Backward*, 56-7.

[51] Hobson, 'Edward Bellamy', 187.

[52] Hobson, 'Edward Bellamy', 186.

However, Bellamy is said to have failed to understand the limits to the efficacy of 'social' incentives, limits which prevent productive activity being wholly motivated by 'the claims of brotherhood and citizenship'.[53] Hobson maintains that even allowing that the demand for some unpleasant work might disappear, and that machinery might take over some proportion of the remaining burden, we would still be left with a significant motivational shortfall that 'social sentiments' could not make up. Social sentiments 'undoubtedly exist', but on their own they are neither 'strong' enough, nor 'general' enough, to cure 'shirking and idleness' and to evoke from everyone 'the best work of which they are capable'.[54] Treading a path between the overly 'anti-social' character of present-day capitalism, and the overly social character of *Looking Backward*, Hobson recommends a combination of 'social and individual incentives'.[55] He sees this compromise motivational combination as in keeping with both the cooperative movement, and some recent ideal commonwealths. He especially recommends *The Real History of Money Island* by 'Mr Flürscheim' for seeking to preserve 'individualism' (not least, in the choice of work and remuneration) in the context of a system of social cooperation based on the 'social ownership of land and credit'.[56]

Both of these threads, in Hobson's review, take a parallel form. Bellamy's ideal society is commended where it is, and criticized where it is not, sufficiently 'realistic'. ('Realism' here connotes the requirement that the structure of, and transition to, the ideal society have the right kind of 'organic' connection to 'known phenomena of present life'.)[57] Where Bellamy is insufficiently 'realistic', Hobson offers his own amendments to the proposed institutions and ethos, endorsing an institutional combination of public and private enterprises, and a psychological mixture of social and individual incentives. These amendments—which license a little less 'machinery' and a little less 'brotherhood'—are seen as consistent with Bellamy's realist aspirations (since they reflect a 'clearer grasp of the structural character of industry' and a 'better knowledge of psychology', respectively).[58]

Of course, some critics had already objected to *Looking Backward* on the grounds that its ideals were inappropriately modest. (Morris for one had understood Bellamy as proposing an unappealing and impossible 'half-change' in which the capitalist economy was somewhat modified, but the

---

[53] Hobson, 'Edward Bellamy', 186.   [54] Hobson, 'Edward Bellamy', 187.
[55] Hobson, 'Edward Bellamy', 189.
[56] Hobson, 'Edward Bellamy', 189. For more on this little known ex-stockbroker and radical, see Lyman Tower Sargent, 'Michael Flürscheim: From the Single Tax to Currency Reform', *Utopian Studies*, 21 (2010), 139–61.
[57] Hobson, 'Edward Bellamy', 179.
[58] Hobson, 'Edward Bellamy', 189. There is, of course, more to Hobson's ideal than this. See, for example, the interesting remarks about democracy in Hobson, *Confessions of an Economic Heretic*, ch. 15.

social and cultural arrangements of bourgeois society were left largely intact.)[59] Hobson could easily be seen as suggesting that the ideal society should be more modest still (with its economic arrangements containing more private enterprise, and 'the motive of individual gain' being utilized to a greater extent).[60]

Hobson anticipates this concern, and offers a response. He accepts that, by comparison with the older type of utopia, he might be said to have endorsed 'humbler ideals'.[61] However, he insists that these 'humbler ideals' have two overwhelming advantages. In the first place, they are 'more convincing in their realism', because they understand and respect the structural and psychological constraints of the present. And second, they are liable (seemingly as a result) to be 'more serviceable in their propagandist uses'; more effective, that is, in bringing about the structural reform of social and political life.[62]

RAWLS AND UTOPIANISM

By comparison with Hobson, Rawls is in less need of an introduction. *A Theory of Justice* (1971) is widely regarded as the most important twentieth-century work of Anglo-American political philosophy. With this book, Rawls was seen not only to have moved academic political philosophy onto new (or, at least, revitalized) terrain, but also to have established a leading position within that terrain for his own views. He overturned the then-dominant view of the appropriate ambitions of political philosophy (as limited to the resolution of certain kinds of linguistic confusion), by re-establishing the formulation and defence of substantive moral and political principles as a legitimate goal. Moreover, within that revitalized discipline, he offered a systematic and influential defence of the nature of social justice. In particular, Rawls advanced a liberal account of the structure of a just society, an account which combined a traditional affirmation of pluralistic toleration and personal freedom, with a concern for social and economic inequalities.[63] Famously, one of the ways in which he motivates support for this account of social justice utilizes the idea of a hypothetical contract in which the fundamental (higher-order) interests of free and equal persons are fairly represented (since a figurative 'veil of ignorance' abstracts from the particular features and circumstances of

---

[59] William Morris, 'Looking Backward', in *William Morris: Artist, Writer, Socialist*, ed. May Morris, vol. II (Oxford: Blackwell, 1936), 502.
[60] Hobson, 'Edward Bellamy', 189.
[61] Hobson, 'Edward Bellamy', 189.
[62] Hobson, 'Edward Bellamy', 189.
[63] See Thomas Nagel, 'Rawls and Liberalism', in Samuel Freeman (ed.), *The Cambridge Companion to Rawls* (Cambridge: Cambridge University Press, 2003), 62–85.

individuals, and eliminates the use of threat advantage). Rawls subsequently (and controversially) presented this theory of 'justice as fairness' as (unambiguously) independent of any particular 'comprehensive' moral doctrine, as a freestanding 'political' conception that might claim the allegiance of all the citizens of a democratic society.

Very roughly, Rawls maintains that the fundamental principles of justice apply primarily to the 'basic structure' of a democratic society (rather than, say, to the choices that individuals make within that structure). The basic structure consists of (some of) the major social institutions of a society—including its constitution, legal order, economic structure, and forms of property—which distribute fundamental rights and duties, and which profoundly influence the division of the advantages of social cooperation. That basic structure is said to be just when it satisfies two principles. The first of these, a principle of strict equality, applies to the political and legal institutions of a society (not least, its constitutional structures and guarantees). These institutions are judged by the extent to which they secure a fully adequate scheme of 'equal basic liberties' to their members (including political liberties; liberties of conscience and freedom of thought; freedom of association; and rights covered by the rule of law). The second of these principles, a principle of permissible inequality, applies to the social and economic institutions of a society (not least, its tax system and employment policies). These institutions are judged by the extent to which the social and economic inequalities that they systematically generate satisfy a two-part condition: that they are attached to positions and offices open to all under conditions of 'fair equality of opportunity'; and that they are required to maximize the benefits that go to the least advantaged members of society ('the difference principle'). Strict rules about the lexi(cographi)cal ordering of these principles prevent equal basic liberties being traded off against anything else, and prevent fair equality of opportunity being traded off against a reduction in socio-economic inequality.

This kind of sketch of 'justice as fairness' will be familiar to many, but it fails to provide much concrete sense of what a Rawlsian society might actually look like. Not least, it gives little idea of what the main institutional features of a society that realized those principles might be. (Even on Rawls's own account we might need some such idea, since reflective equilibrium requires accepting the implications of our principles in particular cases, and that seems to necessitate knowing something about their institutional content.[64]) Rawls is not much concerned in *A Theory of Justice* with that elaborating task, but he subsequently put a little additional social and political flesh on the otherwise abstract bones of principle. Not least, he later provided idealized sketches of five candidate 'regimes' (complete with political, economic, and social

[64] See John Rawls, *Justice as Fairness: A Restatement*, ed. Erin Kelly (Cambridge, MA: Harvard University Press, 2001), 136.

institutions) of which only two are judged to constitute 'well-ordered' regimes of the right sort. In particular, 'laissez-faire capitalism', 'welfare-state capitalism', and 'state socialism' with a command economy are found, in different ways, to fail to satisfy the two principles of justice.[65] (For example, welfare-state capitalism fails, not only because the 'fair value' of the political liberties is undermined by the concentration of wealth and capital in too few hands, but also because it does not recognize a principle of 'reciprocity'—of which the difference principle is one form—in its regulation of economic inequalities.[66]) The two remaining candidate regimes are what he calls 'property-owning democracy' and 'liberal socialism'. Perhaps the most distinctive feature of liberal socialism is that the means of production are socially owned, but economic power is shared amongst firms, which are governed in part by their workforce, and which operate in competitive markets, thereby avoiding too much government control and bureaucratic power.[67] In contrast, a property-owning democracy (like welfare-state capitalism) allows private property in productive assets, but (unlike welfare-state capitalism) is designed to ensure the widespread ownership of such assets and a broad spread of human capital (that is, of education and skills), thereby avoiding both too much concentration of private economic power and the emergence of an underclass.[68] Since both a property-owning democracy and liberal socialism satisfy the relevant principles, 'justice as fairness' cannot decide between them. The choice between these two regimes is rather to be made in the light of the historical context, political traditions, and social forces of each country.[69]

My main concern here is not the justification and elaboration of these principles of social justice, but rather the level of abstraction at which Rawls's theory is initially pitched. He provides an account of (aspects of) an ideal commonwealth, but insists that this ideal is not blind to all of the constraints of what is sometimes called the real world. Justice as fairness is portrayed as 'realistically utopian', as 'probing the limits of practicable political possibility', and thereby as helping us to explore what a just society under 'reasonably favourable but still possible historical conditions' might look like.[70] It is a role

---

[65] Whether its institutions are just is one of four questions to ask of candidate regimes. See Rawls, *Justice as Fairness*, 136–7.

[66] Rawls, *Justice as Fairness*, 137–8.

[67] The first principle includes a right to private personal property, but not a right to private property in productive assets. See Rawls, *Justice as Fairness*, 114–15.

[68] Rawls, *Justice as Fairness*, 138–49; and 'Preface for the French Edition of *A Theory of Justice* (1987)', in John Rawls, *Collected Papers*, ed. Samuel Freeman (Cambridge, MA: Harvard University Press, 1999), 419–20.

[69] Rawls, *Justice as Fairness*, 139.

[70] Rawls, *Justice as Fairness*, 4. See also John Rawls, *Lectures on the History of Political Philosophy*, ed. Samuel Freeman (Cambridge, MA: Harvard University Press, 2007), 10–11. The other roles identified for political philosophy are: first, as a *practical* response to divisive political conflict (for example, seeking to identify agreement between apparently divergent

with a distinguished historical pedigree. In particular, Rousseau's *Social Contract* is identified as a realistically utopian precursor, aspiring to describe a society that is both 'fully just and workable'.[71] Rawls's account of a just society is also intended to be both 'utopian' and 'realistic', but the boundary between these two characteristics is not immediately obvious.[72]

Rawls draws an important distinction between 'ideal theory' and 'non-ideal theory', and identifies *A Theory of Justice* as, primarily, a contribution to the former. The qualifier ('primarily') is needed for two main reasons: first, some issues of non-ideal theory (such as civil disobedience) are discussed in the book; and second, ideal theory is related, in several ways (discussed below), to non-ideal theory. Rawls also maintains that ideal theory is, in some sense, the more 'fundamental' part of theorizing about justice.[73] Both the distinction and this primacy claim require some elaboration.

Ideal theory is concerned with establishing the principles that ought to constrain the design and operation of the basic structure of a democratic society.[74] In pursuit of that task, ideal theory makes both simplifying and idealizing assumptions, but it is the latter that are of interest here.[75] Ideal theory puts aside certain non-ideal features of the existing world, but this process is only to go so far. Certain kinds of ideal theorizing—what one commentator refers to as 'idle utopianism'—are seemingly ruled out.[76] In turn, Rawlsian ideal theory is required to respect certain realistic constraints (in order to explore 'the limits of practicable political possibility' successfully).[77] The precise boundary here—between 'utopianism' and 'realism'—may be difficult to discern, but it is important to see that the divide here is internal to 'ideal theory'.

What we might call the 'utopian' assumptions of ideal theory include what Rawls calls 'favourable circumstances' and 'strict compliance'. First, in

---

philosophical and moral opinions); second, providing *orientation* by helping a people think about their own political institutions and history (for example, providing members of a democracy with a notion of equal citizenship); and third, (in quasi-Hegelian fashion) helping *reconcile* individuals to their society (for example, dampening 'frustration and rage' at society by revealing the rationality and good that exist in its institutions and history).

[71] Rawls, *Lectures on the History of Political Philosophy*, 193. This interpretation is said to be in line with Rousseau's own ambition to take 'human beings as they are and laws as they might be' in *The Social Contract* (opening paragraph of book I).

[72] The term 'realistic utopia' appears only in Rawls's later work, and in adopting it to talk about his work as a whole there is perhaps a danger of underestimating the development of his ideas. However, I take that risk partly because the term does appear to capture something of the impulse behind the discussion of ideal theory in *A Theory of Justice*.

[73] John Rawls, *A Theory of Justice* (Cambridge, MA: Harvard University Press, 1971), 9.

[74] I ignore other (international and individual) dimensions of ideal theory here.

[75] An example of a simplifying assumption might be the restriction of the discussion in *A Theory of Justice* to a closed domestic society.

[76] See A. John Simmons, 'Ideal and Nonideal Theory', *Philosophy & Public Affairs*, 38 (2010), 8.

[77] Rawls, *Justice as Fairness*, 4.

assuming 'favourable circumstances', we assume that the society does not suffer from natural limitations or historical contingencies of the kind that would prevent individuals from being able to support and comply with just principles. In particular, we assume that fortune and history have been kind enough to ensure that the society does not lack either the level of economic well-being, or the kind of political and cultural stability, that make a 'well-ordered' society possible. As a result, citizens of the society can be said to have a (meaningful) choice of whether to support and comply with the principles of justice under consideration. Second, in assuming 'strict compliance', we assume that, confronted with this (meaningful) choice, everyone (or very nearly everyone) chooses to support and comply with those principles of justice (in the ways required by those various principles). Or rather, being careful—and complicating the relation between ideal theory and strict compliance—that is what we initially assume (in order to isolate conceptions of justice for comparison). Recognizing that different conceptions of justice will motivate different degrees of support and compliance, we are subsequently required to take these 'strains of commitment' into account in assessing the comparative merits of different conceptions over time.[78] These are clearly both ideal assumptions. We know that, in the real world, for example, societies can suffer from severe poverty and contain individuals who behave unjustly (conditions which help form the remit of non-ideal theory).

What we might call the 'realistic' assumptions of ideal theory include what Rawls, following Hume (and others), calls 'the circumstances of justice'. These take into account certain 'general facts of political sociology and human psychology', and are said to reflect the historical conditions under which modern democratic societies exist.[79] They have 'objective' and 'subjective' components. The *objective* circumstances of justice include the conditions that make social cooperation possible and necessary. (Note that social cooperation here is a slightly technical notion, involving publicly recognized rules and procedures, some reciprocity of benefits and burdens, and the rational advantage of each participant.[80]) Cooperation is possible because many individuals coexist in the same geographical territory, and because they have sufficiently similar, or complementary, needs and interests. Cooperation is necessary because of 'moderate scarcity', and because individuals are sufficiently alike in their physical and mental powers (not least, similarly vulnerable) that no individual(s) can (stably) dominate the rest. The idea of 'moderate scarcity' asserts that natural and other resources are neither too abundant nor too meagre for cooperation. That is, there are not so many natural resources

---

[78] Rawls, *A Theory of Justice*, 176. Rawls famously judges utilitarianism to fall at this hurdle, since its 'strains of commitment' turn out to 'exceed the capacity of human nature'.
[79] Rawls, *Justice as Fairness*, 33.
[80] Rawls, *Justice as Fairness*, 5.

that cooperation is superfluous (since individuals could just take what they wanted); nor are there so few natural resources that cooperation would always break down (since there could never be enough for all to meet their needs).[81] In conditions of modest scarcity, cooperation makes it possible for all of us to lead a better life than would be possible if we attempted to live solely by our own efforts. The *subjective* circumstances of justice recognize that individuals have different ends and purposes, and that they are preoccupied with pursuing their own plans of life (which need not be self-interested plans).[82] In this context, Rawls would later refer to the 'fact of reasonable pluralism' and the (related) 'fact of oppression'. The first of these asserts that in a democratic society, there will always be 'profound and irreconcilable' differences in the comprehensive (and partially comprehensive) religious, moral, and philosophical doctrines, held by citizens.[83] The diversity of such doctrines in modern democratic societies is not a historical contingency that may pass away, but 'a permanent feature' of the public culture. Nor is that diversity the result of irrationality or malice on the part of individuals, since what Rawls calls the 'burdens of judgment' will scupper even conscientious and sincere attempts to reach agreement on a comprehensive doctrine.[84] The second of these 'facts' asserts that continuing and shared allegiance to one comprehensive doctrine can only be maintained by 'the oppressive use of state power'.[85] This is purportedly true of secular as well as religious doctrines. Thus, a society based on the moral views of Kant or Mill, like a society based on Catholicism, would require the 'oppressive sanctions of state power' in order to remain so.[86] Rawls holds (empirically) that free societies will always be characterized by reasonable pluralism, and (normatively) that sustaining agreement on a comprehensive doctrine could never justify the resulting loss of freedom.

As well as distinguishing between ideal and non-ideal theory, Rawls also maintains that ideal theory is the 'fundamental' part of the theory of justice.[87] This primacy claim is open to misunderstandings. He is not saying, for example, that the problems of non-ideal theory are less urgent (indeed, given the kind of world that we live in, non-ideal theory is 'of first practical

---

[81] Rawls, *A Theory of Justice*, 127.   [82] Rawls, *A Theory of Justice*, 127.

[83] Rawls, *Justice as Fairness*, 3.

[84] This reasonable disagreement results from obstacles including: the complex and conflicting nature of evidence; the ways in which our (different) experience affects our treatment of evidence; the vagueness of concepts; and the difficulty in weighing different kinds of reasons against each other. (This fact also helps explain why a free society cannot itself be a community—given Rawls's idiosyncratic definition of a community as a body of persons affirming the same comprehensive doctrine—although it may, of course, contain several. Rawls, *Justice as Fairness*, 3–4.)

[85] Rawls, *Justice as Fairness*, 34.

[86] Rawls, *Justice as Fairness*, 34.

[87] Rawls, *A Theory of Justice*, 9.

Liberalism and Utopia

importance').[88] Nor is there any suggestion that less time and energy should be expended in the pursuit of solutions to non-ideal problems. Rather, ideal theory is primary in the conceptual sense that non-ideal theory depends on it for the proper specification of its constructive goals. Without ideal theory, non-ideal theory 'lacks an aim'; unless and until we know where we want to go, we cannot properly work out how to get there.[89]

The primary function of non-ideal theory is to map out the various (usually gradual) steps (involving individual actions, policy choices, institutional changes, and so on) that might take us from our particular imperfect present location towards a society with a just basic structure. As a result, non-ideal theory would seem to require knowledge and skills—including empirical information, historical understanding, and social scientific techniques—which ideal theory either lacks, or requires less of. Rawls does not discuss these issues of transition at length, but he does identify some significant constraints on the kind of steps that are required. In particular, these steps should: be 'likely to be effective' (in bringing about the ideal); be 'morally permissible'; be 'politically possible'; and respect a priority rule (tackling more serious injustices ahead of less serious ones).[90] On this 'strongly transitional' reading, it seems that non-ideal theory should choose the next step for society, not on the basis of how close that step might be situated to the eventual goal, but rather by how close to that eventual goal it might eventually enable us to go.[91] As a result, non-ideal theory should prefer a 'third-best' or 'fourth-best' arrangement that would leave the route to the ideal open, over a 'second-best' arrangement which would prevent us from ever reaching that ideal.

On this account, ideal theory is clearly important in the non-ideal context. Three roles might be mentioned here. Ideal theory has the foundational role already discussed; it provides the ultimate destination, in order that non-ideal theory can work out the route to that destination from our own particular imperfect starting point. In addition, ideal theory provides a benchmark for criticizing the existing basic structure. Extant institutions are evaluated in the light of the ideal conception and 'held to be unjust to the extent that they depart from it without sufficient reason'.[92] Finally, ideal theory can also contribute to establishing the priority rule that non-ideal theory needs to respect in its transitional role. For example, the lexical ordering of the

---

[88] Rawls, 'The Law of Peoples (1993)', in *Collected Papers*, 537.
[89] John Rawls, *Political Liberalism* (New York: Columbia University Press, 1993), 285.
[90] See John Rawls, *The Law of Peoples* (Cambridge, MA: Harvard University Press, 1999), 89, and Rawls, *A Theory of Justice*, 303. For interesting analysis of the interpretation and plausibility of this list, see Simmons, 'Ideal and Nonideal Theory', 18–19.
[91] Simmons, 'Ideal and Nonideal Theory', 22.
[92] Rawls, *A Theory of Justice*, 246.

principles of justice might help ascertain which particular injustices count as more serious (and which are therefore to be tackled ahead of less serious ones).[93]

On this Rawlsian account, ideal and non-ideal theory appear as partners rather than rivals. Moreover, they are partners who need each other. Non-ideal theory depends on ideal theory (to specify its ultimate target, to provide a benchmark for its social criticism, and to help identify its priorities). Less obviously, ideal theory also depends on non-ideal theory. In particular, Rawls appears to hold that if ideal theory were construed in such a way as to lack these (or similar) links with non-ideal theory, then it would cease to be worth pursuing.[94] On its own, ideal theory cannot offer workable solutions to the problems of non-ideal circumstances, and it is only because, and to the extent that, it contributes to the solution of those non-ideal problems that ideal theory has any claim to our attention.[95]

HOBSON AND RAWLS: SOME COMPARISONS

There are some striking similarities in the attitudes of Hobson and Rawls towards ideal description. Moreover, these similarities seem to be pertinent to the wider issue of how best to characterize the liberal attitude towards utopianism. (This is not, of course, to deny that there are also differences here—not all of which redound to the advantage of Hobson—and several of these are acknowledged in what follows.)

In order to introduce these similarities (and differences), consider two broad criticisms that might be made of Hobson's enthusiasm for 'humbler ideals', which I will call the conceptual criticism and the practical criticism, respectively. Both complaints could be seen—at least, by what we might call less timid enthusiasts for utopia—as reflecting a failure to take the ideal seriously. In each case, I will consider whether parallel (but not identical) concerns might be raised about Rawls's work.

Some conceptual preliminaries might usefully introduce the first of these criticisms. In thinking about ideal commonwealths, it is often helpful to

---

[93] See Rawls, *A Theory of Justice*, 391.
[94] Much depends on what counts as sufficiently similar. For example, I am not inclined to accept the apparent suggestion of the elaborating sentence that follows this footnote, since I hold that ideal theory might have value independent of its contribution to workable solutions in non-ideal circumstances.
[95] At least, this seems to be implied by his claim that: 'If ideal theory is worthy of study, it must be because, as I have conjectured, it is the fundamental part of the theory of justice and essential for the nonideal part as well.' Rawls, *A Theory of Justice*, 391. I am grateful to Adam Swift for drawing my attention to this particular reference, albeit in a rather indirect manner.

distinguish between the desirability, feasibility, and accessibility, of the social and political arrangements that they propose.[96] Very roughly: by desirability, I mean whether the proposed arrangements are normatively preferable (and not, for example, whether they are psychologically desired by anyone); by feasibility, I mean whether those arrangements are compatible with (what is known about) social design and human nature; and by accessibility, I mean whether those arrangements are reachable by us from where we are currently situated. On this account, arrangements that are desirable might or might not be feasible, and arrangements that are feasible might or might not be accessible.

The conceptual criticism of Hobson is that, at times, he conflates the ideal (the most desirable) with the (best) accessible. Consider, for example, his insistence that the ideal commonwealth requires 'individual' incentives in addition to 'social' incentives, since the latter (although they exist) are neither sufficiently strong nor sufficiently widespread to motivate the required productive activity. At first glance, this might look like a concession to feasibility. That is, Hobson might appear to be advancing a claim about a psychological limit to the generosity of motivations that applies to humankind as such (in any possible context). However, his response to an imagined objection (from a putative subscriber to less humble ideals) suggests otherwise. The imagined objection concedes that the 'altruism' of present-day individuals might be insufficient, but—appealing to the many and various ways in which social structures shape individual motivation—maintains that the 'altruism' of future individuals who have been socialized under a radically altered environment would be sufficient.[97] In his response, Hobson denies neither the desirability nor the feasibility of such wholly socially motivated individuals. His reason for excluding wholly social motivations from the ideal is simply that this kind of motivational structure is not an option 'for man as he is now'.[98] In short, his response seems to allow as ideal only those (desirable and feasible) arrangements that can be reached by us from our present circumstances. On the present account, this is to conflate the ideal with the accessible.[99] That a target is a distant one, not attainable by us from where we are now, is not a good reason for denying its ideal status. We might, after all, just happen to be presently situated a long way from social arrangements that are ideal.[100]

---

[96] For adjacent distinctions, see Allan E. Buchanan, *Justice, Legitimacy, and Self-Determination: Moral Foundations for International Law* (Oxford: Oxford University Press, 2004), 38, fn. 44; and Eric Olin Wright, *Envisioning Real Utopias* (London: Verso, 2010), 20–5.

[97] Hobson, 'Edward Bellamy', 187–8.

[98] Hobson, 'Edward Bellamy', 188.

[99] I am not endorsing the idea that wholly social motivation is the ideal; I am merely insisting that the impossibility of us attaining that ideal from our current situation is not enough to disqualify it.

[100] See also, in this context, Hobson, *Confessions of an Economic Heretic*, 199.

A parallel (but not identical) conceptual criticism can be made of Rawls. At first, this might seem unlikely. After all, Rawls is happy to identify the realistic utopia as a 'long-term goal of political endeavour', which today we can only work towards.[101] He even makes it clear that it might be subsequent 'others', and not we, who 'will someday, somewhere, achieve it'.[102] And he seems explicitly to warn against identifying the ideal with the extant *qua* extant, noting that 'the specific conditions of our world at any given time—the status quo—do not determine the ideal conception'.[103] However, whilst he thereby resists (mis)identifying the ideal with the (best) accessible, some have seen him as making a parallel error—(mis)identifying the ideal with the (best) feasible. In particular, the notion of a realistic utopia seems designed to guarantee that the ideal is consistent with (what is known about) social design and human nature. (It is for this reason that the Rawlsian principles of justice assume, for example, certain facts about moderate scarcity and reasonable pluralism.) And yet that social and political arrangements are infeasible is not obviously a good reason for denying their ideal status. The world might, after all, just be structured in such a way that the ideal is not feasible. Indeed, to rule out that very possibility looks like wishful thinking of the kind that (unrealistic) utopianism is itself often accused of.[104]

Some conceptual preliminaries might also usefully introduce the second of these criticisms. The functions of utopia are many. They variously include: criticism (of the existing world); construction (of a new world); context revelation (illuminating the world they were written in); clarification (both of values, and of the institutions and ethos that might embody them); consolation (providing comfort); and cheer (providing amusement).[105] It is the constructive function that is pertinent here, the utopian ambition to transform the world. And I will assume that ideal commonwealths typically discharge this function by motivating people to change the world, and by providing a target which can help direct their efforts to do so.

The practical criticism of Hobson is that his endorsement of the efficacy of humbler ideals is misplaced. Hobson recognizes and endorses the 'constructive' ambition of ideal description, but insists that 'humbler ideals' are more effective in this role than their less humble counterparts. (Indeed, he suggests elsewhere—in a sharp personal attack on Bernard Shaw—that the practical irrelevance of less humble ambitions can sometimes explain their

---

[101] Rawls, *The Law of Peoples*, 128.
[102] Rawls, *The Law of Peoples*, 128.
[103] Rawls, 'The Law of Peoples (1993)', in *Collected Papers*, 555.
[104] See G. A. Cohen, *Rescuing Justice and Equality* (Cambridge, MA: Harvard University Press, 2008), 254.
[105] See David Leopold, 'What is Utopia For?', unpublished manuscript. I do not suggest that this is an exhaustive list, or that these functions cannot be combined.

adoption.)[106] I take Hobson to be claiming that humble ideals are both more effective motivators, and more effective guides, by comparison with their less humble counterparts. Neither claim looks convincing. That more modest goals are always more effective at inspiring people to change the world is far from obvious. Given the complexity of human motivation and the various costs of political engagement, it seems possible, at least, to imagine circumstances in which the (eventual) promise of more (rather than less) dramatic change is necessary to engage and energize the relevant political will.[107] In addition, that more modest goals always form more effective guides is potentially misleading. Hobson implies that the choice of the social reformer is whether to let more modest or less modest targets guide their constructive ambitions in the imperfect present. This is to misrepresent the alternatives here, and to ignore the role that more demanding and less immediate ultimate targets can play in helping us choose between equally accessible possibilities now. The choice facing those seeking to change the imperfect present might rather be formulated as between using accessible targets (chosen in the light of extensive reflection on both the ideal and the feasible) and using accessible targets (chosen in wilful ignorance of their relation to the ideal and feasible). Framed in that way, it is far from obvious that those interested in social and political reform should opt for the latter.

A parallel (but not identical) practical criticism can be made of Rawls. At first, this might again seem unlikely. After all, Rawls seems to recognize that less humble ideals might be needed to motivate us. For example, it is the 'reasonable hope' that we may one day achieve a just society that he identifies as working (whether or not that hope is fulfilled) to banish 'the dangers of resignation and cynicism' in the present.[108] In addition, and as seen above, he recognizes that ideal theory has a role to play in shaping the recommendations of non-ideal theory (specifying its ultimate target, providing the benchmark for its social criticism, and helping it identify its priorities). Moreover, Rawls endorses Rousseau's view that the 'limits of the possible in moral matters are less narrow than we think', and understands that a realistic utopia might function, not only to help work out how existing ambitions might be realized, but also to expand our ideas about what is possible.[109] Rawls often says that

---

[106] In response to Shaw's view that distributive justice requires the equalization of income, Hobson remarks that 'he leaves himself open to the retort that he must know quite well that such a condition precludes any effective interference with his own large body of wealth', Hobson, *Confessions of an Economic Heretic*, 73. For the original suggestion, see George Bernard Shaw, *The Intelligent Woman's Guide to Socialism and Capitalism* (New York: Garden City Publishing, 1928), 49, 55–6, 68–70.

[107] I am conscious here of engaging in what has pejoratively been called 'armchair sociology'. It is not quite a defence of this practice to observe that Hobson seems to be doing the same thing.

[108] Rawls, *The Law of Peoples*, 128.

[109] Rawls, *The Law of Peoples*, 7, fn. 10. The Rousseau quotation is from *The Social Contract*, book II, ch. 12, para. 2.

the role of ideal theory is to *explore* the limits of practical political possibility, but he clearly appreciates that this exploration also '*extends* what are ordinarily thought of' as those limits.[110] This is important, not least because expanding our understanding of what arrangements are feasible is sometimes a condition for achieving more desirable arrangements (because beliefs about feasibility can constrain what is achievable).[111] And yet looking at Rawls's practical recommendations, some have thought them too 'humble', in that they are inappropriately concessive to less than permanent features of human society and psychology. For example, his ('lax') account of the operation of the difference principle (in a well-ordered society) can seem to tolerate significant inequalities, driven by the provision of economic incentives to the 'well-placed'. These inequalities, it is suggested, are not strictly necessary to make the worse off better off, but rather reflect a compromise with the kind of selfish character—or, if you prefer, the 'inequality-endorsing attitudes'—encouraged by capitalism.[112]

The issues raised by these two broad criticisms are complex, and not to be resolved in any brief concluding remarks. However, enough has been said to indicate and reinforce some of the similarities implicit in the earlier discussion. The broad parallels between Hobson and Rawls are both striking, and illustrative of a neglected aspect of the relation between liberalism and utopia.

Both Hobson and Rawls view ideal description as a potentially legitimate and worthwhile activity. Indeed, they are both happy to use the language of 'utopia' to describe (parts of) their own social and political vision. However, they both are careful to qualify their enthusiasm, maintaining that (in their preferred form) ideal description should not stray too far from the constraints of this world (it should not be *too* utopian). And they both use the language of a 'realistic utopia' to capture the resulting desideratum.

Both component parts of this concept of the 'realistic utopia' are crucial. If either is neglected, it can distort the understanding not only of liberalism, but also of these particular authors.

As an example, of the latter, consider the treatment of Rawls's work in some of the recent critical literature. It has been said, for example, that his theory 'certainly purports to be pure of contamination' by certain facts, and especially 'the facts of history, psychology, economics, sociology, and political science'.[113] (This kind of 'abstractness' is, in turn, identified as making the theory peculiarly ill-equipped, either to understand, or to change the modern world.) However, on the account offered here, such a reading would seem to underestimate both the realist constraints that Rawlsian ideal theory strives to respect,

---

[110] Rawls, *The Law of Peoples*, 6. My emphasis.
[111] See Olin Wright, *Envisioning Real Utopias*, 23.
[112] Cohen, *Rescuing Justice*, 33.
[113] Raymond Geuss, *Outside Ethics* (Princeton: Princeton University Press, 2005), 33.

not least in its account of the circumstances of justice, and the nature of the proposed partnership between ideal and non-ideal theory.

More importantly, Hobson and Rawls's shared commitment to a 'realistic utopia' also casts doubt on the familiar account of liberalism as unremittingly hostile towards utopianism. Whatever the support offered to that characterization by, for example, 'cold-war liberalism', it is apparent that it cannot be sustained in its unqualified form. Not least, our two authors demonstrate that liberalism is capable of a different, more positive, attitude towards utopianism. And, if we are not to mistake the part for the whole, we should acknowledge that variety here.

The temptation at this point is simply to affirm the diversity and flexibility of liberalism as an ideology, and perhaps remark on its ability to adopt a wide range of attitudes towards the discussion of the ideal commonwealth. However, I think we might do a little better.

Notice, in particular, the broad political similarities between our two subjects. Both Hobson and Rawls have plausibly been characterized as 'left liberals'. Obviously a sample of two authors is insufficient to establish any strong claims about the attitude towards utopia of any particular current within the liberal tradition. Yet, on the evidence above, and with all the appropriate cautions in place, I conclude with a (descriptive) hypothesis that might be explored further.

Left liberals, I suggest, are typically willing to engage in ideal description, and they do not share the hostility towards utopianism exemplified by (some) other strands of liberalism. However, their utopian enthusiasms are typically tempered by a commitment to the need for 'realism' in ideal description. Whatever their differences, Hobson and Rawls, for example, are united in their determination not to stray too far from the constraints of this world in envisaging their ideal commonwealth. The advantages and disadvantages of such 'realistic utopias' are in some dispute—not least by those sceptical of the merits of 'humbler ideals'—but need not affect the suggestion advanced here. Namely, that on the basis of evidence from two continents, and either end of the twentieth century, the left-liberal embrace of utopia remains a cautious one.

2

Socialism and the New Liberalism[1]

Ben Jackson

> The discussion turned largely on the relative merits of Liberalism & Socialism, but suffered from the fact that the definitely socialist members & the definite;ly liberal members did not seem to be agreed on what Liberalism & Socialism were.
>
> Minutes of the Rainbow Circle, 1 April 1908[2]

INTRODUCTION

One of the abiding lessons that I learned from Michael Freeden was that the history of British liberal thought contains a rich and radical vein of social democratic political theory, whatever the foibles of the politicians who claim to represent the British liberal tradition at any particular moment. Before I benefited from Michael Freeden's supervision of my doctoral thesis, and a close reading of his own writings, I was more accustomed to the traditional notion that it was 'socialists' who held the monopoly of egalitarian social democratic principle. Freeden's inspirational account of the new liberalism therefore played a salutary and formative role in imparting to me a more pluralistic understanding of the British Left in the twentieth century.[3] But for all its power, Freeden's revisionist account of the British progressive tradition

---

[1] Earlier versions of this chapter were presented at the conference on 'Ideologies, Political Theory, and the Practice of Politics: Themes from the Work of Michael Freeden' in Oxford in April 2008, and at the conference on 'Languages of Politics: Mapping Britain's Long Nineteenth Century' in Durham in April 2009. I am grateful to Jose Harris, Gregg McClymont, Zofia Stemplowska, Stuart White, and the participants on those occasions for very helpful comments.

[2] Michael Freeden (ed.), *Minutes of the Rainbow Circle, 1894–1924* (London: Royal Historical Society, 1989), 173.

[3] See the published version of my doctoral thesis: Ben Jackson, *Equality and the British Left* (Manchester: Manchester University Press, 2007).

nonetheless leaves us with some important unanswered questions regarding the relationship between liberalism and socialism in twentieth-century British politics, and it is this subject that I want to address in this chapter.

In retrospect, the timing of the 'rediscovery' of the new liberals can be placed in an intriguing political context: serious scholarly investigation into new liberal political thought commenced in the late 1970s and achieved its greatest public attention in the 1990s.[4] Thus the ideological crisis of socialism and the electoral crisis of the British Labour Party coincided neatly with the earliest archaeological efforts to dig up a progressive but apparently non-socialist body of radical ideas. Meanwhile, the rebirth of Labour in a sort of progressive alliance with the resurgent Liberal Democrats was the period in which the shared ideological roots of Labourism and Liberalism were widely debated in the pages of British broadsheet newspapers as well as in scholarly journals. Of course, these suggestive historical connections should not be taken entirely at face value. It is not clear, for example, that all of the scholars usually identified as the 'rediscoverers' of the new liberalism straightforwardly sought to furnish contemporary political debate with a language suitable for late twentieth-century political consumption.[5] However, what certainly does emerge from these scholarly writings, and in particular from Michael Freeden's work on the British progressive tradition, is a more sophisticated historical account of the genesis of British social democratic ideas. This account highlights the pattern of mutual influence and indeed intellectual interdependence between theorists who self-identified as liberals and those who saw themselves as socialists but who were subsequently sorted by scholars and political actors into quite separate ideological boxes. As became clear from

---

[4] The key texts for this 'rediscovery' of the new liberalism were Peter Clarke, *Liberals and Social Democrats* (Cambridge: Cambridge University Press, 1978); Michael Freeden, *The New Liberalism* (Oxford: Oxford University Press, 1978); Michael Freeden, *Liberalism Divided* (Oxford: Oxford University Press, 1986); Stefan Collini, *Liberalism and Sociology: L. T. Hobhouse and Political Argument in England, 1880–1914* (Cambridge: Cambridge University Press, 1979). For other contributions, see e.g. Peter Weiler, *The New Liberalism* (New York: Garland, 1982); Gerald Gaus, *The Modern Liberal Theory of Man* (London: Croom Helm, 1983); Raymond Plant and Andrew Vincent, *Philosophy, Politics and Citizenship* (Oxford: Basil Blackwell, 1984); Avital Simhony and David Weinstein (eds.), *The New Liberalism* (Cambridge: Cambridge University Press, 2001). A valuable overview of this literature is Andrew Vincent, 'The New Liberalism in Britain 1880–1914', *Australian Journal of Politics and History*, 36 (1990), 388–405. For the wider public debate about the relationship between liberalism and socialism, see e.g. David Marquand, *The Progressive Dilemma*, 2nd edition (London: Phoenix, 1999); John Gray, 'Goodbye to Rawls', *Prospect* (November 1997), 8–9; John Gray, 'After Social Democracy', in his *Endgames: Questions in Late Modern Political Thought* (Cambridge: Polity, 1997), esp. 25; Marc Stears and Stuart White, 'New Liberalism Revisited', in Henry Tam (ed.), *Progressive Politics in the Global Age* (Cambridge: Polity, 2001); Michael Freeden, 'True Blood or False Genealogy: New Labour and British Social Democratic Thought', in his *Liberal Languages* (Princeton: Princeton University Press, 2005).

[5] Indeed, Stefan Collini's avowed aim was precisely the opposite of this resolutely unhistorical objective: see his *Liberalism and Sociology*, 253.

the (misleading) appropriation of the 'progressive alliance' motif by Tony Blair and New Labour, this is an interpretation of British progressivism that can be instrumentally useful to those engaged in political polemics, whether the 'rediscoverers' of the new liberalism intended it to be so or not.

My primary aim in this chapter, though, is to draw attention to a scholarly rather than strictly political unintended consequence of this revisionist historiography of British social democracy. For as the new liberals became more widely discussed in scholarly literature from the late 1970s onwards, and as the surrounding political climate became more and more anti-socialist, the retreat from socialist language in the British public sphere was increasingly accompanied by a perceptible scholarly retreat from acknowledging the historical importance of socialist ideology to British political development. The careful formula that there was a 'mutual' intellectual exchange between liberals and socialists in twentieth-century Britain became reduced to an overwhelming focus on the role of a hegemonic liberalism in shaping British socialism. The possibility that socialist ideology might itself have exercised some influence over British liberals, although occasionally remarked upon, has been left unexplored by historians and political theorists. In this chapter I aim to step into the breech and make the case that the intellectual influence of socialism on the new liberalism has been understated.

LIBERALS AND SOCIALISTS

In making this case, it is not my intention to take Michael Freeden's work on the new liberalism as a stalking horse or proxy for this neglect of British socialism. Freeden's works on the new liberalism emerged from a very different political context, and they remain justly celebrated milestones in the field. Both *The New Liberalism* and *Liberalism Divided* are books that repay repeated and careful readings. Indeed, both books are wholly persuasive in their identification of the close ideological affinity between leading new liberal theorists and socialist intellectuals and politicians, and both books meticulously document the extent to which such socialists were influenced by the ideas of liberals such as J. A. Hobson and L. T. Hobhouse, not to mention of course by the later work of William Beveridge and J. M. Keynes. The point of this chapter is not that this picture stands in need of substantial revision, but rather that we need to *complete* this revised account of the British progressive tradition by recognizing that new liberal theorists themselves were in turn drawing on arguments and policies that were socialist in their intellectual provenance. I therefore want to stress the symmetry of the ideological influence between the new liberals, or at least new liberal intellectuals, and socialists. To make my task manageable, I will leave liberal politicians to one side in favour of focusing on the socialist influence on liberal intellectuals—it is no part of my case to claim that leading new liberal politicians such as David Lloyd George or Winston Churchill were sympathetic to socialist analysis.

My argument may nonetheless entail a disagreement at some level with Michael Freeden's own interpretation of the progressive tradition. Freeden's aim in his early work was explicitly to deflate the excessively socialist-centric understanding of the changes that occurred within British liberalism in the late nineteenth and early twentieth centuries. As he argued in *The New Liberalism*:

> The theme of this study is to demonstrate that intellectually and ideologically, liberalism itself was fully responsible for, and capable of, transforming its political doctrines (though naturally, one cannot ignore the simple fact that there is always an interflow and exchange of ideas in an open society).

He added later: 'Liberal influences among many socialist leaders and intellectuals seem to have been stronger than the reverse.'[6] This latter observation clearly does not foreclose the possibility that socialist ideology was a strong influence on liberal thinkers in an absolute rather than a relative sense, so it would be excessively argumentative, and rather fruitless, to disagree directly with this claim. I am, however, more sceptical of the idea that twentieth-century liberal revisionism can be understood as basically independent of socialism in its intellectual development. It is not necessary to believe that the new liberals simply copied the ideas of socialists to think that the rise of the labour movement and socialist ideology across Western Europe acted as an extremely powerful influence on the trajectory of liberal thinking.

Clearly, a great deal would need to be said to fully justify this claim and (perhaps fortunately) I do not have space to give such a comprehensive account in this chapter. In order to get some evidence on the table, though, and to sidestep an intimidating phalanx of questions of definition and method relating to how, exactly, one could go about tracing the influence of socialist ideas, I will simply suggest that one illuminating way to track the influence of socialism on the new liberalism is to examine the attitudes of new liberal intellectuals to the social ownership and control of industry. As Freeden has pointed out, the word 'socialism' had a variety of connotations in the early twentieth century, including the description of any measure designed to increase the role of the state in guiding economic and social policy.[7] In this sense, for example, the expansion of the welfare state could be described as advancing socialism. My concern here will be 'socialism' in a strict sense, understood as a method of placing private firms and capital under the

---

[6] Freeden, *New Liberalism*, 21–2, 255; see too the endorsement of this latter point by Ross McKibbin, in his review in *English Historical Review*, 94 (1979), 613.

[7] Freeden, *New Liberalism*, 25–7; Freeden, *Liberalism Divided*, 178–9.

ownership and management of the community rather than private individuals. My working hypothesis is that examining the attitude of new liberals towards this socialist objective gives us some insight into the extent to which they engaged with and accepted socialist arguments.

While certain limited forms of nationalization were espoused by non-socialists for technocratic reasons independent of socialist ideology, historically it was socialism that placed public ownership on the British political agenda. As Kenneth Morgan has observed: 'The public ownership of major industries, utilities and natural resources was inseparable from the socialist idea in Britain from the foundation of Keir Hardie's ILP in 1893 down to the Second World War'.[8] A political programme that envisaged a large strategic role for social ownership, and viewed with equanimity the encroachment on the rights of capital that this entailed, therefore displayed a significant affinity with socialism. Such a programme, I will argue, was articulated by the leading British theorists of left liberalism in the first half of the twentieth century.

One earlier and well-attested example of the importance of socialist thought to British liberalism is John Stuart Mill, who was of course greatly interested in socialist writings in the latter stages of his career.[9] There is a good case for seeing Mill's liberalism as blending into a form of socialism by the end of his life. However, some contributors to the Mill literature seek to draw a distinction between a Millian 'liberal socialism', focused on the need to ensure greater individual freedom through participation in worker-managed firms, and later, more 'statist' liberals or social democrats who, it is argued, prioritized distributive justice through the welfare state rather than Mill's more participative ideals.[10] The remainder of this chapter will, among other things, suggest that this distinction has been drawn too sharply.

The rest of the chapter proceeds in three stages. First, I will investigate the ideas about social ownership found in the works of political theory produced by J. A. Hobson and L. T. Hobhouse before the First World War; second, I will muster some evidence of left-liberal enthusiasm for quite radical forms of social ownership and control drawn from the debate surrounding the future

---

[8] Kenneth Morgan, 'The Rise and Fall of Nationalization in Britain', in his *Ages of Reform: Dawns and Downfalls of the British Left* (London: I. B. Tauris, 2011), 241; see also Jim Tomlinson, 'A "Failed Experiment"? Public Ownership and the Narratives of Post-War Britain', *Labour History Review*, 73 (2008), 230; E. Eldon Barry, *Nationalization in British Politics* (London: Cape, 1965), especially 130–59.

[9] See e.g. Gregory Claeys, 'Justice, Independence and Industrial Democracy: The Development of John Stuart Mill's Views on Socialism', *Journal of Politics*, 49 (1987), 122–47; Bruce Baum, 'J. S. Mill's Conception of Economic Freedom', *History of Political Thought*, 20 (1999), 494–530; John Medearis, 'Labor, Democracy, Utility and Mill's Critique of Private Property', *American Journal of Political Science*, 49 (2005), 134–49.

[10] Bruce Baum, 'J. S. Mill and Liberal Socialism', in Nadia Urbinati and Alex Zakaras (eds.), *J. S. Mill's Political Thought: A Bicentennial Reassessment* (Cambridge: Cambridge University Press, 2007), 99–102, 118–20.

of the coal industry in the years following 1918; and third, I will outline the serious consideration given to socialist planning by William Beveridge, the apparent epitome of a centrist liberal, in the 1930s and 1940s.

FABIAN SOCIALISM AND NEW LIBERAL POLITICAL THEORY

The first point I want to make is an obvious one, but is easily overlooked when discussing the policy prescriptions of the new liberalism, namely that the most eminent of the early twentieth-century new liberal theorists, notably Hobson and Hobhouse, favoured a significant amount of public ownership.[11] It is therefore misleading to present the ideology of the new liberalism as entailing progressive reforms to fiscal policy, labour market regulation, and social policy without also mentioning the strong new liberal commitment to socializing certain forms of industry.

Property ownership was of course an issue of great concern to earlier liberals. Both Gladstonian liberalism and radicalism, for example, clearly had quite firm views about large-scale private land ownership. However, such liberals were extremely reluctant to take this hostility to large concentrations of landed wealth as an endorsement of nationalization, let alone to extend public ownership into the wider industrial sphere.[12] The influence of the labour movement was therefore pre-eminent in shaping the thinking of new liberal theorists with respect to the ownership and control of industry. The support of key new liberal intellectuals for a limited, though substantial, socialization of privately held productive resources in the first three decades of the twentieth century emerged as a result of exposure to trade unionism, the cooperative movement, early British socialists such the Fabians, and syndicalism and guild socialism. In particular, we should distinguish between two separate phases of new liberal engagement with socialism. First, from the late nineteenth century until the years immediately before the First World War, writers such as Hobson and Hobhouse maintained a discernibly Fabian tone in their discussion of public ownership. Second, from the First World War into the 1920s, a new emphasis on worker participation in industry emerged in

---

[11] This point has, however, been noted in passing by Alan Ryan, 'New Labour Needs a Moral Compass', *New Statesman*, 7 February 2000.

[12] Eldon Barry, *Nationalization*, 17–77. We should also note that Gladstone himself remained open to the possibility of the public ownership of the railways: see H. C. G. Matthew, *Gladstone: 1809–1898* (Oxford: Oxford University Press, 1997), 67. For the broader nineteenth-century debate on 'state purchase' of the railways, see Eldon Barry, *Nationalization*, 78–108.

liberal political thought, as the influence of syndicalism and guild socialism began to spread into advanced liberal circles.

To begin with the influence of Fabianism, it is well attested in the secondary literature on Hobhouse that his earliest work was cast in a somewhat socialist and Fabian mould.[13] But the persistence of latter-day stereotypes about the character of Fabian socialism may prevent us from appreciating the full import of this influence. As Kevin Morgan has demonstrated, the early work of the Webbs and their Fabian allies was more sophisticated than they are usually credited with. The Webbs in particular were alert to the broader political significance of working-class associational life, and rested their socialist strategy not merely on the advance of the centralized state—as they are often assumed to have done—but also on the strengthening of municipal socialism, cooperatives, and trade unions.[14] However, it remains fair to say that the Fabians and other like-minded nineteenth-century socialists lacked enthusiasm for significant worker participation in industry, and tended to assume that managerial authority in the public sector should not be subject to direct forms of democratic control.[15]

From the late 1880s, Hobhouse was inspired by the emergence of the 'new unionism'—the efforts to organize unskilled workers into trade unions associated in particular with the 1889 London Dock Strike—and was socially and intellectually close to the early Fabians. In Beatrice Webb's diary, for example, Hobhouse is first mentioned as one of the advocates of Fabianism in Oxford.[16] His 1893 book, *The Labour Movement*, was packed with Fabian arguments, and delineated an emergent labour movement that pursued several interconnected strategies to advance the position of the working class, including a defence of producer cooperatives which he drew directly from the work of Beatrice Webb; an appreciation of trade unionism; and a Webbian advocacy of the social ownership of certain industries and services on a national scale, for example the Post Office (which was already under public ownership) and the railways. In applying these various policies, Hobhouse argued: 'we avoid the waste and friction at present involved in the adjustment of supply and

---

[13] Collini, *Liberalism and Sociology*, 59–71; Clarke, *Liberals and Social Democrats*, 44–6; Michael Freeden, 'Hobhouse, Leonard Trelawny (1864–1929)', *Oxford Dictionary of National Biography* (Oxford: Oxford University Press, 2004; online edition, May 2006, <http://www.oxforddnb.com/view/article/33906>, accessed 28 January 2011).

[14] Kevin Morgan, *The Webbs and Soviet Communism* (London: Lawrence and Wishart, 2006), *passim*. For similar revisionist thoughts, see Julia Stapleton, 'Localism Versus Centralism in the Webbs' Political Thought', *History of Political Thought*, 12 (1991), 147–65; Mark Bevir, 'Sidney Webb: Utilitarianism, Positivism, and Social Democracy', *Journal of Modern History*, 74 (2002), 217–52.

[15] Eldon Barry, *Nationalization*, 168–72.

[16] *The Diary of Beatrice Webb Volume 2, 1892–1905: 'All the Good Things of Life'*, Norman MacKenzie and Jeanne MacKenzie (eds.) (London: Virago, 1983), 85 (entry for Christmas, December 1895), although see also p. 324 for the later distance between Hobhouse and the Webbs.

demand; and we put surplus revenue into the pockets, not of individuals, but of the community. Lastly we introduce a new spirit and a new principle into industry.'[17] This contrast between the moral superiority and efficiency of motives of public service and the corruption of working on the basis of private profit sounded a strikingly anti-capitalist note. Recalling Mill's claim that 'men would some day learn to dig and weave for their country as well as to fight for it', Hobhouse argued that 'we may with still more confidence hope that men may learn to follow earnestly and strenuously the higher calling of directing those who dig or weave for the same end'.[18] 'In time', Hobhouse concluded, 'the community will become the chief, perhaps the sole owner of capital and land. But it will be by gradual steps.'[19]

As is well-known, Hobhouse was to take a frostier attitude towards the Webbs and Fabianism more generally later in his career, but his subsequent work retained a commitment to a certain amount of social ownership, notably of monopolies, whether 'natural' or the result of the emergence of uncompetitive 'cartels'. Examples included industries such as gas, water, transport, and the mines.[20] As I will discuss later, however, there was a clear shift in Hobhouse's post-1918 work, away from his support for a classic Fabian model of state-run and elite-directed public ownership to a hybrid cooperative model involving participation by workers, consumers, and management.

The early work of J. A. Hobson elaborated a view of public ownership that was more far-reaching and clearly worked-out than Hobhouse's. Like Hobhouse, Hobson's formative political and intellectual experiences were characterized by sympathetic dialogue with his socialist contemporaries. Upon moving to London in 1887, he moved in the same circles as Sidney Webb, Graham Wallas, and Ramsay MacDonald, becoming a fixture in the London Ethical Society and then of course the Rainbow Circle.[21] His views on the need for a substantial public industrial sector alongside the private sector also drew on the ideas of his friend, and Fabian essayist, William Clarke. Clarke's account of the growth of monopoly capitalism, and the likely

---

[17] L. T. Hobhouse, *The Labour Movement* (London: T. Fisher Unwin, 1893), 38–41, quote at 41. For the source of Hobhouse's understanding of cooperatives, see Beatrice Potter, *The Co-operative Movement in Great Britain* (London: Swan Sonnenschein, 1891).

[18] Hobhouse, *Labour Movement*, 71–2. Mill quote from J. S. Mill, *Autobiography* (London: Penguin, 1989 [1873]), 176.

[19] Hobhouse, *Labour Movement*, 77.

[20] L. T. Hobhouse, *Liberalism* (Cambridge: Cambridge University Press, 1994 [1911]), 46–7; L. T. Hobhouse, *Elements of Social Justice* (London: Allen & Unwin, 1922), 177–82. For an example of Hobhouse's later account of the shortcomings of Fabian socialism, see his *Democracy and Reaction* (London: T. F. Unwin, 1904), 227–9.

[21] Clarke, *Liberals and Social Democrats*, 51–61; Michael Freeden, 'Hobson, John Atkinson (1858–1940)', *Oxford Dictionary of National Biography* (Oxford: Oxford University Press, 2004; online edition, May 2009, <http://www.oxforddnb.com/view/article/33909>, accessed 28 January 2011).

emergence of new forms of social ownership in response, was indebted to a close reading of Marx's *Capital*.[22] When it came to the specific question of which industries ought to be brought under social ownership, Hobson was not averse to a Labour manifesto-style shopping list of the various industries that he considered ripe for public ownership. In his 1902 book, *The Social Problem*, for example, Hobson argued in favour of the public ownership of banks; insurance; utilities such as water, electricity, and gas; railways; oil; the mines; iron works; engineering shops; cotton; corn; sugar; and possibly agricultural land.[23]

What were the criteria that Hobson felt bound this apparently heterogeneous list of services and industries together as suitable for social rather than private ownership? Hobson proposed three. First, he distinguished between what he saw as standardized, 'routine' industries or services, which supplied goods or services with a fairly predictable demand, and those that supplied goods or services that relied more heavily on the individual abilities or energies stimulated by the incentive of private profit. The former were to be the sphere of various forms of social ownership, the latter to remain the preserve of private enterprise. Second, Hobson argued that the state should undertake to supply directly those goods and services that were required by all citizens: the basic necessities 'of physical, moral and intellectual life'. Hobson's view was that supplying the basic needs of the population would require social ownership of precisely those industries that were the most 'routine' in character: for example, transport or public utilities, but also eventually basic consumption goods such as milk and bread. The idiosyncratic tastes of individuals would be served by the remaining 'non-routine' industries. Third, and like contemporary socialist analysts such as Sidney Webb and Ramsay MacDonald, Hobson argued that public ownership was required to safeguard the public and workers from exploitation by dominant private monopolies. The evolution of enormous companies or 'trusts', seen as an inevitable trend in early twentieth-century capitalism due to the superior efficiency of large-scale production, was said to hand vast power to unaccountable private businesses. The only practicable method of avoiding such 'economic despotism', argued Hobson, was to substitute a public for a private monopoly.[24] In making this point, Hobson was

---

[22] William Clarke, 'The Industrial Basis of Socialism', in George Bernard Shaw (ed.), *Fabian Essays in Socialism* (London: Fabian Society, 1889), 62–101; Peter Weiler, 'William Clarke: The Making and Unmaking of a Fabian Socialist', *Journal of British Studies*, 14 (1974), 90–5; Jules Townshend, 'Hobson and the Socialist Tradition', in John Pheby (ed.), *J. A. Hobson After Fifty Years* (Basingstoke: Macmillan, 1994), 42.

[23] J. A. Hobson, *The Social Problem* (London: J. Nisbet, 1902), 176–7, 193; see also 179.

[24] The arguments in the preceding sentences are taken from Hobson, *Social Problem*, 175–86; and J. A. Hobson, *The Crisis of Liberalism* (London: P. S. King & Son, 1909), 117–32. Hobson's case for public ownership has also been examined by Jules Townshend, *J. A. Hobson* (Manchester: Manchester University Press, 1990), 94–100; and by David Leopold in his chapter of this book.

drawing on widespread progressive sentiments. As the liberal-Fabian philosopher D. G. Ritchie put it, for example, given the rise of the joint-stock company and the salaried manager, 'the state will not so much displace individual enterprise, as substitute for the irresponsible company or "trust" the responsible public corporation'.[25] Once again, Hobson believed that the capitalist enterprises that had evolved furthest in the direction of 'trustification' would also prove to be those engaged in producing standardized goods or services for all.

Hobson made the further, subsidiary argument that large public corporations would also be able to act as model employers, serving as examples to the remaining private sector. In classic Hobsonian (but also Webbian) fashion, he observed that raising the wages and improving the job security of public-sector employees should not be seen as an efficiency loss, since sweated labour entailed significant waste in the working capacity and life chances of working-class families.[26] Clearly, one difference between Hobson's view of socialization and the analysis of his early twentieth-century socialist contemporaries was that such socialists were notionally committed to a much larger, probably all-encompassing, public sector, whereas Hobson was clear that a substantial private sector should remain. Nonetheless, many socialists made the point that they favoured an experimental rather than prescriptive approach to the eventual end-point of public ownership and we should be careful not to overstate the differences between Hobson and socialists such as Webb and Ramsay MacDonald in this period.[27]

As with Hobhouse, Hobson's initial characterization of the structure and organization of the public ownership and management of industry took a Fabian form. In the years before the First World War, Hobson envisaged considerable managerial autonomy in the public sector, with industries run nationally or locally by a board appointed by and accountable to nationally or locally elected politicians.[28] However, Hobson and Hobhouse's view of the most appropriate organizational model for the public sector shifted rapidly in the years around the First World War with the rise of guild socialism and syndicalism. In the next section I will examine this shift in new liberal thinking by focusing in particular on the debate surrounding the ownership of the coal industry immediately after 1918.

---

[25] D. G. Ritchie, *Principles of State Interference* (London: Swan Sonnenschein, 1891), 63–4.
[26] Hobson, *Crisis*, 152–3.
[27] J. R. MacDonald, *Socialism and Society* (London: Independent Labour Party, 1905), 177–9; Philip Snowden, 20 March 1923, *Parl. Deb.*, 4th ser., vol. 161, cols. 2482–4; A. M. McBriar, *Fabian Socialism and English Politics 1884–1918* (Cambridge: Cambridge University Press, 1966), 107–18.
[28] See the organizational model implicit in Hobson, *Crisis*, 140–8.

THE MINES FOR THE NATION: INDUSTRIAL DEMOCRACY AND THE NEW LIBERALISM

The controversy over the future of the coal industry provided a focus for debates about public ownership in the years immediately following the First World War.[29] Confronted by an industry apparently blighted by chronic inefficiency and dogged by acrimonious industrial relations, the post-war coalition government provided the platform for this debate by appointing a Royal Commission on the Coal Industry, chaired by Sir John Sankey, in 1919. Appointed to the Commission were three representatives of the mine owners; three independent businessmen; three representatives of the miners' union, the Miners' Federation of Great Britain (MFGB); and three experts sympathetic to the miners' cause: Sidney Webb, R. H. Tawney, and Sir Leo Chiozza Money.[30] Chiozza Money, a former Liberal MP and leading parliamentary advocate of the new liberalism in the Edwardian period, provides a further example of the extent to which the most radical liberals drew on socialist ideas about public ownership. Even before the War, Chiozza Money advocated the nationalization of the milk trade and the coal industry, a conviction that was confirmed and amplified by his experience as a wartime civil servant. By 1918 he was a Labour parliamentary candidate and in 1920 he authored a substantial monograph entitled *The Triumph of Nationalization*.[31]

One important feature of the context of this post-war debate on the ownership of the coal industry should be emphasized. The period running roughly from 1910 to 1920 can in retrospect be seen as the high-water mark of syndicalist politics, not only in Britain, but also in many industrialized nations. This international current of socialist radicalism, apparently supported on the ground by an enormous surge of labour protest, had a significant agenda-setting power in so far as it succeeded in promoting the idea of industrial democracy nearer to the top of the political agenda. In countries such as Germany, the United States, and Britain, the syndicalist challenge forced political debate, and the mainstream Left in particular, to take seriously models of social ownership that were oriented towards worker participation

---

[29] In the following paragraphs I tread in the footsteps of Freeden, *Liberalism Divided*, 49–77, 177–93, although I think with a different emphasis.

[30] For the background to the Sankey Commission and for an account of its work, see Barry Supple, *The History of the British Coal Industry Volume 4: 1913–46 The Political Economy of Decline* (Oxford: Oxford University Press, 1987), 117–68, details of the Commission's membership on p. 126; for the political context, see Kenneth Morgan, *Consensus and Disunity: The Lloyd George Coalition Government 1918–22* (Oxford: Oxford University Press, 1986), 62–74.

[31] Martin Daunton, 'Money, Sir Leo George Chiozza (1870–1944)', *Oxford Dictionary of National Biography* (Oxford: Oxford University Press, 2004; online edition, September 2010, <http://www.oxforddnb.com/view/article/55929>, accessed 28 January 2011); Leo Chiozza Money, *The Triumph of Nationalization* (London: Cassell & Co., 1920).

in industrial decision-making.[32] In Britain, the labour unrest of these years generated important innovations in socialist thinking, notably the emergence of guild socialism, and the exposition of the syndicalist case famously articulated by a group of South Wales miners in *The Miners' Next Step* (1912) and its sequel, *Industrial Democracy for the Miners* (1919).[33] The syndicalist challenge was indeed particularly potent in the mining industry and by the time the Sankey Commission commenced its work, the mood of the MFGB and its elected officers was sympathetic to an agenda grounded on greater industrial democracy.[34]

Viewed against this background, the proceedings of the Royal Commission, its majority report in favour of public ownership, and the subsequent debate prompted by the government's rejection of the majority's recommendations, all provide fascinating insights into the pro-public ownership progressive alliance that is the subject of this chapter. Evidence in favour of public ownership was taken by the Royal Commission from the leading progressive intellectuals of the period. Webb and Chiozza Money took the unorthodox step of giving evidence themselves,[35] and were followed into the witness box by such luminaries as G. D. H. Cole, Graham Wallas, the future deputy leader of the Labour Party Arthur Greenwood, and, crucially, L. T. Hobhouse and J. A. Hobson. Hobson's evidence contained similar points to those discussed earlier, stressing in particular the excessive power that would be wielded by a unified private mining company and the inefficiency of the existing dispersed organization of the mining industry. To these familiar points, Hobson added a new emphasis on the demand made by the workers in the coal industry for public ownership. This indicated, Hobson argued, that among the workers there was 'a wide-felt preference for a new status as employees in a public service'. Consequently, it was likely that significant efficiency gains could in fact be made under public ownership since the workers actually preferred 'that the state or the municipality should get the advantage of whatever surplus accrues on industry than it should go to the owners of private capital'. Questioned by the General Secretary of the MFGB, Frank Hodges, about his

---

[32] David Howell, 'Taking Syndicalism Seriously', *Socialist History*, 16 (2000), 27–48; Geoff Eley, *Forging Democracy: The History of the Left in Europe, 1850-2000* (Oxford: Oxford University Press, 2002), 97–9, 131–8, 160–4; Marcel van der Linden, *Transnational Labour History* (Aldershot: Ashgate, 2003), 49–84.

[33] See Eldon Barry, *Nationalization*, 207–17; *The Miners' Next Step*, introduced by Merfyn Jones (London: Pluto Press, 1973 [1912]); David Egan, 'The Unofficial Reform Committee and *The Miners' Next Step*', *Llafur*, 2 (1978), 64–80; Richard Price, 'Contextualising British Syndicalism', *Labour History Review*, 63 (1998), 261–76; Marc Stears, 'Guild Socialism and Ideological Diversity on the British Left, 1914-1926', *Journal of Political Ideologies*, 3 (1998), 289–305; Howell, 'Taking Syndicalism Seriously', 36–43.

[34] Morgan, *Consensus*, 62.

[35] A point which Lloyd George used to discredit the Commission when he subsequently turned against it: David Lloyd George, 18 August 1919, *Parl. Deb.*, 5th ser., vol. 119, col. 2001.

view of syndicalism, Hobson indicated that he was opposed to the wholehearted application of such a radical model of ownership, but added:

> I think the development of today has shifted the view of those who would have been reckoned as ordinary state socialists a few years ago, and we recognise it is important that there should be a different representation of the workers in the industry in the administration of that industry.

Influenced by the syndicalist and guild socialist currents then coursing through the British labour movement, Hobson endorsed a hybrid model of public ownership encompassing nationalization of the industry but with its management then subject to the joint democratic control of managers, workers, and consumers.[36]

Hobhouse also endorsed public ownership of the mines in his evidence. Like Hobson, a new note now appeared in his arguments, stressing that for the miners the 'motive of public service' would now be more effective than 'the desire for profit'—this was 'a higher motive in itself', as Hobhouse had earlier argued, but it also indicated the 'double demand' of the post-war worker: 'that the only master a man ought to serve is the community' and that 'as a member of the community he should have some effective ... voice in the control of the conditions under which he works'. In Hobhouse's view, some form of workplace democracy was therefore integral to any public ownership plans.[37]

The contributions of Hobson and Hobhouse cohered with the dominant rhetorical strategy of the advocates of nationalization of the coal industry during the deliberations of the Sankey Commission and in the debate immediately thereafter. They all argued along the following lines, with some differences of emphasis: the existing diffuse structure of the industry was assumed to be inefficient and the choice thus narrowed to a private versus a public monopoly. The immense discretionary power over consumers and workers that would be handed to such a private monopoly meant that the only acceptable organizational model available was nationalization. The efficiency of the industry, it was added, would receive a further boost from the greater willingness on the part of the miners to work in the public service rather than for the gain of private capitalists. Furthermore, the model of nationalization eventually proposed by the majority of the Sankey Commission, and endorsed by the MFGB, was designed to ensure worker participation in the management of the industry. This was felt by the advocates of nationalization to be a critical new reason for public ownership.[38] Compared to later discussions of

---

[36] J. A. Hobson, 25 April 1919, in *Reports and Minutes of Evidence of the Coal Industry Commission Volume Two*, Cmd 360 (London: HMSO, 1919), 473–6, quotes at 474, 476.

[37] L. T. Hobhouse, 6 May 1919, in *Reports*, 560–1.

[38] For different versions of the preceding arguments, compare the evidence given to the Sankey Commission by G. D. H. Cole, Leo Chiozza Money, Sidney Webb, and Graham Wallas: *Reports*, 477–98, 501–44, 548–57, and the arguments put by sympathetic MPs such as William

the coal industry by official bodies, the Sankey Commission was unusual in the extent to which its case for public ownership rested not only on efficiency concerns, but also on the distributive injustice and undemocratic hierarchy created by private ownership of the mines.[39]

The Sankey model did not envisage wholesale industrial democracy but recognized that the miners now had, beyond a desire for higher wages and shorter hours, 'a higher ambition of taking their due share and interest in the direction of the industry to the success of which they, too, are contributing'. Under the Sankey proposals, existing mine owners were to be bought out by the state and in their place each pit would be run by an appointed manager advised by a Local Mining Council. The Local Mining Council would consist of ten members, three managers sitting *ex officio* alongside four members elected by the miners and three members appointed by the District Mining Council. The District Mining Council would in turn comprise a Chairman and Vice-Chairman appointed by the Minister of Mines, four members elected by the miners, four consumer representatives, two technical representatives (e.g. engineers), and two representatives of the commercial side of the industry. The District Mining Councils would appoint the manager of each mine. Atop the District Councils would sit a National Mining Council constituted under the direction of the Minister of Mines and comprising representatives of the District Councils. A standing committee with equal numbers of consumer, worker, and commercial/technical representatives would provide the leadership of this body.[40] The details may have been byzantine, but they undoubtedly signalled a serious engagement on the part of socialist, liberal, and even centrist opinion with the demand for workers' control and the guild socialist-syndicalist critique of capitalist managerial prerogatives. As Tawney put it, under the Sankey model of public ownership, the miners

> will no longer be "hands", employed for the advantage of a profit-making company, but partners in a communal enterprise. It is impossible to exaggerate the significance of that change of status. It is the difference between freedom and something like serfdom.[41]

The radicalism of these objectives partly accounts for the unwavering hostility from employers and Conservatives that greeted the Sankey proposals, and which eventually led to their rejection by Lloyd George's coalition government.

Brace, Vernon Hartshorn, and Aneurin Williams in the parliamentary debates on the Sankey Report: e.g. 11 February 1920, *Parl. Deb.*, 5th ser., vol. 125, cols. 73–99, 135–41, 146–9. See also R. H. Tawney, *The Nationalization of the Coal Industry* (London: Labour Party, 1919); Herbert Smith et al., *The Mines for the Nation* (London: Mines for the Nation Committee, 1920).

[39] David Greasley, 'The Coal Industry: Images and Reality on the Road to Nationalization', in Robert Millward and John Singleton (eds.), *The Political Economy of Nationalization in Britain, 1920-50* (Cambridge: Cambridge University Press, 2002), 51.

[40] Chairman's Report, 20 June 1919, in *Reports*, pp. vii–xi, quote at p. vii.

[41] Tawney, *Nationalization*, 24.

The response of advanced liberals to the majority report of the Sankey Commission was enthusiastic, and they argued that this model could be extended to other industries. *The Nation*, for example, applauded the report as making 'industrial and social history' and noted that its proposals were 'midway between state ownership and administration as conceived by the early socialists, and the full control of the workers which is the aim of guild socialists'. Such nationalization would 'give to the workers new and stimulating aspirations' and 'a degree of control over their own industrial conditions'.[42] *The Nation* acknowledged that radical currents in the labour movement had rightly identified that the worker 'is still in industry what even the bourgeois was in an autocratic or aristocratic state, a subject and not a citizen, called to obedience but denied self-government'. The Sankey solution, *The Nation* concluded, was 'inevitable' for mines, railways, electric power, the post office, and municipal services. But such reforms would also catalyse a wider change in the private sector: 'we cannot for long emancipate the miner and the railwayman from the direct rule of the private owners, and still expect the shipbuilder, the engineer, and the cotton-spinner to remain entirely content with their old status'. *The Nation* therefore envisaged as an initial step in this direction elected worker delegates on the boards of private companies and far greater management consultation with the unions. But the paper did not rule out that in due course some form of guild socialism might eventually emerge.[43]

Hobhouse and Hobson were also enthusiastic about the Sankey model in their later writings. In his *Elements of Social Justice*, for example, Hobhouse argued that nationalized industries could best be managed by joint boards split into three equal sections, representing consumers, the managerial and technical staff, and the workers respectively. Hobhouse regarded the extent of nationalization, and the scope of the other industrial models he saw as plausible (municipal enterprises, cooperatives, and private firms), as an empirical matter, dependent on the results achieved by each model in particular cases.[44] On his account, there was certainly no reason of principle to favour private ownership of the means of production.

Hobson's *Incentives in the New Industrial Order*, published in the same year as Hobhouse's *Elements*, assumed that free competition had already been extinguished in many industries due to the growth in scale of productive units and spoke out for the public ownership of such industries, with nationalization understood to incorporate within its purview 'the substitution of

---

[42] 'State Mines', *The Nation*, 28 June 1919, 382–3.
[43] 'The Future of Industry', *The Nation*, 11 October 1919, 25–6. For similar pieces sympathetic to some form of industrial democracy, see e.g. 'A Question to Property', *The Nation*, 15 February 1919; 'The Miners' Case', *The Nation*, 20 September 1919; 'New and Old in Industry', *The Nation*, 14 February 1920; 'The New Manchesterism', *The Nation*, 1 January 1921.
[44] Hobhouse, *Elements*, 177–84.

representative government for employers' autocracy'. As examples, Hobson cited the usual suspects—mining, railways, electricity, banking, and insurance—but envisaged these as the first instalment rather than the end-point of social ownership. Hobson anticipated the growth of several different forms of social ownership or joint control, each embodying different mechanisms for worker participation: nationalized industries run along the lines of the Sankey Commission majority report; full worker-managed cooperatives or 'guilds'; and private firms with formal mechanisms for consultation with workers and profit-sharing schemes. A National Industrial Council would provide a national forum for discussion between capital and labour and would be invested with certain regulatory responsibilities over industry.[45] Although assigning influences to intellectual developments is a notoriously treacherous business, it is hard to imagine Hobson's thinking, and the new liberalism more generally, manifesting this degree of sympathy for worker participation in the absence of the concurrent ideological shift within the labour movement towards syndicalism, guild socialism, and industrial democracy.[46]

SOCIALIST PLANNING AND THE LIBERALISM OF WILLIAM BEVERIDGE

As a coda to this discussion of early twentieth-century liberalism, it is worth concluding by acknowledging that the pattern sketched so far persisted as British liberalism passed into the later era of Beveridge and Keynes. However, we must at once distinguish between these two seemingly inseparable names. Although both have been classified as centrist liberals who were instrumental in defeating the appeal of socialism by prescribing a dose of moderate liberal interventionism, this description in fact fits Keynes much better than Beveridge.[47]

As Jose Harris has pointed out, during the 1930s and 1940s Beveridge was deeply influenced by, and at times an outright admirer of, economic planning and even the state socialism found in the Soviet Union. It was perhaps not

---

[45] J. A. Hobson, *Incentives in the New Industrial Order* (London: L. Parsons, 1922), 35–6, 5, 100–12, 152–3, 156.

[46] Indeed, as Stuart White has shown, elements of this agenda persisted into later twentieth-century liberal thinking, albeit in a more attenuated form: see his '"Revolutionary Liberalism"? The Philosophy and Politics of Ownership in the Post-War Liberal Party', *British Politics*, 4 (2009), 164–87.

[47] However, Keynes was sympathetic to the growth of public corporations run by experts and professional managers at the expense of large private monopolies, and envisaged such public enterprises playing a significant role in the economy of the future: J. M. Keynes, *The End of Laissez-Faire* [1926], in *The Collected Writings of John Maynard Keynes Volume IX: Essays in Persuasion* (London: Macmillan, 1972), 288–91.

unrelated that the aspiration to give workers a greater say in the conduct of industry did not, however, feature in Beveridge's vision of socialism. After many discussions with Beatrice and Sidney Webb and G. D. H. Cole, and a careful reading of the Webbs' *Soviet Communism*, by the early 1940s Beveridge was convinced that some form of socialist planning, subject of course to democratic control, was the only feasible way to secure economic stability and tackle unemployment. This seems to have been his view at the time he wrote his celebrated 1942 report on social insurance and the rationale behind the famous 'assumption C' of the report: 'maintenance of employment, that is to say avoidance of mass unemployment'.[48] In 1941, for example, Beveridge argued to a private conference held by the Nuffield College Social Reconstruction Survey that 'he was inclined to think that the country might have to go over to a form of state socialism'. He added that he regarded the trade cycle as a barrier to the better world he envisaged, which 'would not disappear while the course of production was determined by a system of profits and prices'.[49] He urged the Nuffield Survey to turn its attentions to 'the state organs necessary for planning under democracy'.[50]

As Jose Harris has also observed, however, this phase in Beveridge's thinking was short-lived and by the time he turned his attention to drafting his *Full Employment in a Free Society*, published in 1944, Beveridge had fallen under the influence of the young Keynesian economists who provided technical advice for the report such as Joan Robinson and Nicholas Kaldor.[51] But in spite of Beveridge's shift in his full employment report towards budgetary rather than physical planning, Beveridge's sympathy for socialism was still palpable. First, the route to full employment Beveridge laid out in the report entailed the public ownership of monopolies to prevent the exploitation of the consumer and the nationalization of certain strategic industries in order to increase the power of the state to stabilize demand. On these grounds, Beveridge floated the possibility of nationalizing transport, power, coal, and steel. Beveridge also suggested the creation of a National Investment Board

---

[48] Jose Harris, *William Beveridge: A Biography*, 2nd edition (Oxford: Oxford University Press, 1997), 302-23, 426-32; William Beveridge, *Social Insurance and Allied Services*, Cmd 6404 (London: HMSO, 1942), 8. See e.g. William Beveridge, 'Soviet Communism', *Political Quarterly*, 7 (1936), 346-67. This interest in the Soviet Union among British progressives of many different hues during the 1930s has been well discussed by Morgan, *Webbs and Soviet Communism*; and John Callaghan, 'Labour's Turn to Socialism in 1931', *Journal of Political Ideologies*, 14 (2009), 115-32.

[49] Minutes of Private Conference of the Nuffield College Social Reconstruction Survey, 4 October 1941, Session I, papers of the Nuffield College Social Reconstruction Survey, Nuffield College Library, M5/1, p. 3.

[50] Minutes of Private Conference of the Nuffield College Social Reconstruction Survey, 5 October 1941, Session IV, M5/1, p. 6. On the background to these conferences, see Daniel Ritschel, 'The Making of Consensus: The Nuffield College Conferences During the Second World War', *Twentieth Century British History*, 6 (1995), 267-301.

[51] Harris, *William Beveridge*, 432-43.

Socialism and the New Liberalism 51

which would coordinate and to some extent control private-sector investment. Beveridge indicated that in any case he thought that no more than 25 per cent of total national investment should be left under the control of private manufacturing industry.[52]

Second, aside from these concrete proposals, Beveridge also indicated that he retained an open mind with respect to further moves towards socialism. He was now satisfied that it was possible to attain full employment and control the trade cycle without full-blooded socialism, but he acknowledged that other arguments might support a greater amount of socialist planning. Beveridge's report supported, he said, the 'socialisation of demand' rather than production, but he also outlined several reasons that might still favour further social ownership of the means of production, namely, to ensure greater cooperation from the workers; to prevent powerful capitalists sabotaging full employment policies or manipulating the political process; and to ensure a more equal distribution of income.[53]

Strikingly, while Beveridge believed that it was eminently feasible to preserve the essential liberties of a free, democratic society while achieving full employment, he excluded one notable freedom from his list of essential liberties that must be retained:

> The list of essential liberties given above does not include liberty of a private citizen to own means of production and to employ other citizens in operating them at a wage. Whether private ownership of means of production to be operated by others is a good economic device or not, it must be judged as a device. It is not an essential citizen liberty in Britain, because it is not and never has been enjoyed by more than a very small proportion of the British people. It cannot even be suggested that any considerable proportion of the people have any lively hope of gaining such ownership later.[54]

Like Hobhouse and Hobson, Beveridge saw the private ownership of productive property as a practical question rather than an issue of fundamental liberal principle.[55] Beveridge therefore did not rule out the abolition of private property in the means of production if it in fact proved to be necessary to maintain full employment. Indeed, if the abolition of private property in the means of production were shown to be essential to full employment, then 'this abolition would have to be undertaken'.[56] If this is the archetypal voice of a

---

[52] William Beveridge, *Full Employment in a Free Society* (London: Allen & Unwin, 1944), 157, 162, 177–8, 203–5.
[53] Beveridge, *Full Employment*, 190–2, 205–7, 252.
[54] Beveridge, *Full Employment*, 21.
[55] A similar point was also made by the later liberal revisionist John Rawls, *A Theory of Justice* (Oxford: Oxford University Press, 1999 [1971]), pp. xv–xvi, 242.
[56] Beveridge, *Full Employment*, 23. This point was also mentioned by Michael Freeden in *Liberalism Divided*, 370, and first drawn to my attention by Jose Harris: see her *William Beveridge*, 432.

liberal, mid-twentieth-century political and economic 'consensus', then the importance of socialist political thought to the architects of this 'consensus' should not be underestimated.

CONCLUSION

This chapter's main aim has been to puncture a certain image of the new liberalism that has assumed too prominent a place in recent debates about British political history. The desire to find an attractive progressive political discourse untainted by the apparent shortcomings of post-1945 Labour socialism has led many commentators and political actors to invoke the new liberalism as a leading candidate for such a discourse. Critics of this tendency, including Michael Freeden, have observed that this underestimates the radicalism of new liberal welfare theory.[57] I have sought to add a different point to this debate: new liberal theorists also supported a significant amount of public ownership and were to that extent as complicit in the formation of the post-1945 Labour socialist agenda as their socialist contemporaries. Although it might fit contemporary political constraints to conjure up a safely non-socialist progressivism, from a historical perspective we should acknowledge that left liberals and socialists alike really did believe in public ownership as an important tool of progressive economic policy. And, as we contemplate the corporate Leviathans that now exercise such a pervasive influence over our democracy, from a political perspective it might even be worth remembering why earlier progressives saw public ownership as critical to the advancement of core liberal ideals.

[57] See, e.g., Freeden, 'True Blood or False Genealogy', 187–8.

3

Liberalisms in India: A Sketch

Rochana Bajpai

INTRODUCTION

Liberalism in India is relatively under-studied as *liberalism*, although liberal ideas have been examined as part of other ideologies, notably nationalism, socialism, and secularism.[1] The labels 'liberalism' or 'liberal' are not in common parlance, and do not possess an established set of referents.[2] A consideration of liberalism in India thus has to contend with questions of definitions and sources at the outset. How is liberalism to be understood, and where should we look for it? Liberalism, of course, comes in many guises. The classical liberalism of Locke, with its belief in the sacredness of private property and limited government, is a very different creature from contemporary liberalism inspired by Rawls, with its emphasis on egalitarian principles and support for welfare states. Late twentieth-century liberal concerns about the equal status of all individuals and distributive justice blur the boundaries between liberalism and democracy that nineteenth-century liberals such as de Tocqueville and J. S. Mill, were keen to preserve.[3] Is there sufficient common ground between the different traditions of liberalism to identify the object of our investigation? And in tracing the shape of liberalism in a non-European context, without the guiding-posts of an established canon, which thinkers or

---

[1] For research assistance, I am grateful to Manjeet Ramgotra; for comments and suggestions, I would like to thank Chris Bayly, Chakravarthi Ram-Prasad, Faisal Devji, Nandini Gooptu, Ramachandra Guha, Ben Jackson, Shruti Kapila, Sunil Khilnani, Prashant Kidambi, Rinku Lamba, Matt Nelson, Thomas Pantham, and David Taylor. I am extremely grateful to Chris Bayly for allowing me to read his unpublished manuscript.

[2] For perceptive suggestions on the usage of the category 'liberal' in India, see Ramachandra Guha, 'The Absent Liberal: An Essay on Politics and Intellectual Life', *Economic and Political Weekly*, 36, 50 (2001), 4663–70.

[3] See, for instance, Bhikhu Parekh's influential essay, 'The Cultural Particularity of Liberal Democracy', *Political Studies*, 40 (1992), 160–75.

texts should we consult? Indeed, is the quest for liberalism worthwhile at all in contexts far distant from its European-Christian origins?

In addressing these questions, this essay is influenced by Michael Freeden's pioneering interventions in debates on liberalism and ideology. Two key concerns animate Freeden's writings, from his early seminal work on new liberalism to his recent path-breaking methodological studies.[4] The first is an insistence that liberalism should not be identified with its historical variants that emphasize the asocial individual, property rights, economic freedoms, and a limited state. While undoubtedly defining an important strand of liberalism, these themes do not constitute its essential characteristics. Liberals have also been concerned with social welfare, community responsibility, and state intervention. Social justice has been a significant liberal concern since at least the late nineteenth century, before Rawls. Second, in order to properly appreciate the richness and complexity of political thought, Freeden has urged that we broaden our net beyond the standard canon of Great Men and texts, to examine the writings of political practitioners such as intellectual politicians and social reformers explicitly responding to the 'burning political and social problems of their times'.[5] Ideology, action-oriented political thinking forged in the heat of public debate, though lacking the consistency and rigour of philosophy, is an important form of political thought. Without a proper appreciation of liberal ideologies, our understanding of liberal thought is radically incomplete. The recuperation of the social strands of liberalism and of the significance of ideologies for political thought are the two themes to which Michael Freeden's writings constantly return, from *New Liberalism* to the recent interventions in comparative political thought.

This essay offers an exploratory sketch of some important distinct strands of liberalism in India in theory and practice. As it has rarely possessed a separate identity of its own, a sketch of liberalism in India is necessarily an exercise in retrieval, involving a delimitation of ideas usually located within other ideological frames. This requires a minimal identification of its object at the outset, however rough. A useful starting point here is Judith Shklar's influential characterization of liberalism as a political doctrine that seeks to 'secure the political conditions that are necessary for the exercise of personal freedom'.[6] Liberals have differed over why the freedom of individuals is valuable: importantly, enhancing personal autonomy is not always

---

[4] Michael Freeden, *The New Liberalism: An Ideology of Social Reform* (Oxford: Oxford University Press, 1978); Michael Freeden, *Ideologies and Political Theory: A Conceptual Approach* (Oxford: Oxford University Press, 1996); Michael Freeden 'Editorial: The Comparative Study of Political Thinking', *Journal of Political Ideologies*, 12 (2007), 1–9.
[5] Freeden, *New Liberalism*, 1–2, 244–5.
[6] Judith Shklar, *Political Thought and Political Thinkers* (Chicago and London: University of Chicago Press, 1998), 3.

the ultimate goal.[7] Liberals have also disagreed over what the political conditions required for the realization of individual freedom are, in particular whether these involve greater or lesser intervention by the state in the economy and society. Nevertheless, advocates of both greater and lesser state intervention in the economy agree that the civil and political liberties of individuals should be protected 'beyond the reach of the coercive claims of the state or society'.[8] Liberalism is fundamentally concerned with political institutions that protect and enhance the freedom of individuals. So construed, does liberalism have a significant presence in India, and if so, who are its exemplars?

This essay will argue, to begin with and contrary to influential opinion, that liberal ideas have had a substantial presence in the Indian polity. I distinguish three strands of liberalism that have been influential in nineteenth- and twentieth-century India: colonial, nationalist, and radical liberalisms. The classification is heuristic and so beset with the usual deficiencies of simplification and overlapping cases, but nevertheless useful. The Indian Constitution, arguably the foundational text of political liberalism in India, is a legatee of these three liberal traditions.[9] In politics, colonial, nationalist, and radical liberalisms in India have been antagonistic, as well as mutually constitutive. In ideological terms, however, important convergences can be discerned, particularly a strong belief in the state as the primary agent of liberal reform, and an acceptance of group-differentiated rights. In the different strands of liberalism in India, while the civil and political rights of individuals are widely affirmed, sustained meditation on why individual freedom is important, and how it might be protected from the incursions of state and society, is rare. The sophisticated accounts of individual freedom in modern Indian thought, found, for instance, in the writings of Vivekananda, Tagore, and Gandhi, are not ultimately focused on the political conditions for individual freedom, and as such, do not fit easily into a liberal frame. At one level, this implies that strong liberalisms are weakly articulated in India, even though weaker liberalisms are more pervasive than their presence in the scholarly literature suggests. The normative importance of the rule of law, universal citizenship, and the inviolability of individuals remain to be elaborated in philosophical terms. At another level, however, the Indian case is a useful reminder of the limits of liberalism as a category. As the dominant ideology of the Anglophone world, liberalism tends to be overused as a normative and analytical frame, its existence taken for granted in Western contexts. However, as Shklar reminds us, even in its European heartland, liberalism has been 'very rare both in

---

[7] Paul Kelly, *Liberalism* (Cambridge: Polity, 2005).
[8] Kelly, *Liberalism*, 10.
[9] See my *Debating Difference: Group Rights and Liberal Democracy in India* (New Delhi: Oxford University Press, 2011).

theory and in practice' in the last two hundred years.[10] In the non-European world, while significant traditions of thought on individual freedom are to be found, the category needs to be used with even more caution: in India for instance, as Dennis Dalton notes, the most sophisticated thinking on individual freedom is best characterized as anarchist.[11] Comparative explorations thus serve as necessary reminders of the ontological and ethical limits of liberalism, and of the significance of other moral horizons for the pursuit of individual freedom.

THE NEGLECT OF LIBERALISM IN INDIA

An exploration of liberalism in India has to contend at the outset with at least three powerful sources of scepticism. The first comes from Marxist and postcolonial perspectives, where liberalism is typically cast as an oppressive ideology, sustained by asymmetrical relations of power, and associated with the rise of capitalism in the modern West and colonialism in Asia and Africa. In Marxian perspectives, liberalism is often dismissed as the ideology of the bourgeoisie, and tends to be identified with neo-liberalism, or with weak egalitarianism. Postcolonial theorists have also sought to unmask the universalist claims of liberalism as serving the interests of particular, privileged groups. A second influential line of scepticism is provided by cultural-difference perspectives, notably those that emphasize the Christian roots of liberal values such as secularism in the history of the modern West. Culturally alien to India and other non-European contexts, unsupported by local religious and normative traditions, liberalism is doomed to unintelligibility and failure.[12] Postcolonial and cultural-difference perspectives converge in their dismissal of liberalism as weakly articulated in India, as normatively inadequate (e.g. secularism is not capable of dealing with the problems of Indian diversity), and as lacking epistemic power (e.g. can Indian realities be adequately comprehended through Western categories?). A third possible reason for the neglect of the study of liberalism in India is that in the narrative of Indian nationalism, liberalism figures as the first, feeble stage. The constitutional liberalism that defined the Congress Party's stance in its early years (1885–1905) seems in retrospect a timid nationalism, ultimately weak and ineffective against

---

[10] Shklar, *Political Thought*, 4. Liberalism has been powerful 'in the United States only if black people are not counted as members of its society' (4–5).

[11] Dennis Dalton, 'The Ideology of Sarvodaya: Concepts of Politics and Power in Indian Political Thought', in Thomas Pantham and Kenneth L. Deutsch (eds.), *Political Thought in Modern India* (New Delhi: Sage, 1986), 275–96.

[12] S. N. Balagangadhara, *'The Heathen in His Blindness': Asia, the West, and the Dynamic of Religion* (Leiden: E. J. Brill, 1994).

colonialism, in large part *because* it was liberal, emphasizing 'constitutional action' for the removal of the deficiencies of British rule.[13] In the standard Indian nationalist narrative, the limits of liberalism are overcome by democracy, with Gandhi's alchemy transforming a mendicant nationalism into a mass movement. It is democracy that provides the master-frame for understanding India's history and future, not liberalism.

For an account of Indian liberalism, some quick points of rebuttal are in order. First, its dismissal derives in many cases from the identification of liberalism with its individualist strands, either rights-based or utilitarian. As Freeden's work reminds us, however, liberalism has a significant welfare tradition, concerned with the social conditions required for individual freedom and the collective provision necessary for enabling individual development. Furthermore, as Rajeev Bhargava has noted, in a context defined by inegalitarian collectivism, individualist ideas, both utilitarian and rights-based, represented an egalitarian impulse.[14] Second, critics of liberalism in India often assimilate liberalism into phenomena with which it was contingently associated in the course of its historical development—capitalism, colonialism, nationalism, and state centralization. As Shklar reminds us, however, historical associations and even psychological affinities are distinct from logical consequences. Third, the historical origins of ideas do not, of course, dictate their subsequent fate. It has been argued, for instance, that Indian liberalism was 'crippled from its origins' in colonial utilitarianism, 'squeezed into a culture that had little room for the individual'.[15] This is an influential view that has merit. However, democratic ideas and institutions were introduced in India by a colonial state, in an anaemic form, in a society that had little place for the idea of social equality. Yet no serious analyst of India claims today that democracy has remained trapped by its origins.

While I am making a case for the study of Indian liberalism, my case is not that liberalism is necessarily strongly articulated in India. Sustained meditation on the importance of constraints on political and social power, of choice for individuals to shape their lives as they will, is hard to come by, even in the writings of defenders of liberalism. It is true that political practice in India has been characterized by greater accommodation of political dissent than many other countries in Asia, Africa, and Latin America. As Chris Bayly notes, India has a long history of liberal newspapers in English and vernacular languages such as Hindi, Bengali, and Marathi dating back to the nineteenth century, which is exceptional not just in the developing world, but also in European

---

[13] Sanjay Seth, 'Rewriting Histories of Nationalism: The Politics of "Moderate Nationalism" in India, 1870–1905', *American Historical Review*, 104 (1999), 102, 107.

[14] Rajeev Bhargava, 'Democratic Vision of a New Republic: India, 1950', in Francine Frankel et al. (eds.), *Transforming India: Social and Political Dynamics of a Democracy* (New Delhi: Oxford University Press, 2000), 34.

[15] Sunil Khilnani, *The Idea of India* (London: Hamish Hamilton, 1997), 26.

terms.[16] However, the protection of civil and political liberties, to the extent to which it exists in India, appears to be more a result, in complex ways, of the functioning of democracy, where intense electoral competition has produced liberal outcomes, as James Manor argues, rather than a consequence of a staunch ideological commitment to the inviolability of the individual.[17] Having conceded that strong liberalism remains weakly articulated in India, I do want to claim that liberalism is more significant in India than is commonly believed. Historically, three main liberal traditions can be identified.[18]

COLONIAL LIBERALISM

The first strand of Indian liberalism, which is associated with British rule and might be termed colonial liberalism, is something of an oxymoron. The Raj, it should be noted at the outset, was not predominantly liberal. Scholars have shown that those who were liberals in Britain were often authoritarian in relation to India, including such distinguished figures as James Mill, James Fitzjames Stephen, and even John Stuart Mill.[19] Moreover, even when the Raj was liberal, it remained hierarchical: Macaulay's famous dismissal of 'the entire literature of India and Arabia' as not worth 'a single shelf of a good European library' stemmed, as Thomas Metcalf notes, not from 'some chance prejudice but the liberal project itself': the 'future triumphs of "reason" demanded as their counterpart the present existence of "barbarism"'.[20] Nevertheless, hierarchical, constrained, and infused with racial superiority as it was, colonial liberalism was an important source for liberal ideas and practices in India, such as the rule of law, equality before the law, and education as a means of improvement. Paternalist reform has remained an enduring liberal impulse in India.

---

[16] Chris Bayly, *Recovering Liberties: Indian Thought in the Age of Liberalism and Empire* (Cambridge: Cambridge University Press, 2011).

[17] I am grateful to James Manor for raising this point in personal communication.

[18] This classification draws upon, while departing from two seminal accounts of Indian liberalism, K. M. Panikkar, *In Defence of Liberalism* (New York: Asia Publishing House, 1962); and Rajendra Vora, 'Two Strands of Indian Liberalism: The Ideas of Ranade and Phule', in Thomas Pantham and Kenneth L. Deutsch (eds.), *Political Thought in Modern India*, 92–109.

[19] Eric Stokes, *The English Utilitarians and India* (Oxford: Oxford University Press, 1959); Javed Majeed, *Ungoverned Imaginings: James Mill's The History of British India and Orientalism* (Oxford: Oxford University Press, 1992); Thomas R. Metcalf, *Ideologies of the Raj* (Cambridge: Cambridge University Press, 1994); Uday Singh Mehta, *Liberalism and Empire: A Study in Nineteenth-Century British Liberal Thought* (Chicago: University of Chicago Press, 1999).

[20] Metcalf, *Ideologies*, 34–5; on imperialism as integral to the development of liberalism from its inception, see Mehta, *Liberalism*, 75.

Colonial liberalism developed in India from the late eighteenth century, at the intersection of debates between those who sought to preserve Indian traditions in the governance of India (Orientalists) and those who sought to remodel Indian practices in line with general principles of law (Anglicists). Liberals of the Raj, of different generations, were for the most part Anglicizers. Early strands of colonial liberalism reflected key concerns of classical Lockean liberalism with the limitation of government power and respect for property rights. Governor-General Cornwallis's policies (1786–93) were driven by Whig doctrines, as Eric Stokes's magisterial study shows, with the Permanent Settlement of Bengal (1793) seeking to limit the discretionary power of the executive and to subject it to the rule of law, through formal enactments that were to be enforced by an independent judiciary.[21] In keeping with Whig notions, the Permanent Settlement also introduced rights to private property in land for the landlords (*zamindars*).[22] The influence of Whig liberalism in India was limited: the Permanent Settlement represented one type of revenue settlement, used in some portions of British India, and in practice it did not achieve a massive shift to Western-style private property rights and capitalist agriculture.[23] From an egalitarian liberal standpoint, the effects of Whig policies were highly illiberal: the increased power of landlords resulted in much greater poverty and oppression of the peasantry. Nevertheless, Whig notions of limited government, fixed laws, and private property rights did represent one strand of liberalism in India.[24]

In the nineteenth century, as utilitarian doctrines gained ground in England, India became a testing ground for projects of reform in law and education.[25] Several scholar-statesmen of the Raj authored programmes for Indian improvement. Utilitarian scholar and head of the India Office James Mill wrote the *History of British India*, which became a training manual for officials of the Raj, and offered a Benthamite diagnosis and remedy for India's ills.[26] English utilitarians and liberals were often authoritarian in relation to India, a useful reminder of the distance that can separate utilitarianism from liberalism, and both from democracy. James Mill favoured good government by experts, noting that so long as India's government was 'well and cheaply performed', it was 'of little or no consequence who are the people that perform it'.[27] While John Stuart Mill held that representative institutions ought to be extended to colonies 'composed of people of similar civilization to the ruling country' such as America and Australia, on India, he largely agreed with his

---

[21] Stokes, *English Utilitarians*, 4. [22] Stokes, *English Utilitarians*, 5, 26.
[23] Cited in Metcalf, *Ideologies*, 36; David Washbrook, 'Law, State and Society in Colonial India', *Modern Asian Studies*, 15 (1981), 649–60.
[24] Stokes, *English Utilitarians*, 6.
[25] Metcalf, *Ideologies*; Mehta, *Liberalism*.
[26] Mehta, *Liberalism*, 89; Majeed, *Ungoverned*.
[27] Metcalf, *Ideologies*, 31.

father, as Mehta has shown:[28] India was 'at a great distance' from being capable of self-government.[29] While detailing the dangers to good government in a colonial situation, such as those arising from the ignorance and the unchecked power of rulers (the despotism of foreigners who do not 'know anything about their subjects, has many chances of being worse than that of those that do'),[30] he saw the government of India by England as justified ('It has been the destiny of the East India Company to suggest the true theory of the government of a semi-barbarous dependency by a civilized country, and after having done this, to perish'), bringing 'constant if not very rapid, improvement in prosperity and good administration'.[31] However not all followers of Bentham in India opposed self-government.[32] For Thomas Macaulay, author of the two most influential liberal reforms of the British era, the penal code, and English-based education, utilitarian and liberal commitments meant accepting the possibility of Indian government, as he argued in his famed speech supporting the liberal Charter Act of 1833 that ended the East India Company's monopoly over trade:

> It would be, on the most selfish view of the case, far better for us that the people of India were... ruled by their own kings, but wearing our broadcloth, and working with our cutlery, than they were performing their *salams* to English collectors and... magistrates, but were too ignorant to value, or too poor to buy, English manufactures. To trade with civilized men is infinitely more profitable than to govern savages...[33]

Macaulay's design for a common criminal law for all of India, enacted eventually in the 1860s, was, as Stokes has shown, unmistakably Benthamite in its emphasis on achieving uniformity as far as practicable, minimizing suffering at the same time as cost, and, above all, in its attempt to eschew existing practice and fashion for a code of law '*ex nihilo* by... disinterested philosophic intelligence'.[34] Macaulay's other influential initiative of liberal reform was his famous minute on education of 1835 that introduced English language as the medium of instruction and English literature as the main subject in the curriculum, intended as a secular instrument of moral

---

[28] On some differences between the views of the elder and younger Mill, see Lynn Zastoupil, *John Stuart Mill and India* (Stanford: Stanford University Press, 1994).

[29] John Stuart Mill, *Utilitarianism, Liberty and Representative Government* (London: J. M. Dent and Sons Ltd, reprinted 1972), 376–737; see also Metcalf, *Ideologies*, 32–3; Mehta, *Liberalism*, 70–1.

[30] Mill, *Utilitarianism*, 383.

[31] Mill, *Utilitarianism*, 393, 390.

[32] Bentham himself was more critical of colonialism than the Mills and less inclined to give weight to racial distinctions: see Jennifer Pitts, *A Turn to Empire: The Rise of Imperial Liberalism in Britain and France* (Princeton: Princeton University Press, 2005).

[33] Cited in Stokes, *English Utilitarians*, 43–4.

[34] Stokes, *English Utilitarians*, 191, 219–20, 222, 225.

training.[35] A humanities-based, liberal-arts-oriented educational curriculum, in which English literature dominated, with its nineteenth-century 'glorification of liberty' and 'the Whig interpretation of British history',[36] was to be the instrument for the liberal transformation of Indian character.[37]

While colonial liberalism in India reached its apogee in the first half of the nineteenth century, liberal ideas of limited government and the rule of law, equality before the law, and education as a means of improvement, remained influential under the Raj, which increasingly allied itself to the cause of moderate self-government for Indians. These ideas were articulated by statesmen such as Ripon[38] and Montagu,[39] in policies of constitutional reform,[40] as well as in professions such as law and civil services.[41] To be sure, liberal ideas had to contend with more 'conservative visions of empire', as well as the 'exigencies of colonial rule', and were rarely fully reflected in policy, let alone practice.[42] The liberal instinct for legal uniformity was held in check—both Cornwallis's reforms and Macaulay's Penal Code steered clear of areas of law seen as governed by religious authority. Conservative imperialists used the existence of legal pluralism in the area of personal law to justify illiberal policies, as in the famous Ilbert Bill controversy (1882–3), where courts upheld the differential treatment of Indians and Europeans.[43] The growth of representative institutions took place alongside the expansion of communal electorates, with representation organized along communities of identity and interest. Although self-government expanded, franchise remained restricted by educational and property qualifications. As such, colonial liberalism provided an uncertain basis for a liberal democratic public sphere of common and equal citizenship. Nonetheless, it represented a distinct variant of liberalism, shaped by the possibilities and constraints of Indian conditions. Colonial liberalism's most enduring influence was perhaps in the institutions of education, law, and representation it created, which served as powerful schools for other Indian liberalisms.

---

[35] Metcalf, *Ideologies*, 40.   [36] Panikkar, *Liberalism*, 9.
[37] Stokes, *English Utilitarians*, 222.
[38] For instance, Lord Ripon emphasized that his local government reforms of 1882 aimed not so much at improving the administration, but were 'chiefly designed as an instrument of political and popular education' (cited in Metcalf, *Ideologies*, 201).
[39] The Montagu-Chelmsford Report (1918–19) echoed Macaulay's idealism, holding that demand for self-government by the Indian educated classes was 'no reproach but rather a tribute to our work'. Metcalf, *Ideologies*, 226.
[40] On liberal imperialism, see, in particular, Peter Robb, *Empire, Modernity and India: Liberalism, Modernity and the Nation* (New Delhi: Oxford University Press, 2007); and Karuna Mantena, *Alibis of Empire: Henry Maine and the Ends of Liberal Imperialism* (Princeton: Princeton University Press, 2010).
[41] The establishment of High Courts served to symbolize 'the supremacy of law' (Panikkar, *Liberalism*, 8–9).
[42] Metcalf, *Ideologies*, 35.   [43] Metcalf, *Ideologies*, 209.

NATIONALIST LIBERALISM

The second strand of liberalism in India, nationalist liberalism, was very much a product of colonial liberalism, of the emerging middle class formed by Western education. Its principal bearers were the professional classes created by the Raj—lawyers, civil servants, and educators—and the organizations that they spawned. These were nationalist to differing extents: full independence from Britain was not desired in all cases, and was not common until the second decade of the twentieth century. Key liberal concerns shaped nationalist endeavour in relation to both Indian society and the colonial state: the assertion of individual reason against the authority of tradition, limits on executive power, freedom of the press, education as a means of improvement, equality before the law, and equality of opportunity in employment. Nationalist liberals were largely drawn from the elite strata of Indian society.

In India, as elsewhere, the emergence of an indigenous modern liberalism is related to a crisis of religious authority. The encounter with the colonial state, Western education, and Christian missionaries produced intense self-questioning and criticism of orthodox religious and social practices. While proto-liberal concerns can be discerned in several impulses for Hindu reform, the accuracy of the label 'liberal' that is often applied to Hindu social reformers is debatable, given a relative lack of interest in politics as a route to achieving desired change. Although individual freedom was a central concern for thinkers such as Swami Vivekananda, the domain wherein its realization was pursued was spiritual and religious. Politics was considered too shallow a pool for the contemplation of freedom. Men, he argued, 'cannot be made virtuous by an Act of Parliament...'; individual freedom required fewer artificial laws. An emphasis on political power was part of a Western 'vanity', reflecting a 'material tyranny'; by contrast, India's distinctive genius was spiritual.[44] Despite resonances of liberal themes in Vivekananda's critique of the caste system noted by scholars,[45] he is more accurately described as a progenitor of the tradition of modern anarchist thought in India.[46]

The exemplary figure for the elaboration of an identifiably liberal programme within the Hindu social reform tradition is Raja Rammohan Roy (1772–1833), described as 'the father of liberalism' and 'India's first indigenous "public man"'.[47] Rammohan Roy pursued the typical causes of Hindu social reform, including campaigns against widow burning, idol worship, polytheism, rituals of purity and pollution, and the monopoly of the priestly class over

---

[44] Cited in Dalton, 'Sarvodaya', 278–9.   [45] Panikkar, *Liberalism*.
[46] Dalton, 'Sarvodaya'.
[47] Panikkar, *Liberalism*, 2; Chris A. Bayly, 'Rammohan Roy and the Advent of Constitutional Liberalism in India: 1800–30', *Modern Intellectual History*, 4 (2007), 29.

education. Religious tenets and practices were to be subjected to the test of individual reason and social utility, and to be discarded if found wanting: Rammohan Roy was, as Thomas Pantham notes, a 'religious Benthamite'.[48] Like British liberals of his time, Rammohan Roy supported the cause of free trade against the monopoly of the British East India Company and defended property rights, seeing capitalism and industrialization as forces that promised emancipation from the servitude of the feudal economy. Rammohan's elaboration of an indigenous liberalism is perhaps most clearly evident in the political causes that he championed, such as a mixed constitution, a free press, and jury rights for Indians, in transnational networks stretching across Britain, Iberia, and Latin America in the early nineteenth century, as Bayly has shown.[49] He argued passionately against restrictions on the press and for a legislative check on executive power on classic liberal grounds.[50] Newspapers 'by introducing free discussion among the Natives and inducing them to reflect and inquire after knowledge' had 'served greatly to improve their minds and ameliorate their condition'.[51] Restrictions on the press prevented 'the Natives from making the Government readily acquainted with the errors and injustice that may be committed by its executive officers'.[52] He advocated the reform of the Westminster Parliament, with representation for Indians and other colonials to exercise a legislative check on the East India Company.[53] This constitutional liberal vision of checks to prevent an abuse of executive power, like other early nineteenth-century liberalisms, was democratic and nationalist only to a limited extent. The British Parliament was to make laws for Indians through consultation with 'gentlemen of intelligence and respectability'.[54] Insistent about the need for the rule of law to curb the excesses of power, Rammohan was more equivocal about equality before the law.[55] Campaigning against restrictions on the Indian press, Rammohan appealed to 'sympathy which forms a paternal tie'[56] between the rulers and the ruled, and was at pains to emphasize that liberties were sought for Indians as loyal British subjects, grateful for the blessings of British rule.[57] Nevertheless,

---

[48] Thomas Pantham, 'The Socio-Religious and Political Thought of Rammohun Roy', in Thomas Pantham and Kenneth L. Deutsch (eds.), *Political Thought in Modern India*, 40.
[49] Bayly, 'Rammohan Roy'.
[50] See Bruce Carlisle Robertson, *The Essential Writings of Raja Rammohan Ray* (Delhi: Oxford University Press, 1999), 235–6, 258.
[51] Robertson, *Essential Writings*, 234.
[52] Robertson, *Essential Writings*, 236. Any limitations ought to be 'legal restraints... inflicted after trial and conviction according to the forms of the Laws of England' (257).
[53] Bayly, 'Rammohan Roy'.
[54] Robertson, *Essential Writings*, 256; Pantham, 'Rammohan Roy', 47.
[55] See Rammohan in Robertson, *Essential Writings*, 219–20.
[56] Robertson, *Essential Writings*, 259.
[57] Robertson, *Essential Writings*, 239; Bayly, 'Rammohan Roy', 32–3.

nationalist cultural concerns do appear in Rammohan's attempt to ground the notion of a mixed constitution in a lost Indian/Hindu tradition of an ancient constitution with a separation of powers between Brahmin legislators and Rajput warriors. He argued, as Bayly has shown, that liberal institutions had, contrary to British misrepresentations, substantial Indian precedents, in ancient judicial institutions such as the *Panchayat*,[58] as well as more recent Mughal India's *akhbarat* and *akhbar navis* (news writers).[59] Through his championing of liberal institutions such as a free press and juries largely denied to Indians under the Raj, Rammohan laid the foundations for the nationalist critique of British rule. A liberalism robustly opposed to restrictions on civil liberties, which was both resolutely cosmopolitan and, simultaneously, nationalist in its sensibilities, became with Rammohan a significant strand in modern Indian public discourse.

In the late nineteenth/early twentieth century, a form of nationalist liberalism was articulated by the early Congress Party leaders known as Moderates, including such figures as Dadabhai Naoroji (1825–1917), Pherozeshah Mehta (1845–1915), Surendranath Banerjea (1848–1925), and G. K. Gokhale (1866–1915). This remains the clearest political referent of liberalism in India. Early Congress nationalists were liberal in their political demands as well as methods, as Seth notes, emphasizing constitutionalism, gradual reform, an appeal to English traditions, and typically rebuking British rule in India for 'failing to live up to its own...historic mission as the bearer of liberal institutions' in India.[60] Many early Congress nationalists, like nineteenth-century British liberals, were comfortable with educational and property restrictions on the franchise, and demanded greater political rights mainly for educated Indians, seeing themselves as the spokesmen of the poor, illiterate masses.[61] With respect to economic liberalism, however, early Indian nationalists were more equivocal, and developed a critique of prevalent doctrines of *laissez faire* in advance of British liberalism of the time. Rejecting cultural and Malthusian explanations for Indian poverty and famine, they argued that these could be tackled through better state policies of irrigation, food storage, and reducing the tax burden on poor peasants.[62]

The most systematic elaboration of nationalist elite liberalism is perhaps to be found in the writings of the Maharashtrian jurist and social reformer, M. G. Ranade (1842–1901). Ranade's *Essays on Indian Economics* (1898) advocated

---

[58] The 'principle of juries under certain modifications' had 'been well understood in this country under the name of Punchayat' (Rammohan in Robertson, *Essential Writings*, 207–8).

[59] 'Rammohan Roy', 37. The *Akhbar Navees* 'published an account of whatever happened', 'to prevent the abuses that are so liable to flow from the possession of power' (Rammohan in Robertson, *Essential Writings*, 257).

[60] Seth, 'Rewriting Histories', 103–4, 100–1.

[61] See Seth, 'Rewriting Histories', 107.

[62] Bayly, *Recovering Liberties*, chs. 6 and 7; also Panikkar, *Liberalism*, 13–16.

the extension of private property rights in agricultural land to both landlords and peasants: freedom of contract and competition were necessary to counter the immobility of Indian capital and labour.[63] Crucially, however, these were not sufficient for achieving economic development, which required state intervention: Ranade was an early critic of *laissez faire*. The key assumptions of classical political economy did not obtain in India ('With us an average Individual man is, to a large extent, the very antipodes of the Economical man'), and were not 'literally true' of any 'existing Community'.[64] German scholars among others had demonstrated that the textbook interpretation of Adam Smith's doctrines[65] was 'essentially English and Insular', 'unsuitable to the Continental Countries':[66]

> ...the Individual and his Interests are not the centre round which the Theory should revolve...the true centre is the Body Politic of which that Individual is a Member...The State is now more and more recognized as the National Organ for taking care of National needs in all matters in which individual and cooperative efforts are not likely to be so effective and economic as National effort.... Education, both liberal and Technical, Post and Telegraphs, Railway and Canal communications, the pioneering of new enterprise, the insurance of risky undertakings, all these functions are usefully discharged by the State.[67]

State-supported capitalist industrialization along the lines found in Europe was sorely needed in India. While acknowledging that the colonial state had invested in a few industries, these efforts were meagre 'as compared with its resources and the needs of the Country', given that 'the State claims to be the sole Landlord and is certainly the largest Capitalist in the country', or relative to the efforts of European states in areas such as the building up of national credit through the banking system, or the protection of local industry from foreign competition.[68] Ranade also pressed for state action on behalf of the poor on paternalist liberal grounds: the fixing of rents, tenures, and rates of interest for tenants were all 'legitimate forms of protection of the weak against the strong', necessary to 'check the abuse of Competition'. For, 'where the parties' were not 'equally matched in intelligence and resources', 'all talk of equality and freedom adds insult to injury'.[69] Ranade's thought and practice reflected characteristic themes of Hindu social reform: a metaphysical

---

[63] M. G. Ranade, *Essays on Indian Economics: A Collection of Essays and Speeches*, 2nd edition (Madras: G. A. Natesan and Co., 1906), 284, 299; Vora, 'Ranade and Phule', 94.
[64] Ranade, *Essays*, 10.
[65] Adam Smith's own views, Ranade argued, were more subtle, unlike those of his successors such as Ricardo and Malthus, who were hampered by a 'too absolute assertion of his doctrines' (Ranade, *Essays*, 16).
[66] Ranade, *Essays*, 19.   [67] Ranade, *Essays*, 21, 34.
[68] Ranade, *Essays*, 35; Vora, 'Ranade and Phule', 95–6.   [69] Ranade, *Essays*, 31.

conception of individual freedom,[70] a critique of the oppression of lower castes and of women,[71] a narrative of decline from an ancient, more liberal past, with proposals for reform supported by appeal to Vedic and Bhakti traditions. Influenced by Herbert Spencer's organicism and evolutionary doctrines, Ranade argued that in order to achieve real, lasting change, reform had to be slow and gradual, without a violent break with the past.[72] Interdependence was 'a law of our nature... what applies to the human body holds good of the collective humanity... the society, or state'.[73] The belief in interdependence and gradualism meant that liberal reform in society, politics, and the economy was interconnected, and for Ranade, as Rajendra Vora notes, the cause of social reform took precedence over that of political freedom. Indians were not yet ready for self-rule and needed to serve 'a period of political apprenticeship'.[74] In a backward country, it was the elites who were the agents of liberal reform, with the educated minority in particular 'the soul of Indian liberalism',[75] whereas the masses were 'unlettered, improvident, ignorant, disunited...', incapable on their own of understanding the value of liberalism.[76] Holding that 'power must gravitate where there is intelligence and wealth', Ranade sought weighted representation in local and provincial government for the educated and property owners through indirect election. He acknowledged that these bodies would be 'far from democratic', but held that the masses were not yet ready for democracy and needed a long period of tutelage.[77] The middle classes needed assistance from the state in order to fulfil their pedagogical role, in the form of state support for higher education, which Ranade favoured over mass education. There was little demand for education among the masses, whereas the middle classes that were seeking higher education, he argued, in particular the Brahmins, were not wealthy.[78]

In Indian nationalist narratives, this limited, elite liberalism is transformed, first, through Gandhi's alchemy, into a mass movement, then through Nehru's socialism, into a vision of the developmental state. Nevertheless, elite liberalism has been influential in post-Independence India, in state policies and discourses informed by paternalistic concern for the masses and 'weaker

---

[70] On Ranade's notion of individual freedom as combining European theistic ideas of the time with Upanishad doctrines, see Vora, 'Ranade and Phule', 98–9.

[71] Ranade's particular focus was on education and marriage reform to improve the status of high-caste women.

[72] Vora, 'Ranade and Phule', 102; Ranade, *The Miscellaneous Writings of the Late Hon'ble Mr Justice M.G. Ranade* (Bombay: The Manoranjan Press, 1915), 117–18, 230–1.

[73] Ranade, *Miscellaneous Writings*, 232.

[74] Vora, 'Ranade and Phule', 104.

[75] Cited in Vora, 'Ranade and Phule', 105.

[76] Cited in Vora, 'Ranade and Phule', 104.

[77] Cited in Vora, 'Ranade and Phule', 105.

[78] Ranade, *Miscellaneous Writings*, 274, 292, 314.

Liberalisms in India 67

sections', as well as civic activism by non-governmental organizations dedicated to the education and betterment of the poor.[79]

Elite liberal concerns are also to be found in Muslim nationalism in nineteenth- and twentieth-century India. Modernist leaders such as Sir Sayyid Ahmad Khan (1817–98), Syed Ameer Ali (1849–1928), and Mohammed Ali Jinnah (1876–1948) were mostly hostile to Indian nationalism in political terms.[80] Different Muslim nationalisms in British India shared a rejection of the Congress claim that it represented all Indians: their core assertion was that Muslims in India were not just a minority, but a distinct nation, and deserved political recognition commensurate with this status.[81] Muslim nationalism also differed from Indian nationalism in ideological terms in that liberal concerns were often articulated within the frames of Islamic history and theology; this deserves fuller treatment than is possible within the scope of this essay.[82] Worried about the numerical weakness of Muslims in a democratic framework, leading Muslim liberals remained more sceptical of democratic institutions throughout, seeking to limit the scope of majority opinion through mechanisms such as separate electorates and the minority veto, demonstrating a greater awareness of the tension between democratic and liberal principles than mid-twentieth-century Indian nationalists.[83] Nevertheless, the thought and practice of leading Muslim nationalists also reflected several preoccupations of Indian nationalist liberalism. This included a rationalist and historicist critique of socio-religious customs, such as women's seclusion or *pardah* and polygamy as subsequent, non-essential accretions, together with the attempt to establish the truth and relevance of the fundamentals of religion (notably the Qur'an).[84] A belief in Western education as the means to progress, and an emphasis on the role of elites as agents of liberalism and the proper spokesmen of the people was also common.[85] Muslim nationalists continued to share significant liberal ground with Indian

---

[79] Middle-class civic associational activity has been a significant strand in Indian politics since the late nineteenth century. See Prashant Kidambi, *The Making of an Indian Metropolis, Colonial Governance and Public Culture in Bombay, 1890–1920* (Aldershot: Ashgate, 2007).

[80] Strands of Muslim opinion in India did support Congress nationalism. For more details, see Wilfred Cantwell Smith, *Modern Islam in India: A Social Analysis* (Lahore: Ashraf Press, 1946); Ayesha Jalal, *Self and Sovereignty: Individual and Community in South Asian Islam Since 1850* (London and New York: Routledge, 2000).

[81] On Sayyid Ahmad Khan, see Faisal Devji, 'Apologetic Modernity', *Modern Intellectual History*, 4 (2007), 72–3.

[82] See, for instance, Farzana Shaikh, *Community and Consensus in Islam: Muslim Representation in Colonial India* (Cambridge: Cambridge University Press, 1989); Devji, 'Apologetic Modernity'; Bayly, *Recovering Liberties*.

[83] Sunil Khilnani, 'Nehru's Judgement', in Richard Bourke and Raymond Geuss (eds.), *Political Judgement: Essays for John Dunn* (Cambridge: Cambridge University Press, 2009), 267.

[84] See Christian Troll, *Sayyid Ahmad Khan, A Reinterpretation of Muslim Theology* (New Delhi: Vikas Publishing House, 1978), pp. xvii, 229; Smith, *Modern Islam*.

[85] On Sayyid Ahmed Khan's elitism, see Jalal, *Self and Sovereignty*, 92–3.

nationalists even after their political divorce. Mohammed Ali Jinnah's famous speech to the Pakistan Constituent Assembly in August 1947 proclaimed liberal values of religious freedom and equal citizenship that he shared with Congress nationalism of the time, to which he remained, poignantly, attached:

> ... in course of time all these angularities of the majority and minority communities, the Hindu community and the Muslim community ... will vanish ... this has been the biggest hindrance in the way of India to attain the freedom and independence. ... You are ... free to go to your temples, you are free to go to your mosques or to any other place of worship in this State of Pakistan. You may belong to any religion or caste or creed that has nothing to do with the business of the State.[86]

A full assessment of Indian nationalism is not possible within the scope of this essay, but some brief considerations are in order. Although liberalism is not the best frame to capture the distinctive cast of the thought of key figures such as Gandhi or Nehru,[87] significant liberal elements are undoubtedly discernible in their ideas. These included an emphasis on the individual as the basic unit of the political community; on moral universalism that transcended differences of race, nationality, and religion; and a belief in progress through individual self-development, as well as in a limited state that respected the civil and political liberties of citizens. Gandhi's notion of freedom as *swaraj* or self-rule was centred ultimately on the individual ('Swaraj has to be experienced by each one for himself'), as Antony Parel argues. Modern Western civilization had to be resisted, but the 'expulsion of the English' was not sufficient, or even necessary in theory, for this.[88] Nationalism required a commitment to liberal principles such as religious freedom:[89] both Gandhi and Nehru were, in different ways, strongly committed to civic nationalism,[90] and as a result, to secularism. Indeed, the project of creating a single Indian nation out of diverse and conflicting religions, languages, castes, and tribes could not but be liberal in key respects if it was democratic. Nehru's thought fits the descriptor 'liberal' better than Gandhi's, although here too liberal ideas were embedded within other ethical frames, notably social democracy. Writing in *Glimpses of World History* of the great declarations of the rights

---

[86] 'Mr Jinnah's Presidential Address to the Constituent Assembly of Pakistan', 11 August 1947, <http://www.pakistani.org/pakistan/legislation/constituent_address_11aug1947.html>, accessed 23 April 2011.

[87] Gandhi's notion of individual freedom was fundamentally spiritual, involving self-discipline and self-transcendence, and is best seen as developing the dominant anarchist tradition of modern Indian political thought. See Dalton, 'Sarvodaya'.

[88] M. K. Gandhi, *Hind Swaraj and Other Writings*, ed. Anthony J. Parel (Cambridge: Cambridge University Press, 2009), 71. For a reading of Gandhi's thought and practice as elaborating a distinctive type of liberalism, see Anthony J. Parel, 'A Gandhian Liberalism?', in Antony Copley and George Paxton (eds.), *Gandhi and the Contemporary World* (Chennai: Indo-British Historical Society, 1997), 289–97.

[89] Gandhi, *Hind Swaraj*, 50.

[90] On civic nationalism in Gandhi, see Parel, 'Introduction' to *Hind Swaraj*, p. xv.

of man of the American and French revolutions, Nehru saw these as the achievements of democracy, which made 'everybody a free and equal citizen'.[91] The expansion of democracy would help to safeguard basic rights of individuals and minorities, as Sunil Khilnani notes.[92] For Nehru, as for Gandhi, although for different reasons, independence from British rule was not sufficient for freedom.[93] While he was critical of the massive material inequalities that persisted under 'formal democracy' and was an admirer of the Russian revolution, Nehru's attachment to liberal values nevertheless meant that he saw the expansion of state power in the dictatorships of the time, communist and fascist, as unacceptable for sanctioning repression, censorship, and the submerging of the individual in the state.[94]

When we turn from the ideas of individuals to nationalist practice more broadly, even a cursory examination suggests that opposition to colonial rule in India focused substantially on liberal causes.[95] In the nineteenth century, these included demands for a free press, separation of judicial from executive power, equality before the law for Indians and Europeans, and, later, equal rights for Indians in judicial, civil service, and legislative arenas. In the twentieth century, key episodes of nationalist mobilization sought freedom from arbitrary arrest, freedom of expression, and freedom to vote for Indians; nationalist declarations affirmed standard liberal rights (notably the Congress Party's Karachi resolution on fundamental rights of 1931).[96] In terms of its ideology at least, Indian nationalism was more liberal than the British colonial state that it opposed, and of course, used this very effectively to undermine its claim to rule. Through nationalist mobilizations, iterated over the first half of the twentieth century, a commitment to liberal freedoms, at least in the form of professed ideals, came to be shared by a widening section of elites. As their expressive document, the Indian constitution could not but be liberal, although it was also influenced by more radical liberalisms.

RADICAL LIBERALISM

The third distinct strand of liberalism in nineteenth- and twentieth-century India might be termed radical liberalism. Most thinkers and movements on

---

[91] Jawaharlal Nehru, *Glimpses of World History* (New Delhi: Penguin Books, 2004), 614.
[92] Khilnani, 'Nehru's Judgement', 268.
[93] Nehru, *Glimpses*, 10.
[94] See his discussion of dictatorships in *Glimpses*, 955–9.
[95] On the liberal ends of Gandhi's campaigns in South Africa, see Anthony Parel, 'Gandhian Liberalism', 290; on liberalism as embedded within nationalism in India, see Bhargava, 'Democratic Vision', 32, 34–5, 52; Panikkar, *Liberalism*.
[96] See Parel, 'Gandhian Liberalism', 293.

the left of the political spectrum in India have defended liberal values. As Bayly notes, even 'in theory, it was difficult to envisage an Indian "socialist" man, similar to his Soviet or Chinese counterparts'.[97] Heterodox Marxists, such as M. N. Roy who advocated radical democratic proposals such as government by people's committees, affirmed a humanist approach to freedom.[98] Perhaps the most politically influential of radical liberalisms in India are to be found among lower-caste thinkers and movements. Although liberalism is not the only frame for their analysis, a sufficient number of liberal themes appear in lower-caste excoriations of Hinduism and Indian nationalism to identify a distinct type of liberalism here. These include an emphasis on the equal dignity of all humans, inalienable human rights, the importance of mass education and of constitutional protections for the lower castes.[99] Historically, anti-upper-caste liberalism also emerged from the institutions of colonial liberalism, such as Western education and employment, and was nationalist in its own way, championing autonomy for lower castes, fired by anger against the Brahmins, and asserting that the oppressed castes were the original inhabitants of the nation.[100] It nevertheless represented a distinct strand from nationalist liberalism in ideological terms with its strongly egalitarian thrust directed primarily against inequalities *within* Indian society. In political terms, too, radical lower-caste nationalism differed in its critique of upper-caste domination of the Indian national movement ('Brahmin-bourgeois' in one formulation), and its insistence on the need for the separate political organization of the lower castes. Two exemplary figures considered here are Mahatma Jotirao Phule (1827–1890) and Dr B. R. Ambedkar (1891–1956).

Phule argued that all men, and, significantly, women, were in nature and by birth, free and equal, possessing inalienable rights bestowed on them by the Creator that were morally beyond the reach of any human authority.[101] In the context of centuries of caste oppression, underpinned by Hindu theology that had little place for a 'strong concept of an original human equality' as Rosalind O'Hanlon notes, this was a radical claim.[102] Influenced by Tom Paine's *Rights*

---

[97] Chris Bayly, 'Indian Liberalism Transcended, 1914–45: Economic Regionalism, Positive Discrimination and Anti-Materialism', *Centre of South Asian Studies Occasional Paper No. 28* (2008), 28.

[98] Bayly, 'Indian Liberalism Transcended', 24–6. On radical thought in India, see Sudipta Kaviraj, 'Marxism in Translation: Critical Reflections on Indian Radical Thought', in Richard Bourke and Raymond Geuss (eds.), *Political Judgement: Essays for John Dunn* (Cambridge: Cambridge University Press, 2009), 172–99.

[99] See Panikkar, *Liberalism*, 12.

[100] This was an important theme in the thought of Phule, though less so of Ambedkar. Gail Omvedt, *Dalits and the Democratic Revolution: Dr Ambedkar and the Dalit Movement in Colonial India* (New Delhi: Sage, 1994), 16.

[101] Vora, 'Ranade and Phule', 107; R. O'Hanlon, *Caste, Conflict, and Ideology: Mahatma Jotirao Phule and Low Caste Protest in Nineteenth-Century Western India* (Cambridge: Cambridge University Press, 1985), 195.

[102] O'Hanlon, *Caste*, 193.

of Man, Phule's thought reflected similar themes, such as an emphasis on the equal natural rights of all individuals that were given by God, attacks on priestcraft and religious texts, and a narrative of an ancient dispossession of original inhabitants by outside invaders.[103] The downtrodden castes—*sudras atisudras* in Phule's influential formulation—had been enslaved and exploited for centuries, through rules, codes, and mythologies devised by devious Brahmins to preserve their own advantage.[104] As Gail Omvedt observes, Phule reversed the Aryan theory of race, arguing, in a historicist vein, that Brahmins were Aryan invaders (*Irani Aryabhats*) who, through violence and cunning, had destroyed an 'originally prosperous and egalitarian society' and used a religious ideology based on inequality to legitimize their rule (*bhatshahi*).[105] He welcomed British rule as 'meant by the Creator to rescue the Sudras from slavery'.[106] While nationalist liberals such as Rammohan and Ranade had sought to recuperate an unsullied Hinduism of the Vedic past, for Phule, Hinduism was beyond redemption because of its denial throughout history of the basic human rights of the lower castes, and had to be destroyed. Nationalist social and political organizations were 'monopolized' by the Brahmins; the Sudras should not be duped again by Brahmin cunning.[107] Instead, they should embrace Western education and scientific knowledge (*vidya*) as 'a weapon' of change and 'cultural revolution'.[108] In contrast to nationalist liberals' preoccupation with higher education, Phule wanted the British government to focus resources on mass education; this would instil 'mental independence' and consciousness of rights among the Sudras.[109] In contrast to nationalist liberals' emphasis on industrialization, as Rajendra Vora notes, Phule wanted agriculture and the peasants to be the focus for achieving economic development, emphasizing that the peasants were the 'primary producers looted by the state', both during the rule of the 'Arya Brahmins' and of the British, through their Brahmin-dominated bureaucracy.[110] It is in Phule's and his successors' critique of upper-caste domination that egalitarian liberal ideals have been most powerfully elaborated in India. Social justice arguably became a central creed of the Indian Constitution because the Indian nationalists were forced, sometimes against their will, to accommodate the demands of the lower castes in order to forge a broad front against British rule.

---

[103] O'Hanlon, *Caste*, 197; see also Vora, 'Ranade and Phule'.
[104] Vora, 'Ranade and Phule', 107.
[105] Gail Omvedt, *Dalit Visions: The Anti-Caste Movement and the Construction of an Indian Identity* (New Delhi: Orient Longman, 1995), 19, 21.
[106] Vora, 'Ranade and Phule', 108.
[107] Vora, 'Ranade and Phule', 108.
[108] Omvedt, *Dalits*, 99.
[109] Vora, 'Ranade and Phule', 108; O' Hanlon, *Caste*, 197.
[110] Omvedt, *Dalits*, 98–9.

If Phule demonstrated the possibilities of radical liberalism as a movement of protest, it is in the work of the brilliant Dalit leader and the architect of the Indian Constitution, Dr B. R. Ambedkar, that the institutional potential of radical liberalism is best discerned. Although Ambedkar disavowed the term liberal, like Phule, his condemnation of Brahminism drew upon liberal values, such as the importance of individual merit, effort, and choice. The Hindu social order, Ambedkar argued, 'does not recognize the individual as a centre of social purpose... there is no room for individual merit and consideration of individual justice...';[111] '...The division of labour brought about by the Caste System is not a division based on choice... It is based on the dogma of predestination'.[112] Ambedkar's thought also reflected themes from early twentieth-century liberalism, such as eugenics.[113] Like Phule, Ambedkar offered a historicist account of the oppression of the Sudras and the untouchables in terms of ancient defeats, seeking to establish that these groups were not inherently inferior, but were just on the wrong side of history, as Bayly has shown.[114] Like liberals elsewhere, he saw entrenched social problems as amenable to human endeavour, and believed that progress could be achieved through better political arrangements. He was an early advocate of universal franchise, arguing in the Franchise Sub-Committee in 1930 against prevailing restrictions on suffrage that excluded most Untouchables, on individualist liberal grounds that the franchise was 'the inherent right of every individual in the State' that ought not to depend upon the 'convenience' of the administration: each individual who was subject to legislation that was likely to 'invade his liberty... his life and his property' 'ought to have the power to defend himself' against it.[115] While his proposals for guaranteed places for Untouchables in the government and public services pushed at the bounds of liberalism, Ambedkar offered liberal and democratic arguments in support of his case. Adapting constitutional liberal arguments, he suggested that quotas were essentially forms of checks and balances, similar to fundamental rights and the separation of powers found in liberal constitutions. These were required to save Untouchables from betrayal by the caste Hindus, from the fate of the

---

[111] Cited in M. S. Gore, *The Social Context of an Ideology: Ambedkar's Political and Social Thought* (New Delhi: Sage, 1993), 262.

[112] B. R. Ambedkar, *Annihilation of Caste with a Reply to Mahatma Gandhi* (Jullunder City: Bheem Patrika Publications, 1968), 47–8.

[113] A division of labour based on caste 'had no basis in race and by enjoining endogamy caste did not secure any advantage from a eugenic point of view' (Ambedkar cited in Gore, *Social Context*, 278). On the coexistence of eugenics and social democratic thought in Britain, see Michael Freeden, 'Eugenics and Progressive Thought: A Study in Ideological Affinity', *Historical Journal*, 22 (1979), 645–71.

[114] Bayly, 'Liberalism Transcended', 17.

[115] *Dr Babasaheb Ambedkar Writings and Speeches*, II, ed. Vasant Moon (Bombay: Government of Maharashtra, 1976), 559.

'Negroes in the United States after the Civil War'.[116] In the absence of constitutional safeguards for minorities such as the Untouchables, a parliamentary system would not be a form of democracy, but of imperialism.[117] Just as Indian nationalists had invoked English liberalism against British colonial rule, Ambedkar turned liberal and democratic arguments against Indian nationalists.[118]

Democracy, for Ambedkar, was fundamentally about equality, not just in material terms, but also that of status.[119] Like other radical thinkers, he held that formal institutions were inadequate for its realization. Freedom from British rule, constitutional government, and universal franchise were not sufficient for democracy, for these were 'no bar against governing class reaching places of power and authority... self-government and democracy become real... when the governing class loses its power to capture the power to govern ...'.[120] For a truly democratic order, guaranteed seats in each political institution for Untouchables were needed that would help to oust the 'governing class' from power. Unlike many radical thinkers, Ambedkar accorded political institutions a central role in social transformation; this, however, required the presence of the 'servile classes' in the bodies of government. Far more than Congress leaders like Gandhi or Nehru, Ambedkar was able to see the potential of political institutions for achieving desired social change. Quotas for Untouchables, together with their enfranchisement and education, would lessen the sense of inferiority and promote social mobility or social endosmosis, a concept that Ambedkar adapted from John Dewey, as Arun Mukherjee has shown, to refer to the ability of individuals to move within the social order, which was blocked in India by the caste system.[121] Most of Ambedkar's colleagues in the Indian Constituent Assembly did not share his vision that the 'principal aim' of a democratic constitution was 'to dislodge the governing class' from power.[122] Nevertheless, nationalist liberals' avowal of the cause of betterment of the downtrodden, as well as the willingness of all sides to compromise to reach agreement, meant that legislative and

---

[116] B. R. Ambedkar, 'What Congress and Gandhi Have Done to the Untouchables', reprinted in *Dr Babasaheb Ambedkar Writings and Speeches*, IX, ed. Vasant Moon (Bombay: Government of Maharashtra, 1979), 232, 173.
[117] B. R. Ambedkar, *States and Minorities: What are their Rights and How to Secure Them in the Constitution of Free India* (Bombay: Thacker and Co. Ltd, 1947), 36.
[118] Ambedkar, *Writings and Speeches*, II, 598-9.
[119] He contrasted equality with liberty, the latter identified with the freedom of contract and resulting in 'economic wrongs' (Ambedkar, *Writings and Speeches*, IX, 446-7).
[120] Ambedkar, *Writings and Speeches*, IX, 444, 448-9; see also 202-4.
[121] Arun Mukherjee, 'B. R. Ambedkar, John Dewey, and the Meaning of Democracy', *New Literary History*, 40 (2009), 345-70; on Dewey's influence, see also Bayly, 'Liberalism Transcended', 18, 20. For a discussion of Ambedkar's developmental and social notion of freedom, see Mukherjee, 'B. R. Ambedkar', 363.
[122] Ambedkar, *Writings and Speeches*, IX, 448.

employment quotas for *dalits* and *adivasis* were eventually accepted by the Indian Constitution-makers, despite the strong misgivings of Jawaharlal Nehru and others.[123] The Indian Constitution is thus a legatee of all three liberalisms: colonial, nationalist, and radical.

COMPARISONS AND CONCLUSIONS

In politics, colonial, nationalist, and radical liberalisms have been opponents. One reading of modern Indian history is to see it as the triumph first of nationalist over colonial liberalism, and then of radical liberalism over nationalist liberalism. In terms of ideology, however, two important convergences can be discerned across the opposed liberalisms in India described in this essay. The first is a strong belief in state action for achieving liberal ends. Most variants of liberalism in India have been welfarist in orientation, seeing the state as 'the agent of individual well-being and flourishing through social reform'.[124] The utilitarian-Whig Macaulay, the Brahmin reformer Ranade, and the anti-Brahmin *dalit* leader Ambedkar, all argued that the initiative, direction, and resources of the state were essential for progress. Macaulay championed intervention by the British Parliament in Indian affairs in support of liberal projects in trade, education, and law. Ranade criticized *laissez faire* as unsuited to the needs of a backward economy, and argued for greater state intervention for economic and social advancement. Ambedkar was a staunch advocate of a strong centralized state for safeguarding the interests of the downtrodden castes, and in his later career went further than even Nehru and other socialists in advocating state ownership of agriculture and key industries.[125] In the diverse liberalisms outlined above, outside of criticisms of communism, it is hard to find elaborations of the classical liberal concern that the expansion of state power posed a threat to the individual. The main concern appears to have been the opposite, namely that unless the state was roused to and empowered to intervene, liberal ends would not be achieved, and individuals would remain trapped in oppressive traditions and exploitative relations. To use Isaiah Berlin's influential distinction, Indian liberalisms of different hues have mostly articulated variants of positive freedom. On the normative significance of negative freedom from the standpoint of the individual, they have remained largely silent.

---

[123] For more details of this process, see my *Debating Difference*.
[124] Michael Freeden, 'European Liberalisms: An Essay in Comparative Political Thought', *European Journal of Political Theory*, 7 (2008), 23.
[125] Bayly, 'Liberalism Transcended', 23.

A second feature shared across the different liberalisms discussed in this essay has been the recognition of group difference, along with a willingness to cohabit with group-differentiated rights. Indian liberals have on the whole been good social theorists, mindful of prevailing social conditions in their prescriptions for desired reform, attentive to the ways in which individual agency is shaped and limited by group membership and the wider social context. This has not always resulted in egalitarian policies. In colonial liberalism, the recognition of group difference often indicated the political or intellectual limits of liberalism, with liberal reformers having to yield large areas of law and policy to religious authority or conservative proponents of the Raj, and notions of racial hierarchy serving to limit the universal application of liberal principles.[126] In nineteenth-century nationalist liberalism, the recognition of group difference often indicated an acceptance of social hierarchy, as for instance in Rammohan's and Ranade's proposals for greater political rights for the educated and propertied. That a later generation of nationalists such as Nehru saw group-differentiated rights as inconsistent with liberal principles, like mid-twentieth-century liberals elsewhere, is not surprising in the light of their association with notions of racial and class superiority, although worries about national unity were as important.[127] Radical liberals like Ambedkar, however, advocated group-differentiated rights on egalitarian grounds. The Indian Constitution of 1950 recognized group-differentiated rights to a much greater extent than liberalisms of its time did elsewhere in the world, instituting special cultural rights for religious minorities, legislative quotas for the downtrodden castes and tribes, and preferential treatment in education and government employment for 'backward' groups. In one sense, the recognition of group-differentiated rights can be seen as an instance of Indian Constitution-makers being ahead of the theory and practice of liberalism of their time, adopting an expansive commitment to justice, elaborating a liberal egalitarian framework for addressing group-based inequalities.[128] However, to the extent that Indian Constitution-makers and their successors have failed to elaborate liberal justifications and mechanisms for group-differentiated rights that strengthen a common citizenship centred on individuals and constrain the exercise of power, these also indicate weaknesses of liberalism in India.[129]

The main exception to the common ground of liberalisms in India discussed in this essay appears to be free-market liberalism, prominent in Indian politics since the 1990s, and often identified with liberalism by those on the

---

[126] Metcalf, *Ideologies*.
[127] See Bajpai, *Debating Difference*.
[128] Panikkar, *Liberalism*, 16; also, Bhargava, 'Democratic Vision'; Gurpreet Mahajan, *Identities and Rights: Aspects of Liberal Democracy in India* (New Delhi: Oxford University Press, 1998).
[129] See, for instance, Guha, 'The Absent Liberal'; Pratap Bhanu Mehta, 'Democracy, Disagreement, and Merit', *Economic and Political Weekly*, 41, 24 (2006), 2425–47.

left. Advocates of the pursuit of economic growth through private accumulation and consumption criticize state intervention in the economy and group-differentiated rights as detracting not only from efficiency, but also from freedom. While neo-liberalism in India does articulate proto-liberal concerns, whether it can be characterized as liberal is debatable, as it has not offered a sustained account of personal freedom or the political conditions within which this can flourish. In theory, it offers at best what Freeden terms in the context of Eastern Europe an 'emaciated liberalism', a 'reactive legacy' of state control of the economy;[130] in practice, it has not been significantly distinct from strands of nationalist liberalism.[131]

To conclude, this essay has sought, in the spirit of Michael Freeden's seminal contribution to the study of liberalism, to explore the main variants of liberalism in nineteenth- and twentieth-century Indian political theory and practice. It has argued that liberalisms have been more prevalent and influential in India than is commonly believed, with thought conventionally characterized as imperialist, nationalist, socialist, and anti-caste exhibiting many liberal features. However, I have also suggested that Indian liberalisms have rarely expanded on the need for constraints on state power for the sake of individual freedom. Further, many sophisticated theorists of individual freedom in India (notably Gandhi) have affirmed liberal values but are not best described as liberal, having focused little on the institutional conditions for individual freedom. At one level, these findings indicate an area of weakness in Indian liberalism, which should be addressed by its defenders in the future. At another level, its limits in India serve as a useful reminder of the boundaries of liberalism as a category for comparative inquiry, of the need also for other frames—religious, anarchist, socialist, and republican—to capture and compare ideas of individual freedom.

---

[130] Freeden, 'European Liberalisms', 17.

[131] Indian national governments pursuing economic liberalization have also continued to expand state action on behalf of the poor, as well as group-differentiated rights.

4

Liberalism and American Stories of Peoplehood

Marc Stears

INTRODUCTION

Across the course of his career, Michael Freeden has done more than probably any other scholar to draw our attention to both the internal diversity of liberalism and to liberalism's place as a competitor amongst other ideologies. There have always been multiple liberalisms, he has insisted, allied by their shared core commitments, and those liberalisms have always had to fight for their place against conservative, socialist, and other competitors. The terms on which these liberalisms compete, moreover, has involved advancing different versions of a group of identifiable core concepts that always place central importance on some notion of human liberty, progress, reason, and sociability. Although liberalism is not always popular, and, therefore, is certainly not always politically persuasive, there is something undeniably attractive about liberalism to many of us, especially in comparison to its rival ideologies, and especially given the fact that its internal contestability has been bounded by an unshakeable dedication to core concepts that many of us would hope should always be central to politics.[1]

Compelling and influential though this interpretation of liberalism undeniably has been, it has always had its doubters and these have been especially prominent when it has come to the politics of the United States. For there, it has often been charged, liberalism has been much more rigidly fixed than it has been in Europe or elsewhere—constantly centred on individualist ethics, hostility to the power of the state, scepticism of social elites, and an intense sense of equality of status—and there also, it has rarely had to fight off any serious challengers, enjoying cultural and intellectual dominance in American

---

[1] See Michael Freeden, *Ideologies and Political Theory: A Conceptual Approach* (Oxford: Oxford University Press, 1996).

public life from the revolutionary war right through to the present. This view, which found its greatest expression in Louis Hartz's postwar masterpiece *The Liberal Tradition in America*, also sees American liberalism as a paradoxical threat to individual freedom. Liberalism here is a dogmatic creed, imposed on all Americans, willing liberals or otherwise, by social pressure and historic expectations. It is an ideology that possesses few of the open, contestable, and liberating characteristics that Michael Freeden's account might be taken to suggest.

Given Michael Freeden's own primary focus on European ideology, he has not yet had an opportunity to respond to this rival interpretation in much detail. The nature of American liberalism has, though, played a prominent part in my own research ever since I was a research student of Michael's in the late 1990s, and I have sought continuously to follow Michael's suggestions as to how to conduct such inquiries. My work has, then, focused not only on the 'great texts' of the ideological tradition but also on a far broader range of ideological forms, including articles in newspapers and periodicals, political pamphlets and manifestos, and even novels and films. Examination of this range of material spread over a long period of time has led me to the view that there is something distinctive about the liberalism of the United States, that it does not work in quite the same way as liberalism in Europe or elsewhere, but that neither does it fit the description provided by Hartz and his followers.[2] American liberalism does not, in particular, engage with its ideological rivals in the way that Hartz would expect, but neither has it had to fight quite as hard for a public hearing as it has had to elsewhere.

In this chapter, I deepen this enquiry into the nature of American liberalism still further by examining a much neglected but fascinating range of events in the American liberal story: the civic festivals that swept across the United States in the immediate aftermath of the Second World War, the moment when American politicians of all parties sought to redefine their nation's identity in opposition to the totalitarianism of both European fascism and of Soviet communism. These festivals, and especially the most successful of them all, the 1947–8 Freedom Train, I will argue, provide a perfect opportunity to assess the status of American liberalism. By examining them, and seeking to understand what two groups of contemporary intellectuals made of them, we can begin to ascertain whether American liberalism was, at this crucial moment of its development, an open, contested, ideological form focused on liberty, sociability, reason, and progress, or a narrower, more doctrinaire creed, threatening the liberties and the experimental-mindedness of the American people.

---

[2] See Marc Stears, 'Change We Already Believe In? The Liberal Tradition and the American Left', in Mark Hulliung (ed.), *The American Liberal Tradition Reconsidered* (Lawrence, KA: University Press of Kansas, 2010), 184–207; Marc Stears, *Demanding Democracy: American Radicals in Search of a New Politics* (Princeton: Princeton University Press, 2010).

THE FREEDOM TRAIN

In September of 1947, President Harry Truman travelled from Washington to Philadelphia to set the 'Freedom Train' on its way around the country. The Train was packed full of historical documents—including the Declaration of Independence, George Washington's copy of the Constitution, and the Bill of Rights—and was part of a Presidential mission to 're-sell America to the Americans'.[3] It was met by near frantic scenes wherever it went. In the words of *The New York Times*, people 'flocked' to the Freedom Train. 'Everywhere', the *Times* continued, the Train's arrival was 'a big day in town, a day for brass bands and patriotic speeches and visiting dignitaries. Schools dismiss. Merchants decorate their windows and the country people come in to see the "Spirit of 1776" with its cargo of "genuine American history"'.[4] Around four million people made it on to the Freedom Train in the nine months it toured the country, but many more participated in the events that surrounded it. In Charlotte, North Carolina, for example, 100,000 citizens lined up to enter the Train, even though only 8,416 were able to get on. Those who were disappointed were at least able to take part in the accompanying 'Rededication Week', in which they recited 'Freedom Promises', 'Freedom Pledges', and even 'Freedom Prayers', before going on to a 'Freedom Fashion Show'. The National Archives estimate that fifty million Americans attended some element of the Train's festivities.[5]

There was never any doubt as to the central ideal that lay behind the Freedom Train. It was given away in the name. But its origins are intriguing nonetheless. The Train itself was the dream-child of United States Attorney General Tom Clark in the immediate aftermath of the War and was first known as the 'Liberty Train'.[6] Clark proposed the idea to President Truman, arguing that as the United States emerged from one hot war and entered a cold one, it was the time to remind American citizens of the glory of the history of a 'free society' and to encourage them to reaffirm their dedication to the political and legal structures and the 'steely virtues' required to maintain such a society over time. America needs a 'civic reawakening', Clark insisted. The plan he

---

[3] For introductions to the Train, see John Bradsher, 'Taking America's Heritage to the People', *Prologue*, 17 (1985), 228–45; Richard Fried, *The Russians Are Coming! The Russians Are Coming! Pageantry and Patriotism in Cold War America* (New York: Oxford University Press, 1998); Robert Griffith, 'The Selling of America: The Advertising Council and American Politics, 1942–1960', *The Business History Review*, 57 (1983), 388–412; Wendy L. Wall, *Inventing the 'American Way': The Politics of Consensus from the New Deal to the Civil Rights Movement* (Oxford: Oxford University Press, 2008).
[4] See G. Bailey, 'Why They Flock to the Freedom Train', *The New York Times*, 25 January 1948.
[5] See Bradsher, 'Taking America's Heritage to the People', 241.
[6] See Fried, *Russians are Coming!*, 14–15.

and Truman eventually settled on would see the great historic documents of American liberty sent around the country for people to see, with each village, town, or city in which the Train stopped encouraged to organize a local celebration of American political structures and to organize rituals allowing local people to reconfirm their dedication to the American story and to the civic virtues necessary for freedom.[7]

Within a month of Clark proposing the basic idea to Truman, the American Heritage Foundation was founded to oversee the plan, drawing in support from the private sector, especially from the Advertising Council of America, which had helped with propaganda during the War, led by Thomas D'Arcy Brophy. Working closely with archivists and historians in the National Archives, the Heritage Foundation selected some 130 original and copied documents and flags, organized for a new locomotive and a set of carriages, and drew up a nationwide itinerary. They also commissioned Irving Berlin to write a song to be performed by Bing Crosby and the Andrews Sisters to wish the collection on its way and to welcome it in cities and towns across the nation: 'Inside the Freedom Train', Berlin's chorus ran, 'you'll find a precious freight, those words of liberty, the documents that made us great!'[8]

In addition to this organization work, the Advertising Council and the Heritage Foundation were also pressed into slightly incongruous historical and philosophical service. Without much input from professional academics, advertising executive Leo Burnett (the creator of 'Marlboro Man') produced a lengthy pamphlet, entitled *The Good Citizen*, reminding every American citizen of the national purpose through a series of telling short stories, pious poetry, and noble sayings along the lines made popular in the Depression years by *Reader's Digest*.[9] The Foundation also prepared the 'Freedom Pledge' which each visitor to the Train was instructed to recite as they boarded, the 'Freedom Prayer' for them to offer in church on Sunday, and 'Nine Promises of the Good Citizen' to which they were asked continually to commit themselves. The 'Promises' were widely distributed and displayed, including in the lobbies of public buildings and the foyers of theatres. They ran as follows:

> Ask yourself,
> "Am I truly a citizen—or just a fortunate tenant of this great nation?"
> Here is a summary of the working tools of good citizenship. Pledge yourself here and now to these nine points—that you, your children and your children's children may continue to enjoy the American heritage of "life, liberty and the pursuit of happiness."

---

[7] See Fried, *Russians Are Coming!*, 29–33, and Griffith, 'The Selling of America', 388–412.
[8] See <http://www.lyricstime.com/irving-berlin-the-freedom-Train-lyrics.html>.
[9] See Steven Gelber, 'A Job You Can't Lose: Work and Hobbies in the Great Depression', *Journal of Social History*, 24 (1991), 741–66.

1. I will vote at all elections. I will inform myself on candidates and issues and will use my greatest influence to see that honest and capable officials are elected. I will accept public office when I can serve my community or my country thereby.
2. I will serve on a jury when asked.
3. I will respect and obey the laws. I will assist public officials in preventing crime and the courts in giving evidence.
4. I will pay my taxes understandingly (if not cheerfully).
5. I will work for peace but dutifully accept my responsibilities in time of war and will respect the flag.
6. In thought, expression and action, at home, at school and in all my contacts, I will avoid any group prejudice, based on class, race, or religion.
7. I will support our system of free public education by doing everything I can to improve the schools in my own community.
8. I will try to make my community a better place in which to live.
9. I will practice and teach the principles of good citizenship right in my own home.[10]

The 'Promises', 'Pledge', and 'Prayer' all ended with the motto of the Train: 'freedom is *everybody*'s job', the invocation of the world of work presumably intended to leave the Train's visitors in no doubt that freedom in the United States was a serious business, in part protected by the social legacy of the past and by the inherited institutions of American governance but also needing a weary citizenry to rededicate itself to the fundamental ideals and the virtues believed essential to its protection and its maintenance across time.

DEBATING CAMPAIGNS FOR LIBERALISM

The Freedom Train was the most spectacular of a series of efforts in the early Cold War years to advance liberal ideology through the telling of the American story. It was joined by an enormous range of similarly extraordinary, if smaller-scale, campaigns. At the same time, the Advertising Council ran a series of national billboards advancing the prosperity-inducing benefits of the 'American Way'; Harding College of Arkansas produced a popular cartoon series widely shown before mainstream movies, which promised a 'complete understanding of the institutions, values, and ideas of liberty and democracy that made our country great'; and the US Office of Education organized an annual 'Voice of

---

[10] 'The Nine Promises of a Good Citizen', 27 August 1948, Port Huron Museum Collection, Port Huron, MI.

Democracy' competition, where schoolchildren from across the country were invited to write essays entitled 'I speak for democracy', with state and regional rounds leading to four children being selected to compete against each other in a national final held at Williamsburg and broadcast nationwide on radio.[11] All of these efforts shared a great deal in common, with a constant emphasis on freedom, on rights, on tolerance, and on open-mindedness, even in controversial areas such as racial affairs, standing out. They were also unarguably patriotic, with their liberalism being clearly and consistently combined with an equally extensive emphasis on the 'exceptional' status of the United States among nations and on the duties that citizens of the United States must fulfil in order to maintain their republic and its freedoms over time.

Despite their ubiquity and their undeniable public popularity, these liberal stories were not met with a uniform response from scholarly critics. In fact, to the sceptics they exhibited all the worst features of the American ideological experience. Of all these voices, it was Louis Hartz, whose *The Liberal Tradition in America* was published just seven years after the Freedom Train had ended its journey, who advanced the most searing critique. In that book, and in a series of scintillating supporting articles published from the late 1940s to the mid 1950s, Hartz argued that the American obsession with telling this kind of story both formally in large-scale events, such as the Freedom Train, and informally, as in political campaigns, small-town newspapers, and even everyday conversation, was responsible for many of the political failings of the United States. It was responsible, in particular, for encouraging Americans to turn their back on the unparalleled creativity and imagination of the New Deal, and to return to the more familiar laissez-faire politics of the early Depression years.

Hartz's critique of liberal stories of peoplehood in the United States had two components and it is vital to understand both of them. *First*, he insisted that the politics of the United States was characterized by an obsessive, dogmatic, and inflexible dedication to what he called the 'storybook' version of 'Lockean liberalism'. Ever since the Founding, he charged, the elites and the citizens of the United States have been almost uniformly dedicated to 'atomistic social freedom'—a doctrine that involved a commitment to individualist ethics, widespread hostility to the power of established authority, a pervasive scepticism towards social elites, and an intense sense of political equality. As a result, Americans of all political persuasions have had to defend all of their favoured policy positions in those terms.

The result of this, Hartz believed, was a form of 'liberal conformity' that posed a grave threat to creativity and innovation within American political

---

[11] For Harding College, see <http://www.youtube.com/watch?v=RG9jjxIF20A>, <http://www.youtube.com/watch?v=FAbqgxPLlE8>, <http://www.youtube.com/watch?v=gqyXJMcozng>. For more examples, see Wall, *Inventing the 'American Way'* and Fried, *The Russians are Coming!*

life, with its almost 'hysterical' emphasis on the core values of American liberalism leading to the 'binding down' of any potential dissenters until they were unwilling, even unable, to challenge established norms, even if it would have been politically useful to do so.[12] The only exception to this rule was the New Deal years when the severity of the crisis combined with the rhetorical prowess of Roosevelt had wrested Americans from their ideological slumber and allowed them to experiment with real political alternatives. Otherwise, Americans were in the grip of a fascination with the liberal tradition and were incapable of seeing the value of political 'eccentrics' or oppositionists, choosing instead always to narrow the range of political commitments that were thought 'decent' or permissible and invoking a vast array of formal and informal social sanctions, stretching from discouragement to effective ostracism, against anyone who dared to disagree.[13] 'Determined to pound loyalty home', he insisted, Americans who embrace their liberalism dogmatically have forgotten that 'dangerous thoughts are an inevitable part of... a free society' and that 'when they do not occur to anyone... that society will have ended, and the need for sedition will indeed be great'.[14]

It was not only the hold of liberalism per se which troubled Hartz, though. For, *second*, he also insisted that the American stories of peoplehood revealed that the elites and citizens of the United States were also unhealthy, obsessed with the nation's own past, liberal or otherwise. The United States, he explained, had never experienced a revolutionary break from feudalism in the way that Europe had. As such, it had never witnessed the overthrow of one domestic political system and its replacement with an alternative. This, in turn, had led to Americans possessing an astonishing reverence for their own past in the mistaken assumption that it was this continuity that was responsible for the relative prosperity and international success of the republic. Such a view resulted, Hartz suggested, in an inability to understand the political future in terms of the discontinuity that was needed for real change. The United States was simply politically incapable of appreciating what other nations understood as the occasional necessity of dramatic political transformation. This ensured that America was destined always to look backwards to the period of the Founding even at periods of intense political introspection rather than forwards to a new polity grounded in an alternative political ideal.[15]

---

[12] Louis Hartz, *The Liberal Tradition in America* (New York: Harcourt Brace, 1955), 185.

[13] See the prolonged discussion in Desmond King and Marc Stears, 'The Missing State in Postwar American Thought', in Desmond King and Lawrence Jacobs (eds.), *The Unsustainable American State* (Oxford: Oxford University Press, 2009), 116–34.

[14] Louis Hartz, 'Goals for Political Science', *American Political Science Review*, 45 (1951), 1003–4.

[15] See Hartz, *Liberal Tradition*, 232, and Hartz, 'American Political Thought and the American Revolution', *American Political Science Review*, 46 (1952), 321–42.

Combining these two critiques, Hartz saw American exercises in stories of peoplehood like the Freedom Train as milder instantiations of the dogmatic, inflexible, backward-looking liberalism that emerged in the early 1950s as the Cold War, which included the 'Red Scares' of McCarthy and his colleagues, took place. This was all part of what Hartz called the politics of 'liberal conformity'. And there is no doubt that there was something in his view. The Freedom Train, for example, exhibited many of the characteristics that Hartz identified and condemned. A form of impassioned and even slightly paranoid liberalism was reflected in all of the Heritage Foundation's publications, especially in *The Good Citizen* and its 'Freedom Pledge' and 'Freedom Promises'. It was also heavily present in public justifications for the project. The Freedom Train was 'intended to combat lawlessness, subversive tendencies and lethargy', Tom Clark told Congress employing a language that would have chilled Hartz's heart.[16] There was also a heavy degree of nostalgia underpinning the Train, running from the selection of the documents that the Train carried to the name of the locomotive that pulled it: 'the Spirit of 1776'. In an editorial in defence of the Train, *The New York Times* indeed brought these themes together exactly as Hartz would have feared. 'Reading in its original parchment the words, "These truths we hold to be self-evident," or the preamble of the Constitution', the *Times* suggested, 'many Americans will...feel a closer relationship to the past, will see behind the words the men who wrote them, will realize that there is such a thing as the "American tradition" and the "American way of life," and will take a new vow to be worthy of these things'.[17]

LIBERALISM IN PERIL

Powerful and influential though the Hartzian argument undeniably was, and has continued to be, there was nonetheless something both too simplistic and too extravagantly critical in its dismissal of the early Cold War stories of peoplehood. The tellers of these stories—the organizers of events such as the Freedom Train—did not, after all, see themselves as reinforcing already widely shared dogmas. They thought, instead, that they were saving an imperilled tradition. American citizens, they believed, had become deeply insecure in their allegiance to a standardized Lockean liberalism during the War. Feelings of alienation, loss, and confusion engendered both by the conflict and the Depression had rendered Americans easy prey to rival political identities and especially to those, such as communism and variants of religious extremism,

[16] 'Clark Explains Funds for Freedom Train', *The New York Times*, 19 June 1947.
[17] 'Freedom Train', *The New York Times*, 7 September 1947.

which offered more dramatic certainties in politics, religion, or other aspects of social life.[18] America's identity as an identifiably liberal order could not be taken for granted, they thus insisted. Rather, it would have to be fought for. As one noted contemporary commentator put it, 'the death pallor will come over free society' unless these versions of the American story 'can recharge the deepest sources of its moral energy'.[19]

The historian Wendy Wall is right, then, when she suggests that those such as the organizers of the Freedom Train saw their mission as *instilling* (or, at the most, *reinstilling*) rather than simply *reinforcing* liberal mores.[20] Some of these storytellers even openly described themselves as taking on 'the task of liberal guardianship'.[21] This by itself, of course, does not prove Hartz wrong. He would have explained all of these anxieties as just another instance of American liberal paranoia, no different to the moral panics about immigrants from Southern Europe that had gripped mainstream opinion in the first decade of the twentieth century or the fears of communists, gamblers, feminists, and alcoholics that irrationally shaped public debate in the years immediately after the First World War. But, whatever his response, this realization does nonetheless take us to Hartz's most powerful contemporary intellectual rivals, an otherwise inchoate group of political thinkers that I call the early cold-war realists, and to whom I now turn.

LIBERALISM AND REALISM

The early cold-war realists—whose work was captured in an array of otherwise dissimilar texts as Reinhold Niebuhr's *The Children of Light and the Children of Darkness*, Arthur Schlesinger's *Vital Center*, Stuart Chase's *Roads to Agreement*, and Ralph Ellison's *Invisible Man*—all began their reflections on American politics with a single assumption. The United States, they charged, was not primarily characterized by a stable liberal consensus, as Hartz believed, but by a deep and dangerous set of domestic disputes, including

---

[18] See Harold Metz and Charles Thompson, *Authoritarianism and the Individual* (Washington DC: Brookings Institutions, 1950), and Franz Alexander, *Our Age of Unreason: A Study in the Irrational Forces in Social Life* (Philadelphia: Lippincott, 1950). For excellent discussion, see Andrew Abbott and James T. Sparrow, 'Hot War, Cold War: The Structures of Sociological Action, 1940–1955', in Craig Calhoun (ed.), *Sociology in America* (Chicago: Chicago University Press, 2007), 281–313, and Mark Leff, 'The Politics of Sacrifice on the American Home Front in World War II', *Journal of American History*, 77 (1991), 1307–12.

[19] Arthur Schlesinger, *The Vital Center: The Politics of Freedom* (New York: Transaction, 1997), 246.

[20] Wall, *Inventing the 'American Way'*, 3.

[21] Ira Katznelson, *Desolation and Enlightenment: Political Knowledge after Total War, Totalitarianism, and the Holocaust* (New York: Columbia University Press, 2003), 131.

racial division, class conflict, and tensions between the several States and the federal government. American politics, Niebuhr thus explained, faced a grave 'internal peril' from such conflicts.[22] Such conflicts, they continued, had their roots in the peculiar history of the United States, prompted especially by the absence of a sense of ethnic unity that characterized most European nations and by popular belief in individualism and capitalistic competition. But they had been horrifically intensified by the social and economic dislocations of the Depression and then further still by the sense of confusion, even moral desolation, which had been the inevitable result of the experience of total war against fascism. 'Beset by feelings of isolation because of the fluid, pluralistic turbulence of [our nation]', Ralph Ellison poetically put it, 'we cling desperately to our own familiar fragment of the democratic rock, and from such fragments we confront our fellow Americans in the combat… which is the drama of American social hierarchy'.[23] The more prosaic result was that modern American politics was characterized by fierce internal rivalries. For Niebuhr, almost each and every citizen possessed 'ambitions, hopes and fears, which set him at variance with his neighbour'.[24]

If conflict was the present danger of American politics for the realists, then their first commitment was to discovering a means of containing those conflicts. It was simply unconscionable to ignore them, as they believed Hartzians did, or to presume that they could ever be fully overcome, as some naïve idealists in the past had aspired to. It was vital, then, to render these disputes peaceful and to ensure that they did not prevent the political process from working smoothly and sustainably. Compromise and conciliation became the political commitments of realists. It was vital to prevent any one group from seeking to dominate others and to prevent the kind of excessive infighting that threatened to inflict irreparable damage on the political system itself, presenting the serious risk that the liberalism of the United States would fail in its competition with authoritarian rivals. Realist politics was thus to be premised on the assumption that 'conflict must be kept within bounds, if freedom itself is to survive'.[25]

The realists were also clear, though, that the spirit of compromise would not come easy. All sorts of Americans—working class and bourgeois, white and black, southern and northern, left and right—would need to develop a 'positive and continuing commitment' to moderate and loyal forms of political action, learning how to give-and-take, to recognize the merits of social stability, and to turn their back on excessive sectional certainties. The difficulty was to

---

[22] Reinhold Niebuhr, *The Children of Light and the Children of Darkness* (New York: Charles Scribner's Sons, 1944), 152.
[23] Ralph Ellison, 'Going to the Territory', in John Callahan (ed.), *The Collected Essays of Ralph Ellison* (New York: The Modern Library, 1994), 504.
[24] Niebuhr, *Children of Light*, 11.
[25] Schlesinger, *Vital Center*, 173.

explain how such a spirit could be built. The beginning of the answer, the realists all felt, lay in the emotions. War and depression had revealed, they believed, that citizens chose how to act politically as much on the basis of irrational, or at least non-rational, impulse as self-interested calculation. Any vision that was to have a chance of success in moderating political conflicts, therefore, would have to have a 'living emotional content'. It was citizen *feelings* that would lead to moderated citizen actions.

But it was not just any passion or emotion that was required. Rather, what was needed was an emotional sense of commonalities drawing together differing individuals and groups.[26] It was only such a lived feeling of commonality, the realists insisted, that could lead erstwhile political opponents to moderate their aggression towards each other such that they learnt to restrain their conflictual urges and treat each other as respected rivals with whom they lived, rather than as enemies that they sought to eliminate. 'Our democracy has to generate a living emotional content, rich enough to rally its members' together whatever their personal or social differences', Schlesinger thus argued.[27]

It was for this reason, then, that the sort of shared story of peoplehood propagated by the Freedom Train was celebrated as a possible solution to the nation's political ills, rather than condemned as an exercise in excessive homogenization and political conservatism. 'If democracy is to survive' in the United States, Niebuhr concluded, 'it must find a more adequate cultural basis', and that cultural basis would have to be the kind of emotionally rich and potentially widely shared story encapsulated by events such as the Train.[28] This is not to say, however, that the realists were not also acutely aware of some of the dangers that were associated with this kind of project. Most crucially, they were insistent that these stories had to emerge at least partly from the lived experience of the majority of the people themselves and should never be imposed by a distant state authority or enforced by any other agency without significant public support. A 'coerced unity', Niebuhr insisted, can only 'produce sadistic cruelties'. That, indeed, was the 'tremendously valuable lesson' to be taken from the study of Nazism. The war, after all, had engendered a deep pessimism about the state and related political agencies, believing that all 'special elites' are constantly 'exposed to the temptations of pride and power'. To leave state authorities in charge of shaping and advancing stories of peoplehood, or at least to do so uncontested, was to invite disaster.[29]

More important than even that, though, was the fact that the emotional unity realists sought was intended to be 'thin'—not invested with too much in the way of controversial assumptions—and open to continual reinterpretation and reinvention. These conditions were required both so that as many groups as possible would feel fairly treated by the story if it became influential and so

---

[26] Schlesinger, *Vital Center*, 189.
[27] Schlesinger, *Vital Center*, 245
[28] Niebuhr, *Children of Light*, 6.
[29] Schlesinger, *Vital Center*, 170.

that it did not stand in the way of political innovation. It was crucial, therefore, that no story of peoplehood that was widely propagated should be fixed, dogmatic, or unreasonably exclusive. As Schlesinger put it, 'a sense of humility is indispensable... The conservative must not identify a particular *status quo* with the survival of civilization; and the radical equally must recognize that his protests are likely to be as much the expressions of his own self-interest as they are of some infallible dogma about society'.[30] The realists hoped, therefore, that a complicated Americanism could be born at this moment. It was to be emotionally intense enough to bind together people who were otherwise hostile to each other, but also light of detail and flexible of interpretation. Social and political conflicts were inevitable in the United States (while performing important functions), the realists insisted, but stories of American national identity could generate a shared sense of collective identity which could moderate those conflicts as they took place, stabilizing the republic and safeguarding it from enemies, both internal and external, as it did so.

The realists were not solely interested in prescription, though. Theirs was also intended to be a descriptive account. To their eyes, the early cold-war years were already witnessing the emergence of just such a complicated, almost ironic, American story in events like the Freedom Train. 'As a nation, we exist in the communication of our principles, and we argue over their application and interpretation as over the rights of property or the exercise and sharing of authority', Ralph Ellison described. And yet despite those arguments, the national story within which these principles were embedded was common and emotionally powerful enough. It was that story that collectively 'influence[d] our expositions in the area of artistic form' and was constantly 'involved in our search for a system... capable of projecting our corporate, pluralistic identity'. It was these liberal stories of peoplehood, Ellison concluded far from Hartz's scepticism, which enabled American citizens to 'interrogate' themselves 'endlessly as to who and what we are', and it is they that 'demand that we keep the democratic faith'.[31]

LEARNING THE LESSONS FOR LIBERALISM

These two very different interpretations of the place of stories of peoplehood in the early cold-war years were premised on two mirror-opposite accounts of the present danger in American politics in the mid twentieth century: excessive consensus, on the one hand, and excessive conflict, on the other.

---

[30] Schlesinger, *Vital Center*, 174.
[31] Ralph Ellison, 'The Little Man at Chehaw Station', reprinted in John F. Callahan (ed.), *The Collected Essays of Ralph Ellison* (New York: Random House, 2003), 505–6.

Comparing and contrasting them is, therefore, extraordinarily different, as at base are two rival, but equally fundamental, axioms. Nonetheless, their arguments also depended on particular empirical judgments, especially concerning the impact of the early cold-war stories of peoplehood on political debate in the United States. As such, then, it remains possible for us critically to evaluate their arguments, to compare them against each other and against political experience, in the hope that by doing so we might learn something of value for our debates today.

The most straightforward of these evaluations is worrying for Hartzians and encouraging for realists. The impact of the widespread attempt to tell stories of peoplehood in the early cold-war years on the nature of public discussion in the United States was unarguably contrary to what a Hartzian would expect. Put bluntly, such attempts did not close down political debate, at least nowhere near as dramatically as Hartz's account suggested. Rather, they appear to have sparked an astonishingly lively public discussion both about the nature of American political identity and the relationship of that identity to everyday politics.

The Freedom Train provides a perfect example. Even a cursory examination of newspaper, radio, and social-movement discussions of the Train demonstrates that its journey enlivened political argument. It did not quash it. Indeed, there were so many groups who felt perfectly comfortable being deeply and very publicly sceptical of the Train that J. Edgar Hoover sent nine reports to Tom Clark worrying that its travels were invoking subversion across the land.[32] As usual, Hoover overreacted. Nonetheless, there were trade unionists who dismissed the Train as an exercise in business-biased propaganda and condemned the absence of the Wagner Act from the collection of documents; civil rights activists who thought it did not go far enough in its dedication to racial justice; Republicans who believed it was all part of the Democratic election machine; and some States' rights activists who were worried by the very idea of a Train travelling through their territory carrying a cargo from Washington.

Crucially, though, this was not open conflict, of the sort the realists feared. Instead, those who contested the message of the Train chose to do so in its *own* terms rather than in the name of a rival ideological tradition or self-interest. The trouble with the Train was thus not said to be its equation of Americanism with some form of liberalism per se, let alone its attempt to tell a kind of American story. Instead, it was criticized either for its failure to advance some aspects of that liberalism over others or for its inability to acknowledge the reality that life in the United States often fell short up to key aspects of its

---

[32] See Bradsher, 'Taking America's Heritage to the People', 238.

professed ideals. The Train offered a common language within which political debate could be joined.

This was especially strikingly true of two movements that might well have been expected to have distanced themselves from the Train: the U.S. Communist Party and the nascent civil rights movement. The leadership of the former group apparently toyed with the idea of a boycott. Eventually, though, they decided that even they were 'in favour of the Bill of Rights', so they chose instead to encourage members to visit the Train as long as they were accompanied by a Party-appointed commentator. The commentator's role was to draw the visitor's attention to the invaluable role that working people had played in struggling for freedom and justice throughout American history.[33] The civil rights movements' relationship to the Train was similar. It found voice in Langston Hughes's much-quoted poem, 'Freedom Train', originally written for *The New Republic*, in which Hughes rejected neither the central liberal ideals of the Train nor the nostalgia with which it was imbued. Instead, he asked: 'Is this here freedom on the Freedom Train *really* freedom or [just] a show again?' Opening with a scathing critique of the injustices faced by African Americans in mid-century America, Hughes concluded on a more optimistic note. Americans, he suggested, should 'let the Freedom Train come zooming down the track', but only so long as it is 'gleaming in the sunlight for white *and* black'.[34]

The resolute unwillingness of the Train's detractors to criticize either the liberal essentials that the Train represented or its nostalgic reconstruction of American history might be thought to lend some succour to Hartz's criticism. But on reflection it is closer to a vindication of the realists' position. Here, it seems, was a popular story of peoplehood that *restrained* conflict without abolishing it, provided an emotional bond between erstwhile opponents, and presented a common language and point of reference which far from preventing dissent and debate actually offered a means by which innovative arguments could be advanced. In the instance of the civil rights movement, indeed, the realists might even have had a more powerful case. For, just as Gunnar Myrdal had famously predicted two years earlier, widespread public discussion focusing on the 'American creed' enabled African-American activists to highlight their cause in terms which powerfully resonated with large sections of the American public.[35] The arrival of the Train in southern cities also witnessed the first major racially integrated civic events since the Civil War, as the Heritage Foundation steadfastly refused to allow the Train to be complicit in segregation. The Train's organizers in Maryland even led one

[33] 'Travelling Heirlooms', *Time*, 22 November 1947.
[34] Langston Hughes, 'Freedom Train', *The New Republic*, 15 September 1947.
[35] See Gunnar Myrdal, with the assistance of Richard Sterner and Arnold Rose, *An American Dilemma: The Negro Problem and Modern Democracy* (New York: Harper and Brothers, 1944).

woman who had been born into slavery, 95-year-old Annie Grey, publicly through the Train to see Lincoln's drafts of the Emancipation Declaration. As one civil rights activist put it, the connection between African Americans and the Train seemed often to be almost inevitably positive because 'we have a special interest when you talk about freedom'.[36]

At its best, then, the Freedom Train provided a powerful response to what Ralph Ellison would later call 'the puzzle of the one-and-the-many', offering a way of considering 'the mystery of how each of us, despite his origin in diverse regions, with diverse racial, cultural, religious backgrounds' can think of himself as 'nevertheless, American'.[37] But before we conclude that the realists' defence of these early cold-war stories of peoplehood was thoroughly successful, it is crucial to note that there remain many reasons for caution.

Most straightforwardly, of course, there were still undeniable limits on what could politically be expressed within the context of the liberal story advanced on the Train. So even if the Train enabled civil rights activists to find a common platform with 'mainstream America', it clearly prioritized some arguments over others. There was little opportunity to contest the structural, economic inequalities between racial groups in America, for example. Moreover, the relentlessly upbeat 'storybook' history that accompanied the Train gave little sense of how grave injustices had ever been propagated in the American past. Everything in the story of liberal America was good, and always had been, rendering it extremely difficult to identify the sources of the injustices that remained or to apportion responsibility and blame for these injustices even if it was widely felt that they were needed and deserved.

But even more important than these restrictions, there was also the question of precisely *how* the orthodox liberal stories could be contested, opened up, and reinterpreted. The realist case for stories of peoplehood was reliant on those stories being told and received with a certain degree of irony, even playfulness. The liberal story of events such as the Freedom Train remained plausible as a site for peaceful political contest and innovation only in so far as it could be constantly reworked and that reworking required that no single part of the story be treated with too great a degree of reverence or seriousness. All aspects of the story, therefore, had to be open not only to formal critique but to pastiche, satire, and even mockery. The possibility of such jocular distancing—what Giorgio Agamben has called 'studious play'[38]—was required for two reasons. First, it provided a means by which groups could dismiss aspects of the story that they found unattractive without causing too great a degree of offence. Second, it was also a way by which groups could come to

---

[36] See Bailey, 'Throng to the Freedom Train', and '13,000 See Freedom Train', *The New York Times*, 23 November 1947.

[37] Ralph Ellison, 'Hidden Name and Complex Fate', in Callahan (ed.), *Collected Essays*, 207.

[38] Giorgio Agamben, *State of Exception* (Chicago: University of Chicago Press, 2005), 64.

cope with unattractive elements of the story that would not go away. If, after all, they could find some kind of *fun* in the story that was offered, even in the parts that might not necessarily gel with their own ideological convictions, then they might be able to overcome their hostility towards it or to others whose own allegiance to the story was less affected.

It was for this very reason that the more light-hearted aspects of the Train's journey were central to its very serious political purpose. For all of their apparent silliness, the public festivities of the 'Rededication Weeks', the entertainers who accompanied the endless lines to climb aboard, the comic-book stories of Mickey Mouse, Popeye, or Captain Marvel's visits to the Train, and even the 'Freedom Fashion Shows' all played their part in engendering the right kind of atmosphere for realist engagement with the liberal story of peoplehood that it offered. They each maintained, in other words, the light touch that was essential to enabling the story to feel widely and genuinely shared rather than exclusive, selective, and coercively imposed. It was almost as if the organizers understood, as Ralph Ellison would later put it, that in order to work effectively stories of peoplehood must provide three things: 'hope, perception and *entertainment*'. It is only if they combined all three, Ellison explained, that they 'might help keep us afloat as we...negotiate the snags and whirlpools that mark our nation's vacillating course towards and away from the democratic ideal'.[39]

Yet just as some aspects of the Freedom Train's journey reveal the sources of this success, they also reveal the beginnings of real difficulties. For onerous and exclusive seriousness was never too far away from the Train's mission. The 'Promises', 'Pledges', and 'Prayers' testified to that, as did the frequent official discussions from Clark and his colleagues about civic virtue, the avoidance of subversion, and the overcoming of apathy. With such seriousness, however, came a dangerous degree of political ossification. It is far less easy to contest and reinterpret a story of peoplehood imbued with the sort of status that places it beyond irony, and beyond challenge. This, we might recall, was Hartz's central objection to the whole endeavour: it was liberal *dogmatism* that Hartz decried, not liberalism itself. And this dogmatism was an undeniable danger of telling the story of American peoplehood in the spirit of 'moral vigor', as Arthur Schlesinger once put it, or of continually emphasizing that 'being an American is an arduous task'.[40]

This inflexible seriousness was, of course, largely a product of fear, both rational and irrational. There was fear of the Soviet Union, of uncontrollable internal dissent, of economic decline, of moral permissiveness. And yet it was this fear that the early cold-war realists seemed to miss almost entirely as they encouraged the telling of American stories of peoplehood. They seemed to

---

[39] Ellison, 'Introduction to Invisible Man', in Callahan (ed.), *Collected Essays*, 487.
[40] Ellison, 'Hidden Name', 209.

believe that those telling these stories in the United States would always have the open, ironic character that was required if those stories were to help keep freedom, contest, and innovation alive. But in this they were mistaken. Even if those characteristics were frequently—if not constantly—displayed in the era of the Freedom Train, that is, they were nowhere near as evident as the Cold War continued. Put simply, the early cold-war years were not the later cold-war years. For all of the nuclear danger there was a 'relatively less oppressive and less terrifying political climate' in the United States in the late 1940s and very early 1950s than there was in later periods, as David Riesman later explained.[41] And while it may have been relatively safe to encourage the telling of stories of peoplehood in times of openness, creativity, and generosity, it quickly became evident that it was much less so in times when fears were almost continually exacerbated and conflicts ever more increasingly intensified.

The next generation, of course, could not fail to notice this limitation. For the 1960s and 1970s witnessed the most ferocious of turns in the 'culture wars', during which stories of peoplehood were invested with a degree of both seriousness and inflexibility that rendered them completely incapable of providing any kind of emotional glue for a divided society. Instead, accounts of essential American political identity—the 'cultural/national issues' as they became—were the stuff of brutal presidential elections, public confrontations between hard-hat-wearing construction workers and student protesters, and even campaigns of civil disobedience.[42] By the late 1960s, then, the idea that a politically proposed, partisan-informed story of national identity could bring conflicting groups together so that they could dispute openly and creatively with one another in an atmosphere of respect seemed a very long way away. It is ironic that the early cold-war realists who were otherwise so alert to the present danger of civil conflict missed the importance of this context almost entirely.

CONCLUSION

The early cold-war realists hoped that liberal stories of peoplehood could play a crucial but undeniably complex role in American politics. Such stories were intended to hold an inevitably conflictual polity together, and to do so without seeking to transcend that conflict or to prioritize a conservative commitment

---

[41] David Riesman, 'Preface to the 1961 Edition', in David Riesman, *The Lonely Crowd* (New Haven: Yale University Press, 2001), p. lvii.

[42] See Byron E. Shafer, *The Two Majorities and the Puzzle of Modern American Politics* (Lawrence KA: University of Kansas Press, 2003).

to the status quo over progressive aspirations for a better tomorrow. By providing a shared conceptual language, a shared political history, and, most importantly of all, a shared emotional experience to the rival groups that comprised the American polity, such stories would shape 'an American people who are geared to what *is*, and who are yet driven by a sense of what it is possible for human life to be in this society'.[43]

There is much that was greatly admirable in this project. The realists understood both the unavoidable limits and the unquenchable aspirations of political life. They were aware of the dangers of division, yet also conscious of the equally worrisome perils of excessive homogeneity. Yet there was also a grave difficulty in their argument, for they failed to emphasize that only a very particular kind of story of peoplehood can play the role they demanded and that it takes a very distinctive social and political context for such a story to flourish.

The question that remains for us is: what can we learn from this debate concerning the early twenty-first-century use of liberal stories of peoplehood in American politics? The answer is a crucially nuanced one. When our attention is drawn to the deep divisions in American politics and to the need to restrain some of the worst consequences of those divisions without seeking to transcend them entirely, then we might well be attracted to the possibilities of a liberal story of peoplehood. In that regard, we might well insist that liberalism does occupy a distinctive position in American politics, that it is able somehow to raise itself above the ideological fray that Michael Freeden has rightly pointed out elsewhere. We must remember nonetheless that only the warm, open-ended, flexible, ironic, even playful variants of this liberalism are, in fact, ever able to play a role in transforming potentially destructive political antagonisms into potentially creative and dynamic political agonisms. As Freeden has so powerfully noted, as with all ideologies, it is the internally flexible, adaptable, open-ended liberalism that is capable of growing and playing the role that is required of it. If the citizens of the United States are fortunate enough to live in circumstances that enable those kind of liberal stories to be told—or even if they are brave enough to be able to help create those circumstances—then such stories may well offer the piece of political magic that their advocates suggest.

---

[43] Ralph Ellison, 'What America Would Be Like Without Blacks', in Callahan (ed.), *Collected Essays*, 588.

5

The Liberal Dilemma: The Economic and the Social, and the Need for a European Contextualization of a Concept with Universal Pretensions

Bo Stråth

INTRODUCTION

There is not one liberalism but several, each of which has contributed to the modernity of Europe. Liberalism—like other ideologies—should not be seen in the conventional view of a more or less cohesive line of thought through history, but as a collection of arguments, which have been used in very different ways and combinations depending on the given historical context. The collection of arguments that we call liberalism reflects the deep historical diversity of Europe, a diversity that since the nineteenth century has had the demarcation among nation states as a point of departure. To argue that each national culture has had its own understanding and experience of liberalism is to underestimate the complexity, however, because in each national setting there have been various more or less contested versions. Nietzsche said that the worst enemy of truth is not the lie but conviction. Over the years many convictions have been pronounced in the numerous attempts to define the right version of liberalism.

There is in other words a need to historicize and contextualize liberalism. Nobody has more convincingly argued for such contextualization than Michael Freeden. His approach to politics and ideologies has emphasized the conceptual in its historical context, where ideologies, rather than being long-term consistent and separated chains of thought, are seen as depositories or arsenals of arguments which can be collected and combined in various ways from various ideological origins contingent on the specific historical situations.[1] Through his long-standing interest in comparative analyses Freeden has demonstrated the variety of liberalisms. Interestingly, however, his starting point in reconstructing the historical trajectory of liberalism has usually been John Stuart Mill. The liberal market tradition stemming from Adam Smith has been much less prominent in Freeden's account of liberalism. This chapter examines that tradition of market liberalism and in particular investigates the way in which liberals have conceptualized the economic. Bearing in mind the need to contextualize liberalism—as well as other ideological collections of arguments—I will nevertheless try to outline some historical long-term trends.

MANCHESTER AND SMITH: TWO DIFFERENT THINGS

Liberalism emerged in the struggle against absolute monarchy and religious orthodoxy. The point of departure was the emerging perspective where the individual saw him- or herself as the basis of law and social organization as opposed to the divine or tradition. Based on such radical individualism, liberalism is closely connected to the idea of limited state power and limited legal restrictions. This version is referred to as laissez-faire liberalism or Manchester liberalism. 'Let-go' liberalism with maximum freedom of trade and minimum state intervention was propagated by the French physiocrats, François Quesnay and others, against mercantilism. Manchester became the headquarters of the Anti-Corn Law League from 1839, an organization that campaigned against agricultural protection so as to reduce food prices for the poor and to increase the competitiveness of manufactured goods abroad. Manchester liberalism grew out of this movement. It was regarded as a challenge to the dominant economic system of Europe between the sixteenth century and the eighteenth century: mercantilism. In 1846, the Conservative MP, Benjamin Disraeli, first used the term 'the School of Manchester'.[2] The term 'Manchesterism' was invented by Ferdinand Lassalle, the founder of German socialism, and was meant as a term of abuse.[3] This meaning it has retained ever since.

---

[1] Michael Freeden, *Liberalism Divided: A Study in British Political Thought 1914–1939* (Oxford: Oxford University Press, 1986); Freeden, *Ideologies and Political Theory: A Conceptual Approach* (Oxford: Oxford University Press, 1996); Freeden, *Liberal Languages* (Princeton: Princeton University Press, 2005).

[2] He used it in a debate in Parliament with Prime Minister Robert Peel, who had just proposed to repeal the Corn Laws. He referred to 'the disciples of the school of Manchester'. T. S. Ashton, 'The Origin of "the Manchester School"', *The Manchester School*, 1 (1938), 24.

[3] According to a note by the leader of the Prussian free trade party, Julius Faucher, from 1870, the term was invented by Lassalle as a *Schmähwort*. Manchesterism provoked a heated debate in

Based on the ideas of popular sovereignty, and of justice and law as the means for peaceful coexistence, liberalism is also connected to an intense philosophical debate on concepts like 'the people', 'nation', 'wealth', and 'security'. Hobbes, Locke, Kant, Montesquieu, Rousseau, de Tocqueville, and many others developed arguments about the relationships between the individual, the nation, and the state, and about what the good society is and how it could be achieved. It was a philosophical debate full of oppositions, ambiguities, and contradictions.

In this very fertile debate the issue of the market emerged. Market language was at its origins connected to the question of the institutions and rules needed to regulate economic activity, and to the image of a free public sphere for the free flow of information necessary for economic exchange. Concerning institutions, the most prominent founding father of the market idea, the Scottish moral philosopher Adam Smith, stated that human beings continuously needed aid from their fellow human beings. It was in vain, however, to expect this aid solely for altruistic reasons. The question was rather how aid to other human beings could be promoted through the mechanisms of self-interest. This was an institutional and organizational collective question far from promoting any idea of individual atomism.[4]

In *The Wealth of Nations* he states in a famous quote that it 'is not from the benevolence of the butcher, the brewer, or the baker that we expect our dinner, but from their regard to their own interest'. However, he also said that in a well-organized society based on the division of labour the baker and the brewer were 'at all times in need of the co-operation and assistance of great multitudes, while [their] whole life is scarce sufficient to gain the friendship of a few persons...Man has almost constant occasion for the help of his brethren, and it is in vain for him to expect it from their benevolence only'.[5]

Adam Smith did not believe that self-interest was the only driving force of human action. He was not a narrow-minded propagator of laissez faire, and never argued that an invisible hand would automatically coordinate economic activities to produce optimal results when left alone. His key question was

---

the German states. It was seen in positive terms in government administration, the business community, and the liberal press. There were also numerous adherents in the universities. Against all these stood the adherents of competing theories, such as Friedrich List's national economics, the corporatism propagated by Hermann Wagener and others, and the egalitarian state socialism outlined by Ferdinand Lassalle. After the 1870s the historical school and the *Kathedersozialisten* in economics, law, and social sciences confronted Manchesterism. For Lassalle as the originator of the term Manchesterism, see Ralph Raico, *Die Partei der Freiheit: Studien zur Geschichte des deutschen Liberalismus* (Stuttgart: Lucius & Lucius, 1999), 29. See also Paul Kennedy, *The Rise of the Anglo-German Antagonism, 1860–1914* (London: Allen & Unwin, 1980), 152.

[4] Smith discussed the term self-interest in particular in *The Theory of Moral Sentiments* (New York, NY: Penguin Books, [1759] 2009). For the reference here, see pp. 154–5 and 277.

[5] Adam Smith, *An Inquiry into the Nature and Causes of the Wealth of Nations* (New York: J. Wiley, [1776] 2010), 15.

what institutional arrangements could canalize self-interest into beneficial outcomes. Smith was empiricist, eclectic, and pragmatic, rather than dogmatic. Self-interest was one of several factors needed to achieve good economic results. The market was not the only and exclusive instrument for the production of wealth but rather a coordinating order to curb self-interest. In that function markets were certainly more than self-propelling machines driven by an invisible hand. They required political rules. Smith opposed government's manipulation of trade, but he acknowledged a decisive role for government to guarantee property rights and justice, build public works, and provide public education.

In the theoretical construction of a growing economy triggered by a division of labour in more intensified and transnational forms, *labour* became a means, not only to maintain the existence of, but also to create, capital. Labour began to connote economic growth through specialization and the allocation of labour through the price mechanism, and economic growth signified more material wealth. Smith never believed in a straightforward progression towards equality through the expansion of market liberties. His position was that markets create *economic* and *social* inequalities, although they undermined traditional *feudal* forms of inequality, which opened up a space for *political* equality. The economic and social inequality was in his theory justified in terms of aggregate economic gains, which provided an increasing pie where all could have a growing share. For such a fair distribution, political equality was important. The distribution would be sufficient to convince even the poorest labourer that he would gain from an order of inequality because of the general growth it brought about. This was an argument against traditional republican ideas that political and economic equality in an uncomplicated way advance hand in hand. Even if there was a connection between political and economic equality, Smith argued, the former could never bring about market equality.

This interpretation of Smith was later to become important in European political debate. In the 1830s, when the social question emerged on the political agenda all over Europe in response to the dark side of industrial capitalism and agrarian proletarianization, the issue at stake was not inequality as such, but the credibility of believing that the growing pie would also give a little piece to the poor.

There is a tension between persuasive utopian utilitarianism and pragmatic reasoning in Smith's text. There has been a strong tendency among later commentators and disciples to overemphasize this utopian element. Such was the case when neoclassical thinkers read Smith a hundred years after he wrote. And such is particularly the case when neo-liberal interpreters do so today.[6] Smith discussed the contradiction between labour and capital and the

---

[6] Emma Rothschild, *Economic Sentiments: Adam Smith, Condorcet, and the Enlightenment* (Cambridge, MA: Harvard University Press, 2001), gives the full evidence for this point.

social problems that follow from this antinomy in a much more sophisticated way than have the many modern theories that refer to him. It was not by chance that Marx called Smith the Luther of political economy.

Although Smith was convinced of the common interests of employers and workers in the long run, through the capacity of a growing economy to provide more goods to all, he was well aware of their short-term conflicting interests. Although the increasing pie through the growing supply of commodities in the new labouring society would lead to increased consumption and general prosperity, which would dismantle class barriers in the long run, he never envisaged a process without problems and social conflicts.

In Chapter VIII of *The Wealth of Nations*, on the wages of labour, he developed his view:

> What are the common wages of labour, depends everywhere upon the contract usually made between those two parties, whose interests are by no means the same. The workmen desire to get as much, the masters to give as little, as possible. The former are disposed to combine in order to raise, the latter in order to lower, the wages of labour.[7]

It was not, however, difficult to foresee which of the two parties would have the advantage in the dispute, and force the other into compliance with their terms. The masters, being fewer in number, could 'combine' much more easily. The law, besides, authorized, or at least did not prohibit, their joint action against the workers, while it prohibited that of the workers.

> We have no acts of parliament against combining to lower the price of work, but many against combining to raise it. In all such disputes, the masters can hold out much longer. A landlord, a farmer, a master manufacturer, or a merchant, though they did not employ a single workman, could generally live a year or two upon the stocks, which they have already acquired. Many workmen could not subsist a week, few could subsist a month, and scarce any a year, without employment. In the long run, the workman may be as necessary to his master as his master is to him; but the necessity is not so immediate.[8]

One rarely heard, Smith continued, of the combination of masters, but frequently of those of workers. However, whoever imagined that masters rarely combine was 'as ignorant of the world as of the subject. Masters were always and everywhere in a sort of tacit, but constant and uniform, cooperation, not to raise the wages of labour above their actual rate. To violate this cooperation is everywhere a most unpopular action, and a sort of reproach to a master among his neighbours and equals'. One seldom heard of this cooperation, or 'combination' as Smith called it, because it was so common,

---

[7] Smith, *The Wealth of Nations*, 60. I am grateful to Thomas Hopkins for important comments and suggestions on my discussion of Smith.
[8] Smith, *The Wealth of Nations*, 60.

'the natural state of things', and so evident that one never talked about it. When masters entered into particular 'combinations' to sink the wages of labour, these were always conducted with the utmost silence and secrecy until the moment of execution. When the workers yielded to such dictates, as they sometimes did without resistance, though they severely felt the cuts, they were never heard of by other people. Such employer agreements, however, were frequently resisted by a contrary defensive union of the workers, who sometimes, too, without any provocation by the employers, unified in order to raise the price of their labour. Their usual pretences were sometimes the high price of provisions, sometimes the great profit which their masters made by their work. But whether their unification was offensive or defensive, it was always abundantly heard of. In order to bring the point to a speedy decision, they had always recourse to the loudest clamour, and sometimes to the most shocking violence and outrage. They were desperate, and acted with the folly and extravagance of desperate men, who must either starve, or frighten their masters into an immediate compliance with their demands. Smith sided with the workers:

> Servants, labourers, and workmen of different kinds, make up the far greater part of every great political society. But what improves the circumstances of the greater part, can never be regarded as any inconveniency to the whole. No society can surely be flourishing and happy, of which the far greater part of the members are poor and miserable. It is but equity, besides, that they who feed, clothe, and lodge the whole body of the people, should have such a share of the produce of their own labour as to be themselves tolerably well fed, clothed, and lodged.[9]

It was in the 'progressive state', where society was advancing towards more wealth and higher levels of economic accumulation, that the conditions of the labouring poor, of the great body of the people, seemed to be the happiest and the most comfortable. Their situation was 'hard in the stationary, and miserable in the declining state'. The progressive state was the cheerful and hearty state 'to all the different orders of the society; the stationary was dull; the declining melancholy'. Here Smith emphasized the role of the state in economic performance and distinguished between different kinds of state in this respect. The liberal reward of labour increased the diligence and industry of the common people. The wages of labour were the encouragement of industry, which, like every other human quality, improved in proportion to the encouragement it received:

> A plentiful subsistence increases the bodily strength of the labourer, and the comfortable hope of bettering his condition, and of ending his days, perhaps, in ease and plenty, animates him to exert that strength to the utmost. Where wages

---

[9] Smith, *The Wealth of Nations*, 70.

are high, accordingly, we shall always find the workmen more active, diligent, and expeditious, than where they are low.[10]

Besides the role of the 'progressive state', Smith emphasized altruistic human values—connected to self-interest—rather than the role of automatically functioning markets in providing an economic distribution for sustainable growth. He developed this altruistic argument already in *The Theory of Moral Sentiments*, which appeared seventeen years before *The Wealth of Nations*. The first chapter is entitled 'On Sympathy', and he begins his reasoning by stating:

> How selfish soever man may be supposed, there are evidently some principles in his nature, which interest him in the fortune of others, and render their happiness necessary to him, though he derives nothing from it, except pleasure of seeing it.[11]

The straight line from Smith to neo-liberal arguments in the 1980s about a flourishing economy without the state is historically inaccurate. If there is a line backward from the neo-liberalism of the 1980s it is to the physiocrats. A strong sense of individualism and private property became the critical component of their *tableau économique* where they designed how the economy would function. Smith appreciated some of the technical merits of the physiocrats, but he was also very keen on not ever being thought of as one of them, a member of their 'sect'. In *The Wealth of Nations* he stated that all things considered he preferred Colbert's mercantilist policies to Quesnay's, the leading physiocrat.[12] Having said that, this does not mean that the line from the physiocrats to neo-liberalism is straight or continuous, either. The physiocrats analysed an agrarian economy, the neo-liberals of the 1980s a post-industrial finance capitalist economy. The contextual difference is huge, which was reflected in their respective theoretical languages. However, irrespective of this difference, and irrespective of Smith's openness to the social issue and the role of politics, Manchester and laissez-faire liberal ideas of a natural order governed by the market thrived against the backdrop of free trade and the increasing global exchange of commodities during the half-century after the Napoleonic Wars. These liberal ideas provided an interpretative framework for the expansion of world trade. However, in several cases this view of the market as a self-propelling machine went hand in hand with an overall emphasis on state responsibility for investments in infrastructure and economic performance, for instance in Scandinavia.[13] Political rhetoric about a

---

[10] Smith, *The Wealth of Nations*, 72.
[11] Smith, *The Theory of Moral Sentiments*, 1.
[12] Smith, *The Wealth of Nations*, 38. See Istvan Hont, *Jealousy of Trade: International Competition and the Nation-State in Historical Perspective* (Cambridge, MA: Belknap, 2005), 100.
[13] For the case of Sweden-Norway, see Bo Stråth, *Union och demokrati: De Förenade rikena Sverige-Norge 1814–1905* (Nora: Nya Doxa, 2005), ch. 5 and, for Sweden, Stråth, *Sveriges historia 6*.

liberal economy did not exclude political practices of state responsibility for economic development.

RADICAL ECONOMIC LIBERALISM

Liberal free-trade language became problematic in the 1870s, however, under the conditions of increasing competition in world markets and a narrowing scope for profits and wages. Protectionism replaced free trade in a development that culminated in 1914 with the outbreak of the First World War.

However, the idea of the optimal self-regulation of a market-oriented economy survived these developments under competition from more state-oriented views provoked by the slowdown of economic growth. Ludwig von Mises in Vienna, the mentor of Friedrich Hayek, warned in the early 1920s against the alliance of the Social Democrats and the Prussian *obrigkeitsstaatliche* bureaucracy. Later on, as this extreme warning ceased to make an impression, he argued against the emerging interventionist state, which, through unemployment insurance, destroyed the stabilizing effects of the market. Friedrich Hayek withdrew in the 1930s to orthodox and methodological deduction without social observation as an explicit opponent of Keynes's heresy. In such views arguments emerged which in the long run provided the market concept with magical power. Hayek came back from his asylum of reflection in the 1970s when the Keynesian form of liberalism ran into trouble.

Hayek's neo-liberal theory that gained momentum in the 1970s and 1980s thus had a long prehistory. In August 1938, some twenty-five people, among them the philosophers Raymond Aron and Louis Rougier, and the economists Wilhelm Röpke, Ludwig von Mises, Friedrich Hayek, Jacques Rueff, and Alexander Rüstow, met for a colloquium on the crisis of liberalism. They did so, on the eve of the Second World War, at the Institut International de Coopération Intellectuelle on rue Montpensier in Paris next to Palais Royal, where the French Revolution had begun. The discussions dealt with the likelihood and preconditions of a liberal renaissance; with markets and crises; with the liberal state; and with an agenda for liberalism. They struggled for a new mobilizing concept for the intellectual movement they planned and which they defined as liberal, although demarcated from conventional liberalism, which since the 1870s had fallen into ever more disrepute. The meeting discussed several concepts, among them neo-capitalism and constructive liberalism. At the

Med framtiden som hägring och hot: Småstaten tar form bland Europas stormakter (Stockholm: Norstedts, 2012), and Lars Magnusson, *Sveriges Ekonomiska Historia*, 3rd edition (Stockholm: Prisma, 2002).

end the participants seemed to find neo-liberalism the most attractive term, although there was no formal agreement or recorded unanimity.[14]

From this point onward the term neo-liberalism began a remarkable career. Neo-liberals at the Paris meeting like Wilhelm Röpke and Alexander Rüstow, and with them Walter Eucken, who was not among the participants, became the *Vordenker* of the German *soziale Marktwirtschaft*. Hayek, on the other hand, developed an alternative view and a theory for the liberalization and deregulation of the world economy, where regulation of social life would emerge through the market without the mediation of the state, which was described as a suffocating apparatus.

However, the new concept of 'neo-liberalism' did not have any immediate success. World War II and its aftermath led to a search for guarantees against a recurrence of the Great Depression in directions which emphasized the role of political management of the economy. J. M. Keynes was the leading architect of this social democratic liberalism, or the 'mixed economy'. Hayek and his neo-liberal project played no part in this Keynesian solution.

The Hayekian moment would come only half a century after the meeting in Paris. On this point it is important to note that Hayek had an alternative interpretation of the term 'neo-liberal' when compared to Röpke, Rüstow, and Eucken, the neo-liberal approach of whom had a remarkable career in Germany under the label of *soziale Marktwirtschaft*.

The participants at the Paris meeting could not imagine the mobilizing force the concept they agreed on would have fifty years later—pro and contra. At the end of the twentieth century, it was viewed as a salvation that would heal the world economy from its sclerosis. Twenty years later, by the beginning of the twenty-first century, it has become an invective, even an insult, a synonym for a ruthless competitive economy which penetrates all areas of life and divides the world into rich and poor, a synonym for predatory capitalism. However, even if they could not imagine these developments in Paris in 1938, there were already there contrary positions. They all agreed on private property in the means of production and freedom to enter contracts as the necessary basis of a functioning market economy. They also agreed on the market economy as the precondition of democracy. The contentious point was

---

[14] F. Denord, 'Aux origins du néo-liberalism en France. Louis Rougier et le Colloque Lippmann', *Le Mouvement Social*, 195 (2001), 9–34; F. Denord, 'Neoliberalisme et "économie sociale de marché": les origins intellectuelles de la politique européenne de la concurrence (1930–1950)', *Histoire, Economie et Societé*, 27 (2008), 23–34; Bernhard Walpen, *Die offene Feinde und ihre Gesellschaft: Eine hegemonietheoretische Studie zur Mont Pèlerin Society* (Hamburg: VSA Verlag, 2004); Philip Mirowski and Dieter Plehwe (eds.), *The Road from Mont Pèlerin: The Making of the Neo-Liberal Thought Collective* (Cambridge, MA: Harvard University Press, 2009); Ben Jackson, 'At the Origins of Neo-Liberalism: The Free Economy and the Strong State, 1930–47', *Historical Journal*, 53 (2010), 129–51.

the role of the state and the location of responsibility for the social. This contention has continued ever since.

It is historically problematic to draw a straight line from Adam Smith to neo-liberal discourse in the 1980s. This was nevertheless what happened in the attempt to legitimize the new Hayekian language historically. It would be as problematic and anachronistic to draw a straight line from the neo-liberals in Paris in the 1930s to the Mont Pèlerin Society that after 1947 institutionalized the ideas of the neo-liberal think tank. The neo-liberals in the 1980s demarcated themselves from the overstretched Keynesian welfare state; the neo-liberals in the 1930s, from the crisis of capitalism hijacked by international price and production cartels. Almost all of the neo-liberals in the 1930s acknowledged some role for the state and were critical of the power of organized capital and corporate business oligopolies or monopolies (and also of the power of organized labour). There were on certain points, to various degrees, commonalities with the suggestions of Keynes. Not least there were connections with the later German social market economy developed by the ordo-liberals in the 1930s, which does not mean that the differences should be underplayed. The only firm adherent of ideas that came close to the neo-liberals in the 1980s was von Mises. His antipode on the left side of the neo-liberal network in the 1930s and 1940s was Walter Lippman with his influential book *The Good Society* in 1937.[15] The major contextual difference between the 1930s and the 1980s was the latter's more or less total neglect of the role of the state and the political capacity to dictate the rules of the game, and disregard of the problems of capital concentration and corporate business.

THE NEO-LIBERAL BREAKTHROUGH

The acceleration of neo-liberal language in the 1990s, with the concept of *globalization* as the key term in a rapidly evolving new semantic field, spread from economics to political science. In a silent conceptual revolution *government* was without much debate replaced by *governance*. The focus shifted in political theories from hierarchy and power to network and soft coordination, from state to civil society. The question of Keynesian political management of the economy disappeared silently from political and academic language. Politics in terms of political management of the economy faded away in political theory, and political language confirmed the imagination of the market as a self-propelling machine. A new kind of teleology was propagated, implying an ahistorical depoliticization of politics and the naturalization of

---

[15] For a concise discussion of the complexity of and ambiguities in the network that the neo-liberals formed in the 1930s, see Ben Jackson, 'At the Origins'.

market performance. Frequent references were made to Adam Smith in this unfolding narrative. He became a kind of principal witness testifying to the truth of this story.[16]

However, as emphasized and demonstrated above, Smith never discussed the market in the pure form he is commonly credited with having done. The theoretical dichotomy between market and state as exclusive entities is also historically problematic. Theoretical and ideological differences between liberalism and socialism have overlapped at the level of political and economic debate and practice, borrowing from and influencing one another. Starting with Smith, and accelerating with Marx and the liberal reaction to him, the theoretical construction of the market has not excluded, but rather included, the state. It has done so under a constant tension. As Michael Freeden has convincingly demonstrated, late nineteenth- and early twentieth-century liberalism developed a positive view of the state.[17] However, a tension undoubtedly emerged within liberalism between the idea of popular sovereignty through political debate and the idea of the good society through autonomous market performance. The original entanglement of the political and the economic was split apart. Instead, liberalism developed into two main trends of argumentation.

TWO ARGUMENTATIVE TRENDS AND THE TENSIONS BETWEEN THEM

One trend reduced the state to a nightwatchman function with the government as an occasional evil. The other trend emphasized civic rights and some kind of social protection as the basis of progress, where politics was the arena to solve social problems and conflicts. The two trends opposed one another on certain points and overlapped on others. For some periods one emerged as predominant and at different times the other prevailed. Adam Smith's argument for some kind of social and institutional embedding of autonomous individuals has historically resulted in much uneasiness in the formulation of liberal politics. During a brief period from the 1840s to the 1870s, liberalism and nationalism went hand in hand with market expansion and international free trade. The unification of liberalism and nationalism emphasized

---

[16] See, for instance, Milton Friedman, 'Free Markets and the End of History', *New Perspectives Quarterly*, 23 (2006), 37–43; Monica Prasad, *The Politics of Free Markets: The Rise of Neoliberal Economic Policies in Britain, France, Germany and the United States* (Chicago: Chicago University Press, 2006), and a vast number of publications from the Adam Smith Institute, <http://www.adamsmith.org>.

[17] See, for instance, Michael Freeden, *The New Liberalism: An Ideology of Social Reform* (Oxford: Oxford University Press, 1978).

popular sovereignty and national freedom as the instrument for individual self-realization.

The drawn-out economic stagnation due to tighter competition and wage and profit pressure on world markets, which began in the 1870s, triggered protectionism and the idea of the nation gained new significance. Protectionism and nationalism became powerful instruments for economic recovery through military expenditure, which opened the way towards 1914. The brief attempt to establish a liberal order in the 1920s failed, as we know. Again, the combined forces of economic depression, protectionism, and nationalism proved stronger than liberal arguments. This time the anti-liberal forces emerged in much stronger and more violent forms, as we also know.

The modernization of Western industrial society over the past two hundred years can be seen as a summary of a number of processes, such as industrialization and technological development, bureaucratization, professionalization, and democratization. These processes oftentimes have different temporal rhythms, which produce tension between them. Industrialization meant, for instance, rapid destruction of economic structures, whereas political institutions in many respects remained unchanged. The time lag provoked social tensions. Economic change, political change, and social change occur at different velocities and with tensions between economic integration and social disintegration. These tensions constitute a fundamental—not to say existential—dilemma for liberalism.[18]

These tensions were at the core of nation and state building in the nineteenth and twentieth centuries. They provoked a variety of solutions to the national and the social questions. The national and the social questions dealt with the political construction of cohesion and community in response to the tensions provoked by these different temporal rhythms. In revolutions, wars, and world wars, the languages of nation and social class were transformed into bloody practice. The images of national and social homogenization—not infrequently in explosive combination—lent wings to the masses and raised expectations about emancipation from the misery that had been handed down to them. Often the two concepts of nation and class brought hopes that a better world would come about more rapidly through violence. The equality and community contained in the two concepts held out the prospect of security in situations where the individual freedom guaranteed by liberalism was experienced as a threat. The invulnerability—in the name of the Enlightenment idea of universal human rights—of individuals and minority groups was violated when they were identified as enemies of the nation—or the class—and became victims of collective aggression. It is important not to

---

[18] For a theoretical development of this argument, see Reinhart Koselleck, *Zeitschichten: Studien zur Historik mit einem Beitrag von Hans-Georg Gadamer* (Frankfurt/Main: Suhrkamp, 2000).

The Liberal Dilemma

forget this violent side of the construction of nations and community. Political liberalism born in the French Revolution was, as we know, in itself pregnant with terror. Economic liberalism provoked terror from forces that made liberalism responsible for the failure of the market.

In *The Wealth of Nations*, Adam Smith discerned a global order based on a transnational distribution of labour through a transnational mobilization of the factors of production. However, he—and his colleagues—never argued that nations and their governments would disappear. On the contrary, the aim and the consequence of market expansion were to reinforce the peoples and their political institutions: the wealth of *nations* rather than individuals. Free trade was thought to be the economic cement of political democracy.

The confidence in this harmonious conceptualization of a world both with and without borders eroded with the advance of industrial capitalism. As we have seen, Smith was aware of social problems. However, with accelerating industrialization these problems proved to be much greater than Smith had envisaged and all of the poor did not believe that they got a fair share of a growing pie. Economic development was not only growth but also speculative bubbles, crisis, depression, and unemployment. Increasing awareness of poverty, which was assumed to be a result of the emerging capitalist system rather than the responsibility of poor individuals themselves, and the ostentatious wealth of a few, provoked the idea that wealth was a matter of class rather than nation. The social issue was put on the agenda everywhere in Europe from the 1830s onwards, when the insight grew that the emerging capitalist order produced damage that went beyond the responsibility of the individual (as in the old view on poverty). Some kind of a systemic dysfunction was diagnosed. The emerging issue at stake was who was responsible.[19]

The debate accelerated against the background of the long economic stagnation beginning in the early 1870s. The tension between economic integration and social disintegration became dramatic, and confidence in free trade was replaced by protectionist practices and politics. 'Unemployment' was a concept invented in the 1880s to cope with a new mass phenomenon. The concept was a social construct.[20] The social borders of economies were emphasized. The social question became the question of the worker, of unemployment, i.e. the class question. *Capital* by Karl Marx in 1867 and the *Manifesto* by Marx and Friedrich Engels in 1848 had already, before the 1870s, given a new shape to the concept of class. The language of class became more intensive from the 1870s on.

---

[19] Michael Freeden, 'The Coming of the Welfare State', in Terence Ball and Richard Bellamy (eds.), *The Cambridge History of Twentieth-Century Political Thought* (Cambridge: Cambridge University Press, 2003), and Freeden, *The New Liberalism*.

[20] Christian Topalov, *Naissance du chômeur 1890-1900* (Paris: Albin Michel, 1994), and Jose Harris, *Unemployment and Politics: A Study in English Social Policy, 1886-1914* (Oxford: Oxford University Press, 1972).

In conservative defence strategies, the social question was mixed up with the national question. The vision of a harmonious unification between liberal emancipation and national unity culminated in the European revolution in 1848. The subordination of individual civic rights to the idea of national sovereignty was a powerful historical mix, which, however, was violently defeated in the reaction of the monarchical order to the uprising. Although the liberal theory of a harmonious free-trade unification of the world remained strong until the early 1870s, despite the outcome of 1848, the problem that the revolution had put on the political agenda remained unsolved, and the social question could in the long run not be ignored. The construction of national community was, from the 1870s onward, closely connected to the social question. Conservatives transformed the social question into a national question in an attempt to canalize dangerous social energy. Protectionism and nationalism went hand in hand with a growing attention to social protests, replacing the earlier tandem of nationalism and liberalism. Liberal discourse about state-bound universalism and general economic wealth declined. Conservative protectionists hijacked the concept of nation from Smith and promised the wealth of nations in other terms.

National socialism was suggested as a conservative response to the emerging project of class-struggle socialism. Swedish conservative political scientist professor Rudolf Kjellén as a matter of fact argued for a national socialism around the turn of the twentieth century in his outline of a conservative home for the people.[21]

A social Darwinian language was another tool that gave this trend meaning. Here one should add that the established and conventional term social Darwinism is misleading. The proper term is social Spencerianism. Herbert Spencer talked about the survival of the fittest several years before Darwin described evolutionary adjustment. There was much less teleology and violence in Darwin's language than in Spencer's.[22] Nations were in social Spencerian language portrayed as in a fight for survival against other nations, with only the strongest destined to survive. Michael Freeden has demonstrated how liberalism responded to this new framework of interpretation and made use of organic and evolutionary imagery to argue against Spencerianism.[23]

Nationalism in response to economic strains and growing protests against social deficiency meant, in Europe from the 1870s, political stabilization and social integration through nationalism. A crucial instrument of social integration was the identification of an 'other'. Nationalist languages

---

[21] Rudolf Kjellén, 'Partier och idéer', *Politiska essayer: Studier till dagskrönikan (1907–1913), andra samlingen* (Stockholm, 1915), 22–5.

[22] Herbert Spencer, *Social Statics* (London: Chapman, 1851), and Spencer, *A Theory of Population Deduced from the General Law of Animal Fertility* (London: G. Woodfall, 1852); Charles Darwin, *On the Origin of Species by Means of Natural Selection* (London: Murray, 1859).

[23] Freeden, *New Liberalism*.

and protectionist practices reinforced categories of 'we' and 'they'. Division according to ethnicity and race was probably the strongest instrument, but the social could also spill over to the religious sphere and join with arguments about religious separation. Arguments about cultural essence and linguistic purity were also in operation. Fichte's and Herder's romanticist ethnic and language communities transformed into racial discourses.[24]

The Smithian theory of the distribution of labour through the invisible hand was translated and transformed into the social Spencerian language of market competition that set nation against nation. From here there was only a short step to military ideals. The economic wheels began to roll again through rearmament politics. The road to 1914 was paved.

The core of the construction of nations at this time was Europe, but the arena of the conflict was global. Colonial expansion and imperialism confirmed national strength. National competition occurred under the overarching assumption of a European/Western superiority.

The key concepts of the liberal message as it was formulated in the French Revolution as an intellectual tool to shape and make the future were freedom and equality. The two concepts were in the revolution kept together in one cohesive *Denkfigur*. 'Freedom' took the individual as the point of reference. 'Equality' emphasized the individual in social context. The two concepts were temporarily unified in the idea of the nation and of national sovereignty, but developments in the long run revealed the latent tension between the two terms, with radical consequences for the whole conceptualization of liberalism. In the British liberal pre-Revolutionary Enlightenment tradition Adam Smith emphasized the liberty aspect, when he interpreted the emerging capitalist order. In that tradition the equality aspect was considered less problematic. He argued that some inequality would emerge, but this had to be accepted, since in the long run all would benefit. On this point he also developed his thought about social solidarity through economic growth.

---

[24] A crucial link in the transformation of views where nations were seen in folkloristic terms, with a focus on language and ethnicity, into languages of race was Richard Wagner. He notoriously argued that those who were ethnically different could not comprehend the artistic and cultural meaning inherent in national culture. Another link was, of course, Herbert Spencer. 'Das Judenthum in der Musik' ('Jewishness in Music') was an essay by Richard Wagner, attacking Jews in general and the composers Giacomo Meyerbeer and Felix Mendelssohn in particular, published under a pseudonym in the *Neue Zeitschrift für Musik* in Leipzig in 1850. It was reissued in a greatly expanded version under Wagner's name in 1869. The article was an important contribution to the emergence of German anti-Semitism and to the stronger nationalistic language for external colonial expansion and domestic social peace from the 1870s. Richard Wagner, *Judaism in Music and Other Essays*, trans. W. Ashton Ellis (Lincoln, London: University of Nebraska Press, 1995); Paul Lawrence Rose, *Wagner: Race and Revolution* (London: Faber and Faber, 1992). See also Miroslav Hroch, 'Introduction: National Romanticism', in Balázs Trencsényi and Michal Kopeček (eds.), *National Romanticism: The Formation of National Movements* (Budapest: Central European University Press, 2007).

As with all powerful languages a tension emerged early on between experiences and expectations. The references to experiences were strong as long as the French, and after them a large number of other peoples, could argue with credibility that they had founded a new society of free and equal people. The language of both liberty and equality functioned as a real force in a real historical process. The concept of liberalism and the charismatic semantic field in which it was embedded became powerful through its reference to a different social experience, the *ancien régime*, and became a force for historical change temporarily hiding the tensions between liberty and equality.[25]

The explorer of liberalism *par préférence*, Alexis de Tocqueville, observed the inherent tension in liberal language. When he came back to France after his visit to the United States in 1831–2 he wrote in *Democracy in America* (Vol. II, 1840) that individual liberty was nothing but an illusion, although an important illusion. The Americans *believe* that there is such a thing as individual liberty, he wrote. They *believe* that it is possible to act independently of their social context and that historically created social ties can be ignored. Of course, human beings cannot do such a thing, de Tocqueville continued, but they *believe* that they can, and that is decisive and is what individualism and individual liberty mean. There is no such thing as an individualistic society where people do not perform and act in groups, classes, or other social formations. Instead, people pretend that they do not do it or have to do it. The importance of the liberal model was not that it produced what it promised but that it was an invitation to political action. The driving force in America, and the bridge between the individual and the social, was in the eyes of de Tocqueville the doctrine of self-interest, which properly understood did not inspire great sacrifices but every day prompted some small ones. By itself it cannot make a man virtuous, but its discipline shapes a lot of orderly, temperate, moderate, careful, and self-controlled citizens. Even if it did not lead the will directly to virtue, it established habits which unconsciously turned it that way. The philanthropic individual constituted through its self-interest the democratic society of voluntary associations in America.[26]

What Karl Marx called the democratic abstraction was nothing but a translation into his own language of the same idea that fascinated de Tocqueville: democratic equality is the individual's permanent striving for an unattainable goal. The democratic individual considers him- or herself an equal in relation to all other individuals, whereas nature and society unceasingly produce unequal individuals. Marx rejected this inherent contradiction in liberal democracy as an illusion, but he was obsessed by the search for the

---

[25] For the charismatic language of the French Revolution, see Lynn Hunt, 'The Rhetoric of Revolution in France', *History Workshop Journal*, 15 (1983), 78–94.

[26] Alexis de Tocqueville, *Democracy in America* (New York, NY: Harper and Row, 1988 [1835–40]), 525–8.

reality behind the illusory idea. He dreamed of a society without classes, but, like Smith, he did not believe in the idea of equality. In his analysis of fixed hourly wage rates versus piece rates in his *Critique of the Gotha Programme* he showed how relative the notion of equality is. The *Critique of the Gotha Programme*, published after his death, and one of Marx's last major writings, was based on a letter to the Eisenach faction of the Social Democratic Party in 1875. In the letter he discussed the dictatorship of the proletariat and the coming communist society. He elucidated the principle of 'to each according to his contribution' as the basis for a 'lower phase' of communist society directly following the transition from capitalism, and 'from each according to his ability, to each according to his needs' as the basis for a future 'higher phase' of communist society. In describing the lower phase, he stated that 'the individual receives from society exactly what he gives to it'. Equality was thus interpreted in relation to achievement. In the higher phase needs were also considered. The 'democratic abstraction' in the phrasing of Marx was an account of the impossibility of equality. De Tocqueville was dead when Marx reached this conclusion, but it would not have made sense to him, because in his view precisely the abstract and imaginary character of liberal democracy was its proper nature and driving force.[27]

NEGATIVE AND POSITIVE, INDIVIDUAL AND COLLECTIVE LIBERTY

The liberal idea that market mechanisms made society self-regulating had a tremendous impact on the intellectual and political order at the end of the *ancien régime*. Quite obviously the liberal model expressed capitalist interests, but it benefited from the fact that in its formulation it was not tied to specific interests but was universally defined. The core of the concept of liberty was the private property rights conquered from the birthrights of the society of estates and privileges. Tensions developed, as has already been mentioned, between the ideas in the emerging class society about individual rights, described as freedoms (and in particular the freedom to own property), and the ideas of equal human relations, once these two sets of argument were brought together and unified in one intellectual construction. In the conceptualization of freedom there is a closure towards others. Freedom is conquered and exerted at the

---

[27] The *Critique of the Gotha Programme* was written in April or early May 1875, and was first published abridged in the journal *Die neue Zeit*, 1/18 (1890–1), and in a full version in *Karl Marx and Friedrich Engels: Selected Works in Three Volumes, Volume 3* (Moscow: Progress Publishers, 1973), 13–30. See also François Furet, *Marx and the French Revolution* (Chicago: Chicago University Press, 1988), 27–8. I am grateful to Thomas Hopkins for comments on this point.

expense of others. The conceptualization of equality tries to break up and open this closure and to prevent liberty from being taken as the right to do something at the cost of others. The historical solution to the tension—conceptualized by Isaiah Berlin as a tension between negative and positive liberty[28]—has often been to emphasize one of the contradictory terms, if not in rhetoric, where one has tried to keep them unified, at least in practice and action.

The philosophical debate about negative and positive liberty has been abstract and has circumvented many of the concrete problems experienced in modern societies. The dichotomy discerns two definitions of liberty, but is an undue reduction of historical experiences, which hint at a continuum of ambiguous and contradictory approaches to liberty rather than a clear-cut choice.

Of relevance here is not the long debate on internal obstacles to individual liberty, which basically deal with free will, but the issue of external obstacles, according to which one is unfree when other people prevent one from doing certain things. Is an employer unfree when a strike prevents him from reducing wages? If this is the argument, one can only add that Adam Smith was more sophisticated on this point, as we have seen. In philosophical pleas for negative liberty—freedom from obstacles—the state and the trade unions have often been depicted as the main hindrances. The state is seen in intentional terms, as an aggregate of personal wills. What about impersonal, unintentional structural forces such as unemployment? Do they not constitute an obstacle to the liberty of those employees made redundant? Hayek's answer—and that of a great number of market-oriented libertarians—is a clear no. Impersonal economic forces, being brought about unintentionally, do not restrict the employees' freedom, they only make them unable to do what they want to do: to work. Freedom is the absence of coercion, where to be coerced is to be subject to the arbitrary will of another.[29] The state and the trade unions have in this view a will and can coerce, whereas bankers who jeopardize the whole economic order are defined as impersonal market forces. The historical experiences of labour markets are hypocritically ignored in this theoretically legitimized cynicism with practical consequences.

Classical liberal authors were more open to the historical complexity of the conceptualization of liberty than the dichotomous reductionists. I have referred to Smith above. Locke is another example. Among the dichotomous defenders of negative liberty, he is seen as defending their case. He did, indeed, explicitly state that liberty is to be free from restraint and violence from others. However, he also said that liberty is not to be confused with 'licence' and that

---

[28] Isaiah Berlin, *Four Essays on Liberty* (Oxford: Oxford University Press, 1969 [1958]).
[29] F. A. Hayek, *The Constitution of Liberty* (London: Routledge and Kegan Paul, 1960), and his *Law, Legislation and Liberty* (London: Routledge, 1982).

'that ill deserves the name of confinement which hedges us in only from bogs and precipices'.[30]

Socialists and egalitarians have tended to claim that the poor in a capitalist society are as such unfree, or in any case less free than the rich. Their notion of what counts as a constraint on freedom is broader. They often call their definition of freedom 'positive', for instance, the freedom to unionize. They claim that freedom requires the presence of abilities or what Amartya Sen has influentially called capabilities.[31] Another tool of attempts to defuse the tension between negative and positive liberty has been the distinction between individual and collective liberty, which has tended to reintroduce the tension, however, through the invitation to choose between the two versions.

The enemy when Berlin distinguished between negative and positive liberty was communism, which might explain the lack of nuance. Attempts to confront the dichotomous tension built into the concept of liberty within democratic societies have moved the divide from negative liberty towards positive liberty, with the latter taken to imply some more encompassing goal. One should add that adherents of negative freedom, even Hayek, recognize that under certain circumstances liberty needs to be restricted. The dividing line is rather what is to be taken as legitimate grounds for this intervention.[32]

The long-term contentious debate on the meanings of liberty produced concepts like economic liberalism and social liberalism, right liberalism and left liberalism, *Rechtsstaat* and *Sozialstaat* or welfare state, neo-liberalism, etc. They emerged in order to mark occupied semantic positions in political practice. The tension has demonstrated the unmistakable limits of the capacity of a universally formulated ideology. In situations of obvious tension new attraction has been generated through the formulation of specific instead of universal interests, such as the examples just referred to. Or the tension has become uncontrollable and brought the model to collapse under the triumph of totalitarian orders.

THE LIBERAL SEMANTIC FIELD: A EUROPEAN AND HISTORICAL PERSPECTIVE

It is problematic to attempt to link the disintegrating term 'liberal' to well-demarcated specific socioeconomic interests or to philosophical, not

---

[30] John Locke, *Second Treatise on Civil Government* [1689], paras 6, 57, at <http://www.sparknotes.com/philosophy/locke/>, accessed 20 October 2010.

[31] Amartya Sen, 'Well-Being, Agency and Freedom', *Journal of Philosophy*, 82 (1985), 169–221, and his *Inequality Reexamined* (Oxford: Oxford University Press, 1992). For the discussion of negative and positive liberty, see also I. Carter, 'Positive and Negative Liberty', in *Stanford Encyclopedia of Philosophy* (2007), at <http://plato.stanford.edu/entries/liberty-positive-negative/>.

[32] I have benefited here from discussion of negative and positive liberty with Thomas Hopkin.

less-demarcated abstractions in analytical approaches. A much more practicable approach is to take the concept as such and the semantic field around it as the point of departure for analysis and to see how it has been used culturally in specific historical situations to produce meaning. How has the liberal semantic field emerged? Who developed the concepts in this field? In conflict/cooperation with whom? Has the employment of this field indicated social polarization or social alliances/compromises? Which interest-formulating and action-orienting capacities has the field conveyed? What degree of closure and openness? To what extent has the liberal semantic field produced more or less consistent interpretative frameworks? This is the approach that Michael Freeden has taken throughout his writings.

Such questions start from cultural practice, where culture should not be understood as a cohesive community but as the production of context and meaning through language and symbols, through social contention and the search for compromises in processes of social bargaining.

Here one can briefly refer to some historical developments of liberalism in Europe. Liberal ideas of how to combine freedom and equality were fundamental for the development of the Scandinavian societies and the strength of the labour movement. The deployment and successive seizure of power by the labour movement was a question of the realization of independently defined humanistic ideals and self-educational goals, which from the 1890s to the 1920s emerged within the countercultural formation that the people's movements, *folkrörelserna*, constituted in a complex interaction of competition and cooperation between social democrats and liberals. The road the Scandinavian labour movements took to the political power centres can be described as an integrative movement from below, which initially used the support of left liberals for suffrage and other reforms and thereafter established itself as the leading progressive party. The liberalism that around the turn of the twentieth century attracted the interest of the labour movement in coalition building was a typical left liberalism, which emphasized social responsibility and was more likely to focus, if the issue had been brought to a head, on equality rather than freedom. In Sweden, there emerged around 1900, in opposition to the social liberal project, social conservative visions about a home for the people, *folkhem*, where everybody irrespective of social position should feel at home. Exactly how such a home for the people should look in all its details was very much an open issue. Different interests had different proposals. Social conservative thoughts broke against and gradually also mixed up with social liberal and social democratic ideals. There emerged an agreement about the concepts of *folk* and *folkhem* as such, which early on became politically attractive, but there was contention about the concrete substance. The struggle for the interpretative priority of the concept and for universal suffrage and parliamentarianism welded the social democrats and the social liberals together during the first two decades of the twentieth century. This concerted action constituted the specific Swedish/Scandinavian distinction in international comparison. The preconditions of the concerted action emerged during the last decades of the nineteenth century with the people's movements' capacity to mobilize and convince. In this coalition one third of the Swedish population was mobilized under the development of social liberal and social democratic interpretative frameworks, with steadiness, education, and justice as key concepts. The concept of justice was later transformed into equality. The lack of a powerful political tradition of Bismarckian patriarchalism meant that social conservative ideas in the long run lost their attraction when they faced the social liberal and social democratic campaign.[33]

What was liberal in the Swedish scenario? The social democrats took on a liberal dimension and the liberals became social liberals with reference to the key concept of *folk*. On the other side, the liberal party in Sweden split on the issue of personal morality. There was an obvious tension between tolerance on the one side, and pietistic moralism/puritanism under the motto of inner improvement on the other; between atheist free-thinkers and pietistic free-church adherents; between urban cultural radicals and rural free-religious liberals; between a focus on individualistic pietistic ideals of a Weberian Protestant ethic and more collective ideals of social responsibility. All these dimensions were kept together in one liberal party until the split in 1923 on the issue of the prohibition of alcohol. When they reunified in 1934, trying to bridge the tensions they chose the name of *Folkpartiet*. However, this was in a situation when the social democrats had just appropriated the interpretative power of the *folk* concept from the conservatives with the *folkhemmet* metaphor as a key instrument. The liberal success under the new name was therefore moderate.

In the counter cultural practice that emerged in Scandinavia in the 1880s, the concept of liberalism neither connoted the values of the French Revolution, nor the liberty of Adam Smith, but rather concepts like universal suffrage and democracy formulated in relation to local peasant communities, and bargaining practices developed there over centuries, which was certainly a different environment and source of inspiration than the streets of Paris in 1789. Concepts of universal suffrage and democracy in political practice did not connote absolute values but political empiricism and pragmatism. The concepts were formed, and in turn formed the political culture, through extensive social bargaining.

In countries like Britain and the USA, where the workers had not needed to fight for suffrage in the same way, they were early on integrated into liberal movements, instead of remaining in autonomous positions looking for alliances (in Britain an autonomous labour movement eventually developed, but later than in Scandinavia and in continental countries like France, Germany,

---

[33] For a discussion of the Swedish case, see Stråth, *Sveriges Historia 6*.

and Belgium). The longer traditions of political democracy created cultures which did not provide the same incitement for the emergence of an autonomous *political* labour movement. It is striking that in American academic debates before 1930, the term 'liberalism' did not appear frequently at all. Even thereafter, 'democracy' was a much more commonly used term in contexts which would today be read as debates on liberalism.[34]

In Germany the social polarization was much stronger than in Britain and Scandinavia. The liberals failed to bridge the growing chasm. The liberals were strong in the *Vormärz* years before 1848 but as *national* liberals. After the failed revolution Bismarck and the conservatives took over the unification project. With the growing presence of the social democrats on the political scene from the 1860s, political polarization increased and decreased the scope for liberal politics. Before 1914, the German liberal political movement suffered from uncertainty regarding its identity and purpose, and 'liberalism' and 'liberals' as political concepts acquired a rather ambiguous meaning after 1848. While before the revolution liberalism connoted progressivism and political freedom, in the second half of the nineteenth century the term came to refer to modernity in general and also acquired a negative connotation. Political liberalism was criticized by conservatives for promoting secularization, social atomization, and materialist-industrialist world views and by the political Left for promoting bourgeois political aims without a social dimension.[35] This critique accelerated and paved the way first towards 1914 and after the First World War again towards 1933.

In Italy, the national liberal project succeeded, but soon after unification, when the deep economic cleavage between the South and the North and the growing social differences and the class language became ever more apparent, the project was taken over by state managers like Agostino Depretis, Francesco Crispi, and Giovanni Giolitti, who tried to bridge the gaps by a mix of radical and repressive measures, corruption, clientelism, and buying out of political adversaries through remuneration in the form of offices (*trasformismo*). The attempts to stabilize the situation by means of imperialism were unsuccessful. In the end, the situation slipped out of the hands of the political entrepreneurs, paving the way towards fascism.

CONCLUDING THOUGHTS

Instead of liberalism steadily unfolding as an Enlightenment project, my analysis presents a history of a long drawn-out crisis of liberalism after the

---

[34] Liisi Keedus, *Omitted Encounters: The Early Political Thought of Hannah Arendt and Leo Strauss*, Ph.D. dissertation, (European University Institute, Florence, 2010), 227.
[35] Keedus, *Omitted Encounters*, 224.

1870s to the 1940s, accompanying another history of untiring attempts to retrieve basic liberal principles in response to the crisis and its challenges. There were European alternatives to the road towards the catastrophes of 1914 and 1933 that was paved in the wake of the economic depression from the 1870s. It is crucial to retrieve such alternatives today as the crisis of liberalism continues. The argument here is not to outline a kind of negative teleology instead of a positive one, but to develop a more realistic historical view on liberalism and its achievements as well as shortcomings.

The argument about a lengthy crisis of liberalism is based on the fact that the crisis of liberalism since the 1870s around the social question continues today, after a brief recovery in the 1950s and 1960s as social democratic Keynesian liberalism. In the 1970s, the conditions of economic depression and mass unemployment returned. The remedy was this time not looked for in anti-liberal alternatives but in more liberalism, in a kind of overdose of liberalism, or, more correctly formulated, in an overemphasis on one of the two historical argumentative trends of liberalism which can be labelled 'economic liberalism', or liberalism without politics, or liberalism as economic reductionism. This was the Hayekian moment. One might wonder at the force of the neo-liberal message propagated by a handful of economists in Chicago. In a few years it took on global hegemonic proportions. One can only understand this development by reference to the revolutionary situation around 1990, a situation that the young Hegel had described, impressed by the revolution two hundred years earlier: reality does not withstand a revolutionized time.[36]

The euphoric, not to say manic, interpretation of liberalism under the label of neo-liberalism and globalization since the early 1990s ('the end of history', as Francis Fukuyama called it in a moment of hubris)[37] came to a full stop with the collapse of the financial markets in September 2008, and the crisis of liberalism returned.

Liberalism emphasized politics as art, politics as creation, politics as an instrument of human self-realization. It ended under the new label of neo-liberalism, where politics had abdicated and the market was invoked as the sole healing force. In neo-liberal globalization language there was no place for doubts and debates. The belief in the unfolding natural force of the market provided religious conviction that ignored facts and empirical observations. This neo-liberal market dream displaced historical experiences and tragic

---

[36] 'Ist das Reich des Vorstellungen revolutioniert, so hält die Wirklichkeit nicht aus'. Letter to Friedrich Immanuel Niethammer in October 1808. *Briefe von und an Hegel, 1, 1785–1812*, ed. Johannes Hoffmeister (Berlin: Akademie Verlag, 1970), 194. Hegel came back to this statement on several other occasions. See, for instance, his letter to Søren Kierkegaard, also in 1808, and Hegel, *Briefe von und an Hegel, 1*, 253. See Steffen Schmidt, *Hegels System der Sittlichkeit* (Berlin: Akademie Verlag, 2007), 18.

[37] Francis Fukuyama, *The End of History and the Last Man* (New York: Free Press, 1992).

ideas, reduced nations to containers of individuals, and the human being to a kind of modern Robinson Crusoe, who always maximizes his or her interests and attends only to his or her own happiness. Neo-liberalism saw society as an aggregation of economic agents. The collapse of the model in 2008 has brought a mix of cynicism, apathy, and resignation rather than viable alternatives.

Opportunities for all was the neo-liberal utopian motto. What does this utopia really mean? The utopia is based on the assumption that there is no tension between equality and freedom, solidarity and liberty. This was the utopia that de Tocqueville described. The neo-liberals in the 1990s squared the circle by arguing that equality and solidarity were in fact not legitimate social goals because they are in conflict with liberty.[38] However, the question is whether the social issue and the problem of solidarity is back on the political agenda again, although not as in the 1870s and onwards as a class language. Cynicism, apathy, and resignation are certainly visible reactions to the neo-liberal project in the wake of 2008. However, there are growing signs of an alternative narrative, a counter-narrative to the language of globalization, visible already well before 2008, but growing in strength since then. This counter-narrative can be epitomized in terms of nationalism, populism, and protectionism. On this point there are historical points of reference to fall back upon as well as to learn from. However, we know from the Enlightenment philosophers that history does not repeat itself. We also know from them, in particular Hegel, that we do not learn from history.[39]

A realistic historical perspective tells another story about a more complex relationship in political practice than the motto of opportunities for all suggests. The meaning attached to central expressions such as equality, solidarity, freedom, and liberty vary to a great extent. Equality for some means inequality for others, freedom for some means unfreedom for others. One's aggression is another's self-defence.[40]

---

[38] See Berlin, *Four Essays*.

[39] 'Was die Erfahrung und die Geschichte lehren ist dies, dass Völker und Regierungen niemals etwas aus der Geschichte gelernt und nach Lehren, die aus der Geschichte zu zeihen wären, gehandelt haben'. G. W. F. Hegel, *Die Vernunft der Geschichte*, ed. Johannes Hoffmeister (Berlin: Akademie Verlag, 1966), 19. See József Czirják, 'Die philosophische Methode in der Darstellung der Geschichtsbetrachtung', in *Hegel-Jahrbuch 1995* (Berlin: Akademie Verlag, 1996), 333.

[40] Martti Koskenniemi, *The Gentle Civilizer of Nations: The Rise and Fall of International Law 1870–1960* (Cambridge: Cambridge University Press, 2001), 61. Koskenniemi demonstrates the fundamental problem of the liberal vision in how to cope with what seems like mutually opposing demands for individual freedom and social order. The liberal attempt to tackle this conflict is by means of reconciliation, or, paradoxically, to preserve freedom by means of the creation of order through the restriction of freedom. See also p. 71.

6

The Problem of Political Parties in Western Liberalism, 1868–1968

Paolo Pombeni

INTRODUCTION

According to Michael Freeden, 'the dual functions of ideology—"binding the community together" and "organizing the role personalities of the maturing individual"—generate a by-product, the legitimation of authority'.[1] It would be enough to refer to this statement to understand the importance of analysing political parties, which are the main instruments of modern liberalism that perform both these functions in constitutional orders, with their final aim being that of legitimizing authority.

What is worth further exploration—and is my aim in this chapter—is how political parties themselves form the outcome of an ideological journey, with the idea of a political party which emerged from the mid-nineteenth-century framework of the 'English Constitution' forming a quite distinct tradition from the constitutional theory of political parties developed in the same period in continental Europe.

The fundamental question could be posed in the following terms: in a constitutional system that is founded on the freedom of the individual and on a representational mechanism in which citizens make rational choices about the general interest, can we permit political institutions that group and regulate the players on the political scene? This is the question that has troubled European liberalism ever since liberals realized that the *demos* referred to not only highly rational and responsible individuals, but also included the 'masses' whose political education was not guaranteed. The conflict between idealistic and realistic approaches to the nature of the *demos* has therefore dogged theorists of liberal constitutionalism since the

---

[1] Michael Freeden, *Ideologies and Political Theory: A Conceptual Approach* (Oxford: Oxford University Press, 1996), 16.

debate first arose in Great Britain with the famous 'leap in the dark' of the 1867 Reform Act, culminating in the explosion of political irrationalism, one hundred years later, when the student rebellions of 1968 undermined, perhaps for ever, people's faith in the capacity of the Western-style party system to regulate the political playing field.[2]

WHAT IS A POLITICAL PARTY?

Discussions of political parties in the constitutional arena have a long pedigree. There is no need to search for previews of the term 'party' in writers of classical antiquity or in the Bible,[3] since it can be traced back to the political struggles of the eighteenth century. Here it was often associated with the term 'faction' and generally used disparagingly. In a strictly political sense, it implied the presence of a political space structured around constitutional legitimization of a representative type, in which the joint organization of competitive forces for the exercise of power, or at least to influence it, had sense and meaning.

The immediate problem, posed from the very beginning, concerned the 'legitimacy' of these mechanisms for the unification of forces. Burke's words, later to achieve a classic status, did not go beyond a vague reference to 'honourable connections' in relation to an *idem sentire de res publica*.[4] Nonetheless, parties tended not to be a voluntary sharing of ideas that would bring about a shared action. Rather, they represented an essential gateway to the exercise of power, or at any rate to influencing it, and were therefore apparently indissoluble without 'betraying' the common goal.

The liberal constitutional system was based, at least theoretically, on the government of opinion. At the same time, at the heart of this system was the image of the citizen who had 'responsibility' as an individual entity, released from all forms of obligation to his class, race, or religion. Given that parties owed their very existence to acts of aggregating opinions, it was no easy matter to find a balance that would permit such acts without violating the principle of free reciprocal influence and discussion. This latter principle implied, by its nature, the continuous reshaping and regrouping of aggregations of opinions.

---

[2] I am presenting here an argument which I developed more fully in my work, *La ragione e la passione. Le forme della politica nell'Europa contemporanea* (Bologna: Il Mulino, 2010).

[3] Some references to these distant origins may be found in the essay by Klaus von Beyme, 'Partei, Faktion', in Otto Brunner, Werner Conze, and Reinhart Koselleck (eds.), *Geschichtliche Grundbegriffe. Historisches Lexikon zur politisch-soziale Sprache in Deutschland*, IV (Stuttgart: Klett-Cotta, 1972), 677–733.

[4] See Edmund Burke, *Thoughts on the Cause of the Present Discontents*, in *The Writings and Speeches of Edmund Burke, Volume II: Party, Parliament and the American Crisis, 1776–1774*, ed. Paul Langford (Oxford: Oxford University Press, 1981), 317–18.

As the field and spectrum of political opinions opened up, this approach to the problem obviously became increasingly problematic. On the one hand, there was the question of thought which was not merely 'critical'[5] but actually 'subversive'. By the time the phase of constitutional revolutions came to an end, the political system had established itself in incontrovertible rationality. Any act prejudicial to its stability, let alone calling it into question, was therefore contrary to reason and as such unacceptable. On the other hand, the extension of citizenship, and hence the right to suffrage, to social groups which could not be relied upon to hold the presumed requisites of 'education to the management of public affairs', equally called for attention.

THE 'CONTINENTAL' APPROACH TO THE PROBLEM OF POLITICAL PARTIES

In this first part of our discussion we will examine some of the answers offered to these questions by writers and politicians of the era between the 1860s and the 1890s.

The first of these is a Swiss-German named Johan Kaspar Bluntschli (1808–81), whose work on parties was widely influential in Europe. Indeed, few writers of the period from the 1860s to the 1920s were able to escape the need to make at least formal references to Bluntschli, whose theory of parties was widely accepted.

Bluntschli's short work from 1869, *Charakter und Geist der Politischen Parteien*,[6] later became chapter XII of the third volume of his general doctrine of the state, which was aptly entitled *Politik als Wissenschaft*. It set down definitively the (continental-European) liberal approach to the question of parties. From one point of view Bluntschli took a very advanced attitude, attempting to legitimize parties by deriving their basis from a pre-political, or at any rate pre-constitutional, sphere. Based on his not very successful youthful studies and influenced by the bizarre Swiss publicist Theodor Röhmer, he introduced a bold parallel between the party system and individual psychology in order to justify parties as stages in the cycle of developing sensibility towards the state, thereby treating them as fully 'natural' phenomena.[7]

Bluntschli based his approach on references to the mythical 'English model', which had been a subject of fascination for *Vormärz* liberalism generally (that

---

[5] Reinhart Koselleck, *Critica illuminista e crisi della società borghese* (Bologna: Il Mulino, 1972).
[6] J. K. Bluntschli, *Charakter und Geist der Politischen Parteien* (Nördlingen: Beckhschen Buchhandlung, 1869; anastatic reprint: Aalen, 1970).
[7] See Monika Hildegard Fassbender-Ilge, *Liberalismus, Wissenschaft, Realpolitik. Untersuchung des 'deutschen Staats-Wörterbuch' von J. C. Bluntschli und K. Brater als Beitrag zur Liberalismusgeschichte zwischen 48er Revolution und Reichsgründung* (Frankfurt: R. Fischer, 1981).

is to say, of the period prior to the 1848 revolution) and which he considered the essential starting point for any system to be qualified as constitutional.[8]

Bluntschli seems to have been heavily influenced by Robert von Mohl, since he equated government with parliamentary government and therefore defined parties in relation to this system (and not to the more general end of public opinion). At the same time, however, mindful of the *Volk* category which was to be so important for German legal theorists from Savigny onwards, he had to find space for at least a few notions that allowed him not to break entirely the relationship between parties and society.

His target was the conservative political philosopher Julius von Stahl who, in a work in 1863,[9] proposed as the hub of politics, according to Bluntschli, the rift between 'revolution' (left) and 'legitimacy' (right). In the middle there was supposedly a centre, split between these two beliefs. Revolution, according to Stahl, was the 'overturning of the very relationships of power, since authority and law belong systematically and permanently among men, in such a way as to stand above them'. Legitimacy meant, on the other hand, recognizing 'a superior order, absolutely obligatory and placed by God above the popular will and above the aims of the dominating classes'. Hence the division between parties: on the one hand, liberals, democrats, radicals, and socialists associated with revolution; on the other hand, aristocracy, army, and ecclesiastics favouring legitimacy.

Bluntschli's comment is trenchant: 'Stahl's doctrine of the parties thereby divides government from the governed and instigates each to consider the other its natural adversary and mutual sparring partner'.

In order to dispute this thesis while legitimizing the existence of parties, but at the same time not binding them to the structure of society (since he did not wish to support Stahl who was proposing a return to the ancient form of society), Bluntschli introduced what he described as the psychological theory (derived from Röhmer). According to this, the life of society corresponds to the life of man, and the phases of intellectual development of this life are represented by the 'four natural parties'. Thus radicalism corresponds to the child, tending to manliness; liberalism to the young man, conservatism to the 'perfect man', and the 'absolutist party' to the old man, when 'the forces of the passive and womanly soul come again to the fore'.[10]

Since, in the end, parties are based on the different natural phases of the individual's development in the natural order of creation, all parties are therefore natural necessities and consequently have a natural right to exist. A policy aimed at annihilating parties in contrast would be an outrage against the universal ethical order. The parties have to fight one another, in order to

---

[8] See Armel La Divellec, 'Les Libéraux du Vormärz et la constitution anglaise', *Revue Française d'Histoire des idées politiques*, 24 (2006), 233–53.
[9] Julius von Stahl, *Die gegenwärtigen Parteien in Staat und Kirche* (Berlin: Hertz, 1863).
[10] J. K. Bluntschli, *Dottrina dello Stato*, trans. F. Trono (Naples: Vallardi, 1879), 464–75.

re-establish and observe the just relationship among themselves, but they must not attempt to destroy one another, because they are necessary for the life of humanity to be fecund. The reciprocal recognition of the parties is therefore a just requirement of humanity and healthy politics.

It would be reductive, however, to stop here, even though it must be pointed out that this response to liberal requirements for the legitimization of the parliamentary system enjoyed much success.

Running parallel to these needs were others which I shall discuss briefly. The first was that of denying in politics the theory of 'thinking through to the end', according to which the radicals would be the real liberals and the absolutists the real conservatives. The psychological theory, on the other hand, explained that government should be reserved for the 'middle manly parties' (*männliche mittlere Parteien*). The second was that of debunking the English two-party model by pointing to the presence there of 'radical Whigs', 'liberals', 'conservative Tories', and 'absolutist Tories'. Bluntschli strengthened his theory by referring in this way also to events on the other side of the Channel as the political model par excellence. The third was to deny the validity of any coalition not based on the middle parties. In this context, however, he considered acceptable both a liberal–radical alliance opposite to that of conservatives and absolutists, that is to say 'the entire party of movement against the general party of conservation', provided both blocks were guided by the moderates, or a liberal–conservative alliance against the extremes, in order to prevent radical or absolutist leadership from the two fields.

This entire construction was possible because Bluntschli had previously posed a theory of parties which was highly significant. His classificatory criterion allowed 'only those parties that have a principle' ('it is not worthwhile for science to concern itself with the others') and proceeded 'by degrees of purity'. The result was that

> the highest and purest form of the constitution of political parties [*die höchste und reinste Form der politischen Parteibildung*] consisted undoubtedly of those parties which were determined only by political principles (not by religious, class, public law or utilitarian antitheses) and which at the same time accompany public life lastingly and freely.

He thought we thus had a superior form of parties (*eine höhere Parteiform*), since political parties everywhere had freed themselves from mingling with other antitheses, and had in the course of time become attached to conscious and free principles.[11]

This passage is central, since it came to weaken those 'institutional' features which the party form nevertheless had to assume, because it needed to order itself in some way, as Bluntschli wrote, as an active community, and to take

---

[11] Bluntschli, *Dottrina dello Stato*, 426–7; for the original, *Charakter und Geist*, 25–7.

part, as an association strictly disciplined for public life, in electoral rallies or legislative assemblies.[12]

The notion of a party system was further weakened when it became closely associated with the state: if a party set itself up against the state it became a 'faction', since it made the *Sondergeist* (particular spirit) prevail over the *Staatsgeist* (spirit of the state). It was for this purpose that the party was denied any constitutional character.

The parties are by no means an institution of public law, but rather a political institution. The political parties are not members of the organism of the body of the state, they are free groups of members, free to belong or not, sharing a particular feeling and orientation towards a common political action. They are a product and a representation of the different divisions of the political spirit, which moves popular life on the basis of a legal and political order.[13]

The problem of liberal political science was, in continental Europe, posed entirely in these terms. It had identified the party as a 'form' of contemporary political organization; it had even identified its 'institutional' features (its regulatory, quasi-military discipline; its assumption of the general will; its capacity to act as a body, etc.). But it had refused to allow this as the essence of the form because this would also have legitimized the 'confessional' parties, the 'class-based' parties (including the nascent workers' parties, etc.), that is to say the enemies of the system.

So the state was posed as superior and at the same time the external legitimization of the parties, in order to exclude these enemies. The significance of the 'middle' party was once again weakened, having become too much identified with government. The disappearance of parties was recommended, since their demands had been accepted by the state, while mergers and alliances were proposed between liberals and conservatives, now parties of the state. The result could only be, and quite quickly, the abandonment of the party form that, having been identified in its embryo, ceased to be cultivated, leaving the monopoly of it to precisely those hostile forces that were feared. But as we have seen, this was a concept shared throughout continental European culture.

THE BRITISH APPROACH TO THE PROBLEM OF POLITICAL PARTIES

Things were rather different in Great Britain. Here there was neither obsession with, nor theory about, the state as in Germany. Nor was there a 'historical' fear over the return of the *ancien régime* or counter-revolutionary legitimization as

---

[12] Bluntschli, *Charakter und Geist*, 12.   [13] Bluntschli, *Dottrina dello Stato*, 415.

in France. Yet here, too, liberalism was shipwrecked on the conception of the party, as it struggled vainly to remove the equation between democracy and the corruption of political conduct that was to weigh so heavily on subsequent developments.

The story is a complex one and I can only summarize its stages very briefly.[14] It began with the Liberal defeat of 1874, when Gladstone seemed to exit dramatically from the political scene and the conservatism of Disraeli seemed to emerge as the beneficiary of the 1867 Reform Act.

In truth, another Act had been fundamental from the point of view of party organization: namely, that of 1832,[15] which had introduced the 'register', that is to say, the obligation for electors to have their names included in public lists, providing documentation of their possession of the necessary qualifications to exercise the vote. This led, as is well known, to the professionalization of the support backing candidates' appeal to their electorates. 'Agents' dedicated to this operation constituted a network defining the 'party', using it, more or less intensely, to attract and discipline groups of electors.

The evolution appears to have taken a considerable period of time. Certainly, the extension of suffrage provided by the 1867 reform, affecting above all urban areas (where press circulation and opportunities for the socialization of ideas were more developed), was a fundamental turning point. This was more than an electoral law: it was the symbol of the political commitment of a generation, almost monumentalized in the *Essays on Reform*,[16] where young and not-so-young scholars of progressive Oxford sought to explain how this reform had opened the political arena to debate over ideas and the desire for progress against the politics of deference.[17]

The law not only allowed the Conservatives to return to power, but the expected Liberal comeback was guided by the hands of a *homo novus,* the Mayor of Birmingham, Joseph Chamberlain, who proposed new forms of political association as means of recovery.

Chamberlain's proposed 'new political organization' broke away from the old pattern of politics of the 1867 generation in one essential respect: it

---

[14] I have illustrated them in more detail in my study, *La ragione e la passione*, 67–260.

[15] On the 1832 Reform Act, see the classic Charles Seymour, *Electoral Reform in England and Wales: The Development and Operation of the Parliamentary Franchise 1832-1885* [1911] (Newton Abbot: David & Charles, 1970); Philip Salmon, *Electoral Reform at Work: Local Politics and National Parties, 1832-1841* (Woodbridge: Royal Historical Society, 2003).

[16] See G. C. Brodrick (ed.), *Essays on Reform* (London: Macmillan, 1867). It is sufficient to glance down the list of collaborators to appreciate the importance of this group, which included G. Smith, J. Bryce, A. V. Dicey, and F. Harrison.

[17] Essential on the context of this liberalism is Christopher Harvie, *The Lights of Liberalism: University Liberals and the Challenge of Democracy 1860-1886* (London: Allen Lane, 1976). On the politics of deference, see F. Cammarano, 'Logiche comunitarie e associazionismo politico nella Gran Bretagna tardo-vittoriana. Procedure elettorali e corruzione', *Quaderni Storici*, 23 (1989), 839-72.

sidestepped classical republicanism and did not have 'freemen' in mind as political subjects. In its first phase, it was able to attract men soaked in Comtism, such as Morley. It could delude itself that it had found some resonance in the thought of a Frederic Harrison, who rediscovered in the pairing of 'order and progress' the role of a strong government, one able to guide change,[18] but it ultimately did not succeed in winning over progressive liberal intellectuals.

The latter were shocked at the realization that political organization was in the hands, not of 'intelligence', but of 'numbers'. In other words, organizing the vote of an enlarged electorate was no longer simply a matter of the voters' communities or communication by the educated press. The age of the masses, as it began to be called, brought into play an electorate made up of 'common people',[19] without specific political training. The nightmare of the 'demagogue', derived from extensive reading about the collapse of the 'democracies' of the classical age (in particular those of Athens and Rome), became increasingly widespread. Gladstone's own success, following his return to the political scene with the 'Bulgarian Agitations' of 1876, provoked a new look at the question of the party.

The fact is that the British system was structured more by a succession of practical experiences than by the application of abstract principles, as Gladstone himself recognized.[20] In truth, this could be said of all systems, including the German one, except that in the latter case political theory was used more extensively to organize reality. In Great Britain there was no similarly extensive or rigorous organization (although it would be too much to say there was none at all).[21]

Bagehot's work was among the first to pose the problem of 'describing' the British 'constitution'[22] (or, in reality, to give it the form the author had in mind). It quickly became canonical, not least because it was considered descriptive and spoke of the parties more or less in the old terms of Burke. The change of direction came when the new 'public' form of the political struggle shifted the electoral problem, from choosing a person to be sent to Parliament on the vague basis of a substantial trust in his prior selection to

---

[18] See Frederic Harrison, *Order and Progress: Thoughts on Government*, ed. M. S. Vogeler (Hassocks: Harvester, 1975 [1875]). On this figure see the exhaustive M. S. Vogeler, *Frederic Harrison: The Vocation of a Positivist* (Oxford: Oxford University Press, 1984).

[19] As Walter Bagehot, always an astute observer, wrote: 'public opinion...is the opinion of the bald-headed man at the back of the omnibus'. See *The Collected Works of W. Bagehot*, IV (London: The Economist, 1974), 378.

[20] W. E. Gladstone, *Gleanings of Past Years*, I (London: 1879-98), 244.

[21] This assertion has long been accepted even by scholars. As proof of it, see the three volumes of the classic Ivor Jennings, *Party Politics* (Cambridge: Cambridge University Press, 1960-2), which contain practically no trace of an attempt to reconstruct a British theory of parties.

[22] Walter Bagehot, *The English Constitution* (1867), in his *Collected Works*, vols. V–VI.

identifying the ground of the person's ideological affinities and programmatic undertakings.

This transformation was made possible by the British newspaper system, which could provide immediate publication of speeches by the great political orators thanks to the telegraph, to the agencies serving even the smaller dailies, and to the modernization of printing technology.[23]

This raised a question, however. The trust that a voter might have in the proposals made in a political speech could be based on personal trust in the case of choosing a 'leader'; but in all other cases it had to be based on the idea that the proposals were part of a 'discourse' of some form of organized presence, since this was what lent credibility to the candidate's proposals.[24] Without this, it would not really have been possible to bring about that 'parliamentary government', founded on the responsibility of ministers, which had long been theorized,[25] nor even that strict interaction between the executive and the chamber of representatives that Bagehot described as the 'efficient part' of the constitution.

Nonetheless, as we have seen, the prevalence of 'political discourse' as the means for legitimization raised the spectre of the 'demagogue'. This shifted the discussion to the American case, to a 'democracy' without deference and 'settled superiorities'. The theme was a European one, but it had greater influence in Great Britain for obvious linguistic and historical reasons. It had exploded with the case of the Birmingham 'caucus', but it was given an academic airing with the publication in 1888 of James Bryce's *The American Commonwealth*.

The fierce reactions to this transformation of the liberal political constitution can be explained in various ways. In part they derived, as in the case of those opposing the so-called 'caucus' of Birmingham, from that intellectual middle class, which saw the fading of its illusion that enlarged suffrage would mean the end—to its own advantage—of a political profession reserved to the upper classes, and which blamed the political machine for this transformation. Ostrogorski merely gave finished form to this chorus of complaints,[26] completely ignoring the fact that the great dispute over Chamberlain's 'new

---

[23] See H. C. G. Matthew, 'Rhetoric and Politics in Britain, 1860–1950', in P. J. Waller (ed.), *Politics and Social Change in Britain* (Hassocks: Harvester, 1987), 34–58.

[24] 'This is the essence of the ideological act, or thought-practice, and it is performed equally by regular actors in a political system, by professional politicians, and by ethico-political philosophers—in short, by all who endeavour to fashion or to react to the political world around them by developing languages of public participation rather than of investigation'. Michael Freeden, 'Ideology and Political Theory', in Michael Freeden (ed.), *The Meaning of Ideology* (London: Routledge, 2007), 17.

[25] See, for example, Lord Grey, *Parliamentary Government Considered with Reference to a Reform of Parliament* (London, 1858).

[26] See Paolo Pombeni, 'Starting in Reason, Ending in Passion: Bryce, Lowell, Ostrogorski and the Problem of Democracy', *Historical Journal*, 17 (1994), 319–41.

political organization' had already destroyed the myth of the American 'caucus'.[27]

It was the idea of mass politics that dominated now, but in Great Britain, unlike Germany, there was no likelihood of the 'state' posing itself as the instrument for social discipline. This hypothesis had been outlawed by the 'conservative revolution' of 1688/9, and confirmed by subsequent constitutional developments. The 'politics of deference', which had to some extent contained the parties within the limits of traditional community stratifications,[28] had been eroded by the social transformations of the mid nineteenth century and these channels were no longer accessible. Indeed, to do so would have left the field open to the men of progress, whether liberals or radicals, with their alleged anti-community and individualistic claims (in reality more brandished by their adversaries than actually practised by them).

Now the Conservatives, too, had to face the question of organizing the electorate. As for their adversaries, organizing did not mean simply gathering faithful voters or finding ways to acquire or even 'buy' new ones. Rather, it meant 'motivating' consensus, building an identification, as long-lasting as possible, of potential voters with the political proposals they intended to field.[29]

THE GLADSTONIAN TURN OF MIND

Gladstone had made a fine job of this with his 'Midlothian Campaigns', his electoral tours in his Edinburgh constituency. This in fact was a safe seat under the patronage of Lord Rosebery, where propaganda was not actually needed to obtain Liberal votes. But it served as a stage from which to address the nation,

---

[27] See, for example, T. D. Woolsey, *Political Science or the State: Theoretically and Practically Considered* (London: S. Low, Marston, Searle & Rivington, 1877), 563–5.

[28] The question of a society based on 'deference', that is to say, on voluntary acceptance of elite government by the rest of the population, which accepts the situation as in its own interests and not as an imposition, is complex and naturally varied over the course of time. As J. G. A. Pocock reminds us in 'The Classical Theory of Deference', *American Historical Review*, 81 (1976), 516–23, the notion, if not exactly the vocabulary, developed in the eighteenth century in both Great Britain and America. It is often held that it was Walter Bagehot who gave popularity to the idea of a 'society of deference', by underlining the British people's tendency to admire and venerate the 'upper class', or even the nobility. As has been noted by David Spring, 'Walter Bagehot and Deference', *American Historical Review*, 81 (1976), 524–31, the position of the father of the idea of the English constitution is more ambiguous, since in reality Bagehot also noted the decline of this sentiment which, while it remained rooted in popular psychology, nevertheless played a waning role in politics, and in electoral contests in particular.

[29] For the story of the Conservative Party in this respect, see Richard Shannon, *The Age of Disraeli 1868–1881* (London: Longman, 1992).

to create the mass following that was to transform him into a mythical figure, the 'Grand Old Man' (the legendary GOM) adored by the electorate.[30]

His technique became one of no longer presenting 'the old question between Whig and Tory', since 'what we are disputing about is a whole system of Government, and to make good that proposition that it is a whole system of government will be my great object in any addresses that I may deliver in this country'. This passage, from a speech of 1879,[31] did not pass unobserved, and aroused the ire of *The Times* which wrote indignantly: 'In a word, everything is overdone... Does it [the country] wish the conduct of public affairs to be at the mercy of excitement, of rhetoric, of the qualities which appeal to a mob rather than to those which command the attention of a Senate?'[32]

Gladstone had already replied to these observations in 1877, responding to a Conservative critic who accused him of protesting against the government's foreign policies in the public arena (the famous 'Bulgarian Agitations')[33] instead of fighting his battle in the Houses of Parliament. 'I suppose it may be said that the House of Commons represents the country; but still it is not the country, and, as people have lately drawn a distinction between the country and the Government, so there might be circumstances in which they might draw a distinction between the country and the House of Commons'.[34]

Might the political parties better represent the 'people' than the House of Commons? Gladstone would certainly have given a cautious answer to this question, since in his vision it was the leader who had the right to appeal to the people, even though the party remained an excellent organizational instrument, whether for contesting elections or for coordinating the parliamentary actions of the elected.

What is not in doubt is that his example was promptly taken up by the Conservatives, not merely, as already suggested, for the purpose of organizing the electorate, but also for the purpose of building a 'political identity' in support of what would later be described as constructing a 'social bloc'.[35]

It was Robert Cecil, later Lord Salisbury, who gave the Conservatives a political theory that freed them from being merely a party founded on the

---

[30] Eugenio Biagini, *Liberty, Retrenchment and Reform: Popular Liberalism in the Age of Gladstone 1860–1880* (Cambridge: Cambridge University Press, 1992).

[31] Quoted from the introduction by H. C. G. Matthew to *The Gladstone Diaries*, IX (Oxford: Oxford University Press, 1986), p. lxvi.

[32] Editorial in *The Times*, 29 November 1879.

[33] Richard Shannon, *Gladstone and the Bulgarian Agitation 1876* (London: Nelson, 1963).

[34] Quoted in Matthew, *The Gladstone Diaries*, IX, p. lxix.

[35] The use in a different context of the Gladstonian turn of mind reminds me of what Michael Freeden wrote: 'political concepts acquire meaning not only through accumulative traditions of discourse, and not only through diverse cultural contexts, but also by means of their particular structural position within a configuration of other political concepts', *Ideologies and Political Theory*, 4.

power of certain social elites, from being the 'stupid party', as the intellectual elite dubbed it. The Prime Minister of the anti-Liberal backlash (1886–92; 1895–1902) had been a brilliant polemical writer in the *Quarterly Review* and an active Conservative politician who came to the fore in the fight against the 1867 Reform Act.[36]

It is worth dwelling here on a question which was to change considerably the perception of how politics functioned: substantially, the meaning to be attributed to elections.

Salisbury, whose adversaries described him as an 'Elizabethan relic', gradually developed a vision that made a slightly different use of the appeal to the electorate than Gladstone's. It was no longer a question, as with the latter, of a leader calling upon the people to confirm his right to produce 'progress', but of a representative of the institutions asking the people if they truly agreed with that progress which the elite they had sent to Parliament wanted to produce.

In his first phase, Salisbury identified the key institution for this task as the House of Lords. This was the well-known 'referendal theory', which charged this institution with ensuring that the House of Commons did not exceed the mandate it had received from the electorate and obliging it to refer to the Lords' judgment where necessary.[37]

This removed the control of politics from the vague notion of 'public opinion', of which Parliament was one of the mirrors, the press and maybe 'agitation' itself being the others. Since 1861 Salisbury had been convinced that, for Conservative parliamentarians, 'public opinion' was not the beacon, but that it was necessary 'frankly to acknowledge that the nation is our master, though the House of Commons is not, and to yield our own opinion only when the judgment of the nation has been challenged at the polls and decidedly expressed'.[38]

Perhaps unexpectedly for his critics, the Conservative leader attached for this reason great importance to the institution of the party. For him it was no longer simply an instrument for organizing parliamentary presence; it was an opportunity to construct a popular identity. This had become indispensable from the moment in which elections were carried out as 'referenda' on the validity of the reforms proposed by the government. Criticizing the Conservative leaders who had preceded him, Salisbury stated that the party could not be just a (parliamentary) faction, since 'all the members of a party are enlisted in common to serve one great unselfish cause'.[39]

---

[36] On this phase see Peter Marsh, *The Discipline of Popular Government: Lord Salisbury's Domestic Statecraft, 1881–1902* (Hassocks: Harvester, 1978); Andrew Roberts, *Salisbury: Victorian Titan* (London: Weidenfeld & Nicholson, 1999).

[37] A careful and very stimulating analysis of this problem is given in Corinne C. Weston, 'Salisbury and the Lords, 1868–1895', *Historical Journal*, 25 (1982), 103–29.

[38] Weston, 'Salisbury and the Lords, 1868–1895', 120.

[39] Quoted in Peter Marsh, 'The Conservative Conscience', in Peter Marsh (ed.), *The Conscience of the Victorian State* (Hassocks: Harvester, 1979), 233.

For Salisbury, the loyalty of the 'head of the party' to his formation was a duty, as he wrote in an article in the *Quarterly Review* in 1865: 'The position [of Prime Minister gained through the elections] gives him an influence far beyond what could be commanded by any personal qualities. He has accepted that position, and the influence which attaches to it from his party for the purpose of giving effect to their political opinions'.[40]

The question of referring to the judgment of the electorate, however, was not as simple as it seemed. As the Conservative leader had written in October 1862, the governing class should not be given 'unlimited power': 'They must be kept checked by constitutional forms and watched by an active public opinion, lest their rightful pre-eminence should degenerate into the domination of a class. But woe to a community that deposes them altogether'.[41]

In this context parties obviously assumed great importance, since they were the determining factors in a system that increasingly based itself on an appeal to the voters as a means of legitimizing politics and keeping any deviations in check. Parties therefore needed to 'discipline' that public opinion which no longer belonged merely to 'philosophers' thinking in public, as in the Age of Enlightenment, or 'philosophers in action', as Burke had once described them. In short, parties needed 'ideology', in the terms explained by Michael Freeden.

It is not possible here to reconstruct in detail the stages by which European constitutional liberalism came to accept, *obtorto collo*, the inevitability of the 'party form' as a necessary step towards the handling of an enlarged political citizenship.[42] To understand how bitter the surrender was, we need only cite the conclusion of James Bryce's *Modern Democracies* where he writes, remembering the lively polemics of Ostrogorski and the debate deriving from them:

> Must there then always be parties? No one has yet shown how such governments could get on without them. [And he adds in a note:] Political philosophers have incessantly denounced parties, but none seems to have shown they can either be prevented from arising or eliminated when they exist.[43]

This book was published in 1921 and concluded the long career (and life) of a man who had been crucial to formulating Anglo-Saxon constitutional thought in the long nineteenth century, and who especially promoted a greater awareness of the American system.

---

[40] The extract from the article is reproduced in H. J. Hanham (ed.), *The Nineteenth Century Constitution* (Cambridge: Cambridge University Press, 1969), 232.
[41] Quoted in Michael Pinto-Duschinsky, *The Political Thought of Lord Salisbury 1854–1868* (London: Constable, 1967), 115.
[42] I have done so amply in my *La ragione e la passione*.
[43] James Bryce, *Modern Democracies* (London: Macmillan, 1921), 138.

BEYOND 'CLASSIC' LIBERALISM?

What induced constitutionalism of liberal origins (though largely unaware of this fact)[44] to rethink its approach to the question of the party in the post-Second World War period? Why did it revise both the fundamentally Anglo-Saxon tradition of parties as structures for organized mediation between civil society and political society, on the one hand, and on the other the continental European tradition of parties as articulations of an imprecisely defined nature with the functional purpose of channelling consensus towards the state? In my opinion, this was the point where the question of political citizenship was shifted from a simple right to intervene in the sphere of public decisions to a new right of control over the mechanisms for creating and distributing welfare.

Undoubtedly the most important party form in the latter half of the twentieth century was what the German political theorist Otto Kirchheimer happily described as the 'catch-all party'. This formula became widely known with the publication of his essay on the transformation of parties in Western Europe, an essay that appeared in English in the mid 1960s.[45] Over the next decade this theory became increasingly intertwined, predominantly at the hands of German political theorists, with the notion of a 'popular party' (*Volkspartei*).[46] Nonetheless, Kirchheimer's innovation had a more distant starting point, even if we set aside here his Weimar background and his relations with Carl Schmitt.[47] It was during his French exile, followed by his years in the United States, that Kirchheimer began to reflect on the mutations of 'democracy' to the extent that, when he dedicated himself to observing postwar Germany, he stated clearly the novelty, in his opinion, of the party forms that were being created. As early as 1954, in analysing the German political scene, Kirchheimer had identified the key to the transformation.[48] After noting that the 'absence of any real foreign policy alternative is an important factor in Germany's internal stability', since this had pushed the SPD into the role of a 'loyal opposition', Kirchheimer explained the 'moderation' of the policies of the German parties in that period in these terms: 'none of these followed what one might consider a

---

[44] Paolo Pombeni, 'Antiliberalism and the Liberal Legacy in Post-War European Constitutionalism: Considerations on Some Case Studies', *European Journal of Political Theory*, 7 (2008), 31–44.

[45] See Otto Kirchheimer, 'The Transformation of the Western European Party Systems', in Joseph La Palombara and Myron Wiener (eds.), *Political Parties and Political Development* (Princeton: Princeton University Press, 1966), 177–200.

[46] See H. Kaste and J. Raschke, 'Zur Politik der Volkspartei', in W. D. Narr (ed.), *Auf dem Wege zu ein Parteistaat* (Opladen: Westdeutscher Verlag, 1977), 26–71.

[47] See Otto Kirchheimer, *Costitituzione senza sovrano. Saggi di teoria politica e costituzionale*, ed. A. Bolaffi (Bari: De Donato, 1982). See also Frank Schale, *Zwischen Engagement und Skepsis. Eine Studie zu den Schriften von Otto Kirchheimer* (Baden-Baden: Nomos, 2006).

[48] See Otto Kirchheimer, 'Notes on the Political Scene in Western Germany', *World Politics*, 6 (1954), 306–21.

characteristically German procedure, namely to build a whole political system on the basis of their particular grievances. Instead, they were content to pursue their claims through the normal channels of lobby and pressure-group activities'. This seemed to him an 'un-Germanic approach', dominated by an 'almost Anglo-Saxon fashion'.[49]

Kirchheimer's analysis was very detailed and took into consideration the beginnings of the phenomenon of social change leading towards a 'welfare society'. He not only underlined the decline of the great ideological battle with the disappearance of phenomena such as attempts at 'converting the militants', consigning to memory the political 'eternal soldier' of the Weimar period. He also insisted on the fact that there existed 'the trend towards privatization, a turning inward of interests and a concentration upon private affairs', adding that 'in the scale of preoccupations, political interest, especially among young people, ranks well behind sports, dancing, and in fact the sum total of private and personal considerations'. These observations explicitly connected to ongoing sociological research, especially that of Helmut Schelsky who was specifically referred to in a note.[50]

But Kirchheimer's 1954 essay went further still. Enquiring into the possible form that the German party system was likely to assume, Kirchheimer asserted that the current situation could be described as the 'first phase' of a two-party system, with a 'Conservative' party and a 'Labour' party.[51] However, while on the one side there already existed 'a conservative catch-all party', on the other side there was only the embryo of a party of that kind, since SPD policies were founded upon 'Schumacher's [the leader of SPD] principle of austerity by concentrating on requirements of basic industries rather than consumer goods production'. Hence the straight question: 'Will the SPD develop into a catch-all mass party rather than a democratic working class party, and thus retain the possibility of leading an alternative government?'[52] The notion of the 'catch-all party' was not only present but, of equal interest, it was related to the problem of the diffusion of what might be described as the democracy of welfare.

This is a very important concept, one which has profoundly changed perceptions and the actions of European political parties. Certainly, it belongs in a more general context that saw a change in the role of the government, from an institution destined to 'manage the present' (even under the control of representative assemblies), to one destined first and foremost to 'promise the future'; to announce, that is, important changes and happy solutions for

---

[49] Kirchheimer, 'Notes on the Political Scene in Western Germany', 307–8, 310–11.
[50] Kirchheimer, 'Notes on the Political Scene in Western Germany', 312–14.
[51] The obsession with the two-party system as the perfect form of politics was, for most political theorists of the postwar period, a surrogate of the myth of the perfection of the English model which had dominated the nineteenth century.
[52] Kirchheimer, 'Notes on the Political Scene in Western Germany', 317–18.

everyone.[53] Obviously, in a system in which 'government by the parties' was by now the dominant form, every party aspiring to such a role had to present itself as the bearer of a project for the future, for the most part concerning welfare.

Kirchheimer returned to some of these concepts a few years later while, as far as I am aware, the specific theme of the 'catch-all party' did not emerge again until the well-known essay of 1966. If we examine two very interesting writings, one from 1957 and the other from 1958, which are modestly presented as bibliographical surveys,[54] we find an assessment of the evolution of the political scene close to Ostrogorski, with the difference that in this case 'realism' prevails, and hence an acceptance of the situation that is coming about as 'normal'.[55] In the first essay Kirchheimer noted that the traditional antonym between state and society had been, to some extent, overcome, given that 'organizations with millions of members are no less interested in avoiding conflict than are representatives of constituted authority'. This was because 'the traditional *Weltanschauungspartei* has been undergoing a fundamental transformation': the SPD was gradually losing 'its faint Marxist coloration' while the CDU was 'an interdenominational catch-all of "Christian politics"'. In order to understand this, he accepted a sociological analysis of the new Germany as a country with relatively few political tensions ('the unruffled waters of the Bonn political establishment') and a broad consensus deriving from having become 'a homogeneous middle-class society'. This leads to two conclusions: that the political system is necessarily 'oligarchic', founded on political professionalism; and that citizens are not interested in taking part (they go to vote and that is all), delegating management of the public sphere to the state, which itself was colonized by the parties.

> All German parties today are of necessity "integration parties", i.e., potentially democratic mass organizations. This determines their constitutional status; it also makes them different from their nineteenth-century predecessors. Important though all this is, it should not obscure the fact that party contest in present day Germany is a very orderly affair, almost as orderly as competition in the German cartel-dominated "free market economy".[56]

In his 1958 essay, Kirchheimer, in contrast to Sigmund Neumann (the coordinator of extensive research on political parties), rejected a fundamental

---

[53] On this point, which seems to me of a certain importance, see my essay 'Ideology and Government', in Michael Freeden (ed.), *The Meaning of Ideology* (London: Routledge, 2007), 59–74.

[54] Otto Kirchheimer, 'The Political Scene in West Germany', *World Politics*, 9 (1957), 433–45; Kirchheimer, 'The Party in Mass Society', *World Politics*, 10 (1958), 289–94.

[55] Although Kirchheimer, in this 1958 essay, distanced himself from his one-time master Carl Schmitt, praising the critical work by Peter Schneider on the legal theorist of the Reich, he nevertheless maintained Schmitt's methodological realism (see 'The Political Scene', 438–9).

[56] Kirchheimer, 'The Political Scene', 437, 440, 441.

distinction between democratic states and totalitarian states: 'The functions of the democratic system of government—in accordance with the people's radically changed expectations—have become almost as all-embracing as those of the totalitarian state'. Kirchheimer saw a separation between 'political formulas', which remained with the parties as an instrument of struggle, and 'executive decisions', which belonged only to the government, with its corps of technicians and administrators (and he recalled that this had been defined, in the political jargon of the French constitutionalist Maurice Hauriou, *pouvoir minoritaire*). The parties lay siege to governments with their 'shock troops—organized interests' and with their 'foot soldiers—the distant electorate', but the government neutralizes these actions, transforming everything into technical questions.[57]

The fundamental question remained, therefore, about the link between social transformations and new forms of political organization. This was not the responsibility of the electoral system, as had been argued by Maurice Duverger (whom Kirchheimer had implicitly criticized in his 1958 essay), but of a change in people's attitude towards politics, as he wrote very clearly at the end of an essay in 1960:

> [The citizen] is content to opt for parties converted by the inherent logic of industrial society into catch-all aggregates, or, like the CDU, into vast interest markets held together by the prestige of the chief and the magic of prosperity. [...] Yet the 1950s bequeathed to the uncertain 1960s one sole asset: for the first time in a long while the German citizen has been given a chance to enjoy existence without having to fear self-propelled engines of national destruction'.[58]

All this was true not only of Germany; aside from a few specific features, it could be said of Western Europe as a whole. The assumption of 'welfare' as the fundamental parameter of politics was not new in an absolute sense, given that politics as the 'pursuit of happiness' had a long history, but now, not least as a result of the social sciences, it assumed a different meaning. It was no longer simply a matter of guaranteeing the conditions under which the individual might live his own life as well as possible; nor was it even a question of guaranteeing certain 'standards' in 'civil' life (as was the case with the horizons opened by the famous Beveridge Report of 1942, when welfare became a necessity to be extended to everyone). Rather, it had now become a question of ensuring potential access for all to the consumer universe, which was now becoming a 'mass' universe.[59]

---

[57] Kirchheimer, 'Party in Mass Society', 290–2.
[58] Otto Kirchheimer, 'German Democracy in the 1950s', *World Politics*, 13 (1961), 265–6.
[59] On Beveridge and the ideology of welfare, see Michael Freeden, *Liberalism Divided: A Study in British Political Thought 1914–1939* (Oxford: Oxford University Press, 1986), 366–71; Michael Freeden, 'The Coming of the Welfare State', in Terence Ball and Richard Bellamy (eds.), *The Cambridge History of Twentieth-Century Political Thought* (Cambridge: Cambridge University Press, 2003), 7–44.

Paradoxically this opened the pathway to 'another story'. The student revolts of 1968, by questioning the reduction of 'welfare' to 'consumption' (according to Marcuse's mythical book on one-dimensional man), laboured under the illusion that they could relaunch opinion as an open door towards utopia. In doing so they spread an ephemeral nostalgia for the party, not only of *Weltanschauung*, but of teleological progression towards some 'end of history'.

Deprived of a proper ideology about parties as structural agents of disciplining and channelling public opinion, Western constitutionalism saw its liberal roots put into question. In a certain sense the old desperate consideration of James Bryce in 1921 came back to the fore. It is easy to criticize parties, but without agencies structured to mould opinion, how can we organize political discourse and legitimize authority without falling into a totalitarian horizon that solves these problems by force?

Part II

Ideologies and Political Theory

7

Liberalism and Analytical Political Philosophy

David Weinstein

> Historical and metaphysical self-consciousness, we think, is the best precaution against barren scholasticism.
>
> Richard Rorty[1]

INTRODUCTION

Michael Freeden deems what he calls 'American philosophical liberalism' deeply problematic and for some good reasons. Its achievements are considerable, as even Freeden would readily concede. But these achievements, as he would also insist, have been paid for dearly by ideologically and historically decontexualizing liberalism and the liberal tradition.

Analytical political philosophy has always been insensitive to its own tradition and origins, causing analytical political philosophers to marginalize predecessors while regarding themselves as more innovative than they really are. Because of their limited historical memory, they revere a skewed canon of scattered and disconnected heroes that somehow anticipated philosophical problems we now take for granted as fundamental. The narrative that we have learned to tell about ourselves is linear and truncated, leaping between distant figures struggling with philosophical problems anticipating our own, until finally and fortuitously coming of age in places like Harvard and Oxford after the Second World War.

---

[1] Richard Rorty, 'Analytic and Conversational Philosophy', in Richard Rorty, *Philosophy as Cultural Politics: Philosophical Papers*, vol. 4 (Cambridge: Cambridge University Press, 2007), 130.

By marginalizing so much of its origins and collapsing its tradition, especially its liberal tradition, analytical political philosophy has equally marginalized itself as a critical political voice. By forgetting predecessors to its professionalization who were public intellectuals and not just highly specialized disputants fluent in the latest philosophical jargon, analytical political philosophy has become increasingly irrelevant for all its conceptual sophistication. The more professional it has become, the less it has flourished ideologically.

In what follows, I will eschew saying more about contemporary political philosophy's retreat from robust political relevance. Rather, I will stick to speculating about why analytical political philosophy acquired such bad habits in narrating its past. I will also explore how these exegetical habits have affected how political theorists in particular have misinterpreted J. S. Mill and have forgotten Henry Sidgwick. Moral philosophers have done better with both, though not unproblematically.

HISTORICITY, HISTORICISM, AND THE HISTORY OF POLITICAL PHILOSOPHY

Richard Rorty has suggested that whereas analytical philosophy deals in problems, continental philosophy trades instead in proper names. Continental philosophers tend to see themselves as belonging to a chronological tradition of proper names that typically gets underway with Kant. For them, different historical contexts have generated different philosophical problems and therefore evolving philosophical responses typically attached to representative figures. Rorty concurs, insisting that our historical context therefore has its own particular philosophical problems and solutions whose uniqueness is best appreciated as following on earlier contexts, problems, solutions, and their representative figures. By studying these, we acquire critical purchase on our own philosophical problems, much as visiting alien cultures helps us think critically by exposing and undermining our own prejudices and assumptions. Continental political philosophy is consequently more historically self-conscious and sensitive. It thrives on a sense of historicity that analytical political philosophy, with its ahistorical problem-solving focus, lacks.[2]

---

[2] Simon Critchley likens the continental tradition to a 'vast textual archive for contextually specific philosophical problems'. We do better grappling with our contemporary philosophical problems and preoccupations by reaching into our tradition's archive. The 'way one moves forward philosophically is by looking backwards in a fresh manner'. Hence, like Rorty, he sees continental philosophy as being more historically self-conscious than analytical philosophy. But unlike Rorty, he sees continental philosophy as trading in problems as much as in names. See Simon Critchley, *Continental Philosophy* (Oxford: Oxford University Press, 2001), 59.

Historicity is not historicism however. We can be historically self-conscious without becoming philosophical relativists. The history of political philosophy can just as easily reinforce our belief in enduring philosophical problems and truths as it can convince us that all philosophizing is not only contextual but also non-objective. The continental tradition has produced Strauss as well as Heidegger and both in Germany at the same time. But either way, continental philosophy's greater historical self-consciousness has dissuaded continental philosophers, relative to their Anglophone counterparts anyway, from constructing an overly simplified canon and from reinventing theoretical solutions with false, though plainly more sophisticated, novelty.

The menu of basic conceptual issues that analytical political philosophers are taught to value early on in their professional education tends to stay with them as self-evidently important. Naturally, they pass on this importance to the next generation with modest modifications at best. While this disciplinary professionalization has produced erudite results, it has not always been kind to its pre-analytical past. Pre-analytical political philosophers are typically evaluated by how well they purportedly anticipate the problems that preoccupy us. And since analytical political philosophy is predominantly liberal, liberal predecessors get awarded canonical status to the extent we succeed in discovering our conceptual preoccupations already emerging in them. We canonize Mill, especially for his seminal thinking about freedom, but we ignore much of the continental tradition notwithstanding Wittgenstein's legacy to our practice. We also dismiss Leo Strauss and politely ignore Alasdair MacIntyre because they fit so imperfectly into what we have been taught is important. The ongoing Strauss wars in the American academy surely are the product, in part, of analytical political philosophy's construction of its abridged self-understanding. Contrary to what many analytical political philosophers may think, we need history, particularly much better history of political thought. Philosophical liberals need this most of all.

Concepts have complicated histories. They are unstable. They constitute and are constitutive of their times. Philosophical liberals should therefore become conceptual historicists, or at least take conceptual historicism more seriously, and forgo trying to refine our political philosophical concepts into exquisitely finished principles, hoping to solve the many political and fundamental normative dilemmas that plague our world. We would do well to heed Rorty's admonition that you 'can change a concept by changing usage, but you cannot get a concept right once and for all'.[3]

No doubt, then, avoiding conceptual confusion and trying our best to draw out the meanings of the political philosophical concepts we take as central is worthwhile philosophical work. Conceptual inconsistency is to be avoided at

---

[3] Rorty, 'Analytic and Conversational Philosophy', 123.

all times. But liberalism has always been, and remains, a changing constellation of concepts or ongoing rearranging of conceptual furniture as Freeden would say.

Nevertheless, Anglophone political philosophy has never been immune to continental influences. The history of political philosophy is not that hermetic and tidy. Late nineteenth-century and early twentieth-century British idealism and liberalism were deeply informed by Hegel. But the introduction of logical and conceptual analysis through Bertrand Russell and G. E. Moore after the turn of the century put an end to idealism and, with it, explicitly normative political theorizing. The rejection of idealism was the beginning of logical positivism and emotivism perfected by A. J. Ayer, prompting Peter Laslett to declare famously the 'death' of political philosophy in 1956.[4]

Laslett's pronouncement was, of course, premature. Rawls published 'Justice as Fairness' in 1958, which was followed by H. L. A. Hart's *The Concept of Law* in 1961 and Brian Barry's *Political Argument* in 1965. And while Berlin's 1958 'Two Concepts of Liberty' is on one hand a highly polemical narrative aimed at exposing liberalism's unintended theoretical contribution to totalitarian ways of thinking, it more famously articulated a conceptual distinction that continues to inform assumptions so dear to contemporary analytical political philosophy. Though much less neatly dichotomous than it seems at first sight, Berlin's distinction between negative and positive freedom remains intractably paradigmatic to this day.[5] In short, by the late 1950s, Anglophone political philosophy had begun rediscovering its voice, becoming theoretically ambitious if not more politically engaged. But despite its purported rigour, or perhaps because of it, this re-energized philosophizing lost sight of its past, compressing and simplifying it for reasons already alluded to.

Now, whatever these reasons and however condensed the history of political philosophy has become as a consequence, recovering what has been forgotten is hardly straightforward especially if concepts, including notably political philosophical concepts, are historically contextual or, better, historical artefacts. If their meanings are unstable, if these meanings are continuously drifting and realigning, then reclaiming marginalized episodes of the liberal tradition poses daunting interpretive challenges. Once we give up as futile

---

[4] I am greatly indebted to Jonathan Wolff's account of the impact of logical positivism on the decline of Anglophone normative political theorizing. Wolff particularly underscores the influence that T. D. Weldon's 1953 *Vocabulary of Politics* had on reducing political philosophy to a variety of emotivism. See Jonathan Wolff, 'Analytical Political and Legal Philosophy', in Michael Beaney (ed.), *Oxford Handbook of the History of Analytical Philosophy* (Oxford: Oxford University Press, forthcoming).

[5] See my 'English Political Theory in the Nineteenth and Twentieth Centuries', in Gerald Gaus and Chandran Kukathas (eds.), *Handbook of Political Theory* (London: Sage Publications, 2004), 410–26, for an account of ambiguities in the distinction between negative and positive freedom that Berlin introduces in a long and mostly ignored footnote in the essay.

trying to get our seminal, political philosophical concepts right once and for all, then we relinquish a crucial criterion for narrative unity, if not narrative unity entirely, for constructing our canon whether traditional or improved.

But that is not all. Ceaseless conceptual drift and realignment make accessing past conceptual understandings or practices exceedingly problematic. For however one might prefer to retell the canon by resurrecting marginalized figures and perhaps demoting major ones, one must begin by trying to figure out what these marginalized philosophers meant in writing what they did. Recent Anglophone and continental hermeneutics offer alternative ways to think about this dilemma and for coming to terms with it. Two of them, identified with the Cambridge School on one hand and with Gadamer on the other, rather dramatically capture what is at stake.

Not unlike 'new historicism' in literary theory, Quentin Skinner and J. G. A. Pocock have argued strenuously over many years that we need to situate political philosophical texts carefully but firmly in their historical contexts in order to properly interpret them. Skinner and Pocock recommend different strategies emphasizing different contextual dimensions as their preferred methods for getting at what past political philosophers meant by their claims and arguments. And both Skinner and Pocock have somewhat shifted their thinking about their methodological approaches in their more recent writings on theory and method.[6]

Notwithstanding the differences between them as well as changes in their respective approaches to proper textual interpretation, Skinner and Pocock by and large assume that political philosophical texts possess objective meanings that can be displayed or uncovered more or less through reconstructing their contexts. For both, there is something in the text to be discovered through systematic contextualization, though Pocock is more interested than Skinner in how every reading, old or recent, invariably produces meaning, raising doubts about whether texts are really there to recover at all.

Pocock's Cambridge method, therefore, is not wholly unlike Gadamer's philosophical hermeneutics. With Pocock and Gadamer, philosophical traditions converge. Anglophone and continental intellectual histories overlap, making reconstructing political philosophy's canon similarly problematic. For Pocock, no less than for Gadamer, our own historicity is not some contingent

---

[6] For Pocock's understanding of how his method of interpretation has evolved and how it differs from Skinner's, see Pocock's succinct 'Preface' to his recent *Political Thought and History* (Cambridge: Cambridge University Press, 2009). See, in particular, his claim that he has tried 'to press beyond the establishment of "what an author was doing", in Quentin Skinner's famous phrase of 1978—in other words, how the author's "intentions" shaped and were shaped by the language context in which they were expressed—to the question of "what he/she turned out to have done", from illocution to allocution, to borrow language once again from Skinner'. That is, Pocock has also tried to 'inquire how authors were understood by readers, and how the response of the latter both shaped and was shaped by the original author's speech act', p. xiv.

and accidental prejudice that we can and should try as best we can to neutralize but, instead, fundamentally constitutes our ontological condition.

Perhaps, then, when we interpret texts, resurrect marginalized thinkers, or recover forgotten conceptual constellations, we are more properly *mediating* philosophical perspectives than we are *reconstructing* them. As Gadamer insists, presuppositions and biases 'are simply conditions whereby we experience something—whereby what we encounter says something to us'.[7] When we interpret texts, we neither just destroy their original meanings by replacing them with radically new ones nor reproduce them magically in their own terms. Rather, we 'explicat[e] them within our "own horizons" and from our "own concepts", thus giving them "new validity"'.[8]

INTERPRETING NINETEENTH-CENTURY ANGLOPHONE LIBERALISM

Analytical political philosophy is not uniquely prejudiced about its past but is simply differently prejudiced. Rival ways of doing political philosophy have produced alternative narratives some of which have been no less anachronistic and unusual. Different traditions have different canons. They create dissimilar ancestries and write incongruous genealogies, which is not to say that these ancestries and genealogies do not overlap. They compress, marginalize, and forget differently but again, not without intersecting. For instance, Leo Strauss's history of political thought ignores much Anglophone theorizing though he views Hobbes, and Locke to a lesser extent, as having invented liberalism, which is the beginning of historicism leading straight to Nietzsche, political nihilism, and Europe's twentieth-century disasters. MacIntyre tells a parallel story of philosophical and concomitant political decay, but his narrative features more Kant and some classical utilitarianism, logical-positivism, and Anglophone emotivism. And like Strauss, he looks back to Plato and Aristotle for consolation if not reprieve. Continental political philosophy, of course, tells other generally more complex narratives.

---

[7] Hans-Georg Gadamer, 'The Universality of the Hermeneutical Problem', in Hans-Georg Gadamer, *Philosophical Hermeneutics* (Berkeley: University of California Press, 1976), 9.

[8] Hans-Georg Gadamer, 'Semantics and Hermeneutics', in *Philosophical Hermeneutics*, 94. More broadly for Gadamer, reality and not just textual reality, 'does not happen "behind the back" of language; it happens rather behind the backs of those who live in the subjective opinion that they have understood "the world" (or can no longer understand it); that is, reality happens precisely *within* language'. See Gadamer, 'On the Scope and Function of Hermeneutical Reflection', in *Philosophical Hermeneutics*, 35. Hence, for Gadamer as well, it 'is obvious to us that understanding the historical significance of an action presupposes that we do not restrict ourselves to the subjective plans, intentions, and dispositions of the agents'. See Gadamer, 'The Philosophical Foundations of the Twentieth Century', in *Philosophical Hermeneutics*, 122.

But like Freeden, I am more interested in the narratives that Anglophone analytical political philosophers continue to tell about the liberal tradition and how these narratives are not so much distortions as they are marginalizing compressions that, in addition, attribute false novelty to much contemporary liberal theorizing. Contemporary analytical philosophy has, in particular, mostly ignored British new liberals and idealists because of their purported eclecticism, historicism, conceptual imprecision, and general philosophical sloppiness. Much of this disinterest stems from Russell and Moore's rejection, noted before, of idealist metaphysics and epistemology in the name of philosophical analysis in the early twentieth century.

Green, though, has received some attention thanks to Berlin's appropriation of him as a historical stalking horse of positive freedom. For Berlin, Green borrowed from Hegel all to bad effect on the liberal tradition in both theory and in practice. Berlin's appropriation of Green to illustrate positive freedom's conceptual flaws and political dangers has nevertheless not generated strong interest in Green, and other new liberals and idealists for that matter, by contemporary proponents of positive freedom like Charles Taylor. New liberals and idealists remain marginal to analytical liberalism's historical narrative in all its permutations.

Analytical liberalism's equally marginal interest in classical utilitarians like Henry Sidgwick is odder and less easy to explain. Moral philosophers and historians of moral philosophy, notably J. B. Schneewind and Bart Schultz, have successfully done much to restore appreciation of Sidgwick's significance to the invention and refinement of classical utilitarianism no less than to his equally important contributions to the beginning of Anglophone analytical philosophy through his formative influence on Moore in particular.[9]

Contemporary analytical liberals' indifference to Sidgwick is particularly puzzling, however, because Rawls's debt to him is so profound. *A Theory of Justice*, in a large measure, is an effort to justify elemental principles of justice that avoids appealing to traditional intuitionism in all its alleged ambiguity on the one hand and Sidgwick's classical utilitarianism on the other.[10] Nonetheless, Rawls's reflective equilibrium draws heavily from Sidgwick's strategy for justifying basic moral rules.

---

[9] We should distinguish between logical analysis developed by Russell from conceptual analysis practised by Moore. Whereas the former has been concerned with the logical status of propositions, including especially ethical propositions, the latter has stressed argumentative clarity, rigour, and precision utilizing the fewest possible basic concepts, all the while deploying (sometimes far-fetched) hypothetical examples. Sidgwick's moral theorizing helped initiate this kind of conceptual argumentation, which has come to dominate contemporary Anglophone political philosophy especially after Rawls. Ironically, then, Freeden's dissatisfaction with analytical political philosophy has its roots in Sidgwick, whom analytical political philosophy has otherwise largely discarded.

[10] See especially John Rawls, *A Theory of Justice* (Oxford: Oxford University Press, 1999), pp. xvii-iii.

In contrast, analytical political philosophers and political theorists especially have never forgotten about Mill, though the Mill they remember is mostly from his *On Liberty* and not from his *Utilitarianism* and related essays. No doubt, their indifference to Mill's utilitarianism is likewise, in part, due to their general lack of interest in utilitarian moral theory, classical or otherwise. Rawls had, after all, purportedly laid the latter to rest once and for all, demonstrating how it failed to take seriously distinctions between persons.

MILL

In 'Burton Dreben: A Reminiscence', Rawls insists:

> When lecturing, say, on Locke, Rousseau, Kant, or J. S. Mill, I always tried to do two things especially. One was to pose their problems as they themselves saw them, given what their understanding of these problems was in their own time. I often cited the remark of Collingwood that "the history of political theory is not the history of different answers to one and the same question, but the history of a problem more or less constantly changing, whose solution was changing with it".[11]

We might expect, then, that those of us doing nineteenth- and twentieth-century history of Anglophone political thought in the shadow of *A Theory of Justice* would be more sensitive to contextualizing texts in the manner recommended by Skinner, Pocock, and others. We should expect more contextualization, for instance, from those who have otherwise done so much recently to bring Mill's *liberal* utilitarianism back into focus by showing how Millian utilitarianism worked hard, and perhaps succeeded, in taking very seriously distinctions between persons, in contrast to what has been argued by Rawls.[12]

Rawls's reminiscences about Dreben also reveal that Rawls eschewed strict contextualism nevertheless or, at least, that he thought it was inadequate by itself. Rawls continues:

---

[11] John Rawls, 'Burton Dreben: A Reminiscence', in Juliet Floyd and Sanford Shieh (eds.), *Future Pasts: Perspectives on the Place of the Analytic Tradition in Twentieth-Century Philosophy* (New York: Oxford University Press, 2000), 427. Rawls says, too: 'If I saw a mistake in their [canonical thinkers'] arguments, I supposed those writers saw it too and must have dealt with it. But where? I looked for their way out, not mine. Sometimes their way out was historical: in their day the question needed not be raised, or wouldn't arise and so couldn't then be fruitfully discussed', p. 427. Also see Barbara Herman's 'Editor's Forward' in John Rawls, *Lectures on the History of Moral Philosophy*, ed. Barbara Herman (Cambridge, MA: Harvard University Press, 2000), p. xvi. In contrast to most analytical liberals and their critics inspired by him, Rawls maintained a lively interest in the history of moral and political philosophy.

[12] See especially Jonathan Riley's masterful *Liberal Utilitarianism: Social Choice Theory and J. S. Mill's Philosophy* (Cambridge: Cambridge University Press, 1988).

The second thing I tried to do was to present each writer's thought in what I took to be its strongest form. I took to heart Mill's remark in his review of [Alfred] Sedgwick: "A doctrine is not judged until it is judged in its best form." I didn't say, not intentionally anyway, what I myself thought a writer should have said, but rather what the writer did say, supported by what I viewed as the most reasonable interpretation of the text. The text had to be known and respected, and its doctrine presented in its best form. Leaving aside the text seemed offensive, a kind of pretending. If I departed from it—no harm in that—I had to say so. Lecturing that way, I believed, made a writer's views stronger and more convincing, and a more worthy object of study.[13]

Rawls, then, seems to believe that perfecting a historical text's philosophical argument on its author's behalf is legitimate interpretation especially in so far as one admits that this is what one is doing. Though Rawls seems unprepared to go as far as Karl Popper who thinks that reconstructing historical texts by perfecting their arguments well beyond their authors' own formulations is legitimate intellectual history, Rawls's interpretative method is nevertheless, then, anything but rigorously contextualist.[14] Consequently, the mostly imaginative excursions into the history of political thought by analytically trained political philosophers should be less than surprising. In particular, Rawls's commanding legacy for the way it continues to shape debate about utilitarianism, combined with the way he approaches doing intellectual history, has probably done much to encourage recent, highly ingenious interpretations of Mill as 'intending' to accommodate liberty and utility, which Mill, like ourselves, supposedly recognized as problematically deeply challenging. Surely, the authoritative and encompassing shadow of Rawls has at least discouraged reading Victorian liberals like Mill with sufficient sensitivity to their different and suitably unfamiliar contexts.

Besides Rawls and like-minded deontological liberals, other very different philosophers have been unkind to classical utilitarians like Mill but on other grounds. Strauss, G. E. M. Anscombe, and MacIntyre have viewed classical utilitarianism as little more than a distinctive and particularly unwelcome mode of Enlightenment liberalism.

---

[13] Rawls, 'Burton Dreben: A Reminiscence', 427.

[14] See, for instance, Karl Popper, *The Poverty of Historicism* (London and New York: Routledge, 1997), 3, where Popper concedes that he was not so much interested in interpreting what past philosophers actually said as he was interested in 'building up [on their behalf] a position really worth attacking'. Ian Jarvie has called this interpretative strategy 'Popper's Hermeneutic Rule', which stipulates: 'Always try to reformulate the position under discussion in its logically strongest form'. This principle 'enjoins us that where an author has formulated a promising position in a way that is vulnerable to some obvious objection, the commentator should first try to improve upon it before subjecting it to criticism—not for the author's sake but for the sake of the inquiry'. See Ian Jarvie, 'Popper's Ideal Types: Open and Closed, Abstract and Concrete Societies', in Ian Jarvie and Sandra Pralong (eds.), *Popper's Open Society After 50 Years* (London and New York: Routledge, 1999), 77–8.

For Strauss, utilitarianism, which began with Hobbes, 'underlay philosophy's turn to history', empowering historicism with the 'fire and passion which gave it victory in afterdays'. And as far as Strauss was concerned, this victory has remained permanent and all to no good.[15] Similarly for MacIntyre, utilitarianism has never amounted to more than a 'motley party of defenders of liberal individualism', which has come to characterize modernity's demise after virtue.[16]

In an important 1958 essay, 'Modern Moral Philosophy', Anscombe describes the history of ethics, much like Strauss had a few years earlier, as Aristotelianism giving way to divine law with the rise of Judaism and Christianity and then finally collapsing into consequentialism so characteristic of modern moral philosophy, neo-Kantianism notwithstanding.[17] For her, modern moral philosophy in all its unfortunate permutations is simply the futile search for 'retaining a law conception without a divine legislator'.[18] And this futility has left modern moral thinking thoroughly disoriented, though Anscombe goes neither as far as Strauss nor as far as MacIntyre in seeing little hope for us condemned as we are to nihilism after virtue.

Anscombe also explains why modern moral philosophy went so sour, basing it on reasons similar to MacIntyre's. According to her:

> Anyone who has read Aristotle's *Ethics* and has also read modern moral philosophy must have been struck by the great contrasts between them. The concepts which are prominent among the moderns seem to be lacking, or at any rate buried or far in the background, in Aristotle. Most noticeably, the term 'moral' itself, which we have by direct inheritance from Aristotle, just doesn't seem to fit, in its modern sense, into an account of Aristotelian ethics... If someone professes to be expounding Aristotle and talks in a modern fashion about 'moral' such-and-such, he must be very imperceptive if he does not constantly feel like someone

---

[15] Leo Strauss, *The Political Philosophy of Hobbes* (Chicago: University of Chicago Press, 1963), 108. See also Leo Strauss, *Natural Right and History* (Chicago: University of Chicago Press, 1953), 6 and 169, where Strauss links 'liberal relativism' to 'political hedonism' purportedly invented by Hobbes.

[16] Alasdair MacIntyre, *After Virtue* (London: Duckworth, 1985), 260. See also the chapter on 'Some Consequences of the Failure of the Enlightenment Project', where MacIntyre casts utilitarianism, along with Kantianism, as successive episodes in the Enlightenment's failure. For MacIntyre, to repeat in somewhat more detail, the failure of classical utilitarianism (represented by Bentham, Mill, and Sidgwick) led to Moore's failed efforts to substitute anti-naturalistic intuitionism in its place which, in turn, led to the disaster of emotivism. And emotivism was little more than Anglophone philosophy's version of Nietzsche.

[17] As best I can ascertain, Anscombe's essay introduces the term 'consequentialism' into philosophy for the first time. For her, Bentham and Mill were 'old-fashioned' utilitarians, whereas Sidgwick reformulated utilitarianism, transforming it into 'consequentialism'. Modern moral philosophy has never been the same ever since and most lamentably so. Though Mill's utilitarianism was plainly 'stupid', Sidgwick's consequentialism was hardly any better, being mostly 'shallow'. See G. E. M. Anscombe, 'Modern Moral Philosophy', *Philosophy*, 33 (1958), 9–12.

[18] Anscombe, 'Modern Moral Philosophy', 13.

whose jaws have somehow got out of alignment: the teeth don't come together in a proper bite.[19]

In other words, though many of our moral concepts originated with Aristotle, the meanings have changed, causing us to misinterpret him in such a way that invariably feels awkward, though we cannot quite figure out why. Furthermore, now that so many of our basic moral terms have got detached from their original classical contexts, including their semantic context of *related* terms that we no longer regard as normative, and though they retain a certain psychological power over us, they nevertheless have lost their content. They hang in the air and no longer quite make sense. It is as if, as MacIntyre says, we now speak a language we no longer fully understand. Modern moral philosophy (and presumably modern political thought by implication) has become so much half gibberish. As Anscombe puts it regarding the concept 'morally wrong', these days 'all the atmosphere of the term is retained while its substance is guaranteed quite null'. Because 'morally wrong' has got 'cut off from the *family of concepts* from which it sprang', it seems to have no 'discernible content except a certain compelling force, which I should call purely *psychological*' (my italics).[20]

Moral philosophers, then, similar to political theorists such as Berlin who view Mill as the consummate champion of liberty, have never ceased paying attention to Mill. Some contemporary moral philosophers continue looking to Mill for inspiration in their efforts to prove Rawls and Bernard Williams wrong for insisting respectively that utilitarianism cannot take seriously the distinction between persons and for undermining personal integrity. Others have judged such efforts to rescue utilitarianism, by rescuing Mill as a genuine liberal through-and-through, as misbegotten, as bound to prove Rawls's assessment of utilitarianism correct once again. And finally, other moral philosophers, such as MacIntyre and Anscombe, who are committed to valorizing virtue ethics by nostalgically looking back to Aristotle, typically blame Mill as well as Sidgwick for playing such important roles in leading modern moral philosophy, and associated varieties of liberalism, so disastrously astray.[21]

---

[19] Anscombe, 'Modern Moral Philosophy', 1-2.

[20] Anscombe, 'Modern Moral Philosophy', 17-18. Anscombe is specifically referring here to how the concept 'morally wrong' has also become detached from its later divine law context and meaning. She could have just as well said the same thing about such concepts as justice, happiness, and the like.

[21] Nadia Urbinati has recently argued that, to the contrary, Mill's understanding of the good life, particularly in book VI, ch. XII of *A System of Logic*, was considerably informed by Aristotle. See Nadia Urbinati, 'An Alternative Modernity: Mill on Capitalism and the Quality of Life', in Ben Eggleston, Dale E. Miller, and David Weinstein (eds.), *John Stuart Mill and the Art of Life* (Oxford: Oxford University Press, 2010). Also see Eugenio F. Biagini, 'Liberalism and Direct Democracy: John Stuart Mill and the Model of Ancient Athens', in Eugenio F. Biagini (ed.), *Citizenship and Community* (Cambridge: Cambridge University Press, 1996). See especially where Biagini concludes: 'Thus, according to Mill, a free and democratic society ought to be characterized, first, by the greatest possible popular participation in public life; second, by the

So we moderns, for better or worse, and for diverse reasons of blame or praise, refuse to forget Mill. He remains significant to *us* and therefore canonical for *us*. Surely this accounts for why we continue to have so much trouble interpreting him one way or another. We keep trying to reconstruct him through what concerns us. We want him to fit us. We assume that our conceptual templates and constellations were surely his as well. But as Peter Nicholson warns: 'Mill is close enough in time for us easily to assume that his problems and his answers to them are not too dissimilar from ours and that we have immediate access to them. But it is not quite like that. There have been changes, and it requires some exercise of historical imagination to recapture some of Mill's concerns'.[22]

Mill was a great philosopher. But we should not mistake his greatness as a license to reconstruct him in contemporary analytical terms. Riley, as I mentioned, has helped us see just how relevant Mill remains to our ongoing efforts to systematize liberalism by combining it with varieties of consequentialism, yet without forgoing robust moral rights, thus insuring that it remains ethically appealing to those who put a premium on liberty. Riley and others, such as Gray in his early work, have *used* Mill very effectively to construct sophisticated utilitarian versions of liberal consequentialism. For them, liberalism is not necessarily incompatible with utilitarianism. Meaningful moral rules and moral rights can be successfully integrated into stringent decision procedures with the principle of utility in a fashion that Mill first suggested, though not without ambiguity, and which we, armed as we are with habits of greater analytical rigour, have discovered how to eliminate. Besides liberal utilitarianism, we now also call this kind of improved utilitarianism, which Mill purportedly anticipated, 'indirect' utilitarianism or 'rule' utilitarianism in the case of Brad Hooker, Richard Brandt, and the like.

But however much we may be tempted to interpret Mill as what we would now call a liberal or an indirect or a rule utilitarian or whatever, we must guard against reading these subsequent conceptual reformulations and innovations

---

greatest individual freedom in the sphere of 'self-regarding' actions (a sphere which is historically relative); and third, by the fullest possible development of free discussion, both as a habit of inquiry and as a method of government founded on persuasion rather than coercion. Classical Athens—at least the one of Pericles' speech and of Grote's *History*—was to Mill an unparalleled model because it possessed all these characteristics in the highest degree', p. 36.

[22] Peter Nicholson, 'The Reception and Early Reputation of Mill's Political Thought', in John Skorupski (ed.), *The Cambridge Companion to Mill* (Cambridge: Cambridge University Press, 1998), 488. Nicholson continues: 'Mill saw himself, and was seen by others, as addressing public debates and contributing to political activity. He was, in the terms Stefan Collini has recently elucidated so fully, a "public moralist". We should bear in mind that there was then no separate, and isolated, profession "philosophy" and "moral and political theory": the rise of philosophy as a distinct academic discipline began to occur only in the last years of Mill's life. He was in the thick of public debate—and not just during his brief spell as a Member of Parliament—and his writings were read as contributions to it, not as detached scholarly treatises. It follows that his merits were judged partly by political and ideological criteria, and that his reputation was bound to reflect that', pp. 488–9.

back into Mill. Whatever kind of utilitarian he was in his own terms, he was not a utilitarian in the meaning of these contemporary terms.

None of this is to say, of course, that Mill did not see himself as improving Bentham's utilitarianism by placing greater emphasis on moral rules.[23] Nor did Mill's contemporary critics fail to notice these refinements and to take him to task accordingly. F. H. Bradley, for instance, criticized Mill's version of utilitarianism for incoherently trying to combine meaningful moral rules with the principle of utility. Regarding Mill's endeavour to adapt an 'almanac' of moral rules to the principle of utility, Bradley writes:

> For obviously, (1) circumstances get into strange tangles, which cannot be provided against; and the course laid down in the Almanac as a law may, in peculiar cases, lead to pain instead of pleasure; and here I must disregard the Almanac. And obviously, (2) not outward situations only, but men's temperaments differ. What brings pleasure to one brings none to another; and so with pain. You can speak generally beforehand, but it may not apply to this or that man. And the consequence is, that the Almanac and its moral rules are no authority. It is right to act according to them. It is right to act diametrically against them. In short they are *not laws* at all; they are *only rules* and rules, as we know, admit of and imply exceptions (my italics).[24]

We have since come to call this kind of criticism of rule utilitarianism the 'incoherence objection'. And no one has pressed contemporary rule utilitarians harder than David Lyons for incoherently trying to join moral rules possessing decisive 'moral force' with the principle of utility.[25]

---

[23] See especially John Stuart Mill, 'Bentham' [1838] and 'Dr Whewell's Moral Philosophy' [1852] in *The Collected Works of John Stuart Mill*, ed. John M. Robson (Toronto: Toronto University Press, 1985), vol. X.

[24] F. H. Bradley [1876], *Ethical Studies* (Oxford: Oxford University Press, 1988), 102. One should note that Mill did not respond to Bradley's criticisms because *Ethical Studies* was published in 1876, three years after Mill died. Mill was probably familiar with James Fitzjames Stephen's version of this objection, which was published as 'A Note on Utilitarianism' in the *Pall Mall Gazette*, 1869. Stephen included this note in his 1874 *Liberty, Equality and Fraternity* (Chicago: Chicago University Press, 1990).

[25] See especially David Lyons, 'Utility and Rights', in John W. Chapman and J. Roland Pennock (eds.), *Ethics, Economics and the Law: Nomos*, 24 (New York: New York University Press, 1982). See also John Gray, *Liberalisms* (London: Routledge, 1989), 218–24, where Gray likewise insists that utility and moral rights are irreconcilable, though in his earlier *Mill on Liberty: A Defence* (London: Routledge, 1983), he argued that Mill succeeded in showing that they were. See, too, Alan Ryan, *The Philosophy of John Stuart Mill* (London: Macmillan Press, 1987), 223 and 228 for discussion of this issue. For Freeden's discussion of the compatibility of utility with moral rights possessing genuine 'moral force', see Michael Freeden, *Rights* (Minneapolis: University of Minnesota Press, 1991), ch. 6. There, Freeden argues that goal-based theories, including suitably 'constrained' utilitarian ones, can 'include as a central goal the protection of those attributes that rights-based theories deem precious', p. 98. For an extended discussion of how Mill's contemporary critics like Bradley and Stephen faulted him for arguing 'incoherently' as Lyons would say, see my 'Interpreting Mill' in Eggleston, Miller, and Weinstein (eds.), *John Stuart Mill and the Art of Life*.

Our family of political philosophical concepts and conceptualizations are no longer Mill's, though his nonetheless *seem* so familiar, so contemporary. Mill is all too easily read as though he were writing directly to us some one hundred and fifty years later. But he was not writing to us nor could he have been. Though it would be an exaggeration to say that he knew very little of the refined conceptual distinctions that consume us today, he was nonetheless not writing as an analytical political philosopher for fellow analytical political philosophers. We should therefore avoid treating and reading him as one. We should think more than twice about interpreting him as a rule utilitarian, an indirect utilitarian, a liberal consequentialist, a negative or positive freedom theorist, or any other such thing. We may indeed find ourselves in Mill. We might even discover that his critics were beginning to criticize him as we now criticize alternative versions of contemporary consequentialism. But it is *we* who always do the finding and discovering.

SIDGWICK

We continue to claim Mill as canonical for better or worse. And we should be claiming Sidgwick as no less canonical for at least three of the reasons alluded to earlier. Firstly, *A Theory of Justice* is a response to *The Methods of Ethics* more than to any other work, even though Rawls could have said so more explicitly. Both Rawlsians and their opponents err in not taking a better account of Sidgwick, which is to say that contemporary liberals, especially contractualists and neo-Kantians, ought to be taking more seriously than they do the entire utilitarian tradition from Bentham and his precursors right up to Hooker today. Political theorists particularly need to pay more attention to utilitarianism and its extended family of novel forms of contemporary consequentialism such as those of Samuel Scheffler, Wayne Sumner, and Amartya Sen.

Secondly, again, Sidgwick's moral theorizing contributed importantly to the beginning of Anglophone conceptual analysis that began flourishing with Moore and that we now take so much for granted. Since what we take for granted, whether as moral philosophers or as political theorists, owes more than a little to Sidgwick, we ought therefore to feature him in our canon for this reason alone.

Finally, if Anscombe is correct that Sidgwick, along with Mill, was so decisive for Anglophone moral philosophy's decline by marginalizing Aristotle and virtue ethics, then this would also be grounds enough alone to rehabilitate the interest in Sidgwick. And even if Anscombe is mistaken, the *fact* that she and others like MacIntyre and Strauss blame classical utilitarians like Sidgwick for causing so much philosophical havoc, should persuade historians of moral and political thought to pay more attention to Sidgwick in order to figure out why he has received this blame.

Historians of moral philosophy have begun reconsidering Sidgwick in recent years. They disagree, though, about just how far Sidgwick fell out of fashion for much of the twentieth century and why. John Deigh insists that *The Methods of Ethics* was never received well in Sidgwick's lifetime, or for decades afterwards, as the 'towering work of British moral philosophy that we [at least some of us anyway] now see it as'.[26] Indeed, Deigh agrees with Schultz that Sidgwick's reputation declined measurably after his death in 1901 though Deigh attributes this decline to developments within the emerging analytic tradition and modern logic, which rendered the intuitionist epistemology grounding *The Methods of Ethics* obsolete.[27]

By contrast, Anthony Skelton has challenged Deigh, arguing that Sidgwick's reputation and influence never abated and remained just as robust after his death as during his lifetime. For Skelton, Sidgwick remained topical right up through W. D. Ross's *The Foundation of Ethics* (1939), which may help account for why Rawls had Sidgwick in mind and in his sights from early on.[28]

Schneewind's remarkable *Sidgwick's Ethics and Victorian Moral Philosophy* resurrected almost single-handedly interest in Sidgwick as a moral philosopher, assuming that Deigh and Schultz are probably more correct than Skelton. Regrettably, moral philosophers' renewed attention to Sidgwick has not translated into political theorists' renewed interest in him, Rawls notwithstanding. Schneewind's study contextualizes Sidgwick beautifully in his own Victorian terms, trying hard not to reconstruct him through our own, often different and highly conceptualized philosophical problems. Schneewind nevertheless sometimes interprets Sidgwick using conceptual terminology that he would have found unfamiliar and maybe even puzzling at first sight

---

[26] John Deigh, 'Some Further Thoughts on Sidgwick's Epistemology', *Utilitas*, 22 (2010), 87. Also see John Deigh, 'Sidgwick's Epistemology', *Utilitas*, 19 (2007), 19.

[27] Schultz also blames declining interest in Sidgwick on the impact of the Bloomsbury Circle on philosophical fashions. See Bart Schultz, *Henry Sidgwick: Eye of the Universe* (Cambridge: Cambridge University Press, 2004), 4. Schultz, moreover, contends that while Sidgwick has indeed become a 'much-prized member of the philosophical canon', some like Alan Donogan have exaggerated his importance especially by seeing Sidgwick as far more significant for us than Mill. For Donagan, writing in the late 1970s, aspiring young philosophers could safely ignore Sidgwick's contemporaries such as Spencer, Green, and Bradley as now philosophically irrelevant. Moreover, they needed not 'expend much labor even on Sidgwick's predecessor and master, John Stuart Mill, or on his pupil and critic, G. E. Moore'. But they dared not ignore *The Methods of Ethics* 'in the principate' of Rawls. See Alan Donagan, 'A New Sidgwick?', *Ethics*, 90 (1980), 283. For Schultz, Mill was no less eminent than Sidgwick who 'took his point of departure' from the 'real' Mill. See Schultz, *Henry Sidgwick: Eye of the Universe*, 14. Furthermore, for Schultz, while much recent utilitarian moral theorizing often references Sidgwick, such appeals are mostly 'opportunistic', p. 255.

[28] Anthony Skelton, 'On Sidgwick's Demise: A Reply to Professor Deigh', *Utilitas*, 22 (2010), 70–7.

in any case. For instance, Schneewind wonders whether the 'central position Sidgwick assigns to rules in the utilitarian method raises the question of whether the version of the theory he works out should be considered a "rule utilitarian" version'.[29] Schneewind ultimately concludes that Sidgwick 'is not a methodological rule utilitarian'.[30]

Now, in asking whether Sidgwick should be considered a 'rule utilitarian', we must ask *by whom*? Clearly, Sidgwick's contemporaries did not consider him one simply because such conceptual considerations were historically unavailable to them. Presumably, then, Schneewind is asking whether he should be considered a 'rule utilitarian' *by us*. But if we are the ones doing the considering, then we are no longer interpreting Sidgwick in his own terms. We are asking whether Sidgwick represents what we now call rule utilitarianism from our later analytical perspective. Asking such questions is entirely legitimate as long as we are sufficiently aware of what we are doing in asking them, as long as we keep firmly in mind that our answers are not so much interpretations as they are first and foremost reconstructions.[31]

My own limited work on Sidgwick has likewise endeavoured to contextualize him by showing how he was received by his Victorian critics as diverse as Spencer and Green. I have also explored how Sidgwick responded to them, often indirectly and implicitly. For example, Chapter VI of Book II, 'Deductive Hedonism', of *The Methods of Ethics* is fundamentally, though not so obviously, a vigorous rejection of Spencer's unconventional deductive utilitarianism, which Sidgwick viewed as wrong-headedly trying to combine *absolute* moral rights with the principle of utility.[32] Though not cast with quite the conceptual meticulousness we have become accustomed to, Sidgwick suggests why indefeasible moral rights and utility are so difficult to reconcile conceptually, why they are such mismatched pieces of conceptual furniture. More so than Mill, Sidgwick therefore helps us think through the conceptual challenges of combining liberalism with utilitarianism. Maybe we should therefore not be

---

[29] J. B. Schneewind, *Sidgwick's Ethics and Victorian Moral Philosophy* (Oxford: Oxford University Press, 1977), 340–1.

[30] Schneewind, *Sidgwick's Ethics*, 348.

[31] Schneewind also says that 'some features of Sidgwick's position may be brought into focus by using the [our rule utilitarian] distinction, if we specify it appropriately'. Schneewind, *Sidgwick's Ethics*, 341. Here, Schneewind appears to want to keep interpretation separate from reconstruction as much as possible. He seems to think that reconstructing complicated, and often ambiguous, past philosophical texts in our later, more carefully worked-out terminology can often assist us in seeing implications and problems not readily apparent to their authors as well as their contemporary proponents and critics. And, in my view just as crucially, by bringing a past text into 'focus' by reconstructing it, we sometimes expose our own analytical deliberations to critical perspectives that we otherwise would not have encountered.

[32] See my 'Deductive Hedonism and the Anxiety of Influence', *Utilitas*, 12 (2001), 329–46, special symposium on Henry Sidgwick. For a discussion of Sidgwick in relation to Green, see my *Utilitarianism and the New Liberalism* (Cambridge: Cambridge University Press, 2007), 54–5.

so surprised that Sidgwick looks to us much more thoroughly utilitarian and decidedly less liberal than Mill.

But we need to be just as careful handling Sidgwick as we are handling Mill. As with Mill, the conceptual discourse available to Sidgwick, and deployed and modified by him, is no longer the same as ours. Handling Sidgwick carefully, interpreting him in his own context and in his own terms, fortunately may be easier than interpreting Mill accordingly. We may be better positioned to minimize reconstructing Sidgwick through the lens of our own conceptual biases and worries than we are regarding Mill. Simply because we have forgotten about Sidgwick far more than we have forgotten about Mill, we have not fallen as much into the lazy habit of appropriating him as a contemporary supposedly addressing us directly. Having been more forgotten than Mill, Sidgwick is easier to engage with less anachronistic prejudice. Because we are therefore better positioned to interpret him less anachronistically, we are more likely to learn from him. We can more profitably take advantage of his different philosophical perspective as a source of provocative critical purchase on our own.

CANONIZING MILL AND FORGETTING SIDGWICK

Berlin is as responsible as anyone for canonizing Mill as a liberal primarily concerned with liberty above all else, therefore causing political theorists to ignore Mill's utilitarianism and tempting them to see him as our contemporary. According to Berlin, Mill 'founded modern liberalism', whose *On Liberty* 'remains the classic statement of the case for individual liberty'. Mill prioritizes liberty, 'that is, the rigid limitation of the right to coerce, because he is sure that men cannot develop and flourish and become fully human unless they are left free from interference by other men within a certain minimum area of their lives, which he regards as—or wishes to make—*inviolable*' (my italics). In sum, at 'the centre of Mill's thought and feeling lies, not his utilitarianism ... but his passionate belief that men are made human by their capacity for choice'.[33] For Berlin, liberty, rather than utility, was the conceptual centrepiece of Mill's

---

[33] Isaiah Berlin, 'John Stuart Mill and the Ends of Life', in Isaiah Berlin, *Four Essays on Liberty* (Oxford: Oxford University Press, 1969), 173, 174, 190, and 192. Berlin's essay on Mill was first delivered as the Robert Waley Cohen Memorial Lecture to The Council of Christians and Jews in London in 1959. It must therefore be read, just like his more famous 1958 'Two Concepts of Liberty', in the context of the aftermath of World War II and the height of the Cold War. Whereas, as mentioned earlier, the latter essay interprets Green, another nineteenth-century English liberal, as a proponent of positive freedom and faults him accordingly, the former essay interprets Mill as a champion of negative freedom who therefore deserves great tribute in light of twentieth-century fascism and communism.

political thinking around which all other concepts, including especially the concept of utility, circled with lesser significance.

Berlin's postwar reading of Mill as a liberal first and as a utilitarian second, combined with Rawls's legacy of so severely tarnishing classical utilitarianism's reputation, continues to handicap interpreting Mill especially among political theorists. They revere Mill as canonical but it is mostly the Mill of *On Liberty* and not the Mill of *Utilitarianism*, even though the latter was published just two years after the former, in 1861. Their prejudice against utilitarianism has, in turn, interfered with their willingness to take up Sidgwick, let alone Bentham. They not only know very little about the utilitarian dimensions of Mill, but next to nothing about Sidgwick, which is, as I have suggested, surprising given Sidgwick's legacy and importance to Rawls.

Moral philosophers, by contrast, can hardly be accused of ignoring Mill's underlying commitment to the principle of utility as his fundamental criterion of right action. Indeed, for some time now, the best Mill scholars (as well as the best Sidgwick scholars) have been moral philosophers and historians of moral philosophy rather than political theorists and contributors to and readers of journals like *Political Theory*. But while moral philosophers have not forgotten that Mill was a utilitarian first and foremost, their versions of Mill are not without distorting fixations. Too often straitjacketed by dichotomous thinking, such as utility vs moral rules, they tend to reconstruct Mill accordingly as we have seen. For many of them, stringent moral rules are logically incompatible with utility. For others, rule utilitarianism is not incoherent and Mill pioneered the way forward. For both contemporary rule utilitarians and their adversaries, Mill is important and original because he tried to accommodate moral rules and utility. Whether he succeeded or not, he has become for proponents and opponents alike the first serious rule utilitarian.

A Theory of Justice has fostered such dichotomized conceptual thinking as well as encouraging us to impose it on Mill. Whereas Berlin has encouraged political theorists to ignore Mill's utilitarianism altogether, Rawls has encouraged too many moral philosophers to dismiss all versions of utilitarianism as incompatible with liberalism. Once again, Rawls's legacy has been considerable in ways he probably never intended. Moreover, by contrasting classical utilitarianism with his Kantian constructivist alternative, he prompted moral philosophers to read the history of modern moral philosophy too simplistically as a struggle between intuitionism and utilitarianism initially, and then subsequently as a clash between improved versions of rule utilitarianism and neo-Kantianism. Consequently, in the aftermath of Rawls, many moral theorists have focused on showing why rule utilitarianism does or does not work and, in so far as it does not, why deontological alternatives are much to be preferred.

In sum, Rawlsian 'philosophical liberalism', to borrow Freeden's terminology again, has cut a wide and powerful wake. It has reinvigorated political theorizing, but at the cost of oversimplifying the liberal tradition by diluting its complexity and weakening its conceptual flexibility, thus cramping its discourse and compressing its conversation. 'Philosophical liberalism's' impact on *moral*, and not just *political*, theorizing has been no less problematic. As I have been suggesting, it has encouraged dualistic thinking, pitting, for instance, deontology against consequentialism and rights and moral rules against utility. It has desensitized us to the complexity of moral philosophizing, including the history of this complexity, much like it has desensitized us to the liberal tradition's complexity. And in desensitizing us to the former complexity, it has simultaneously marginalized as eclectic, confused, and lacking analytical rigour past moral philosophers who cannot be read through the straitjacket of our dualistic thinking. It forgets what it refuses to see and then cannot see what it has forgotten. It then proceeds to discover what it has forgotten, mistaking this rediscovery for originality. And so it goes with recent sophisticated analytical attempts to accommodate stringent moral rights with utility. And so it also goes with recent equally sophisticated interpretations of Mill, which too often seem more novel than they really are. While many contemporary Mill scholars (moral philosophers and *not* political theorists) have explored the purported incoherence of Mill's 'rule' utilitarianism with nuance, skill, and logical rigour, Mill's contemporary critics like Bradley had long before identified this problem as elemental for Mill. Though Bradley knew nothing of what *we* call rule utilitarianism such as so admirably defended recently with great precision by Hooker and others, he could certainly spot a potential theoretical inconsistency of significant import when he saw one.

CONCLUSION

Rorty contrasts Kant with Dewey as exemplifying the two basic modes of moral philosophical discourse. Kantians, following misbegotten philosophical ambitions going back to Plato, are forever 'trying to shortcut the ongoing calculation of consequences by appealing to something stable and permanent, something whose authority is not subject to empirical test'. Deweyans and fellow-travelling Hegelian historicists like Green, on the other hand, recognize that moral principles are pragmatic responses to our changing circumstances, which stabilize as intuitions only 'in so far as they lead [typically and repeatedly] to good consequences'.[34]

---

[34] Richard Rorty, 'Kant vs. Dewey', in *Philosophy as Cultural Politics*, 192. Dewey was early on influenced by Green, so Rorty's mentioning him in conjunction with Dewey is not coincidental. See, for instance, John Dewey, 'Self-Realization as a Moral Ideal', *Philosophical Review*, 2 (1893), 652–64. Rorty's essay does not mention Sidgwick despite Rorty's praise for Rawls's reflective

By characterizing modern moral philosophy as an ongoing quarrel captured by the differences between Kant and Dewey, Rorty engages in the kind of dichotomized history of philosophizing that is best avoided. Nevertheless, however contrived his characterization, it underscores why moral philosophers need to pay more attention to Green and why political theorists need to pay more attention not just to him but to utilitarians as well. Political theorists will likely continue ignoring classical utilitarianism for the most part though. They have got too used to reconstructing the liberal tradition by applying conceptual templates inherited disproportionately from *A Theory of Justice*. They have become too comfortable with Rawls's taste for arranging conceptual furniture, which disregarded all arrangements that feature utility as a centrepiece. We still need more political theorists to do for classical utilitarianism what Freeden has been doing for new liberals, never forgetting, of course, that *doing for* is always *doing to* in some measure.

Political theorists ought therefore to be reading more Green along with Dewey as well as Hegel, utilitarians, and the like. And if they should be reading more Green, then they should also be reading more new liberals like Hobhouse, Hobson, and Ritchie. Freeden has known all of this for a long time and has worked hard to show us how we should go about doing it. He has long appreciated the magnitude of new liberals for fashioning novel conceptual permutations, which have too often been dismissed by Rawlsians as clumsy at best and just really bad philosophizing at worst. Political theorists, in sum, need to take Green and new liberals more earnestly no less than they also need to take Sidgwick's *The Methods of Ethics* and Mill's *Utilitarianism* earnestly.[35]

---

equilibrium and for Schneewind's account of how moral philosophizing should be done. For Rorty, following Schneewind, moral theorizing never consists of deducing inferences from purported rational or self-evident moral principles: 'Rather, when we find such a principle plausible, and realize that accepting it would lead us to change our ways, we attempt to obtain what John Rawls calls "reflective equilibrium." That is, we go back and forth between the proposed principle and our old intuitions, trying to fabricate a new practical identity that will do some justice to both. This involves imagining what our community would be like if it changed its ways, and what we would be like as a member of this reformed community. It is a detailed comparison of imagined selves, situations and communities that does the trick, not argument from principles. Formulation of general principles is sometimes useful, but only as a tool for summarizing the results of imagining such alternatives', p. 201.

[35] I have tried to do some of this stocktaking in *Utilitarianism and the New Liberalism*. More work also needs to be done by political theorists on the British idealists along the lines of Peter Nicholson's carefully crafted *The Political Philosophy of the British Idealists* (Cambridge: Cambridge University Press, 1990) and Colin Tyler's *Idealist Political Philosophy* (London: Continuum, 2006).

8

Political Ideology and Political Theory: Reflections on an Awkward Partnership

Andrew Vincent

INTRODUCTION

There are two concepts that have figured in virtually all writings on politics, from the late nineteenth century to the present day: that is, ideology and political theory. This does not mean that the large bulk of such usage has been precise. Far from it, their deployment in political or social discussion frequently relies on vagueness. Historically, ideology is probably the more promiscuous of the conceptual duo.[1] The present essay is not designed to provide any comprehensive genealogy of the two concepts. Rather, it focuses on something more specific: namely, the *relationship* between them. It is the core argument of this essay that this *relationship* has not really been clearly delineated. Sometimes the terms are taken as synonyms, at other points they are sworn conceptual enemies. However, they continue to subsist, for historical and conceptual reasons, as continuous, if often profoundly reluctant bedfellows. The present argument is not denying that there have been many conceptions of this relationship. However there has never been a systematic and *comprehensive overview* of the diverse ways in which the relation has been understood. The argument concentrates on the internal structure of the *relation* between political theory and ideology. It does not aim to resolve this relation, although it will indicate more profitable ways of dealing with it.

After a very brief introduction concerning the concepts of political theory and ideology, the debate over the relationship between them will be analysed and presented systematically in terms of the following typology. First, it will unpick attempts to fully integrate ideology and political theory; in other words to make the two terms virtually indistinguishable. This is referred to as the

---

[1] It can indicate virtually any form of thinking. In fact, thinking itself—in some uses—can become ideology.

integration thesis. Second, the analysis turns to the opposite stance, namely, the efforts to completely demarcate their usage. This is categorized as the *segregation thesis*. In addition, both the integration and segregation arguments have *positive* and *negative* poles, that is to say, there are both negative and positive sets of reasons for both integration and segregation. This dimension of the analysis therefore gives rise to two further subcategories for each thesis. This analytical matrix will form the structure for the discussion. The paper concludes on the issue of future strategies for research on the relationship.

IDEOLOGY AND POLITICAL THEORY

One prior historical point to mention here is that in examining the relation between these two concepts we are dealing with something which (despite appearances) is comparatively novel. The compound term 'political theory' is of fairly recent historical vintage, certainly in the manner that we now employ it.[2] It is a product largely of the late nineteenth and early twentieth centuries. In the mid nineteenth century, the word 'theory' often had pejorative connotations, being seen as equivalent to 'mere speculation' or 'untested facts'.[3] In this context, the compound term political theory in the nineteenth century was probably closer in meaning to our current sense of political utopianism. Political theory, as a more practically orientated form of justificatory value-based reasoning, only became a commonplace (as distinct from notions such as utopianism or ideology) during the twentieth century.[4] Similarly, as is well known, the concept of ideology is also a neologism dating from the early 1800s, and not in any recognizable form until the 1840s, and again, not in any popular format until the early twentieth century.[5] Its first use focused on the Enlightenment-oriented idea of an 'empirical science of ideas'.[6] It had no immediate political connotations, certainly not until minimally the 1830s. In Marx and Engels's usage, in the 1840s, it took on a more definite political and critical sense, although with a very particular theoretical orientation. It was not

---

[2] For a fuller discussion of this point see Andrew Vincent, *The Nature of Political Theory* (Oxford: Oxford University Press, 2004), chs. 1 and 2.

[3] This is still reflected in some of the senses indicated in the *OED*, namely, where a theory can denote a 'mere hypothesis or conjecture'.

[4] Initially, no hard and fast distinction is drawn between political philosophy and political theory. In many ways, the relation between these terms remains unresolved and often obfuscates the way we discuss the whole question.

[5] See Andrew Vincent, *Modern Political Ideologies*, 3rd edition (Oxford: Blackwell-Wiley, 2009), ch. 1; also Michael Freeden, *Ideologies and Political Theory* (Oxford: Oxford University Press, 1996), ch. 1.

[6] See Brian Head, *Ideology and Social Science: Destutt de Tracy and French Liberalism* (Hague: Martinus Nijhoff, 1985).

until the mid twentieth century that it really came into its own within the vernaculars of both political and social science-based discussion. It is also at this point that its rather peculiar relation with political theory comes to the fore. Given that 'political theory' was also, as indicated above, etymologically a somewhat novel term, also dating (in more popular usage) from the later nineteenth century, neither concept can really claim great longevity, except rhetorically or imaginatively. Oddly, though, despite the commonplace usage of ideology in both academic and ordinary speech, it still remains the often-vilified cousin of political theory. The argument now turns to the conceptual matrix (outlined above), which allows an examination of the various ways in which the relation between political theory and ideology has been configured over the last two hundred years.

NEGATIVE INTEGRATION

Thus, beginning with the *negative integration* thesis: one of the first to address the relation (in a somewhat indirect way) between political theory and ideology was Karl Marx. Without delving into the minutiae of Marx's adoption of the term ideology, the broad upshot of his position—certainly from the late 1840s onwards—was that political theory and political ideology should be considered largely synonymous; although it is still never wholly clear why Marx adopted the concept 'ideology' as such. However, Marx and the subsequent Marxist tradition do present a complex, variegated picture. Primarily, political theory and ideology were reduced to more or less the same category, and *both* regularly denoted illusion or mystification of actual social and political realities. As is well known, for Marx the material conditions of economic life, understood via political economy, form the *real* basis to social and political existence. Cultural, ideational, and political structures could only be understood via these material conditions and the ensuing class struggles. Since the material basis was considered primary, all ideas had to be explained via their complex connection to the material base. They could not be explained in themselves. They therefore comprised the 'ideology' of a society, an ideology that was constituted through the conflicts that existed between certain classes. Marx, in one of his synoptic semi-autobiographical pieces of writing, the *Preface to the Critique of Political Economy*, famously called the above idea the 'leading thread' of his studies.[7] It is understandable, in this reading, that Friedrich Engels, Rosa Luxemburg, Karl Korsch, and V. I. Lenin, amongst many others, should thus also have configured ideology (including

---

[7] Karl Marx and Friedrich Engels, *Selected Writings* (London: Lawrence & Wishart, 1968), 182.

within this undifferentiated concept the idea of political theory) as illusion or false consciousness. The chief delusion of ideology is its inability to see its own class and material base and the manner in which it distorts consciousness. The history of ideology (and thus political theory) is therefore subsumable under a history of class interests. In fact, to believe in ideology and its purported veracity is equivalent to being an 'Idealist' (in the philosophical sense). Very crudely, in the Idealist case, ideas or consciousness become crucial determinants of the characterization of reality. Political theorists, in this critical reading, are quite literally professional ideologists, that is, skilled purveyors of social and political illusions. The social and particularly economic sciences are therefore needed, in turn, to explain the eruptions of ideology and political theory, within a social scientific framework. Put cleanly, ideology and political theory both become 'social objects' to be explained within the broader structure of the social or economic sciences.

Switching focus slightly to a resonant theoretical development: much twentieth-century empirical sociology—both structural and functional—has also viewed both political ideas and ideologies in a parallel manner to Marxism, that is, as aspects of a broader 'science of society'. In fact, for sociologists such as Émile Durkheim and Talcott Parsons, sociology per se contained a complete and comprehensive social epistemology, which provided clear and unequivocal answers to all the older classical problems of social and political knowledge. Humans (and their cognitive existence) thus had no distinctive or unique attributes outside of a general theory of society, understood as a collective whole. A science of society could, as such, therefore explain more adequately and thoroughly the character and substance of the key issues that had previously engaged political theorists and ideologists.

With the rise of empirically oriented social and economic theory in the mid twentieth century, the 'illusory' or 'social object' status of both political theory and ideology came markedly to the fore. The general frame, for example, of the 'end of ideology' perspective in the 1950s and 1960s caught this general drift of argument. Social science, in effect, offered a general science of society. The development of empirically oriented theories conventionally demanded value-free rigour and clear verification or falsification processes unsullied by appeals to justificatory political theory or ideology.

The only salvation (or future) for either political theory or ideology was therefore to mutate into a helpmate for some form of rigorous empirical theory, namely, where viable social scientific hypotheses could be falsified or verified. This, of course, was the general view of the behavioural movement in social science during the 1950s and 1960s, although it is an idea that still hovers under the rubric of rational choice theory. Consequently, David Easton, amongst a number of North American empirical theorists, was clear that political theory, in the future, would have to be much more empirically rigorous in order to survive academically. Easton, in his famous article, 'The

Decline of Political Theory' (1951), saw political theorists in general as simply academic parasites, feeding on past ideas and retailing useless information about purported universal values, with little or no grasp of complex empirical realities. Herbert Simon, at the same time, bewailed that 'there will be no progress in political philosophy if we continue to think and write in the loose, literary, metaphysical style...The standard of rigour that is tolerated in political theory would not receive a passing grade in an elementary course in logic'.[8] In fact, in Easton's vision a purified political theory must *become* empirical theory. As William C. Mitchell signalled optimistically in 1969, political theory in the future 'will become increasingly logical, deductive, and mathematical. In terms of its content we will make increasing use of economic theory, game theory, decision theory, welfare economics, and public finance'.[9]

In summary, both political theory and political ideology were seen to persist with a use of theory 'that lingered from an earlier period in the discipline's history'. As James Farr has commented:

> In being empirical and explanatory...theory in behavioural research was to be value-free and objective. There was, it was argued, a logical gulf between fact and value, between "is" and "ought", which in no way could be spanned. Normative topics like freedom, justice, or authority—the staple of a pre-scientific study of politics—were best understood in terms of one's subjective emotions or expressive states. They were also laced with a "strong dose of metaphysical discourse"[10]

For the end-of-ideology proponents, both ideologies and political theories could serve indirect cohesive functions in developing immature societies; however, in large industrialized democratic societies, where empirical social science had developed in sophisticated ways, they were largely redundant or merely decorative practices. As Edward Shils commented, 'science is not and never has been part of an ideological culture. Indeed the spirit in which science works is alien to ideology'.[11] For the empirical theorists of the end-of-ideology school, consensus on basic social, economic, and political values had been largely agreed. All the rest (including the substance of both ideology and political theory) was mere gesture and intellectual froth. The upshot therefore of the negative integration thesis was, in more general terms, the prioritizing of

---

[8] Herbert Simon, 'The Development of the Theory of Democratic Administration: Replies and Comments', *American Political Science Review*, 46 (1952), 494–6. See also David Easton, 'The Decline of Modern Political Theory', *Journal of Politics*, 13 (1951), 36–58.

[9] William C. Mitchell, 'The Shape of Political Theory to Come: From Political Sociology to Political Economy', in S. M. Lipset (ed.), *Politics and the Social Sciences* (New York: Oxford University Press), 129–30.

[10] See James Farr and Raymond Seidelman (eds.), *Discipline and History: Political Science in the United States* (Ann Arbor: University of Michigan Press, 1993), 204. See also Heinz Eulau, *The Behavioural Persuasion in Politics* (New York: Random House, 1962), 8–10.

[11] Edward Shils, 'The Concept and Function of Ideology', *International Encyclopaedia of the Social Sciences*, VII (1968), 74.

empirical theory, the diminution of political theory and ideology (as basically part of the same outdated pre-modern category) and their ultimate absorption into empirical theory.

The only slight alleviation to this latter argument was the development of an 'under-labourer' or second-order conception of political philosophy in the same period. The growth of this latter perspective in political theory coincided directly with the rise of empirical political theory, behavioural political science, and the end-of-ideology debates of the 1950s and 1960s. The relation between these elements was not fortuitous. There was some mutual massaging taking place. Empirical political science could pose as the 'first-order' provider of genuine empirical political knowledge, for which a much more circumscribed political theory could function as a 'second-order' handmaid, clarifying speech and logic and acting as a philosophical gatekeeper for genuine empirical social science. The earliest and most strident expression of this new under-labourer idea was logical positivism. Logical positivism developed initially in the 1920s and 1930s in Vienna amongst a group of mathematicians, scientists, and philosophers. Its most notable philosophical voices were Moritz Schlick, Rudolf Carnap, Friedrich Waismann, Otto von Neurath, Herbert Feigl, and Victor Kraft. In Britain, the most well-known exponent was Alfred Ayer. However, many of the initial Viennese group, such as Carnap and Feigl, became émigrés to North America during the 1930s and had a considerable impact on the burgeoning empirical perspective within political studies.[12] The basic premises of this logical positivism were, first, a strong belief in empiricism, namely that all genuine knowledge was founded on testable experience, and, second, that mathematics and logic were independent of direct experience. Logical positivism, in particular, had a vision of a unified scientific enterprise across all the disciplines. The only valid knowledge was therefore scientific. This argument was central to the vision of empirical theory. It followed that any attempt to advance normative or ideological theory was treated with profound suspicion. Both were regarded as equally flawed and superfluous enterprises. Their salvation lay in empiricism.

POSITIVE INTEGRATION

Moving to the second component of the matrix concerned with *positive integration*: in this scenario the integration of political theory and political ideology is accepted, but regarded optimistically. It is not a matter of any theoretical concern that the two concepts are synonymous. There are again, however, different perspectives and sets of reasons within this general

---

[12] In Carnap's case, for example, at the University of Chicago, his courses were of great interest to the new generation of American political scientists.

analytical argument to account for this synonymy. Many, for example, adhere unwittingly (on a common-sense level) to the positive integration of these terms, namely, where ideology becomes simply a verbal shorthand—in ordinary discourse—for political theory. Thus, one often encounters quite unself conscious references to 'liberal ideology', 'feminist ideology', and the like, in discussions which otherwise appear to be quite sophisticated academic debates. Ideology, in this sense, can thus just *appear* as a synonym for political theory and vice versa.

Ironically, this more unwitting merging of concepts appears within the revisionist history of political theory writings from the 1970s. This is, in fact, doubly ironic given the movement's overtly close attention to language and context, and the avoidance of conceptual anachronism.[13] If we bear in mind here that the term 'ideology' itself is a comparatively recent neologism, dating from the early 1800s, carrying a contested baggage of uses, it is, to say the least, odd to find Quentin Skinner, in a number of writings, referring to, for example, 'History and Ideology in the English Revolution' or 'The Ideological Context of Hobbes' Political Thought'.[14] James Tully, explicating Skinner's method, also reflects this underlying synonymy. Thus, for Tully, the new historical method of the revisionist writers demands that we place all political theory texts in an 'ideological context'. Tully continues that an ideology for Skinner 'is a language of politics defined by its conventions and employed by a number of writers. Thus, scholasticism, humanism, Lutheranism and Calvinism are ideologies and both scholasticism and humanism comprise the general ideological context of the Italian city-states during the Renaissance'.[15] Luther and Calvin thus become mainstream political ideologists. Placing an idea or text in context—the mantra of revisionist theories—makes 'political theory...a part of politics, and the questions it treats are the effects of political action'. Tully continues that 'since a political ideology represents a political action...to change some of the conventions of the ideology is to change the way in which some of that political action is represented'.[16] Consequently, Tully describes Skinner's whole substantive two-volume *The Foundations of Modern Political Thought* (1976) as 'a map of the great political ideologies of early modern Europe'.[17] Thus, political theory and ideology become—within this general methodological account—indissolubly and positively *one and the same* entity. One searches in vain, in such contextualist methodological

---

[13] See Margaret Leslie, 'In Defence of Anachronism', *Political Studies*, 18 (1970), 433–47.
[14] See Quentin Skinner, 'History and Ideology in the English Revolution', *Historical Journal*, 8 (1965), 151–78 and his 'The Ideological Context of Hobbes' Political Thought', *Historical Journal*, 9 (1966), 286–317.
[15] James Tully (ed.), *Meaning and Context: Quentin Skinner and His Critics* (Cambridge: Polity Press, 1988), 9.
[16] Tully, *Meaning and Context*, 10–11.
[17] Tully, *Meaning and Context*, 12.

writings, for a glimmering of recognition that the concept of ideology itself is a deeply troubled, comparatively quite new idea, containing deep unresolved internal tensions.

However, not all in this methodological sphere are quite as unacquainted with the idiosyncratic genealogy of the concept of ideology. In an open and quite explicit use of ideology to denote both political activism and political theory, Richard Ashcraft commented that, 'only an ideologically grounded approach with respect to current political problems can provide a bridge between the traditions of political philosophy and the perception of what counts as "political" phenomena'.[18] Political theorists and philosophers are, or should be, considered therefore as unequivocal ideologists. In response to the idea that philosophy (in particular) is something higher, critical, or more balanced than ideology, Ashcraft responds, 'how is it even possible for...epistemological presuppositions to stand apart from the very conflict they propose to "study" and are assumed to transcend'.[19] Ashcraft directs his critical fire here at both historians of political theory and analytical political philosophy, arguing that 'some of the responsibility for the divorce of traditional political theory from present concerns of political life rests squarely with those teachers of political theory who have encapsulated the meaning of politics within the frozen worlds of "analysis" or "history"'.[20] As Ashcraft continues, for many political philosophers, the title ideologist is consequently often regarded as 'the original sin'.[21] Ideology, in turn, appears to relinquish all claims to universality. For Ashcraft, however, this particular perception of universality is well worth losing. He suggests that most political theorists in the past *were* actually concerned about problems in society (at a particular time or historical juncture) and were quite rightly—what we now think of as—political ideologists. To make someone such as Hobbes into an abstract universalist political theorist is just a modern academically inspired self-indulgence.

Although it is an abrupt intellectual jump, it is nonetheless worth noting here, on this positive integration argument, that twentieth-century neo-Marxism has not always adopted the negative integration argument. Unexpectedly, neo-Marxism can also take a very positive view of the integration of political theory and ideology. Thus, probably the most influential twentieth-century Marxist, Antonio Gramsci (although the earlier writings of György Lukács, such as *History and Class Consciousness* (1968), would also be deeply relevant on this same point), saw proletarian ideology as a profoundly effective tool of political struggle against bourgeois ideology. The more Crocean-inspired notion

---

[18] Richard Ashcraft, 'On the Problem of Methodology and the Nature of Political Theory', *Political Theory*, 3 (1975), 20.
[19] Ashcraft, 'Problem of Methodology', 26.
[20] Ashcraft, 'Problem of Methodology', 19.
[21] Richard Ashcraft, 'Political Theory and the Problem of Ideology', *Journal of Politics*, 42 (1980), 695.

of the 'hegemony' of political ideas, developed in his *Prison Notebooks* (1929–35), was thus considered by Gramsci of immense importance in revolutionary struggle. Political theorizing consequently took on a 'partial autonomy' from the material base. In this context, there could be an authentic and effective Marxist ideology (understood as *synonymous* with political theory), which could function as a crucial aspect of effectual class struggle. In a similar manner to Ashcraft, Gramsci argued that intellectual argument could be used systematically to bring about social and political change. In fact this was its *raison d'être*. Socialist intellectuals—as practising ideologists—could formulate an effective counter-hegemony. Aspects of this 'partial autonomy' argument are reflected in a wide range of twentieth-century theorists, such as Ernesto Laclau, Stuart Hall, Edward Said, Terry Eagleton, or more obliquely Pierre Bourdieu.[22] This is also the general perspective undergirding a great deal of mid to late twentieth-century 'critical theory' writing on ideology. Roughly the same argument has also been a mainstay of much constructivist theorizing in the late twentieth century. Ideology and political theory are envisaged as being both equally enmeshed in social action. To analyse this process is the self-appointed task of, for example, discourse analysis, structuralist-inclined Marxism, critical theory, psychoanalysis, semiotics, and much postmodern genealogy. *All* these theoretical accounts stress the constructive or engaged role of language.[23]

Another related dimension to the above critique concerns the traditions of twentieth-century non-foundationalism. Although not directly focused on the integration thesis, there have been a number of arguments within this non-foundational tradition (taken as a broad category), which, once again, facilitate the conceptual overlap of political theory and ideology. For example, for non-foundationalists there are no givens and no raw empirical data in the world. The idea of an empirical 'given' is seen as a myth to be debunked.

In a parallel theoretical vein, for Richard Rorty poetic creativity replaces representational accounts of reality; irony and gaming are set over against epistemological claims. Rorty's work embodies, in many ways, the general drift of this whole non-foundationalist argument. He suggests, for example, the utter uselessness of 'the distinction between "ideology" and a form of

---

[22] 'Symbolic violence', which is developed in a number of Pierre Bourdieu's works, is largely his way of rethinking Gramsci's concept of hegemony. See Pierre Bourdieu, *Outline of a Theory of Practice* (Cambridge: Cambridge University Press, 1977), 192; for his broader unease with the term ideology, see his *Pascalian Meditations* (Cambridge: Polity, 2000), 181.

[23] This latter critique of language was especially characteristic of Michel Foucault's writings. Foucault suggested abandoning the concepts of ideology and political theory altogether. They would be replaced by painstaking genealogical explanation, which examined *how* certain discourses and regimes of truth (*epistemes*) came about. See Michel Foucault, 'What is Critique?', trans. K. P. Geiman, in James Schmidt (ed.), *What is Enlightenment? Eighteenth Century Answers and Twentieth Century Questions* (Berkeley and London: University of California Press, 1996), 393.

thought... which escapes being "ideology".[24] In this context, there are no clear criteria to differentiate them. If political philosophy still claims a special universal insight into the world, as distinct from other forms of thought, such as ideology, then it is quite simply mistaken. Consequently for the non-foundationalist, the representational perspective of some philosophers is better understood as a *pathology* rather than philosophy. As to the relation between political theory and ideology, the upshot of the above range of arguments integrated is clear on one level. The two terms minimally are considered to be positively integrated.

NEGATIVE SEGREGATION

However, the above picture here is still inadequate in terms of encompassing the diverse ways in which the *relation* has been configured. The discussion turns at this point to what is termed the *negative segregation* thesis. This dimension forms the more conventional response of much mid to late twentieth-century Anglo-American political theory. A common and pervasive view of philosophy during the twentieth century has been to see it as a more elevated, sophisticated, and critical practice. No matter what the philosophy espoused, it is seen as distinct from ideology. The most characteristic conception invoked of ideology is that of a tainted, uncritical, or debased product, which lacks all the virtues of political philosophy. In this interpretation, political philosophy (or theory) is generally marked out by a reflective openness, intellectual rigour, critical distance, a focus on following the logic of the argument regardless, and an awareness of human experience that transcends the partialities of political struggles. Ideology, on the other hand, is viewed as the precise opposite. It closes reflection, throws itself into partisan struggle, its ideas are designed instrumentally to manipulate actors, close argument, and ultimately to achieve political power. It therefore has no concern with truth.

A large number of twentieth-century political theorists have held variations of the above argument: for example, Dante Germino, Hannah Arendt, Michael Oakeshott, Eric Voegelin, and Leo Strauss.[25] Strauss was quite typical here of a more general trend. Philosophy was seen as an ancient quest for wisdom and universal knowledge, that is, 'the knowledge of God, the world and man'.[26] Political ideology, however, was wholly indifferent to the distinction between

---

[24] Richard Rorty, *Contingency, Irony and Solidarity* (Cambridge: Cambridge University Press, 1989), 59.
[25] See, for example, Dante Germino, *Beyond Ideology: The Revival of Political Theory* (Chicago: Chicago University Press, 1976) or Michael Oakeshott, *Rationalism in Politics and Other Essays* (London: Methuen, 1962).
[26] Leo Strauss, *What is Political Philosophy?* (Illinois: The Free Press, 1959), 11.

knowledge and opinion, was tied indissolubly to historical contingencies, and was concerned with the uncritical espousal of myths over knowledge. Ideology denoted for Strauss both modernity and nihilism. The broader theme that underpinned this argument, in Strauss, was the debate between the ancients and moderns. For Strauss, the modern era has seen essentially a deeply injurious and nihilistic decline of political philosophy *into* ideology.

Unexpectedly, this negative appraisal was also reflected, in different terminology, in the twentieth-century analytic and linguistic tradition of political philosophy. In logical positivism (as indicated earlier), for example, philosophy was viewed as a second-order activity. It did not contribute any first-order knowledge, as in the empirically based natural sciences.[27] Propositions, which might loosely be grouped under the label 'normative' or 'metaphysical' or 'ideological', did not tell us about the world; rather they revealed the emotional or psychological states of the individuals who uttered them. In this sense, ideology, with other evaluative and normative domains of thought, became equivalent to subjective emotional gush. Further, in early ordinary-language philosophy, the task of philosophy was perceived to pay close attention to the ordinary uses of words and concepts. However, the ordinary-language perspective was still largely in agreement with logical positivism that philosophy could not include any justifications or prescriptions. The same point held for the philosophy of the later Wittgenstein, in relation to *The Philosophical Investigations* (1953). Political philosophy definitely had a more substantive role to play here, but it was still a second-order activity distinct from any direct normative claims.

One important facet of the portrayals of political philosophy during this period was still the implicit or explicit separation from ideology. Ideology, in this case, always looks suspect. It was this kind of analysis which forms the backdrop to the bulk of Anglo-American political philosophy from the mid to late twentieth century. Thus, for example, David Raphael—in a popular political-theory textbook from 1976—concluded that ideology is simply 'a prescriptive doctrine that is not supported by argument', although he offers no argument for this assertion. In other words, ideology was simply equivalent to subjective emotion. This has been a widely accepted credo, even to the present day.[28] This might be described as the standard liturgy of more analytically inclined conceptual introductions to political theory, throughout the second half of the twentieth century.

---

[27] As T. D. Weldon remarked: 'It is not the job of philosophy to provide new information about politics...or any other matters of fact. Philosophical problems are entirely second order problems', T. D. Weldon, *The Vocabulary of Politics* (Middlesex: Penguin, 1953), 22.
[28] See D. D. Raphael, *Problems of Political Philosophy* (London: Macmillan, 1976), 17; for similar judgements see Alan Gewirth, *Political Philosophy* (New York: Macmillan, 1965), 2, or Gerald Gaus, *Political Concepts and Political Theories* (Boulder Colorado: Westview Press, 2000), 36–42.

Even for significant normative political thinkers, such as John Rawls, a similar background credo holds. In his *Political Liberalism* (1993), Rawls argued, for example, that philosophical abstraction was always required when social divisions were deep. He commented that in 'political philosophy the work of abstraction is set in motion by deep conflict'. He continues: 'Only ideologues...fail to experience deep conflicts'.[29] Again, Rawls offered no argument concerning the point that ideology (*vis-à-vis* 'ideologues') never deals with either deep conflict or abstraction. Ideology appears, once again, as relatively simple-minded and unreflective prejudice, which simply embodies the intractable content of social and political conflicts. In this context Rawls equates liberalism with an abstracted philosophical perspective.

However, contrary to Rawls's argument, political ideology in general is usually abstract through and through and 'liberal ideology' (in its various formats) has always, in fact, suggested exactly the same kind of reasonable agenda that Rawls advocates. It is not quite clear here where liberal ideology ends and where liberal political philosophy begins. Further, the fact, for example, that Rawls's writings were often utilized extensively during the intense 1980s *ideological* debates in Britain and America over public policy and social justice, might make one pause for a momentary reflection as to precisely how distanced Rawls's work is from ideology. Despite what its promoters and advocates say, the above negative segregation of political philosophy and ideology is not a time-honoured immemorial position concerning the real nature of philosophy, but is rather part of the theoretical stratagem of a very specific perception of mid-twentieth-century political theory. However, the general upshot of these arguments is still to demarcate political theory and ideology, usually on stringent philosophical grounds. In this case political theory presents us, prima facie, with a more reasonable and universalist face, set against the severe limitations and narrowness built into the practice of ideology.

POSITIVE SEGREGATION

The negative segregation argument held a dominant position, particularly within the Anglo-American academy, up to the later 1990s. This was true for those both within as well as those outside the more mainstream analytically inclined tradition in political theory. Thus, despite their other substantive differences, John Rawls, Brian Barry, Michael Oakeshott, and Leo Strauss were *all* equally adamant that the conceptual segregation between political

---

[29] John Rawls, *Political Liberalism* (New York: Columbia University Press, 1993), 44.

theory and ideology had to be maintained and that, in the final analysis, ideology was the distorting, weak-minded, and corrupting influence. However, this argument also left a series of unresolved questions. Had political theory successfully demarcated itself from ideology? Did political theory actually ever seriously address itself to the realities of everyday politics? What was the exact relation between, for example, liberal political philosophy and liberal political ideology? These questions, amongst others, gave rise to the final and most neglected set of arguments, focused on the *positive segregation* of political philosophy and ideology. The nub of this set of arguments agrees that there are marked differences between the practices of political theory and ideology, but argues conversely that both (in a more ecumenical sense) make a valuable and unique contribution to our social and political understanding. This body of argument represents a more recent intervention in the debate (although it clearly has antecedents). To date it has not had that many proponents. Ecumenism never works quite as well as vigorous principled proselytism.

The intellectual root for one important dimension of this approach can be found in the writings of Clifford Geertz, for example, in his essay 'Ideology as a Cultural System' (1964). Geertz is not directly concerned with the 'relation' question—although the relation of ideology and science does figure. Nonetheless, his essay is immensely suggestive. In effect, Geertz sees the bulk of the social sciences as embodying a 'flattened' and distinctly utilitarian view of human mentalities. He therefore reconfigures human thought semiotically, that is as the manipulation of symbol systems.[30] In effect, humans make themselves, or construct themselves, by means of the cultural symbol systems to hand. Philosophers such as Ernst Cassirer in *The Philosophy of Symbolic Forms* (1955) and Nelson Goodman in *Ways of Worldmaking* (1978) had also suggested something very similar to this. However, for Geertz, every conscious perception is 'an act of recognition, a paring in which an object (or an event, an act, an emotion) is identified by placing it against the background of an appropriate symbol'. Social action is therefore always symbolically mediated. Geertz integrates, in part, the more negative reading of ideology here by suggesting that symbols can *both* distort *and* legitimate. We perceive, understand, judge, and manipulate the world through symbol systems. He adds that it is 'not truth that varies with social, psychological, and cultural contexts but the symbols we construct in our...attempts to grasp it'. Thus, cultural symbol systems (such as ideologies) become 'extrinsic sources of information' and 'templates or blueprints for organizing social and psychological processes'. In this sense, for Geertz, ideologies should be seen as ordered systems of symbols—that is, elaborate metaphors that embody social meanings. They provide cognitive symbolic maps that order our social and political space.

---

[30] Semiotics refers to theories regarding symbolism and how people glean meaning from words, sounds, and pictures.

As Geertz comments, 'it is through the construction of ideologies, schematic images of social order, that man makes himself for better or worse a political animal'.[31] One implication of this is that, given that symbol systems do differ quite extensively, there will inevitably be competing ideologies that mark out divergent paths. Diversity, pluralism, and complexity are thus unavoidable in politics.

What is significant about Geertz's semiotic approach to ideology is that he makes it a source of valuable 'extrinsic meaning'. Ideology is not a distortion of some 'other' reality. The cultural symbols constituting ideology *are* the social and political reality. All social action is therefore symbolically mediated and ideology performs that mediating role. It is the language of *actual political life*. Ideology therefore authorizes, legitimates, and enables everyday human understanding.

Although Geertz's focused reflections on political theory are few and far between, he does nonetheless have certain critical observations on the topic, which, if anything, weaken the role of political theory as against ideology. In one late essay, he thus remarks that one problem is that contemporary 'political theorists tend to operate at levels well above [the] thickets of characterizations, distinctions, particularities'. With their eyes firmly set on rationally purifying certain core values, such as justice or equality, they tend to drift high above ordinary human complexity, 'perhaps for fear that descending into it will expose them to the sort of endless, conflicting detail that so often overwhelms anthropologists'. Such thickets of everyday detail for the political theorist also appear too 'emotional, creaturely, irrational, dangerous'.[32] Political theory thus often stays the intellectual course with 'synoptic musings about essentialized principles'.[33] For Geertz, what is needed in the future is a more capacious and ecumenical sense of political theory, namely one that, in addition to pure reflection, tries to confront and understand such complexity. It will therefore aim 'to expose and interrogate the order of difference, rather than perfecting classroom visions of Hobbesian war or Kantian concord'. Writing in 2000, Geertz suggests that such a novel conception of political theory still 'barely exists'.[34]

Despite Geertz's pessimism, there has been minimally one recent sophisticated attempt to rethink the relation of ideology to political theory; this is the work of Michael Freeden. For Freeden, ideologies are not the poor relation of political philosophy. Conversely, both provide equally valid, if different, insights into the political world. As Geertz also argued, ideologies *both* reflect *and* produce social and political realities. They are also far more subtle and pervasive than commonly

---

[31] Clifford Geertz, 'Ideology as a Cultural System', in Clifford Geertz, *The Interpretation of Cultures* (London: Harper Collins, 1993), 212–18.

[32] Clifford Geertz, 'The World in Pieces: Culture and Politics at the End of the Century', in Clifford Geertz, *Available Light: Anthropological Reflections on Philosophical Topics* (Princeton: Princeton University Press, 2000), 225–6.

[33] Geertz, 'The World in Pieces', 227.

[34] Geertz, 'The World in Pieces', 250.

Political Ideology and Political Theory

understood. Consequently, as Freeden argues, to neglect the study of ideology is to 'weaken our comprehension of political thought'.[35] Freeden views his own approach as 'conceptual morphology'. It is semantically based, focusing on the core question: 'what are the implications and insights of a particular set of political views, in terms of the conceptual connections it forms?' For Freeden, it grasps 'internal ideational arrangements'. Meaning is always dependent on frameworks of interpretation. An ideology is therefore viewed as ordinary human 'thought-behaviour', embodied in commonplace spoken and written language. Ideologies are accordingly defined as 'those systems of political thinking, loose or rigid, deliberate or unintended, through which individuals and groups construct an understanding of the political world they, or those who preoccupy their thoughts, inhabit, and then act on that understanding'.[36] Ideologies thus provide (like Geertz) maps for navigation of the political realm, containing core, adjacent, and peripheral conceptual value components.

What then is the relation of political philosophy and ideology? For Freeden, ideological 'thought-behaviour invariably includes, but is not identical with the reflections and conjectures of political philosophers'.[37] Freeden thus sees political theory as a capacious category containing both political philosophy and ideology as subcategories. He is basically trying to recapture the importance of ideological analysis for political theory. He consequently separates out the history of political theory, political philosophy, and political ideology.[38] For Freeden, ideology regularly contains elements of political philosophy, but it is not the same as the work of political philosophers. He contends, however, that an overemphasis, in much recent political philosophy, on synchronic abstracted reasoning can lead to a virtually semi-private professional academic language, which bears little or no relation to the realities of politics, as perceived by the mass of ordinary citizens. Thus, given the dominance of the negative segregation theory within the academy, political philosophy can often be given an unwarranted precedence (over ideology) within discussion of politics. Freeden adopts a more ecumenical understanding, allowing both practices to coexist with mutual tolerance. Each has distinct and unique roles to play in political understanding. However, he also sees his task as

---

[35] Freeden, *Ideologies*, 2. See also Michael Freeden, *Ideology: A Short Introduction* (Oxford: Oxford University Press, 2003).

[36] Freeden, *Ideologies*, 3 and 125.

[37] Freeden, *Ideologies*, 2.

[38] Morphology combines a diachronic approach (which traces in effect the historical development of language) with a synchronic approach (which examines language as it actually is at a point in time with no reference to historical argument). Morphology balances both dimensions, superimposing a 'diachronic on synchronic analysis and multiple synchrony on the examination of a single system', Freeden, *Ideologies*, 5. This provides a handle for understanding his view of political philosophy and the history of political theory. Political philosophy has tended (to date) to be overly focused on the synchronic dimension. Overall, Freeden argues for 'mutual fertilization', see Freeden, *Ideologies*, 110.

recapturing the important role of ideology, a role that he suggests has been widely misconceived throughout the bulk of the twentieth century.

IDEOLOGY AND CRITIQUE

However, there is one awkward question in both Freeden's and Geertz's positions which remains unanswered: can ideologies deceive us or distort the political world? By what means could one know that such a distortion had taken place? The issue here is that once one allows ideology to populate the realm of the political (at a more ordinary or everyday level), how does one engage in any effective critique of ideological distortion? The political can in some renderings literally become the ideological. Yet, admitting that a distortion or manipulation has taken place implies that there is some non-ideological domain that enables us to judge the content of ideologies. Some critics have therefore suggested that we need some standard—external to ideology—to make any secure judgement. Thus, what is the process by which one ascertains that something is a distortion? The negative segregation argument has frequently underscored this particular censure of ideology.

One example of such a critique has been Jürgen Habermas's powerful arguments concerning the necessity for a *critique of ideology*. Basically, ideology fails to do justice to what Habermas thinks of as the *real* communicative structure underlying social relations. Ideology, for Habermas, is implicitly in conflict with the comprehensive 'power of reflection', that is to say, genuine communicative reasoning in Habermas is distinct from ideology.[39] Without trying to unpack the detail of Habermas's theory, there are a series of arguments which suggest that there is a form of underlying consensual reality present in the way that we communicate with one another, which is embedded in ordinary human discourse and knowledge claims. This reality is essentially concerned with what we *presuppose* when we speak and try to understand each other genuinely and rationally. Habermas argues that there are common normative consensual underpinning rules which function in any discourse and these, in turn, embody ethical and political implications. The gist of this perspective, for Habermas, is that any speech act raises 'universal validity claims...that can be vindicated'. The validity claims are notions such as comprehensibility, intelligibility, truthfulness, sincerity, and rightness. In so far as anyone wants to 'participate in a process of reaching an understanding, [the agent] cannot avoid raising... validity claims'.[40] The normative content is

---

[39] Jürgen Habermas, *On the Logic of the Social Sciences* (Cambridge, MA: MIT Press, 1996), 170.
[40] Jürgen Habermas, *Communication and the Evolution of Society* (London: Heinemann, 1979), 2.

thus presupposed in all genuine communication. In point, it is only by engaging in such intersubjective communicative practices that we can arrive at any conclusions about what constitutes a morally worthwhile or autonomous life. Distortion-free dialogue and reasonable communication are the heart of Habermas's enterprise.[41]

It is clear though, for Habermas, that not all speech acts are aimed at genuine communication; many are purely strategic, instrumental, or manipulative, aiming to further an agent's or a group's interest. A truly *communicative* use of language is thus wholly different from a *manipulative* use of language. Unfettered rational reflection (the power of reflection) will usually in fact reveal the power and manipulation implicit within certain language use. This is the essence of what Habermas sees as 'ideology critique'. If we wish to grasp ideology we have to see it in the field of power, manipulation, and distorted communication. Ideology is thus pseudo-communication. In essence, ideology is about the subjugation of the communicative structure of reality. Thus, communicative reason is equivalent to the 'real' and is distinct from ideology, understood as something that is manipulative and instrumental.

Habermas undoubtedly provides a powerful construal of the argument concerning ideological distortion. He would thus judge Freeden and Geertz as both mistaken about the character of ideology. For Habermas, we need to keep genuine rational communication distinct from ideology. Yet, if we refer back to the conceptual matrix of this paper, Habermas's argument, once again, invokes (in a novel format) a familiar claim central to the *negative segregation* thesis. Habermas argues, in effect, that reason can, at will, step outside the manipulative distortion of ideology and become a completely pristine self-critical mode of abstract philosophical reflection. As Hans-Georg Gadamer argued, in his critique of Habermas, this idea of objective neutral reason is itself a product of the prejudices of the unfinished Enlightenment tradition. For Gadamer, Habermas has in fact solved nothing here, except that he has succumbed, almost unwittingly, to the deepest of the Enlightenment utopian illusions, namely, the idea of a comprehensive overarching critical social science of humanity, premised on pristine philosophical reason.

To argue that reason can step outside all ideology and tradition is, by definition, just another language-based prejudice. For Gadamer, to be outside prejudice and tradition is to be outside of language and human understanding.[42] The idea that 'ideology critique' can reveal something extra, something more fundamental about language, is itself an unargued assumption. The important argument that gives more substance to Gadamer's point here is his insistence on the

---

[41] This theory forms the basis for Habermas's understanding of both discourse ethics and ultimately deliberative democracy.
[42] Hans-Georg Gadamer, *Philosophical Hermeneutics* (Berkeley and London: University of California Press, 1977), 31.

ontological character of language. Reality does not happen 'behind the back of' or 'outside of' language. There is no conceptual clarity, empirical reference, moral truth, or logical self-consistency, which magically exceeds language. This argument is *not* saying that language determines reality. However, it is arguing that everything is, nonetheless, internal to language and interpretation, nothing exceeds it. One may merge with different linguistic horizons, which will, in turn, radically change the nature of description and explanation of the world. One may even have the impression that one has stepped outside of language. Ideology critique can give this impression. However, it is nonetheless an illusion for Gadamer. The Habermasian 'ideal speech situation' and 'discourse ethic' can thus be seen as yet another surreptitious attempt to stop time, history, and human mutability and attain a still point of unchanging 'foundational calm' within the purity of reason. Such a task is impossible.

CONCLUSION

There are certain limited conclusions that can be drawn from this conceptual matrix argument. First, I would concur with the Gadamerian argument that it is impossible to escape from the sphere of language. As Gadamer remarks, 'being that can be understood is language'.[43] It is only in language that we understand and are at home in the world. Language is not something that mirrors or represents the world; conversely, 'it is the living out of what is with us—not only in the concrete interrelationships of world and politics but in all the other relationships and dependencies that comprise our world'.[44] Language is the *whole* process. In effect, we are temporal, finite, historically situated creatures and our language inevitably reflects these factors. There are no ultimate universal foundations and no way of stepping outside our historical finitude. We are irremediably historical beings and our language reflects this. The problem of distortion is not therefore to be solved by an appeal beyond ideology to some timeless rational principle. The solution is much more pragmatic. Some ideologies, in certain circumstances, are just intolerable for human beings, others are tolerable. There are though no absolute timeless rational truths that will tell us this or rationally demonstrate it. On the other hand, we sense this is the case and in many instances it becomes customary to accept it as the norm of social existence. Yet there is no absolute guarantee that it will remain so.

In consequence of the above arguments, something like the *positive segregation* thesis appears to be the more balanced and rational way to go with

---

[43] Gadamer, *Hermeneutics*, 103.   [44] Gadamer, *Hermeneutics*, 32.

future research. This is not an argument that denies the idiosyncratic roles of normative justification, ideology, or history. However, the study of ideology is nonetheless seen to be as serious and equally valid as political philosophy. There is a difference between the more synchronic themes of much recent political philosophy and the more applied semiotic focus of ideology. However, one should not try to make the difference too deep-seated. As such, this theoretical ecumenism looks like a more hopeful way forward as a research strategy, although it still carries its own deep endemic problems. Nonetheless, it does have the virtue of providing an intellectual space for different modes of reflective inquiry and allows us to reconsider the awkward partnership with more intellectual care and subtlety. Further, to gain any sense of the true complexity of this relation of political theory and ideology, something like the present conceptual matrix has to be taken on board. The matrix has been formulated primarily as a way of orientating future reflection on the issue. It is not intended to be definitive, but it is one of the first systematic attempts at such an overarching scheme. The paper is therefore more of a critical conceptual summation of the different ways in which the relation has been understood, particularly over the last two hundred years. As this discussion has demonstrated, there are clearly different and quite legitimate perspectives on this issue that need to be considered.

9

Ideology, Political Philosophy, and the Interpretive Enterprise: A View from the Other Side

Gerald Gaus

MICHAEL FREEDEN AND THE TRADITIONAL STUDY OF IDEOLOGY

The study of ideology has had a complex relation to the activity of political philosophy. As John Plamenatz long ago pointed out, the *philosophes* such as Voltaire hoped that a 'science of ideas' could take us beyond (mere) philosophic speculations: as Newtonian science advanced beyond Cartesian speculation, so too might we become scientific in our thinking about society.[1] And just as Newton showed the errors of Descartes, so too would a scientific study of social ideas show how traditional political doctrines were confused and mistaken; by correcting these mistakes we could be led to a better society. Right from the beginning, the study of ideology was seen not simply as an alternative—but also as a corrective—to philosophical speculation.

Much of the subsequent development of the ideological approach to political ideas stressed its scientific credentials; under the influence of Karl Mannheim, the study of ideology became a general sociology of knowledge.[2] Increasingly, it came to stress causal or functional explanations over reasoned internal analysis. Theorists of ideology such as Marx postulated the causes of political ideas and their consequences, or explained them in terms of the roles they play in social systems. The conviction that all this constituted an unmasking of political philosophy's claims to revealing the truth about the proper structure of political life not only persisted but was re-emphasized:

---

[1] [Francois Marie Arouet] Voltaire, *Philosophical Letters*, trans. Dilworth Ernest (Indianapolis: Bobbs-Merrill, 1961), 60–78. See John Plamenatz, *Ideology* (London: Macmillan, 1970).

[2] Karl Mannheim, *Ideology and Utopia* (London: Routledge and Kegan Paul, 1936), 68–9.

A View from the Other Side 179

philosophy itself became just another form of distorted consciousness with its assigned historical role to play. Hegel's *Philosophy of Right* became *The German Ideology*.

Michael Freeden's magisterial work, *Ideologies and Political Theories*, is a key contribution to contemporary political theory, leading the study of political ideology back in an interpretive and analytic direction. Freeden developed the systematic study of political ideologies in terms of their conceptual 'morphology'. His path-breaking three-tiered analysis examined the components of a political concept, a political concept, and a system of concepts.[3] Ideologies 'decontest' the meaning of political concepts: at the third level—that of conceptual systems—political ideologies are systematic relations of such concepts, with some concepts accorded core status, while others are pushed to the periphery. The morphological approach is immensely useful: it leads us away from the supposition that the study of ideological thinking is causal and functional, and instead sees it as interpretive and analytic. I have learned an immense amount from Freeden's work, and I welcome the opportunity to express my gratitude and deep appreciation.

While Freeden's interpretive turn distinguishes him from the earlier great students of ideology, and although he certainly rejects the extreme debunking claims of Marx or Mannheim, he seems to share a core conviction of the other great theorists of ideology—that the universalistic and rationalistic pretensions of philosophy should be called into question and (although I am not sure about this) in the end rejected. As a student of political ideology, he conceives of political philosophies—like all ideologies—as engaged in 'the inevitable act of decontesting the essentially contestable'.[4] But to see a reflective activity as devoted to decontesting what is essentially contestable must be to call into question its universalistic and rationalistic self-image, for it sees itself as rationally clarifying what at first seems murky and confused and, because of this, contested. Nowhere, I think, is this clearer than in Freeden's treatment of 'American philosophical liberalism': 'Despite initial attempts to present itself as non-ideological, through claims both to universalism and to non-bias,' he tells us, 'contemporary philosophical liberalism *is an ideological phenomenon like any other liberal doctrine*'.[5] Here Freeden is not merely saying that one can view American philosophical liberalism as a political doctrine to be studied as one does conservatism or socialism; he disputes its claims to universalism and non-bias. Like previous students of ideology, he claims to see *through* the

---

[3] Michael Freeden, *Ideologies and Political Theory: A Conceptual Approach* (Oxford: Oxford University Press, 1996), 75.
[4] Michael Freeden, 'Ideology, Political Theory, and Political Philosophy', in Gerald Gaus and Chandran Kukathas (eds.), *The Handbook of Political Theory* (London: Sage, 2004), 16.
[5] Freeden, *Ideologies and Political Theory*, 226. Emphasis added. See also Freeden's essay, 'Ideology: Balances and Projections', in Michael Freeden (ed.), *Reassessing Political Ideologies: The Durability of Dissent* (London: Routledge, 2001), 198.

Rawlsian self-image to the *real* picture. Indeed, on my reading this seems to be the main thrust of his extended treatment of American philosophical liberalism in *Ideologies and Political Theory*. We are told, for example, that 'the non-specifity claimed by Rawls for his political liberalism is chimerical' and 'the range of compatibility between political liberalism and "comprehensive" moral doctrines...is much narrower than Rawls would have us believe'.[6] Rawls is simply *wrong* that political values can be stated in a way that is free-standing in relation to 'moral, religious and philosophical viewpoints'.[7] Ronald Dworkin's claims are criticized in a similar way. Dworkin is said to make distinctions that are not 'sufficiently watertight' and which are 'contestable';[8] he 'marginalizes' crucial problems by 'perfunctory remarks' that are 'designed to acknowledge a difficulty without meeting it'.[9] As I read this, Freeden is not simply viewing the project of American philosophical liberalism from a different perspective—focusing, say, on the way in which American philosophical liberalism can be understood as a social and cultural system of meanings held together by its emotional attractions and used to justify claims of power—it is to see *through* its distorting self-image to *what it really is*. For all his important innovations, in this respect Freeden strikes me a descendant of Voltaire.

This chapter considers—or I should say 'reconsiders' in so far as it constitutes a rethinking of the account I gave in *Political Concepts and Political Theories*[10]—the relation of political philosophy, ideologies, and the study of political ideologies. I focus on two sets of questions. (1) Can we adequately distinguish, say, liberalism as an ideology from philosophical theories of liberalism? Although Freeden often stresses that American philosophical liberalism is within the domain of ideology, at other times he explicitly refers to 'the line between liberal philosophy and ideology'.[11] Is there a line, and if so how might we draw it? (2) Turning from the first-level activity of constructing ideological and philosophical doctrines to the study of such doctrines, we need to inquire whether an analytic (as opposed to a causal or functionalist) approach to the study of political ideologies and philosophies can itself be a critical enterprise. Does taking a stand on the normative and argumentative adequacy of American philosophical liberalism mean that Freeden is, in the

---

[6] Freeden, *Ideologies and Political Theory*, 233.
[7] Freeden, *Ideologies and Political Theory*, 234.
[8] Freeden, *Ideologies and Political Theory*, 235.
[9] Freeden, *Ideologies and Political Theory*, 235.
[10] *Political Concepts and Political Theories* (Boulder, CO: Westview, 2000), 33–42. In that book I drew a great deal on Freeden's way of distinguishing the study of political theory from political ideology, as I did in 'Ideological Dominance through Philosophical Confusion: Liberalism in the Twentieth Century', in Freeden (ed.), *Reassessing Political Ideologies: The Durability of Dissent*, ch. 2.
[11] He remarks that this line is 'more blurred' in France and Germany than in the Anglo-American world. Freeden, 'Ideology: Balances and Projections', 199.

end, offering his own normative alternative to the Rawlsian view, and so cannot be seen as offering an interpretive study of Rawlsian political doctrine? Can we say of Freeden's analysis of Rawls something very similar to what *he* says *of* Rawls: 'Despite initial attempts to present itself as non-ideological, through claims ... to non-bias', Freeden's normative and conceptual analysis is an ideological phenomenon like any other critique of a substantive liberal doctrine? In short: can (what I shall call) a second-level study of political doctrines normatively criticize a first-level theory as resting on false claims without itself becoming just another first-level theory?

FIRST-LEVEL NORMATIVE STRUCTURES: THE POPULAR AND THE REFINED

A Line between Activities in the Same Domain?

Our first question, then, is the relation between philosophy and ideology as first-level enterprises. Freeden refers to the line between them, yet he is also clear that 'political philosophy itself occupies a domain of ideological contestation'.[12] The view of their relation presented in *Ideologies and Political Theory* is complex and subtle. On the one hand, Freeden seeks to show that both ideology and political philosophy are genuine forms of political thought.[13] Yet, while showing how both are modes of political theorizing, he also provides an extensive list of criteria by which to distinguish the methods and aims of the political philosopher from that of the ideologist while, in the end, giving an ideological analysis of American philosophical liberalism. The chapter analysing Rawls's philosophical system appears in the midst of chapters analysing other, more familiar, ideologies. We can, Freeden tells us, give an ideological as well as a philosophical reading of Rawls's work.[14]

Although we may initially be perplexed by this combination of distinguishing the philosophical from the ideological while also treating them as both subject to ideological analysis, the appearance of contradiction disappears when we keep firmly in mind the crucial distinction between first- and second-level analyses, between 'ideologizing' and 'the analysis of ideology'.[15] At the first level—that of theory construction—the philosopher and the ideologist are said to engage in different activities with different aims. The philosopher, say, seeks to construct an impartial, objective, system of thought

[12] Freeden, 'Ideology: Balances and Projections', 198.
[13] Freeden, *Ideologies and Political Theory*, 27.
[14] Freeden, *Ideologies and Political Theory*, 44–5.
[15] Freeden, *Ideologies and Political Theory*, 27.

aiming at the truth about political life while the ideologist aims at a practical doctrine that has wide appeal and will energize and mobilize. And certainly we do make some such distinction in specific contexts. We may, for example, call someone an ideologue rather than a philosopher if it is clear that, despite her construction of an elaborate doctrine, it is the conclusions (say, advocacy of a certain account of distributive justice) rather than the doctrine's arguments and analyses, to which she is truly committed.[16] Certainly it is part of the self-image of the philosopher to get things right, and to reason well. Although at the first level the self-image of these activities may be quite different, at the second level, that of the study of theories of ideology (rather than the production of such theories), we can see that both the ideologist and the philosopher are performing an ideological function. It is here then the student of ideology appears to *see through* the philosopher's activity in a way that she does not see through the ideologist's. For the ideologist seems to be more self-aware of what he is doing: he is constructing a practical doctrine with certain political ends in mind. The student of ideology can analyse this doctrine, point out its functions, and also evaluate it on various counts (more on evaluation anon). Contrast this to the philosopher: supposedly she *thinks* she is engaging in the pursuit of universalistic and timeless truth but she is *really* constructing another ideological system. The philosopher, says Freeden, 'assumes that the mask reflects the face'.[17] Thus the second-level activity of the study of philosophy-as-ideology appears to unmask political reality as well as the pretensions of the philosopher in a way that does not apply to the pretensions of the straightforward ideologist.

Although in certain contexts we certainly do distinguish the activity of political philosophy from that of ideology, I believe that Freeden sometimes tends to overdraw the contrast. The philosopher's self-image, I believe, is often considerably more complex than Freeden suggests. That is, even at the level of theory construction, the line between philosophy and ideology is much more contextual than it may first appear.

The Philosopher and the Sophists

One way that Freeden distinguishes political ideologies from political philosophies is in respect to their normative commitments. The study of the morphology of ideologies, he holds, has *fewer* normative commitments than

---

[16] Thus one might say, as I have done, that most contemporary political philosophy is really the advocacy of ideology (a certain conviction about distributive justice), rather than an attempt to understand and analyse the proper nature of the political realm. See my essay 'The Property Equilibrium in a Liberal Social Order (Or How to Correct Our Moral Vision)', *Social Philosophy and Policy*, 28 (2011), 74–101.

[17] Freeden, *Ideologies and Political Theory*, 31.

does first-level political philosophy. Philosophical systems, he says, purport to stand or fall on standards of good arguments,[18] while the connections between ideas in ideological systems are less concerned with logical and coherent connections and admit emotional and non-rational elements.[19] 'Logic and consistency must remain important [in ideological thinking], but not overwhelming.'[20] 'Ideologies do not dispense with reason. All major ideologies, bar the extreme right and even then not entirely, require some degree of reflectiveness and internal coherence.'[21]

It seems that the picture is, roughly, this: the creator of ideology does not especially care if he makes some suspicious logical moves—his aim is to motivate political activity according to some political programme or plan. If we imagine the philosopher in her study, and the political scribbler pounding out a newspaper article, the philosopher is deeply concerned that her arguments be good ones, while the scribbler wishes to mobilize political action. It is hard not to think here of the difference between Socrates and the Sophists: both are engaging in persuasive discourse, but one has the primary aim of uncovering the truth, the other of moving the audience. The student of ideology, it seems, is at least as interested in the Sophist's rhetoric as in the philosopher's argument.

Justificatory Structures

Is this, though, really a distinction between two types of reflective-practical activity, or between informal and formal modes of essentially the same activity? There is much to say for the idea that it is more a matter of degree of self-consciousness and care than difference in kind. After all, if we accept Freeden's analysis of Rawls's philosophical liberalism, it is chock-full of manifestly bad arguments; and even the scribbler does not wish to commit logical and argumentative howlers. And that leads to the crucial question: *Why* does the political scribbler wish to avoid howlers? Why is the 'ideologist' concerned a good deal, but not totally, with coherence and reason? In the end, I believe that the answer is that, albeit in a modest way, he is proposing a justificatory structure. He is seeking not simply to motivate political action, but to justify it to his audience: to show them that their cause is right, fair, just, good, or Godly. Of course he may not care if he is really justifying the cause; the intentions of the creator are not always expressed in his creations. Some philosophers have advanced arguments to embarrass opponents or to win

---

[18] Freeden, 'Ideology, Political Theory, and Political Philosophy', 4.
[19] Freeden, *Ideologies and Political Theory*, 29.
[20] Freeden, *Ideologies and Political Theory*, 37.
[21] Freeden, *Ideologies and Political Theory*, 29.

prizes. Why one does what one does is always open to dispute, but both the political philosopher and the scribbler are creating justificatory structures that seek to show their followers the righteousness of their cause and the advisability of certain lines of action. That is why a creator of a political ideology is different from a rabble rouser: a rabble rouser may be very effective in generating political action ('Let's teach them a lesson they will not forget!'), but we do not get a conceptual structure that can be interpreted as rational because there is no claim to have advanced any sort of justificatory structure.

Of course the standards of justification vary in different contexts. It is certainly true that the justificatory standards of a pamphleteer will be different than those in a philosophical treatise, but within philosophy itself we also find disagreements about justificatory standards. Rawls advances an accessibility condition of acceptable arguments in political philosophy.[22] As far as possible we should rely on 'plain truths, now widely accepted, or available to citizens generally'.[23] He explicitly maintains that 'convincing philosophical argument' is not sufficient for political justification.[24] Rawls aims to apply the ideal of toleration to philosophy itself. He is thus searching for a conception of justification between the pamphleteer and the constructor of a refined philosophical system. This alone should warn us against any simple dichotomy between the philosopher's pursuit of truth-in-itself and the ideologist's articulation of a popular justificatory structure.

Justification, Bounded Rationality, and Biases

It is, then, of the first importance not to fall into the erroneous identification of philosophy with justification in terms of truth, full rationality, or the absence of biases. A fundamental dispute *among* philosophical theories is whether justification should address agents as boundedly rational, or whether justificatory discourse should be addressed only to those with full rationality and full information. Amos Tversky, Daniel Kahneman, and other cognitive psychologists have uncovered a variety of cognitive shortcuts and biases that humans employ when making judgements. We appeal to stereotypes, our judgements on the same matter markedly differ depending on the way the issue is 'framed' (we are much more likely to approve of a policy if we are informed of the number of lives it saves rather than the deaths that will occur), we are bad at probabilistic reasoning, we ignore abstract evidence in favour of vivid stories,

---

[22] Gerald Gaus, *Justificatory Liberalism* (New York: Oxford University Press, 1996), 132–7.

[23] John Rawls, *Political Liberalism*, paperback edition (New York: Columbia University Press, 1996), 225.

[24] Rawls, *Political Liberalism*, 338–9.

and so on.[25] Philosophers disagree whether these are non-rational biases that should be discounted in justification or whether what counts as good reasoning is determined by the actual ways of thinking that people employ, and which generally do a good job in helping them live their lives.[26] So within philosophy there is deep dispute about the extent to which folk reasoning counts as good reasoning. But clearly, if that is so, the line between philosophy, which focuses on 'good reasoning', and ideologies, which build on people's actual reasoning, with all its flaws, blurs, and perhaps even disappears.

Reason and the Emotions

Nor should we think that, while the philosopher constructs his system simply on the basis of logic and reason, the ideologist appeals to emotion.[27] Since at least Hume, modern philosophy has been well aware of the importance of emotion for normative thought, and recent investigations of moral thinking have led to a renewed appreciation of the fundamental role of our sentiments in morality[28] and, we might say, in 'socio-political interaction'.[29] As I argued (quite a long time ago, now)[30] the best account of the very idea of value 'assigns emotional import' to value[31]—indeed, more than that, it sees value as primarily an emotional response. So philosophy, no less than more popular justificatory structures, can—and should—put the emotions at the very heart of the analysis.

The One and the Many

Sometimes Freeden suggests that a core difference between ideology and philosophy is that philosophy is the creation of an individual thinker, while

---

[25] See e.g. Richard E. Nisbett and Lee Ross, *Human Inference: Strategies and Shortcomings of Social Judgments* (Englewood Cliffs: Prentice-Hall, 1980); Daniel Kahneman, Paul Slovic, and Amos Tversky (eds.), *Judgment Under Uncertainty: Heuristics and Biases* (Cambridge: Cambridge University Press, 1982); Daniel Kahneman and Amos Tversky (eds.), *Choices, Values and Frames* (Cambridge: Cambridge University Press, 2000).

[26] For different views see Gaus, *Justificatory Liberalism*, 54–62; Stephen Stich, *The Fragmentation of Reason* (Cambridge, MA: MIT Press, 1990). See also Gerd Gigerenzer, *Adaptive Thinking: Rationality in the Real World* (Oxford: Oxford University Press, 2000); Vernon L. Smith, *Rationality in Economics: Constructivist and Ecological Forms* (Cambridge: Cambridge University Press, 2008).

[27] See Freeden, 'Ideology, Political Theory, and Political Philosophy', 11–12.

[28] See Shaun Nichols, *Sentimental Rules: On the Natural Foundations of Moral Judgment* (New York: Oxford University Press, 2004).

[29] Freeden, 'Ideology, Political Theory, and Political Philosophy', 11.

[30] Gerald Gaus, *Value and Justification: The Foundations of Liberal Theory* (Cambridge: Cambridge University Press, 1990), part I.

[31] Freeden, 'Ideology, Political Theory, and Political Philosophy', 11.

ideology is the construction of groups.[32] There is certainly something to this: popular justificatory structures tend to reflect widespread popular understandings, while philosophies tend to be individual constructions of creative thinkers. But again, the question is whether this really marks off a difference in kind. One of the disputes within normative philosophy is the extent to which philosophic systems should be simply a refinement of ordinary understandings, or whether, based on claims to superior insight, they can constitute a sharp break with popular justificatory structures. The relation between common-sense moral practice and moral philosophy offers a useful analogy. One view would see their relation as akin to Freeden's distinction between ideology and political philosophy: moral practice is the creation of the Everyman (or at least the articulate Everyman) whose eye is set firmly on practice and results, while moral theory is the product of a philosopher in his study. Think, though, about Sidgwick's *Methods of Ethics*. On his view the philosophical method of common-sense morality appeals to the '*consensus* of mankind—or at least that portion of mankind that combines adequate intellectual enlightenment with a serious concern for morality'.[33] The philosopher of common sense sees moral truth as generally revealed through the actual practices and judgements of (more or less) ordinary individuals as they live their lives, though the philosopher certainly may see herself as qualified to point out contradictions and errors in this morality of Everyman. Here we see a complex dynamic between the popular justificatory structure and philosophical articulation of it—one does not collapse into the other, but neither can we say that one is the creation of a collective and the other of an individual mind.

Rawls's understanding of political philosophy approximates such a view. The philosopher's construction begins with concepts generally accessible in the political culture, though the ultimate way these are brought together may well lead to new insights into justified political structures. (Compare Bosanquet's claim that the dominant system of social ideas is never quite harmonious and so stands in need of rationalization: 'the general will is a process continuously emerging from the relatively unconscious into reflective consciousness'.[34]) To be sure, Freeden rejects Rawls's claim to have rationally articulated common concepts; he approvingly cites Bernard Yack's assertion that Rawls 'merely superimposes his philosophically designed conception upon something he calls our popular culture'.[35] The point here, though, is that a long-standing self-image of many philosophical projects has been that popular justificatory structures constitute the starting place and supply the

---

[32] Freeden, 'Ideology, Political Theory, and Political Philosophy', 11.
[33] Henry Sidgwick, *The Methods of Ethics*, 7th edition (Chicago: University Of Chicago Press, 1907), 215. Emphasis in original.
[34] Bernard Bosanquet, *Science and Philosophy* (London: Allen and Unwin, 1927), 267.
[35] Freeden, *Ideologies and Political Theory*, 233 n.

THE SECOND-LEVEL INTERPRETIVE ENTERPRISE

Conceptual Analysis and the Pull of the Normative

Thus far I have been questioning the idea that we can distinguish the study of ideology from political philosophy by sharply distinguishing two different first-level enterprises—the ideological and the philosophical. The relation between the popular and the refined is itself a matter of internal controversy within philosophy: there is no Archimedean point from which to depict their true relation that remains outside the fray. Any proposal for a dividing line takes place *within* the realm of philosophical dispute.

Let us, then, turn to the key question: the relation of the first-level activity of the ideologist/philosopher to the second-level activity of the student of ideology/political theory. Now the earlier generation of theorists of ideology had no doubt that their second-level activity was entirely distinct from the activity they studied. Whatever else one says about Marx's theory of ideology, his materialism provided a clear basis for unmasking the self-image of philosophy and other ideologies. Philosophy insists that it is regulated by truth and reason: Marx replies that, like all other practical activities, it is ultimately a servant of the mode of production and its dominant interests.

> The production of ideas, of conceptions of consciousness, is...directly interwoven with the material activity and the material intercourse of men, the language of real life.... Men are the producers of their conceptions, ideas, etc.,—real, active men, as they are conditioned by a definite development of their productive forces and of the intercourse responding to these...
>
> ...The ideas of the ruling class are in every epoch the ruling ideas, i.e. the class which is the ruling *material* force of society, is at the same time its ruling *intellectual* force.[36]

Marx had a secure perspective outside of the normative realm, which philosophy claims to rule, and from this outside perspective he unmasked its self-understanding by showing the extent to which the normative realm is an expression of material forces. Political philosophers are simply 'ideologists, who make the perfecting of the illusions of the class about itself their chief

---

[36] Karl Marx and Friedrich Engels, *The German Ideology*, ed. C. J. Arthur (London: Lawrence & Wishart, 1974), 47, 64. Emphasis in original.

source of livelihood.'[37] Marx can reveal the truth about philosophy without being philosophical.

But Freeden, quite rightly in my view, has abandoned the sociology of knowledge in favour of interpretation and analysis. Given this, what resources does he have to criticize Rawls's and Dworkin's normative views except to claim a superior normative understanding? His extensive critique of Rawls must amount to a claim to superior insight about the limits of Rawls's normative claims in Rawls's own theory. Every claim of Freeden's cited in section I (above) was a claim that Rawls's or Dworkin's view was normatively inadequate: Rawls or Dworkin purported to provide decisive reasons for accepting a view but, Freeden claims, *there are no such decisive reasons*. But this appears to assert a *privileged normative perspective*, where one has a more comprehensive view of the justifiability of a philosopher's claims and the reasons to accept them than the philosopher himself has obtained. And there seems no escape from doing this once one forsakes the sociology of knowledge for an analytic and interpretive approach to the study of ideology. There is no non-normative perspective from which one can dispute the normative soundness of American philosophical liberalism.

Consider, for example, Freeden's key notion that concepts are logically indeterminate, and so 'decontesting' them in one way or another is a manner of 'selection' or choice, not simply logic.[38] This is itself a controversial philosophical doctrine. To maintain it is to advance a philosophical position backed by arguments, claiming that one's arguments and analyses are superior to those of others. When Freeden claims that political philosophers act ideologically in asserting that their preferred exposition of a concept is rationally superior to competitors, he is himself taking on the mantel of linguistic philosopher, criticizing the claims of philosophers who base their political analysis on a faulty account of concepts. After all, if Plato is right, and concepts are real universals that can be partly grasped by reason, then the underdetermination thesis is simply false. Or if Wittgenstein's view in the *Tractatus* is correct, Freeden's appeal to the *Investigations* is normatively objectionable.[39] All of these are disputes between those broad justificatory structures that are properly understood as philosophical.

The focus on the morphology of political concepts pulls the study of ideology back to first-level normative positions as to what counts as a good argument and an adequate account of concepts, and so the student of ideology must make judgements about when arguments and conceptual analyses fail. When Rawls asserts that the best analysis of our shared concept of political

---

[37] Marx and Engels, *German Ideology*, 65.
[38] Freeden, *Ideologies and Political Theory*, 45.
[39] Freeden, *Ideologies and Political Theory*, 53. On these points, see my *Political Concepts and Political Theories*, ch. 1.

liberty derives from the idea that free and equal citizens possess political autonomy, Freeden objects that this disregards important ties between heteronomy and freedom.[40] The analysis of what counts as an acceptable interpretation of freedom commits Freeden to his own controversial normative claims about significant uses of freedom and what constitutes the best reasons for excluding some uses as unimportant or peripheral; if Rawls has a powerful reason for excluding some use of 'freedom' then we would hardly think it significant if his theory does not take account of it.

So Freeden must be committed to a certain normative analysis. However, we can see that this does not mean, after all, that he is simply engaging in first-level normative political philosophy. The study of political ideologies can be a different task than constructing first-level normative theories in political philosophy, and it can lead to taking some normative positions on first-level philosophical disputes. To understand the distinction between first-level normative justification and the normative study of ideology we need to know *how it can be that an interpretive activity is distinct from first-level normative theorizing yet inevitably takes positions on such theorizing, and when so doing engages in that very first-level normative activity that it is studying.* When we understand how this is not only possible, but necessary, we will better see the relation of the study of ideologies to political philosophy.

The Interpretive Activity

To see how we can usefully distinguish first-level justificatory structures from 'second-level' interpretation and analysis of such structures, consider a case with which every reader of this chapter will be familiar: the distinction between Hobbes's and Locke's political theories, and our teaching of these political theories to our students. Seldom is teaching Hobbes and Locke anything like simple advocacy of Hobbesian or Lockean theory. We do not merely repeat their arguments, but we explore their assumptions, investigate the moves they make, the way they define their concepts, and so on: we interpret and analyse their justificatory structures. But note that when we do that, we cannot help but evaluate them as well. We do not simply describe Hobbes's model of humans and his claim that they will be in a state of war unless ruled by a sovereign; we chart out the arguments, but we question them too. Our second-level activity of interpreting the canon pulls us into first-level normative analysis: we cannot help but evaluate as we interpret. Teaching can go very wrong in two ways: it may either lapse simply into first-level advocacy in which what should be an interpretation of a text becomes either a battle for

---

[40] Freeden, *Ideologies and Political Theory*, 238.

it or against it, or it can become no more than an exegesis, in which the claims are clarified, but still essentially merely repeated. Neither is an adequate interpretive stance.

The second-order interpretation of those justificatory structures we call ideologies and political philosophies is broadly similar. It is neither itself a first-level argument nor simply a description of another's first-level argument. As Freeden's work exemplifies so well, it feels the pull of the normative without entirely giving into it and so becoming yet another first-level justificatory endeavour. Why must good interpretation be like this, being pulled towards the normative, but always able to draw back?

INTERPRETATION, ANALYSIS, AND THE RATIONAL

Making the Natives Intelligible

To interpret a theory via analysis is to make it intelligible. When we approach a political theory, we are usually confronted by a diagnosis of some political or social problem, some basic claims about the way the world operates and the nature of humans, and a plan or prescription about how to deal with the problem. Now the preferred first step in making all this intelligible—to make sense of it—is to see it as rational. If the problems Hobbes points to are real, if his analyses of their causes are well-grounded, and if his prescriptions would indeed solve the problem, Hobbes's political theory immediately becomes intelligible to us. Because, despite all of our shortcomings in this regard, we are still rational creatures who can grasp other's thoughts best when we see those thoughts as rational and sensible, our first task as interpreters is to render our objects of study as rational as we can. We are generally intelligible to each other because we are rational, and can understand the actions and beliefs of others as rational. To make a system of thought intelligible is, likewise, to see it as rational and sensible.

This leads to the importance of the principle of charity in our second-level interpretations. An anthropologist studying a native culture seeks to render their culture intelligible, and to do that she must see what they are up to as sensible and rational. And a first step in doing that is to interpret what they think in such a way as to render it true. As Donald Davidson stressed, the first step of the anthropologist is

> assigning truth conditions to alien sentences that make native speakers right when plausibly possible, according, of course, to our own view of what is right. What justifies the procedure is the fact that disagreement and agreement alike are intelligible only against a background of massive agreement. Applied to language, this principle reads: the more sentences we conspire to accept (whether or not

through a medium of interpretation), the better we understand the rest, whether or not we agree with them.[41]

The student of ideology and political theory is like an anthropologist confronting a native culture that she does not share, but is trying to make sense of. How is she to interpret Hobbes's statements that 'nothing can be unjust' in the state of nature and that under some conditions one has an obligation to keep covenants in the state of nature?[42] Like an anthropologist who seems to confront natives who are uttering contradictory sentences, the student of political theory sees her 'native' as appearing to contradict himself. But this makes it all puzzling and unintelligible to us. To make sense of Hobbes is, at least in the first instance, to show that what he says is consistent and, if possible, well-grounded.

Levels of Intelligibility

There are, of course, different ways in which we can make another intelligible. Although Davidson maintained that the principle of charity supposes that our aim is to render true the statements that are the object of our interpretation, often we can render them intelligible and yet stop far short of rendering them true. Sometimes we can simply see how they are rational or reasonable; we can see why someone in a certain situation would rationally come to believe something, even if we can now see that what they believed is not true. We might, for example, think that Hobbes's claim that the state of nature is a state of war is rational if we think of human interactions in the state of nature as something like one-shot Prisoner's Dilemmas, but we still might think he is quite wrong to see human interactions under anarchy in those terms. However, even in this case we would have to think it is at least reasonable for him to have understood human interactions as something akin to one-shot Prisoner's Dilemmas. If it was really unintelligible how he could come to see human interactions as akin to one-shot Prisoner's Dilemmas, it will not make Hobbes fully intelligible to say that *if* one sees them in that way, *then* we can understand how the state of nature will be a state of war. That would simply push the ultimate unintelligibility of the project back one step.

And yet, pushing the unintelligibility back a step does help the project of interpretation. One of the reasons why—at least in my view—Freud's work is of continuing interest is that he shows how we can make an action that is totally unintelligible more intelligible but still not reasonable. Consider one of his cases—a nineteen-year-old girl with obsessional sleep ceremonies:

---

[41] Donald Davidson, 'Radical Interpretation', in his *Inquiries into Truth and Interpretation* (Oxford: Oxford University Press, 1984), 125–39, quote at 137.
[42] Thomas Hobbes, *Leviathan*, ed. Edwin Curley (Indianapolis: Hackett, 1994), 78 (ch. 13, para. 13), and ch. 14.

> The pillow at the top end of the bed must not touch the wooden back of the bedstead...The eiderdown...had to be shaken before being laid on the bed so that its bottom became very thick; afterwards, however, she never failed to even out this accumulation of feathers by pressing them apart.[43]

At this point the behaviour is simply incomprehensible. Freud appeals to reasoning—albeit still odd reasoning—to make some sense of it. In the course of her therapy:

> [s]he found out the central meaning of her ceremonial one day when she suddenly understood the meaning of the rule that the pillow must not touch the back of the bedstead. The pillow, she said, had always been a woman to her and the upright wooden back a man. Thus she wanted—by magic, we must interpolate—to keep man and woman apart—that is, to separate her parents from each other, and not allow them to have sexual intercourse...
> If a pillow was a woman, then the shaking of the eiderdown till all the feathers were at the bottom and caused a swelling there had a sense as well. It meant making the woman pregnant; but she never failed to smooth away the pregnancy again, for she had been for years afraid that her parents' intercourse would result in another child...[44]

As Freud notes, these are 'wild thoughts'. Admittedly, if 'wooden bedstead = father', and 'pillow = mother', then we can see a sort of reasoning in keeping bedstead and pillow apart. If she was correct in thinking that what she does to the bedstead and pillow affects what her parents do at night, then keeping the bedstead and pillow apart has a certain sort of rationality to it. But, still, we have made progress: what was simply incomprehensible now is becoming intelligible as it is becoming a bit more rational—but we still need to know why she believes these things.

In interpreting political doctrines, though, we aim at deeper intelligibility: we seek not only to make doctrines less crazy, but reasonable pretty far down. Here, Freeden is surely correct that we will treat refined and popular justificatory structures differently. We expect a refined political doctrine to be intelligible pretty 'far down', though even here there may be limits, as when we see that a conclusion ultimately rests on a doctrine that is wildly implausible—think of Bosanquet's claim that reality is ultimately composed, in some sense, of ideas. However, we are apt to come to the conclusion of implausibility quicker when interpreting more popular doctrines, which may well rest on widespread convictions that we find not only hard to credit, but sometimes 'wild'. The study of fascism, especially Nazism, is a case in point: beliefs about the identity of the 'Aryan race' and its relation to modern Germans was

---

[43] Sigmund Freud, *Introductory Lectures on Psychoanalysis*, trans. James Strachey (Harmondsworth, UK: Penguin, 1973), lecture 17.

[44] Freud, *Introductory Lectures on Psychoanalysis*, lecture 17.

mythical, and about as sensible as Freud's patient's belief in the efficacy of keeping the bedstead from touching the pillow.

By the Interpreter's Lights

As Davidson says, though, to make a view sensible is to make it true (or reasonable) *by our own lights*. Neither the student of political ideologies nor the anthropologist can stand outside of her own normative commitments about what is sensible and rational in her efforts at interpretation. Here is the pull of the normative in one's interpretation: to make Hobbes's conceptual scheme sensible is to make it sensible by one's own lights, and so the process of interpretation is inherently normative. Every interpretive move is normative: we are trying to see how a conceptual structure is rational and sensible. If we see it as normatively sound, then we immediately see it as an intelligible creation: we understand the conceptual structure that confronts us, and we begin to know our way around in it. The more we can plausibly see a conceptual structure as rational and well thought-out, the more intelligible it is to us.

Thus the complexity of second-level analysis of systems of thought. Our aim is to understand classical liberalism, the new liberalism, American philosophical liberalism, or socialism, not to engage in first-level normative disputes with them. We do not wish to enter the fray. But to understand a justificatory structure we are required to apply our normative criteria of what constitutes good reasoning, plausible premises, and reasonable views about the world. We endeavour to make it intelligible against a background of standards of intelligibility that appeal to our own first-level normative commitments. In my own *Political Concepts and Political Theories* I sought to investigate the normative and conceptual structures of versions of liberalism, conservatism, and socialism; my aim was to understand and make intelligible. But any reader will see that liberalism comes out better, because given what I see as the plausible normative criteria, it makes more sense, and is more easily intelligible, than the others. Similarly (although on a much more impressive scale), it is manifest that in *Ideologies and Political Theory* Freeden finds it easy to make the new liberalism intelligible, and finds it quite a hard job to make Rawls really sensible, or to see how libertarianism can be intelligibly seen as an important part of the liberal tradition.

My own advisor, John Chapman, spelled this out wonderfully in his essay on 'Political Theory: Logical Structure and Enduring Types'—a paper that has shaped my own thinking about political theory throughout my career.[45] The

---

[45] John W. Chapman, 'Political Theory: Logical Structure and Enduring Types', in *L'Idée de Philosophie Politique*, annales de philosophie, vol. 6 (Paris: Presses Universitaires de France, 1965), 57–96.

range of intelligible political theories is set by one's understanding of possible logical structures, and how—and whether—various metaphysical, moral, psychological, and political views can be coherently combined. The student of political theory comes to his work with commitments about possible logical structures and this will deeply inform his analysis and his ability to render some justificatory structures intelligible. And it will lead him to be critical of others as normatively flawed. So even if he tries as hard as he might not to appeal to his own specific normative commitments in his analysis of political doctrines, his deeper understanding of what is logically or conceptually coherent must inform his study.

INTERPRETATION, UNMASKING, AND THE APPEAL TO ERROR

Walking a Tightrope

The student of political thought, then, has to walk a tightrope. She cannot but help draw on her own normative commitments throughout her analysis. However, because her aim is to make a first-level justificatory structure intelligible, as an interpreter her first response cannot be to unmask the pretensions of first-level justificatory discourse. There is always the temptation to 'see through' first-level discourse as deeply flawed and implausible. To quickly draw on one's normative commitments and views to see through the pretensions of first-level political doctrines may make for good first-level disputation, but it is to fail in the interpretive task. For unmasking often tends to make our subject *un*intelligible to us. How could the creators have been so unaware of their faults? Did they really fail to see that they sought the impossible? How could they have made such ridiculous claims to objectivity when all along it is so clear they were grinding their own axes? So far from making our subject intelligible we now need an *additional* explanation: one that makes sense of the failure to construct a rationally intelligible view of the world. Unveiling the reality behind a justificatory structure can render our subject less intelligible in much the same way that translating a native language as chock-full of falsehoods renders their form of life unintelligible to us.

We can press the anthropological analogy further. One of the dangers of fieldwork—to which early anthropology succumbed—is to assume an easy superiority over one's subjects, so that *of course* the anthropologist sees things so much clearer than does the native. If the anthropologist takes this attitude, then her default supposition will be that her subjects are wrong because they fail to see nearly as far as she does. And so her field journal will be a study in obvious errors. This is exactly the attitude that encourages lack of understanding of one's subjects; to assume that one sees much further than do they undermines the supposition that one's aim is to see how their views are true or reasonable. Much the same holds true for the study of political theories and doctrines. Interpretation requires a hefty dose of allegiance to the principle of charity, *and so using one's basic normative commitments to help make sense of what others think, rather than to reveal their errors and follies.* The deep flaw of the unmasking approach to political ideologies is its too-easy assumption of a superior perspective, from which one sees so much further, and so much deeper, than first-level political doctrines. Confidence that one sees much deeper is always a barrier to good interpretation, for it tempts us to assume that others are blinkered and wrong.

The Intelligibility of Error

As always, there is a complication: sometimes the best way to make others intelligible is to see them as making a common error.[46] Think back to the use of heuristics (pp. 184–5), and suppose we hold that relying on them is not rational. Once we have good evidence that people tend to make these mistakes, we can appeal to them in our interpretations of why people believe and act as they do, but when we do so we make their beliefs and actions explicable by showing they are *not* rational.

Consider an example from some of my other work. Based on empirical evidence as well as theoretical work concerning complex social systems, I have argued that it is extremely difficult to make accurate and precise social predictions, and that this undermines a great deal of what goes on under the name of public policy.[47] Yet, I have argued, audiences are extraordinarily resistant to this analysis: in the face of a great deal of evidence, they continue to believe that they can accurately predict the future of social systems. In explaining this I appeal again to the work of Kahneman and Tversky, which indicates that people consistently ascribe high levels of probability to very faulty predictions. Indeed, they report that 'subjects are most confident in predictions that are most likely to be off the mark'. '[P]eople are prone to experience much confidence in highly fallible judgments, a phenomenon that might be called the illusion of validity'.[48] So we can understand people's

---

[46] See David Henderson, 'The Principle of Charity and the Problem of Irrationality (Translation and the Problem of Irrationality)', *Synthese*, 73 (1987), 225–52.

[47] 'Social Complexity and Evolved Moral Principles', in Peter McNamara (ed.), *Liberalism, Conservatism, and Hayek's Idea of Spontaneous Order* (London: Macmillan, 2007), 149–76.

[48] Daniel Kahneman and Amos Tversky, 'On the Psychology of Prediction', in Kahneman, Slovic, and Tversky (eds.) *Judgment Under Uncertainty: Heuristics and Biases*, 47–68, quote at 66.

insistence that *they* can make accurate predictions not by seeing how they are rational to think this, but by showing that it is the result of a common human bias.

We can extend the idea to the study of political doctrines. Explicability may be better furthered by supposing a doctrine rests on an error than by supposing that its claims are true, or justifiable, or at least reasonable. This leads us right back to our starting point: the Marxian causal/functionalist view of ideology. We can think of Marx as proposing that all of philosophy is explained by one grand 'cognitive bias'—philosophers produce doctrines that serve the interests of the ruling class. *That* is what renders their content intelligible. But notice how this tack moves us away from intelligibility through analysis back to the original causal/functional perspective of the study of ideology. The more we make a doctrine explicable by citing common human error the less we see it as an object to be made intelligible through analysing its structure and the reasoning behind it. It is also a risky move; it supposes the superior perspective and insight of the unmasking approach, and so always runs the risk of failing to appreciate the reasonableness of its subject by a too-easy assumption that it is riddled with errors from which one is free. Although we cannot say that intelligibility can never be furthered through pointing to common error, it is a temptation to a biased claim to superiority unless very solidly grounded in compelling evidence.

CONCLUSION: A VIEW FROM THE OTHER SIDE

The subtlety and difficulty of the interpretive enterprise is all too clear. Our aim is to understand the subjects of our study as at least reasonable articulations of the political world, and to do that we must exercise considerable charity in interpreting their content. Even if we do not interpret their claims as true we at least aim to make them rational or reasonable. But our project of making a political doctrine intelligible may fail: we may be confronted by some seemingly 'wild' thoughts at the basis of the doctrine, and to that extent we may be puzzled why people would believe it. But, then again, sometimes we can employ psychological or economic theory to show why the 'wild' error is explicable, and then we can further advance the interpretive project, even past the bounds of rational intelligibility. However, to appeal to common error when interpreting a doctrine is to run the risk of forsaking interpretation for unmasking, for again we are claiming to see through our subjects and their false consciousness. And yet the background of all our interpretive efforts is our own normative commitments, and these will enter into our interpretive analysis.

Freeden is correct in suggesting that 'wild' thoughts, and making them explicable by pointing to common error, are more common when analysing popular justificatory structures. I remain unconvinced, however, that there is a distinction in kind between the tasks of interpreting refined and popular justificatory structures. Writing from the philosophy side of the philosophy/ideology divide, I see as much the same the work of the interpreter of philosophical doctrines and that of the interpreter of the popular justificatory structures that are called 'ideologies'. In both, a fine touch is needed to know when we have exhausted intelligibility through rationality and must resort to explicability through common error. In neither is the unmasking approach helpful as a mode of interpretation, though it is a tried-and-true method of first-level normative disputation.

I began by pointing out that Freeden engages in extensive criticisms of Rawls's and Dworkin's normative claims and I asked: Is such criticism consistent with the interpretive enterprise, or does it show merely first-level engagement? It should now be clear that normative criticism is part and parcel of interpretation; to interpret is to draw on one's own standards, but this will inevitably lead to disagreement as well as rationalization. There is no incoherence at the root of the critical interpretation: indeed, criticism and interpretation go hand in hand.

Of course, we are still confronted with the more difficult question of whether an interpretation resorts too quickly to criticism, and so lapses into unmasking or simple first-level dispute. From my view of the divide over 'American philosophical liberalism'—a version of liberalism that, in its basics, I believe is sound—I tend to think that Freeden's treatment comes close to being a first-level disputation rather than a second-level interpretive enterprise. I can certainly understand how this happens. There is, let us say, considerable resistance to Rawls's general approach: those trained in political science from both sides of the Atlantic see it as overly abstract and unworldly;[49] on the European side of the Atlantic, philosophers are perhaps apt to agree with the political theorists (on the Western side, they are certainly split). However, while it is understandable to be tempted into a first-level argument with Rawls, and while that is the bread and butter of first-level normative dispute, I am not, in the end, convinced that the treatment in *Ideologies and Political Theory* has a sufficient dose of the principle of charity. When a reader confronts an interpretation that describes a theory as characterized by 'superficial allusions',[50] 'artificial dichotomies',[51] and 'false antitheses' of which it is 'unduly fond',[52] claims that are 'chimerical'[53] and 'startling',[54] and which exemplify

---

[49] For which Rawls refuses to apologize. *Political Liberalism*, p. lxii.
[50] Freeden, *Ideologies and Political Theory*, 227.
[51] Freeden, *Ideologies and Political Theory*, 259.
[52] Freeden, *Ideologies and Political Theory*, 254.
[53] Freeden, *Ideologies and Political Theory*, 233.
[54] Freeden, *Ideologies and Political Theory*, 259.

an 'artificiality'[55] that leads to 'a serious indictment of its viability'[56] and is based on a 'peculiar American notion'[57]—in such a case one has a hard time accepting that one is encountering a charitable interpretive enterprise. As I have stressed, one cannot be sure, for all interpreters have limits as to what they can see as plausible. In the end, I cannot help but see Freeden as, in this instance, taking off his gloves and entering the normative fray, criticizing Rawlsian liberalism as normatively inferior and empirically inadequate. He may be right or wrong, but I suspect that here he occupies the position of a participant in the first-level philosophical dispute, not a student of political doctrines.

[55] Freeden, *Ideologies and Political Theory*, 253.
[56] Freeden, *Ideologies and Political Theory*, 253.
[57] Freeden, *Ideologies and Political Theory*, 270.

10

Civil Society and the Reconstruction of the Public Sphere: Ideologies between Theory and Politics

Gayil Talshir

INTRODUCTION

The analysis of political ideology is notoriously lacking from the recent volumes on democracy and political philosophy.[1] Indeed, ideology is often treated as the unwanted child of political thought: while the former addresses the eternal questions of the good polity, the just society, the sought values, and the right conceptual framework, ideology supposedly deals with the mere reflections of these sublime concepts in the murkiest water of real politics as manifested in the ideas of actual leaders, organizations, and people. Similarly, the empirical analysis of liberal-democratic politics lacks almost any study of the changing sphere of political ideologies.[2] Whereas comparative politics uses quantitative methods and statistical data to account for the changing nature of liberal democracies, the students of ideology offer interpretative analysis of concepts, views, and sets of ideas that thus hardly qualify as a 'real' (political) science.

The contention of this paper is that the analysis of political ideology exposes a fundamental dimension of politics. Rather than being the unwanted child

---

[1] Thomas Christiano, *Philosophy and Democracy: An Anthology* (Oxford: Oxford University Press, 2003); Frank Cunningham, *Theories of Democracy* (London and New York: Routledge, 2002); Jan-Erik Lane and Svante Ersson, *Democracy: A Comparative Approach* (London and New York: Routledge, 2005).
[2] Bruce Cain et al., *Democracy Transformed?* (Oxford: Oxford University Press, 2003); Richard Gunther et al., *Political Parties* (Oxford: Oxford University Press, 2002); Russell Dalton and Martin Wattenberg, *Parties Without Partisans: Political Change in Advanced Industrial Democracies* (Oxford: Oxford University Press, 2000).

of political philosophy, or the stepsister of hard-nosed comparative politics, the analysis of ideology reveals an essential facet of the changing nature of politics and can be a decisive tool in judging between competing theories of the nature of these changes. Moreover, the study of ideology serves as an essential bridge between the separate tables of political philosophy and comparative politics, thus summoning them up to sit by the same table and cement the discipline of political science.

The argument has three steps. The first one has to do with the rise of civil society as a third dimension of the public sphere and its influence on the ideologies of the traditional political parties. Perhaps the most dramatic change of contemporary theory of the public sphere was the transformation from a binary world of private/public dichotomy into a threefold analysis of the public space with the emergence of civil society as a third constitutive realm. The binary opposition of the private and the public, fundamental to a liberal conception, was also embedded in the way the party system was shaped. During the twentieth century, the main contention on which the ideological spectrum was divided up was precisely about the relationship between the private and the public, also reflected in the dichotomy between the economic and the political. The liberal tradition encompassed a dialectical relationship whereby the individual enjoyed negative freedom, which protected his private sphere, i.e. his economic interests, from the interference of the government, but each individual was free to act in the public domain. The major issue between the Left and the Right's rival positions was about the question of the interference of government in the free market in the economic sphere. Thus, the private/public, substantiated in the distinction between the first and second sphere—the economic and the political respectively—was reflected in the Left/Right dimension of the party system. The Right wanted less intervention of the government; the Left sought distributive justice through governmental policies. In the late twentieth century, civil society became a focal point of theoretical and empirical research, with implications to the theory of deliberative democracy and identity politics. However, the reaction to the rise of civil society as a third dimension of the public sphere was rarely analysed from the perspective of the traditional players in liberal democracies, namely, political parties and their distinct ideologies. The first part of the paper therefore analyses the four ideological families of contemporary politics—the conservative Right, the moderate Left, the radical Left, and the extreme Right—studying in particular the reshaping of their ideology, given the rise of civil society and following the modifications they underwent in order to accommodate the changing public sphere.

The second step involves bringing this analysis to bear on one of the central theoretical debates within comparative politics today: that between dealignment and realignment. While dealignment scholars argue that the traditional patterns of analysing politics in liberal democracies—voting patterns in relation to social cleavages and parties—is no longer applicable in today's advanced democracies, the realignment camp suggests that rather than a total decline of voting alignments, it is actually smaller changes which imply realignment that explain today's party systems. The ideological analysis of the four major players in the political system will demonstrate the adaptability of the parties to the new structures of the public sphere as well as the gradual transformation of their own world views, thus contributing decisively to the latter theory. The concluding discussion addresses the nature of political science, demonstrating how political ideology can actually build a bridge between political philosophy and empirical study of the body politic.

THE STUDY OF IDEOLOGY

That democracy itself is not perceived as an ideology, though its rivals—dictatorship and totalitarianism, on the regime side, communism and fascism on the ideational side—are, is a well-established perception. In the cold-war context, ideology was strictly identified with democracy's enemies, whereas democracy itself was never perceived as an ideology. However, the ideological dimension is a quintessential part of democracy, even according to the most stringent and minimalist political scientists, be they Downs, Schumpeter, or Sartori.[3] In fact, as long as modern democracy is 'unthinkable save in terms of parties',[4] the democratic breath of the party system is that of ideological struggle over different world views among competing parties.

How, therefore, to account for the lacuna in ideological studies? Part of the blame rests on the theory and theorists of ideology: Marx notoriously associated ideology with part of the superstructure, and not the base, and a long line of analysts—Marxists, neo-Marxists, and post-Marxists—[5]followed in his footsteps. In fact, even after the 'linguistic turn', when language was no longer treated as transparent but rather as a discourse pregnant with values, ideas, and perceptions, many of the school of critical discourse analysis were still analysing ideology as biased-producing frameworks; thus, the Frankfurt school called their trade critical theory and not ideological studies.[6] The

---

[3] Giovanni Sartori, 'What is "Politics"', *Political Theory*, 1 (1973), 5–26; Joseph Schumpeter, *Capitalism, Socialism and Democracy* (London and New York: Routledge, 2010); Anthony Downs, *An Economic Theory of Democracy* (Boston: Addison Wesley, 1957).

[4] Elmer E. Schattschneider, *Party Government* (New York: Reinhart, 1942).

[5] See M. Freeden, *Ideologies and Political Theories: A Conceptual Approach* (Oxford: Oxford University Press, 1996), ch. 1.

[6] For a historical account of the transformation in the study of ideology see Gayil Talshir, 'The Objects of Ideology: Historical Transformations and the Changing Role of the Analyst', *History of Political Thought*, 26 (2005), 520–49.

near exclusion of ideology studies from the corpus of political theory and comparative politics is therefore intriguing, making Michael Freeden's project of turning the analysis of ideology into a viable tool in the toolkit of political philosophers, an ongoing project. The presupposition of this project, as manifested in the *Journal of Political Ideologies*, is that a political conflict has almost always an ideational aspect, and the struggle over perceptions, ideologies, and world views is immanent to the study of politics.

Another facet of the decline of ideology study has to do directly with the dealignment thesis, and the crisis of legitimation of liberal democracy. In the vein of 'the end of ideology', 'the end of history', and 'the end of politics', recent research has found that there is a decrease in all patterns of traditional analysis of the political process, such as electoral turnout, party membership, and trust in political institutions. The contemporary literature on advanced democracies suggests that the 'decline of long-term predispositions based on social position or partisanship should shift the basis of electoral behavior research to short-term factors, such as candidate image and issue opinion'.[7] Thus, the argument seems to be that given the changing nature of the political process over the last generation—personification, issue-based politics, and electoral volatility, signifying structural changes in the way the electorate perceives the political sphere itself—ideology has no longer any substantial role to play. This paper challenges this trend of analysis through ideological study of the transformation of the political world view of the major party families in liberal democracies and examines the implications that emerge from this study for the dealignment thesis.

CIVIL SOCIETY AND THE PUBLIC SPHERE: FROM THEORY TO IDEOLOGY

Democracy was once thought to be inconceivable save in terms of party democracy. Yet it has been extensively argued—both by political comparativists and social theoreticians—that in an age of political dealignment, civil society is a key actor in the context of the crisis of legitimation and the future of democracy. Thus, civil society surprisingly serves as a potential positive force both to comparative political scientists and social theorists. Looking beyond the structural differences, it seems increasingly the case that both 'separate tables', to reiterate Almond's characterization of the internal cleavage within political science,[8] are actually highly concerned by the crisis of

---

[7] Dalton Russell and Hans-Dieter Klingemann (eds.), *The Oxford Handbook of Political Behavior* (Oxford: Oxford University Press, 2007).

[8] Gabriel Almond, *A Discipline Divided* (London: Sage, 1990).

democratic legitimacy; moreover, both genres of political study perceive civil society as the only possible way out of the crisis. To take but two examples, Iris Marion Young contends:

> This chapter has supported the claim that a free, active and diverse civil society is crucial for democracy. Associational activity promotes communicative interaction both in small groups and across large publics. It fosters democratic inclusion by enabling excluded or marginalized groups to find each other, develop counter-publics, and express their options and perspectives to a wider public... Civil society limits the ability of both state and economy to colonize the lifeworld, and fosters individual and collective self-determination.[9]

Complementarily, empirical research on party politics has led many scholars to think the hope for the regeneration of democracy lies within civil society. One such example is the expected role of the new collective actor within civil society—the social movements. Ibarra and his colleagues, in *Social Movements and Democracy*, argue that 'once the social movements really acquire protagonism in the different networks of *governance*, once the political process of decision making incorporates different actors including the social movements, the process is more democratic'.[10] In the same manner, Russell Dalton concludes in *Parties without Partisans*:

> The dealignment thesis implies that we are witnessing a broad and ongoing decline in the role of political parties for contemporary publics—not a temporary downturn in public satisfaction with parties as others have argued. Dealignment also suggests that new forms of democratic politics—such as the expansion of direct democracy, the opening of administrative processes to public input, and the expanding use of the court by citizen groups—will develop citizen shift to non-partisan forms of action.[11]

In the face of political dealignment and the breakdown of the patterns of political representation viewed as essential to party democracy, civil society rises as a potential realm in which new politics emerges.[12]

Civil society is also the centrepiece of the alternative model of democracy, namely deliberative democracy. For theorists such as Benhabib and Gutmann and Thompson,[13] working from within a broadly Habermasian framework, civil society has the power to create a diverse public sphere in which communicating actions of different communities and groups mould a discursive

---

[9] Iris M. Young, *Inclusion and Democracy* (Oxford: Oxford University Press, 2002), 188–9.
[10] Pedro Ibarra (ed.), *Social Movements and Democracy* (New York: Palgrave, 2003), 16.
[11] Dalton and Wattenberg, *Parties Without Partisans*, 23.
[12] Thomas Poguntke, *Alternative Politics* (Edinburgh: Edinburgh University Press, 1993).
[13] Seyla Benhabib, 'Towards a Deliberative Model of Democratic Legitimacy', in S. Benhabib (ed.), *Democracy and Difference* (Princeton: Princeton University Press, 1996), 67–94; Amy Gutmann and Dennis Thompson, *Why Deliberative Democracy?* (Princeton: Princeton University Press, 2004).

process of relegitimating the principles of democracy, based on a rational and dialogic discussion in the decent society. These interactions thus strengthen democracy and enhance civil engagement and social participation.

Furthermore, civil society plays a crucial, if more latent role in the multicultural debate. For once the arena of identity transforms itself from universal nationalism to multiculturalism, the obvious loci of these instantiations of actual communities engaged in the debate over minority rights are the boundaries of civil society—be it global, cosmopolitan, or more often than not, statist. Multicultural societies are usually nation states which, through a gradual process since the 1960s, have developed a diversified civil society. Civil society is populated by cultural, ethnic, national, religious, sexual, and gender groups. It is a multilayered arena, inhabited by new social movements, non-governmental organizations, international bodies, and local communities, encompassing new political styles and building new institutions, but also by immigrants' and foreign workers' communities, fundamentalist associations, New Age groups, neo-fascist and anti-immigrant organizations—and many others.[14]

Within advanced industrial democracies both structural and substantive changes have taken place, changes which are reflected in the transformation of political ideologies and in the wider public discourse. On the structural level, a major reshuffling occurred in the apprehension of the public arena. Liberal democracies have by and large endorsed the separation between the public and the private spheres. Going back to classical liberalism in the seventeenth and eighteenth centuries, the public arena was identified with political institutions, the private sphere with individual interest and the economic realm. This basic demarcation was strengthened during the nineteenth century, with the advent of the nation state and the development of representative democracies. It was crystallized in the structuring of the ideological spectrum around the relations between state and the individual: pro-interventionists to the left, anti-interventionists to the right. In the course of the two world wars and the emergence of the welfare state, the cohesiveness of the political, economic, and social realms substantially grew. The neo-liberal rebellion sought to bring back a clearer separation between the private and the public, by rolling back the state and making the free market the main mechanism for social interactions.

However, in post-industrial societies this picture has radically changed. Civil society has become a part of how we perceive society today, a pillar of contemporary theoretical and social discourse.[15] Civil society has become a

---

[14] There is an extensive literature on civil society. Crucial for our argument is to look at both sides of the argument. See, for example, Simone Chambers, 'A Critical Theory of Civil Society', in Simone Chambers and Will Kymlicka (eds.), *Alternative Conceptions of Civil Society* (Princeton: Princeton University Press, 2002), 90–111.

[15] For good overviews, see Simon Sudipta Kaviraj and Sunil Khilnani (eds.), *Civil Society: History and Possibilities* (Cambridge: Cambridge University Press, 2001); Chambers and

key concept in understanding the value system of contemporary discourse, reflecting these changes in advanced democracies.[16] The new patterns of understanding the public sphere, inextricably linked with processes of globalizing markets, waves of immigration, growing levels of higher education, and mounting concerns about environmental problems and indigenous cultures, also enabled a shift in the substantive make-up of the ideological arena. Crucially, this shift was generated on the fringes of the established political system, in an interesting interaction between the radical Left and the far Right, from where it moved onto the centre stage of the public arena. The hegemony of neo-liberalism, which was instated during the 1970s and 1980s, generated a fundamental reaction—against materialism, imperialism, economic globalism, and consumerism—which brought to the fore an alternative set of concepts. Community, sustainability, diversity, grassroots democracy, deliberation, and multiculturalism emanated from a critique of the dominant ideology, but acquired a life of their own in theory, ideology, and public discourse.

This section analyses the incarnation of the structural and substantive changes in contemporary ideologies. Since the 1960s, civil society has emerged as a third dimension of the public sphere. While the main ideological contention since the late nineteenth century has had to do with the relationship between the economic and the political, and whether governmental policies should interfere with the free capitalistic market, the rise of civil society had major implications that transcended the dichotomous political/economic rift. How would the traditional political parties react to the rise of civil society? In what way would it cause a restructuring of their ideology? How would they account for the relationship of institutional politics, the economic realm, and civil society? Would it change their world view? What role would civil society have in their remoulded ideology? The discussion exposes the different responses of the four ideologies to the relations between the political, the economic, and civil society.

In order to analyse these ideological transformations, four contemporary exemplary parties were chosen, all competing for election in 2009-10: the Conservative Party in Britain, the German Greens, the National Front in France, and New Labour in the UK. All these parties adopt a tertiary division: they no longer see the world through the dichotomy of the economic and the political spheres, but perceive civil society as part and parcel of the structure of the public sphere; however, the ideational outcomes in each are fundamentally

---

Kymlicka (eds.), *Alternative Conceptions of Civil Society*; L. Jean Cohen and Andrew Arato, *Civil Society and Political Theory* (Cambridge, MA: MIT Press, 1992); John Ehrenberg, *Civil Society: The Critical History of an Idea* (New York: New York University Press, 1999); Adam Seligman, *The Idea of Civil Society* (Princeton: Princeton University Press, 1992); Charles Taylor, 'Modes of Civil Society', *Public Culture*, 3 (1990), 95-118; Michael Walzer, 'The Idea of Civil Society', *Dissent*, 38 (Spring 1991), 293-304.

[16] See Cohen and Arato, *Civil Society and Political Theory*, p. ix.

different. Their interpretation of this threefold division, in turn, is closely linked with the way they conceptualize issues of identity, culture, community, and their model of democracy. Thus, analysing the role of civil society in the ideologies of contemporary political parties will demonstrate the powerful ideational transformation they all underwent, as well as the different paths of incorporating civil society into the world views that each of them has chosen.

The Big (Civil) Society: Conservative Ideology Refashioned

Thatcher unforgettably declared in 1987 that 'there is no such thing as society':

> I think we've been through a period where too many people have been given to understand that if they have a problem, it's the government's job to cope with it. 'I have a problem, I'll get a grant.' 'I'm homeless, the government must house me.' They're casting their problem on society. And, you know, there is no such thing as society. There are individual men and women, and there are families.[17]

David Cameron, the incoming prime minister of Britain, put forward his own big idea: 'You can call it liberalism. You can call it empowerment. You can call it freedom. You can call it responsibility. I call it the Big Society.'[18] He declared in his first speech outside 10 Downing Street on 12 May 2010 that 'real change is when everyone pulls together, comes together, works together, where we all exercise our responsibilities to ourselves, to our families, to our communities and to others'. Cameron is situated within the Conservative tradition, hence he re-embraces individuals, embedded in families, as his ideological building blocks. However, Cameron goes beyond the family to suggest the community as the social agent critical for his renewed world view. 'Community' facilitates a different reading of the concept of 'society', from the organized workforce which was the focal point of Thatcher's attack to a notion of 'civil society' in which individuals voluntarily take care of themselves and their communities. Cameron explains his idea of the Big Society:

> The Big Society is about a huge culture change where people, in their everyday lives, in their homes, in their neighbourhoods, in their workplace don't always turn to officials, local authorities or central government for answers to the problems they face but instead feel both free and powerful enough to help themselves and their own communities. It's about people setting up great new schools. Businesses helping people getting trained for work. Charities working to rehabilitate offenders. It's about liberating the biggest, most dramatic redistribution of power from elites in Whitehall to the man and woman on the street.[19]

---

[17] Margaret Thatcher, talking to *Women's Own* magazine, 31 October 1987.
[18] David Cameron, *Big Society Speech*, Liverpool, 19 July 2010.
[19] David Cameron, *Big Society Speech*.

Cameron consciously challenges the Conservative tradition and his ancestor, Thatcher, on two fundamental issues: 'community' has entered his discourse as a leading agent of the polity, beyond individuals and family (and the nation) in the traditional reactionary world view; and crucially, society is endorsed by Cameron, cast as his one big idea, the key component of his ideology. There is here an obvious conceptual restructuring of the Conservative discourse.

But is it a fundamental change that transforms their ideology? Has the Conservative world view revised itself a generation after the Iron Lady forged together neo-liberalism and nationalism?[20] Actually, the concept of 'society' they talk about is fundamentally different: Thatcher identified the social factor with socialism, and in particular with the trade unions with their close ties to central government, and sought to shift the balance, to minimize the role of government and leave the terrain for the individual-driven market. For Cameron, society is something completely different, though the sentiment is the same:

> We've got to get rid of the centralized bureaucracy that wastes money and undermines morale. And in its place we've got to give professionals much more freedom, and open up public services to new providers like charities, social enterprises and private companies so we get more innovation, diversity and responsiveness to public need.

Charities, social enterprises, and private companies are all agents of *civil society*. The role of civil society in Cameron's discourse is precisely the role of limiting the state and reducing the power of government: 'For a long time the way government has worked—top-down, top-heavy, controlling—has frequently had the effect of sapping responsibility, local innovation and civic action.' Civic action and innovation are used to reduce state powers and devolve them back to the people. Thus, at the end of the day, these agents of the Big Society work for the same Conservative goals: reducing governmental interference and enhancing the market: 'We want to turn government on its head, taking power away from Whitehall and putting it into the hands of people and communities.'[21] Thatcher wanted to abolish society in order to achieve that goal; Cameron uses civil society organizations, a very different agent of society, in order to get to the same ends.

The idea of society as a third realm between the state and the economy has implications for the role of the government, its policies, and for the public service:

> The Big Society runs consistently through our policy programme. Our plans to reform public services, mend our broken society, and rebuild trust in politics are

---

[20] Desmond King, *The New Right: Politics, Markets & Citizenship* (London: Macmillan, 1987).
[21] David Cameron, *Structural Reform Plans*, The Civil Service Live Event, 8 July 2010.

all part of our Big Society agenda. These plans involve redistributing power from the state to society; from the centre to local communities, giving people the opportunity to take more control over their lives.[22]

As for the public service: 'Our public service reform programme will enable social enterprises, charities and voluntary groups to play a leading role in delivering public services and tackling deep-rooted social problems.'[23] The Conservatives' aim is one and the same as it was a generation ago: 'Our aim is to increase the private sector's share of the economy in every part of the country by boosting enterprise and creating a better business environment.'[24] In terms of policy, Cameron concludes, it boils down to this: 'The rule of this government should be this: If it unleashes community engagement—we should do it. If it crushes it—we shouldn't.'[25] Thus, while there is a clear conceptual refurbishing, and an acknowledgment of the three realms of the public sphere—state, economy, and civil society, civil society is taken as an executor of the traditional Conservative role—that of transferring power for the state to the market, from government to 'the people'. So has the 2010 Conservative Party revoked Thatcherite ideology? It most definitely changed the conceptualization of society; however, the restructuring of society enabled a renewed prominence of the traditional ideology. The way the Conservative manifesto aptly explains it is: 'There is such a thing as society, it's just not the same thing as the state.'[26]

The German Greens: Challenging the Borders between the Social and the Political

The Conservative view of civil society is apparent even in the agents of civil society they have chosen to designate for their ideological revival—charities, voluntary organizations, and aid groups. All these forms of association go back to the mid nineteenth century; however, the newest forms of social actors which have emerged since the 1960s in liberal democracies—the new social movements, non-governmental organizations, protest groups, and the Greens—lie at the heart of new democratic theory. Theories of deliberative democracy were highly influenced by the emergence of the collective actors in civil society. Political theorists seek to maintain side by side the political realm, i.e. representative democracy, and civil society—characterized by deliberating

---

[22] The Conservative Party, *The Conservative Manifesto 2010* (London: Conservative Party, 2010), 37.
[23] The Conservative Party, *The Conservative Manifesto 2010*, 37.
[24] The Conservative Party, *The Conservative Manifesto 2010*, 23.
[25] David Cameron, *Structural Reform Plans*.
[26] The Conservative Party, *The Conservative Manifesto 2010*, 45.

communities. Against representative democracy, against emphasizing universal participation as embodied in elections among parties, and against reducing citizenship to the right to vote, deliberative theorists advocate concrete forms of active participation.

Benhabib is a good case in point. She explicates: 'The procedural specifications of this model privilege a *plurality of modes of association* in which all affected can have the right to articulate their point of view.'[27] With the change from the established political realm to an extended social arena comes the centrality of civil society as the prime locus of interaction manifested in deliberation. Benhabib continues: 'It is through the interlocking of these multiple forms of associations, networks, and organizations that an anonymous "public conversation" results.'[28] Not only does civil society gain primacy as the realm of the public sphere where most of the networks and organizations operate, but the unique feature of this realm is public discourse, argumentation, and communication. An alternative model of democracy emerges. Legitimacy, rationality, and associations become quintessential to the normative power of deliberative democracy. Communication becomes an act of participation, a manifestation of active citizenship, extended to civil society and measured not by voting, legislating, or policymaking, but by engaging in debate on the nature of society on different levels, through diverse networks, by a plurality of collective actors. Yet, just as with communitarianism and multiculturalism, the collective actors become the prime unit in this political analysis.

The green movement was always a key actor in the imagined participatory democracy. Interestingly, while capturing the imagination of political theorists, the activists of the new social movements have developed a world view of their own. Thus, the German Greens who emerged in civil society in the 1980s were from the beginning the actor which above all sought to transform politics: they developed a distinct notion of the role of civil society in the re-politicization of liberal democracies. The Greens challenged the borders between the political and the social, seeking to transform the meaning of the 'political'. The 2010 Manifesto of the Greens in Germany reads:

> Democracy needs civic engagement. Exactly because our party has sprung from the movements and sought cooperation... we know the significance of civic engagement. Civic engagement must be an integral part of our society and not the business of the government. We see engagement as a need and an opportunity for society, as well as its goal. Engagement means social and cultural participation and further personal growth for each and every one of us. In the future we want engagement to engender creativity and solidarity... A lively civil society needs the involvement, creativity, and participation of many people.[29]

---

[27] Benhabib, 'Towards a Deliberative Model', 73.
[28] Benhabib, 'Towards a Deliberative Model', 73-4.
[29] Bündnis 90/die Grünen, *Der Grüne Neue Gesellschaftsvertrag* (Leck: CPI Books, 2010).

The Greens' main ideological concern is with disparate groups that are disadvantaged on political, economic, social, cultural, or environmental grounds. The Greens attempt to incorporate them into an alternative vision of a participatory democracy. This, in turn, allows issues of ecology, the underclass, ethnic minorities, Third-Worldism, or gender inequality to find their place within the broader conceptual structure of their modular ideology. Indeed, the cement between these different disadvantaged groups is the principle of inclusion. This, together with respect for others, tolerance, social justice, participatory politics, and grassroots democracy has been at the heart of their ideology.[30] The idea of inclusion stands in close antagonistic relations to that of exclusion, which is fundamental to the conception of the extreme right.

The Greens sought a post-national multicultural democracy in which cultural, national, and ethnic communities are endorsed and collective identities—other than national ones—are cherished. Civil society is used to revitalize the established political system and endow a different kind of polity, with grassroots democracy based on active participation in local, national, regional, international, and global politics. It was embedded in a new kind of politics: 'we want with our electoral program to create passion for politics'. Politics is a life-long process, politics is a way of life: 'We should not decide for our future only in the ballot box, but everywhere and every day.' The Greens 'want to make politics with people, not only with their votes'.[31] Civil society challenged the established party system and the very understanding of what is the 'political'. The politicization of society was the role ascribed to civil society in the new Left.

While in the 1990s they were strong advocates of cultural rights, the Greens have realized the problem with pursuing the politics of collective identity to the full. Without giving up their vision of a multicultural democracy, their 2003 new fundamental manifesto, replacing the basic programme of 1980, opens: 'At the centre of our politics stands the person, with his dignity and freedom. The prohibition to interfere with one's dignity is our starting point.'[32] For the first time in an ideological document, the individual is placed at the centre of the Greens' world view, and the relations to nature, community, state, and the world are deduced from one's inalienable rights to dignity and freedom. The return to individual rights as the basis of culture, community, and participatory democracy may have been too late as the relegitimation of collective identity and primordial communities already had struck an ancient chord with their principal opponent, the far Right.

---

[30] Gayil Talshir, *The Political Ideology of Green Parties: From Politics of Nature to Redefining the Nature of Politics* (London: Palgrave, 2002).

[31] Bündnis 90/die Grünen, *Wahlprogramm* (Berlin: Bündnis 90/die Grünen, 1994).

[32] Bündnis 90/die Grünen, *Grün2020—wir denken bis übermorgen: Entwurf für das Grundsatzprogramm* (Berlin: Bündnis 90/die Grünen, 2001), 8.

The National Front: National Identity against Multicultural Civil Society

The French National Front placed the struggle against the multicultural society at the heart of its contemporary ideology, constructing a double helix of the foe–friend framework classic of the extreme Right: designating the enemy from within (ethnic cultures and social disintegration) and the enemy from without (cosmopolitan, imperial, American-led mass culture and the European Union). The ideology of the National Front perceives French civilization as constituted by organic ties embedded within history, tradition, and collective values, bonded by French citizenship. Universalism is endorsed by generalizing the natural feeling of national solidarity and portraying it as a universal emotion, which is part of human nature. The National Front therefore claims to be not racist, for it recognizes the universal impulse of nationhood. France is for the French, this is its modest claim; other people can have their own countries. In the words of Le Pen: 'We have one vocation: to serve France so it will remain French.'[33] The climax of the programme of the 2002 National Front reads:

> The rejection of the multicultural society in the name of the identity of France is the fundamental struggle of the National Front. Identity is to the nation what personality is to the individual. They are the conditions for its life and liberty.[34]

Indeed, national identity is the central pillar of the National Front's programme. The first part of the programme is therefore immigration, stating that immigration is the biggest problem France is facing, making the reversal of the immigration flux the primary goal of the National Front, calling to stop all further immigration and rejecting the 'politics of assimilation'.[35] Against immigration and the ethnic communities that are its manifestation, the National Front puts forward the reactionary vision of the family and the nation. The family, the basic unit of society, is facing an economic and social crisis. The prevailing notion is one of disintegration of the basic unit of identity. The 2010 'family and children' programme reads: 'the family is the sole base of our society ... The family, like the nation, is today at the centre of the attacks ... four pillars support the national edifice: the family, the school, the religion and the army. Since 1968, the silent revolution of anarchy and globalism have tried to ruin them. The traditional family is at the heart of conveying the great moral and social

---

[33] Bündnis 90/die Grünen, *Grün2020*, 3.
[34] National Front, *Programme du Front National* (2002), 26.
[35] See <http://www.frontnational.com/?page_id=1095,2010>.

values that constitute our people.'[36] The crisis of the French family is conceived as inextricably linked with the hedonistic and egotistic '1968 culture',[37] which legitimized abortions and children out of wedlock, and ultimately led to the expansion of divorce. The French family—taken to be the natural building block of a national society—is also a microcosm of its disintegration. The prime source of '*dissociété*'—the breakdown of the natural ties—is immigration.

> The presence and development, year after year, of colonies of people, supported by a very auspicious social and legal system and delirious propaganda of favouring strangers, christened as 'the fight against racism', is for our national identity a death threat: it modifies profoundly the very nature of the French people. The formation of closed communities, based on ethnicity, evidently contradicts the entire history of the French society.[38]

This manifests the National Front's reaction to civil society: immigration is the bedrock of multicultural communities, and is therefore rejected as part of the post-1968 outcomes. Opposing multiculturalism in the interests of French identity, they call for the reversal of the current flood of immigration, a ban on all future immigration, and the return of immigrants to their country of origin. It is justified by demanding the reaffirmation of the basic code for nationality and citizenship—being French-born to both a French mother and father. Only French citizens will be accorded the right to vote.[39] The 2010 'Solidarity' manifesto of the National Front in France therefore named as its main objective the establishment of broad national solidarity, from cradle to grave, 'based on the principle of national preference'.[40]

Neither civil society nor multiculturalism is mentioned as such in the 2010 National Front's programmes; however, they are omnipresent as the root of all evil. The development of civil society on both accounts of the National Front—the 1968 silent revolution generation which is manifested in the new social movements in civil society, and the ethnic communities of immigrants which the New Left defends at the expense of French nationals—signifies the deed that needs undoing. Yet from another perspective, if one looks at the actual politics of the National Front—its mobilization, demonstration, virtual politics, activism, and civic engagement—it is clear that the National Front and other extreme right groups were able to capitalize on the emergence of civil society as the locus of their new, more 'legitimate' xenophobia which they fashioned as their new ideological core. Moreover, the far Right can be

---

[36] See <http://www.frontnational.com/?page_id=1116,2010>.
[37] National Front, *Programme du Front National*, 11.
[38] National Front, *Programme du Front National*, 22.
[39] National Front, *Programme du Front National*, 28.
[40] See <http://www.frontnational.com/?page_id=1179,2010>.

counted as part and parcel of the same civil society they so deplore. The boundaries between Left and Right are much less clear-cut in civil society. This can be demonstrated by the fact that both the nationalist, extreme right camp and the radical leftist crowds were marching shoulder to shoulder against the coalition which fought in Iraq and Afghanistan. Indeed, the slogan of the anti-war campaign in the 2000s—'no blood for oil'—was first used by Le Pen himself in the first war against Iraq.

New Labour: Civil Society and the Moral Sentiment

In contrast to the other ideological families, in which the role of civil society had to be reconstructed and its implicit meaning retrieved, the concept has a prescribed role in the renewal of social democracy: 'The fostering of an active civil society is a basic part of the politics of the third way... Civic decline is real and visible in many sectors of contemporary societies... It is seen in the weakening sense of solidarity in some local communities and urban neighbourhoods, high levels of crime, and the break-up of marriages and families.'[41] Third-way thinking, established by Anthony Giddens—a distinguished sociologist who was an adviser to Tony Blair, the first Labour Prime Minister since 1979—relied on civil society to relieve the welfare state of the burden of social justice by ascribing a growing role to local communities and voluntary associations. In return for their greater role, the government expected these associations to play a part in forging a new solidarity towards the nation state. The community thus acquires a role within the cosmopolitan state, and facilitates a growing democratization of society, since democracy is not confined to the party system but to the diversity of civil society.

For Tony Blair, the Third Way was not old left or new right but a new centre and centre-left governing philosophy for the future. The political task was to distance himself from Old Labour and Thatcherism without alienating the two major political blocks, which composed both camps. In economic terms, Blair followed Giddens's footsteps in transforming the role of the state from owner and regulator to a guiding partner: 'The purpose of economic intervention is not that Government can run industry, but that it should work with it so that industry is better able to run itself.'[42] It is this notion of working together, of enabling and facilitating that the government acquires.

Crucially, this understanding of economics generated a vacuum in social cohesion. The welfare state, with Marshall's perception of social rights, held society together through the social net which the state provided. The market economy relinquished this trust in the system and created a vacuum: 'The

---

[41] Anthony Giddens, *The Third Way* (Cambridge: Polity Press, 1998), 78.
[42] Labour Party, *Ambition for Britain, Labour's Manifesto 2001* (London: Labour Party, 2001).

Conservatives have systematically divided our nation and eroded the social fabric that holds us together... For far from creating a classless society, the gap between classes has become a gulf.'[43] The individualism of the marketplace, which Blair did not offset, generated a vacuum of solidarity and trust; the alternative would be the sense of community: 'At the heart of my beliefs is the idea of community... I mean that our fulfilment as individuals lies in a decent society of others. My argument to you today is that the renewal of community is the answer to the challenge of a changing world.'[44]

But what kind of community did he have in mind? This is where the ascribed role of civil society comes into play: 'We understand the benefits of open markets... But we believe also in an active civic society, founded on the basis of solidarity that provides a helping hand for people to realize their potential.'[45] At the heart of Blair's politics were the concepts of community, solidarity, partnership, and civic society. However, in contrast to neo-liberal, consumer-oriented civic society, and fragmented ethnic cultures advocated by the New Left, for Blair civic society was the prime tool for creating solidarity for 'one Britain':

> The Third Way needs a concept of a modern civic society that is founded on opportunity and responsibility; rights and duties go together. Society has a duty to its citizens and its citizens have a duty for society... But—and here is the deal that is at the heart of a good, decent, modern civic society—in return for that opportunity we are entitled to demand law-abiding behaviour... We believe, therefore, in this concept of strong, modern civic society and we can be equally fierce in our defence of racial and religious tolerance as in our attack on crime and social disintegration. What people are looking for today is a country free from prejudice but not free from rules. They want a strong society bound by strong rules. That society should be fair and it should give the equality of opportunity that people need but it should also demand that responsibility back from them as citizens of that society.[46]

The basic unit of civic society in this vision is the individual, bearing rights and responsibilities. It is *civic* society, as its components are equal citizens, bounded by civic laws and entitled to civic liberties. It is where racial and religious tolerance is practised, and also where social disintegration is tackled. Civic society—the community of British citizens—was central for his polity. He sought 'to create a one-nation Britain where all share in our country's prosperity, not only a privileged few.'[47]

---

[43] Labour Party, *Manifesto 2001*, 14.
[44] Tony Blair, speech, Women's Institute, London, 7 June 2000.
[45] Tony Blair, speech, Sao Paulo, Brazil, 30 July 2001.
[46] Tony Blair, 'Speech to the South Africa Parliament' (1999), cited in Norman Fairclough, *New Labour, New Language?* (London: Routledge, 2000), 38.
[47] Tony Blair, speech, Washington, 18 February 2003.

But if this marks a return to classical liberalism with its emphasis on individual citizens within a political community, what did New Labour think about ethnic, religious, and cultural minorities? 'Labour believes that Britain can be a model of multicultural, multi-racial society... Now it is time to build the inclusive society in tune with British values. Our commitment to protection of every citizen is expressed in the 1998 Human Rights Act.'[48] The ideal of a multicultural society was rooted in protecting individuals. Their social communities had a role to play in cementing the new national solidarity:

> Voluntary and community organizations are key to Labour's vision for Britain. From large national charities to local community groups and faith-based institutions, these sectors are a vital and diverse part of national life... Labour will build on its Compact with the voluntary sector, as we develop more far-reaching partnerships for the delivery of services and the renewal of our communities.[49]

Thus, we came full circle: the role of civil society for New Labour, analogous to neo-liberalism, was to relieve the welfare state from its social burdens by using voluntary, religious, and local communities. In return for this role, they were to generate national solidarity. However, this world view was much more national than Giddens's cosmopolitan democracy, and much more committed to reducing the gap between rich and poor than the neo-liberal view. Gordon Brown, the Chancellor of the Exchequer and the successor of Blair as Prime Minister, would add political moralism as his own contribution to the shaping of Third Way ideology.

Indeed, Brown had founded his view of civic society in a central speech on 'civic society in modern Britain', where he argued that civic society was a longstanding British tradition:

> I see our free and cooperative association in civic society as having its roots in what the Scottish Enlightenment philosophers called the moral sense, by which they meant a set of moral sentiments or dispositions that all human beings possess in common. These philosophers argued that the true source of human sociability lies not in self-interest but in a shared feeling of mutual sympathy.[50]

Civic society was perceived as the means to arrive at the caring society, the fair society, derived, according to Brown, from a shared moral sense of altruism:

> In my view, two important consequences follow for the character of civic society, both central to my themes today. First, the new covenant—and the society it leads to—will be one in which we extend opportunity and demand responsibility in

---

[48] Labour Party, *Manifesto 2001*, 33.
[49] Labour Party, *Manifesto 2001*, 34.
[50] Gordon Brown, *Civic Society in Modern Britain*, 17th Arnold Goodman Charity Lecture, 20 July 2000.

return. And secondly, the outcome will be an active civic engagement, not a passive civic obedience, restoring the principles of voluntary and community action to a central social place.

Thus, civic society facilitated a philosophical transition which is apparent in other dimensions of Brown's political thought:[51] one that drifts away from social democracy towards Scottish Enlightenment values and political liberalism. The realm of moral sentiment, of altruism, was completely detached from the state, though the state should be 'an enabling state', in Brown's terms, to facilitate it. Active civic society should nevertheless act in favour of each and every individual and lead to a fair society. Whether this was indeed reflected in Brown's policies, or in his strong endorsement of the state as a key actor, is a different question. In his philosophy, he imagined this role for civil society and for the moral realm, which was never as strong in political reality.

Whereas for Giddens the reliance on civil society was to relieve the state from some of its welfare burden, and for Blair it was a way to transform the state to a more standard-setting, regulating body, for Brown civil society was an independent realm, a true third arena of the public space, which is not run by self-interest like the economic realm, or public interest like the political realm, but by moral sentiment and shared community ideals.

Civic Society—from Theory to Ideology

Advanced liberal democracies have experienced a fundamental restructuring of the perceptions of the public sphere from a private/public divide into three autonomous realms of politics, economics, and civic society. These changes were absorbed into the four dominant ideological families in Europe today, facilitating, in each case, their own internal renewal. For scholars of ideology, that means there are 'guiding concepts' through which a fundamental, cross-ideological change can be explored. However, in each ideology the role of civic society, as manifested in its relation to the other two spheres, was distinctly different. Conservatism constructed civil society as a vehicle to liberate state-occupied public goods, thereby hoping to generate a greater societal good by freeing the creative forces of society from the centralized grip. The idea of citizenship was transformed from a political notion into an economic one and was placed in the economic realm of citizens as consumers. The New Left, manifested in the Greens' ideology, sought to challenge the relationship

---

[51] Simon Lee, *Best for Britain? The Politics and Legacy of Gordon Brown* (Oxford: Oneworld, 2007).

between the political and the social by devising a grassroots democracy of communicating communities. The politicization of civil society, based on collective identities, entailed an opportunity which the extreme Right seized. They sought 'civic peace' in an organic society in which economic chauvinism, national identity, citizenship, and social integration would be coextensive. For the Third Way, civil society was crucial in transferring responsibility from the welfare state to the communities, based on a moral ideal of regenerating a shared solidarity through the voluntary, religious, and local organizations of civil society, thus cementing anew the national community.

The restructuring of the public sphere also had implications for the substance of these ideological families. The main argument here is that in setting the political agenda there is a crucial role to the fringe, opposition, and radical movements. While the main left and right parties focus on the median voter, seeking to capture the centre of the ideological spectrum, it is oftentimes the radical parties which have the capacity to place new political issues on the public agenda. Thus, the discourse of multiculturalism, politics of identity, and communitarianism arose from the reaction against the neo-liberal hegemony of both ruling parties. For neo-liberalism methodological individualism is crucial: each person is a pursuer of interests, whether he is an immigrant, a foreign worker, an employer, or unemployed. There is no room for cultural communities besides the civic space operating on market demand. The neo-conservatives came thus to hold the contrary position, in which their economic agenda encouraged waves of immigration, while their traditional nationalism dictated prohibitions on the naturalization of these immigrants, thus generating an underclass. The reaction of the New Left was a full endorsement of the new disadvantaged groups, including both economically exploited—foreign workers, homeless, immigrants—and culturally disadvantaged—ethnic, religious, national, and sexual minorities. The new sense of community enabled transcendence beyond national identity to the local and the global communities. However, the New Left thus jeopardized the universal commitment to the individual as the basic unit of the political vision. The centrality of groups, and collective identity, was abused by the far Right. Far from being indifferent to the new discourse of identity and culture introduced by the New Left, the extremists built on the relegitimation of collective communities, to return to politics of (national) identity. Whereas their agenda was an exclusionist one, seeing national preference as a natural policy outcome, the Third Way was as nationalistic, but of an inclusionist type. It sought to relegitimize its own understanding of liberal nationalism. The cultural and religious communities were to become part of the national project of a renewed solidarity based on citizenship.

IDEOLOGICAL ANALYSIS AND THE DEALIGNMENT/REALIGNMENT DEBATE

Comparative political research decisively demonstrates that traditional patterns of political behaviour—social position as determining political alignments, electoral turnout, party membership, trust in democratic institutions, party identification, and more—are in decline. One political theorist comments:

> In nearly all advanced industrial democracies for which long-term survey data are now available, partisan ties have weakened over the past generation. Similarly, there has been a decrease in party-line voting and an increase in partisan volatility, split-ticket voting and other phenomena showing that fewer citizens are voting according to a party-line or group-determined lines.[52]

Thus, the argument goes, processes of dealignment erode dramatically the role of parties. If liberal democracy was once unthinkable save in terms of party democracy, the dealignment scholars ask us to 'think the unthinkable'.[53] The weak opposition to this school suggests that rather than dealignment, we are witnessing processes of realignment; that is, not a breakdown of all electoral patterns but a different alignment of social and political attachments.[54] What evidence can the ideological analysis of the four party families in liberal democracies bring to this theoretical debate?

The decline of party democracy has different facets; some dealing with the role parties play in the eyes of the electorate, others with the way parties themselves act. Thus, some of the new trends that have been identified are the personification of politics, issue-based politics, and ideological conversion. The ideological analysis goes back to the primary theory of democracy of Schumpeter and others, taking party competition for voters, by virtue of contrasting campaigns and ideological battle, as the original position. Has the decline of the parties been reflected in their ideological stagnation, and has their leader orientation diminished their distinct world views?

What the ideological analysis has revealed can be introduced on three levels. First, the parties of the early 2000s still perceive the production of electoral manifestos as a central way of explaining themselves to the public. Whether the programmes provide a chance for the new leadership to voice itself, as in the cases of Cameron, Clegg, and Miliband in Britain, or whether it is a participatory process which encourages party members to take part in a meaningful way, like the German Greens, the production of ideology is still a viable vehicle for internal cohesion of the parties today. True, each manifesto

---

[52] Dalton and Klingemann (eds.), *Oxford Handbook of Political Behavior*, 10.
[53] Dalton and Wattenberg, *Parties Without Partisans*, 16.
[54] Peter Mair, *Party System Change* (Oxford: Oxford University Press, 1997).

is also on the party's website, there are video clips on YouTube, and other virtual means of communicating with the technophile electorate, but the party manifesto is still a primary tool in today's electoral campaigns. Second, the world view of the parties as reflected in the manifestos expresses a serious conceptual undertaking by the party. Rather than ideological stagnation or flashy programmes of policy issues which would better fit the bill of issue-based politics, each party has attempted to produce a cohesive and coherent world view. Moreover, each of the party families has reacted to the transformation of the public sphere and incorporated the concept of civil society—and thereby the alternative structuring of the polity—as part of its reformation. Thus, rather than adopting some shared or similar way of relating to civic society, each party has undergone an internal process of ideological refashioning, and created distinct and conflicting views of the role of civil society *vis-à-vis* the traditional economics/politics dichotomy. The very process of internal rethinking and reshaping of the ideology signifies the livelihood and adaptability of the parties. The different products of this rethinking process reveal both the viability of the parties and their distinctness.

Thus, what emerges from the ideological analysis is a refurbished left/right continuum. The conservative Right has challenged its own tradition of revoking society, only to mould the Big Society, manifested in charities, voluntary groups, and private associations as a way to reduce the role of the state, to reform the public services, and to encroach upon the regulative authority of the government, thereby reproducing itself as a neo-liberal agent. The social democratic Left has adopted civic society as a vehicle for changing the role of the state to an enabling, regulative state which sets the standards and values, and regulates the free action of society. It also found new ways of incorporating minority groups by giving them more autonomy, demanding in return greater national solidarity. For the radical Left, civic society is the way to enliven democracy and produce a more participatory, accountable, and engaging society. Meanwhile the extreme Right developed a reactionary position, blaming the ethnic groupings of immigrants in civil society and its political protégé—the New Left—as the root cause of social disintegration. While the big parties voice the traditional struggle over intervention in the economy in terms of the Left/Right, the radical parties are bringing to the ideological spectrum issues of political identity as their quintessential view.

The implications of that to the dealignment/realignment debate are clear: each party has reshaped its own ideological vision in contemporary terms and demonstrated both adaptability and self-identity. Rather than dealignment, ideological analysis supports the thesis of realignment, with a strong emphasis from the traditional big parties, especially in view of the recent economic crisis, on the economic-cum-political dimension, while the small parties focus on identity politics. This shows a secondary realignment within the ideological camps of the Left and Right.

CONCLUDING DISCUSSION: THE ROLE OF IDEOLOGY STUDIES IN POLITICAL SCIENCE

In order to re-examine the role of the study of ideology, this paper has tackled two fronts: that of political theory and that of comparative politics. The theoretical analysis has demonstrated the penetration of theoretical debates and grand theory into real politics. All major ideological families enhanced the new structuring of the public sphere into economics/politics/civil society, but also used these transformations to refashion their own ideological view: each party family has chosen to relate to different agents within civil society as their own take on the polity, and devised a different role for the state, a unique perception of citizenship and a distinct model of democracy. This at once symbolizes the viability and adaptability of the key players of representative democracy—the political parties. As for comparative politics, the ideological account brought to the fore the realigned left/right spectrum: the two dominant parties still differ on the issue of economic intervention, while their smaller counterparts to their right and left emphasize identity politics as their big theme. There is a realignment but only of a secondary importance as it is happening at the margins of the dominant ideological spectrum. However, it signifies the crucial role that the study of ideology plays within political theory and comparative politics, and as a bridge between them. Ideology continues to provide the battlefield of politics today, despite the growth, over the last hundred years, of the apparent feeling that the end of liberal democracy as we have known it has arrived.

11

In Defence of Political Understanding?[1]

Michael Kenny

PREFACE

Over the course of his distinguished career, Michael Freeden has emerged as one of Europe's most important, innovative, and stimulating political theorists. Having forged an impressive scholarly reputation for his interpretation of the New Liberalism of the early twentieth century,[2] he has more recently branched out to develop a stimulating body of interpretative and methodological arguments about the nature and boundaries of political thinking, and how it should be studied. His landmark volume, *Ideologies and Political Theory* (1996), achieved the rare feat of reaching out to scholars in both the 'Anglo-American' and 'Continental' communities. It has done an enormous amount to establish the legitimacy of the proposition that political thinking can be analysed in relation to its ideological patterning, as well as broached through the normative analysis of concepts and the historical study of the meanings of individual authors and texts. His assessments of various ideological traditions in this book, together with a series of enormously fertile editorial essays in the *Journal of Political Ideologies*, and other collections of essays that he has published,[3] represent a rich and highly original corpus of work.

---

[1] I am grateful to Stefan Collini for discussions about Bernard Crick's work, and his thoughts on an earlier draft of this chapter, and also to the editors of this volume for their perceptive feedback on an earlier draft. I would also like to take this opportunity to signal my immense gratitude to Michael Freeden for the friendship, guidance, and intellectual inspiration he has provided over many years.

[2] See Michael Freeden, *The New Liberalism: An Ideology of Social Reform* (Oxford: Oxford University Press, 1978); and *Liberalism Divided: A Study in British Political Thought, 1914–1939* (Oxford: Oxford University Press, 1986).

[3] See, for instance, the essays collected in his *Liberal Languages: Ideological Imaginations and Twentieth-Century Progressive Thought* (Princeton: Princeton University Press, 2004); and *Green Ideology: Concepts and Structures* (Oxford: Oxford Centre for the Environment, Ethics and Society, 1995).

One of the hallmarks of Michael's career has been his commitment to supplement his scholarly work with the hard labour involved in establishing institutional spaces and forums that create new communities of scholarly interest. He was, for instance, the founding editor and guiding force behind the *Journal of Political Ideologies*.[4] He was also instrumental in establishing the innovative Centre for Political Ideologies at the University of Oxford.[5] Latterly, he has been active in promoting the intellectual case for a more rigorous understanding of comparative political theory, bringing together scholars from different countries to develop this enterprise collaboratively.

Michael's work is characterized by the unceasingly creative and enquiring approach he has taken to the study of political ideas. In a field of enquiry that sometimes rewards the formulaic and familiar over the unusual and the heterodox, his writings have been a beacon for the idea of studying political thinking in its historical incarnations and contemporary guises with an eclectic methodological toolkit and intense intellectual curiosity. His work has provided an important source of stimulation and guidance for those who have sought to push beyond the presumptions and predilections associated with the prevailing historical and philosophical approaches to political theory.

Two themes have become especially prominent in his scholarship since he began his extensive labours in the fields of modern political ideology. One of these has been his acute critique of the distorting implications of the approach to political thinking associated with the leading strands of normative Anglophone theory. The other has been his growing frustration at the tendency of academic practitioners to overlook fundamental features of everyday political thinking. This latter commitment has led him most recently to undertake a typically ambitious and challenging study examining the alienated relationship that persists between much political theorizing and recurrent features of politics itself.[6]

---

[4] The *Journal of Political Ideologies* was founded in 1996 under the editorship of Michael Freeden. It has developed into one of the leading political theory journals in the Anglophone world.

[5] He was also an important supporter for the establishment of a 'sister' centre at the University of Sheffield—an unusual example of cross-institutional collaboration at a time when competition has been the predominant norm.

[6] See for instance, Michael Freeden's 'What makes a Political Concept Political?', paper delivered at the Annual Meeting of the American Political Science Association, Washington, DC (2005); 'What Should the "Political" in Political Theory Explore?', *Journal of Political Philosophy*, 13 (2005), 113–34; 'Political Thinking as Power', in K. Dowding (ed.), *Encyclopedia of Power* (London: Sage Publications, 2011); 'Thinking Politically and Thinking about Politics: Language, Interpretation, and Ideology', in M. Stears and D. Leopold (eds.), *Political Theory: Methods and Approaches* (Oxford: Oxford University Press, 2008); 'The Arrogance of Politics: Political Thinking as Boundary-Setting', talk delivered to the Centre for Political Ideologies, University of Oxford, available at <http://www.ucl.ac.uk/spp/seminars/political-theory-downloads/UCL_09.pdf (2009)>; and 'Languages of Political Support: Engaging with the Public Realm', *Critical Review of International Social and Political Philosophy*, 12 (2009), 183–202.

In Defence of Political Understanding?

This chapter is primarily concerned with identifying the limits and consequences of a marked trend in recent political commentary. This involves a widespread return to the insights of Bernard Crick's landmark text, *In Defence of Politics* (1962). In the course of my discussion, I alight upon several arguments that Michael has developed regarding the nature and interpretation of political ideas. My treatment of his writings is necessarily truncated as my primary focus falls elsewhere. But I hope to convey to those unfamiliar with his most recent writings a sense of their richness and importance, and their pertinence to current debates about the standing of, and challenges facing, democratic politics.

INTRODUCTION

The turn back to the account of, and arguments for, politics associated with the late Bernard Crick is a striking feature of recent political journalism and academic commentary in Britain. This trend is closely linked to a growing anxiety about the standing of politics and politicians. This worry has been considerably deepened by the MPs' expenses scandal that dominated politics at Westminster for most of 2009, which continues to reverberate in the consciousness of the public. In the wake of this minor political earthquake, numerous politicians, pundits, and academics have taken to articulating the rationale for politics, and many have sought to claim anchorage in Crick's work.[7] This renewal of interest surfaced too in the various obituary pieces and subsequent assessments that appeared in the wake of Crick's death in 2008.[8]

---

[7] Crick's work is cited in Peter Riddell, 'In Defence of Politicians—In Spite of Themselves', *The Hansard Society Parliamentary Affairs Annual Lecture*, 25 February 2010, available at <http://www.hansard-society.org.uk/blogs/recent_events/archive/2010/02/24/2376.aspx>;
Tony Wright, 'Doing Politics Differently', *Political Quarterly*, 80 (2009), 319–28; P. Evans 'Do We Need Political Parties?' (2009), blogpost available at <http://blog.localdemocracy.org.uk/2009/02/10/do-we-need-political-parties-a-prelude/>; and M. Flinders 'In Defence of Politics', *Political Quarterly*, 81 (2010), 309–26.

[8] See the following obituaries: 'Sir Bernard Crick', *The Daily Telegraph*, 21 December 2008, available at <http://www.telegraph.co.uk/news/obituaries/3884593/Sir-Bernard-Crick.html>; 'Sir Bernard Crick', *The Guardian*, 19 December 2008, available at <http://www.guardian.co.uk/politics/2008/dec/19/past>; 'Sir Bernard Crick: Political Theorist and Orwell Biographer who Advised the Government on Citizenship Teaching in Schools', *The Independent*, 22 December 2008, available at <http://www.independent.co.uk/news/obituaries/sir-bernard-crick-political-theorist-and-orwell-biographer-who-advised-the-government-on-citizenship-teaching-in-schools-1207412.html>; 'Sir Bernard Crick', *The Times*, 22 December 2008, available at <http://www.timesonline.co.uk/tol/comment/obituaries/article5379600.ece>; and Sunder Katwala, 'On Reading Bernard Crick', *Open Democracy*, 23 December 2008; blogpost, available at <http://www.opendemocracy.net/article/ourkingdom-theme/on-reading-bernard-crick.>

After a long period in which *In Defence* was known primarily because of its ubiquitous status on reading lists for secondary and University-level courses in Politics, its recent retrieval is connected to a significant waning of confidence in the standing of representative politics and the health of the wider civic culture. As a growing number of citizens in Western democracies turn away from political involvement, and disenchantment with politics appears ever more acute, it is perhaps not surprising that Crick's warning that humans are in perpetual danger of taking the value of politically regulated societies for granted, seems especially prescient.

But the factors animating contemporary concerns are very different to those that shaped Crick's argument. For contemporaries, it is an abiding worry about the implications of the rise of powerful new trends such as individualism, the decline of social trust, and the percolation of the ethos of consumerism into the public domain, that informs the return to his thinking. Pundits and theorists writing from a variety of political perspectives have united in calling for a renewal of the virtues that a democracy supposedly requires. The appeal of Crick's argument lies in its emphasis on the importance of civic virtue to the health of a political system, and its call for an improved form of political understanding among the public at large. In an era when some commentators suggest that we place too much value on what the political system 'delivers' to us, and when levels of knowledge about, and interest in, politics have declined considerably, his insistence on the need to inculcate such virtues as restraint, compromise, and an appreciation of the public interest, strike a powerful chord.

But I want to introduce a note of caution in relation to this renewal of interest in his work. Crick's account is neither quite as directly relevant to our times, nor as unproblematic in its assessment of how to defend and rejuvenate politics, as recent commentary has tended to assume. There has been a considerable underestimation of the degree to which this book was tailored to the period when it was written. Its treatment of different types of political thinking and attempt to advance a republican conception of politics provide an arresting, but problematic, basis for understanding politics and political ideas.

DEVELOPMENTS IN POLITICAL THEORY AND SCIENCE

Some of the themes of Crick's book have resurfaced within a variegated body of academic scholarship that has criticized the treatment of political phenomena by some of the major theoretical paradigms within political science and theory. Among political theorists this critique has taken different forms and been developed from a range of competing normative standpoints, including republicanism, communitarianism, and post-Marxism. One widely aired criticism is of the application of normative models derived from moral philosophy to the realm of politics.[9] Several recent studies are animated by the commitment to theorize the standards, characteristics, and virtues that are deemed unique to the domain of politics, but which are occluded by the 'normativity' associated with much contemporary political theory.[10]

Political science has also of late become increasingly focused on the nature and importance of the political, as a growing body of work has sought to explore the changing culture and attitudes of citizens in Western democracies. Some commentary has suggested that a key element within the basic ethos of democratic politics—that collective action can be organized in order to effect change for the better—has begun to wither on the cultural vine. With the disappearance of this conviction go the 'habits of the heart' that sustained citizenship in earlier eras.[11] The democratic public is increasingly prone to fragment into a set of quarrelsome groups making narrow calculations about what can be gained from the political system.[12] The implied solution to this analysis of the democratic malady is somewhat different from that sketched above. On this view, we need to revive the institutions, spaces, and traditions that once undergirded the civic culture (or 'social capital' in the less inspiring contemporary phrase), or locate contemporary equivalents for them. With the decline of important forms of secondary association, such as political parties and trade unions, which inculcated the qualities of patience, public spiritedness, and compromise, the virtues required for mass politics are in much shorter supply.

These interpretations of the problems afflicting democratic politics chime with some of the main lines of thinking in British political circles. They infused the arguments that were deployed in favour of the introduction of Citizenship as a subject within the national curriculum, which the Labour government introduced into secondary education in 2002. This programme was intended

---

[9] See the different arguments on this theme advanced by, for instance, John Dunn, *Cunning of Unreason: Making Sense of Politics* (London: Harper Collins, 2001); Benjamin Barber, *The Conquest of Politics: Liberal Philosophy in Democratic Times* (Princeton: Princeton University Press, 1989); and Glen Newey, *After Politics: The Rejection of Politics in Contemporary Liberal Philosophy* (Palgrave: Basingstoke, 2001).

[10] See, for instance, Raymond Geuss, *History and Illusion in Politics* (Cambridge: Cambridge University Press, 2001); and Mark Philp, *Political Conduct* (Cambridge, MA: Harvard University Press, 2007).

[11] This theme has been the source of intense debate among American political theorists and commentators for a good while. See, for instance, Robert Bellah (ed.), *Habits of the Heart: Individualism and Commitment in American Life* (Berkeley: University of California Press, 1992); and Barber, *Conquest of Politics*.

[12] See, for instance, Todd Gitlin, *The Twilight of Common Dreams: Why America is Wracked by Culture Wars* (New York: Metropolitan Books, 1995).

both to improve the 'political literacy' of children and young adults, through instruction in the history of key institutions such as Parliament, and to enable and inspire young people to play the role of civic agents, becoming more engaged in their local communities and in activities such as volunteering.[13] The principal architect of this curriculum was none other than Bernard Crick, appointed as an adviser by his former student, then Labour Minister David Blunkett. As well as leaving his institutional imprint upon citizenship education in England, Crick bequeathed a substantial intellectual legacy in the form of his elaborate argument for the importance of defending politics through the reanimation of civic virtue.

THE RETURN TO CRICK

This is the backdrop to the renewal of interest in Crick's attempt to provide a theoretically grounded account of the legitimacy and purpose of politics. That this book has become such a popular reference despite the quantity of recent empirical and theoretical literature emanating from Anglophone political science communities on this topic, is itself noteworthy. This testifies in part to the widening gap in the last twenty years between literature produced for academic audiences and books that reach across to non-specialist publics. While Crick's argument was couched in terms that demanded much from general readers and academically based ones alike, it was developed in a manner which suggested his confidence that a wider public ought to be detained by his thinking.

What is it about his ideas and our own political times that make his work seem so relevant now? Several recent publications provide us with some important clues. In a pamphlet published by the Fabian Society in 2005, political scientist Meg Russell took Crick's reflections as the starting point for her own discussion of the burgeoning mood of political disenchantment.[14] Crick himself is the author of its Preface, where he describes his continuing 'inner rage' at the gap between what is promised and what is delivered; between the 'is' and the 'ought' of politics.[15]

Russell observed the coalescence of a number of cultural, social, and political trends that have, in combination, generated a potential gap between what politicians promise, and what they can, in practice, achieve. Our political

---

[13] See, for instance, Terence McLaughlin, 'Citizenship Education in England: The Crick Report and Beyond', *Journal of the Philosophy of Education*, 34 (2000), 541–70.

[14] See, for instance, Meg Russell, *Must Politics Disappoint?* (London: Fabian Society, 1995).

[15] Bernard Crick, 'Preface', in Russell, *Must Politics Disappoint?*, 1.

processes and culture have, she argues, 'simply never adjusted to the challenges of mass politics':

> Politicians and the media fail to communicate the very essence of politics—that it is about negotiation and compromise, difficult choices, and taking decisions together as a society—to the extent that it is now seen as something divorced from everyday life, where politicians are expected to 'deliver', and increasingly talk their profession down rather than up, within a media environment that is hostile rather than supportive.[16]

While a good deal of her analysis refers to developments and factors that have emerged since *In Defence* was first published, Russell sought to apply the conceptual structure of Crick's argument to the conditions of today. She retained his twin assumptions that there is a knowable essence to politics, and that this should be couched in the broadly 'realist' terms that Crick favoured. And she endorsed his emphasis upon the processes and values that enabled the institutionalization of consensus, stability, and negotiation: 'Politics is, in short, a process by which complex societies take decisions...', and: 'To maintain a stable and fair society it is the job of politicians to take account of these competing interests in deciding public policy. Politics is fundamentally a process of negotiation and compromise.'[17] She maintained too that the wrong kinds of perceptions of, and expectations about, politics are themselves a crucial variable in creating a climate of disillusion and disenchantment.

She also echoed Crick's republicanism: 'Only by having a frank conversation with people as citizens, rather than consumers, can politics hope to survive.'[18] The main presupposition of consumerism—that in areas where its logic prevails, we are entitled to expect to attain what we desire—is anathema to politics. The latter implies the instantiation of a public realm regulated by the governing principle that the preferences and interests of others need to be factored into decisions taken in the public interest. Russell gives lucid expression to what has become a widely held sentiment—that the penetration of the ethos of consumerism across civil society has encouraged an inflated and overly self-interested sense among citizens of what politics should deliver. We need, therefore, a more clearly demarcated difference between the realm where we engage as citizens and that where the laws of the market apply. 'Politics must unashamedly carve out its own sphere, driven by the rules of citizenship.'[19] And the experience and wisdom generated by the opportunities for civic involvement are for her, as with Crick, vital conduits through which citizens come to appreciate and internalize the values of politics itself.

Russell's extended engagement with Crick is relatively unusual. He is more typically invoked as an unquestioned source of wisdom about politics and his ideas rarely considered at anything more than cursory length. Thus in a recent

[16] Russell, *Must Politics Disappoint?*, 4.
[17] Russell, *Must Politics Disappoint?*, 7.
[18] Russell, *Must Politics Disappoint?*, 5.
[19] Russell, *Must Politics Disappoint?*, 14.

public lecture political commentator Peter Riddell, for instance, reiterates Crick's view that:

> politics is about the peaceful reconciliation of different interests. It recognizes, even celebrates, the clash of views and groups, but within a framework—that of representative democracy and broadly based parties. This requires mutual respect, and mutual constraints, between politicians and their supporters.[20]

Former MP and Chairman of the Public Administration Select Committee, Tony Wright, began a valedictory lecture in 2009 with a salute to *In Defence*. He echoed Crick in calling for a more balanced appraisal of the role of politicians:

> Somebody has to do the messy business of accommodating conflicting demands and interests, choosing between competent options, unwelcome trade-offs, and taking responsibility for decisions that may often represent the least worst course of action.[21]

Signalling Crick's influence on a younger political generation, General Secretary of the Fabian Society, Sunder Katwala began an obituary essay on Crick by asserting the importance of *In Defence* for this thinking.[22] And political scientist Colin Hay has recently written approvingly of Crick's understanding of 'politics as the means by which we struggle to fashion collective ... solutions to collective problems'.[23] In his book *Why Politics Matters,* Gerry Stoker cites Crick as one of a select group of influences upon his own argument. He echoes the latter in regarding the decline of political understanding within the social cultures of democratic states as an important source of the difficulties which politics itself now faces.[24] More unusually, Stoker distances himself from the 'rather noble image of the way that politics works'[25] associated with Crick's republican leanings. This note of dissent is, I will suggest below, well made.

And, finally, Andrew Gamble has recently suggested that Crick's most important insights stem from his acceptance of the ineradicability of pluralism and interest-fuelled conflict in diverse and complex modern societies. He celebrates Crick's assertion that politics represents 'the only way of holding a free society together' and his view of political systems as continually required to dispel popular illusions about what politics is for.[26]

---

[20] Riddell, 'In Defence of Politicians'.
[21] Wright, 'Doing Politics Differently', 320.
[22] Katwala, 'Bernard Crick'.
[23] Colin Hay, *Why We Hate Politics* (Cambridge: Polity, 2007).
[24] See Gerry Stoker, *Why Politics Matters: Making Democracy Work* (Basingstoke: Palgrave, 2006).
[25] Stoker, *Why Politics Matters*, 75.
[26] Andrew Gamble, 'Bernard Crick', in G. Lodge and A. Thomas (eds.), *Radicals and Reformers: A Century of Fabian Thought* (London: Fabian Society, 2000).

CONTEXTUALIZING CRICK

The understanding of politics outlined within the pages of *In Defence* was, however, far more tethered to its times than its latter-day enthusiasts tend to appreciate. This is a point that Michael Freeden has himself indirectly made, in the course of a recent historical discussion of the ways in which British political scientists have conceptualized politics in the last century, alluding to 'the extraordinary impact of the Cold War on political theory, from Berlin to Rawls to Talmon and hundreds of others'.[27] Crick's work does indeed exhibit some of the key features of much political theorizing from the early 1950s to the mid 1960s, notably a highly antinomian conception of which political perspectives count as 'legitimate' in relation to democratic politics, and which ideological forces do not.

A close conceptual relationship emerges on the pages of *In Defence* between the main contemporary 'enemies' of politics—including nationalism, democracy, ideological thinking, and technology—and 'totalitarianism'. Crick defined the latter in the spirit of other leading contemporary intellectual figures, like Michael Oakeshott and Isaiah Berlin, as the product of an ideologically produced monism which sought to override the wisdom associated with Britain's established traditions, including its commitment to the value of individual liberty. He determined to draw a clear line between doctrines that framed politics in terms of unavoidable disagreement shaped by divergent social interests, on the one hand, and those who believed that a greater or hidden truth could be delivered either through the capture or suppression of politics itself. The heavily dualistic framework which this conviction shaped—between politically regulated societies committed to the values of pluralism and individual freedom, and regimes characterized by anti-politics and a dearth of institutionalized liberties—bears a strong resemblance to the writings of other leading anti-socialist intellectuals in this period. It is revealing then that *In Defence* received positive endorsements from, among others, Edward Shils and Isaiah Berlin, doyens of the anti-communist liberalism that was intellectually dominant in this period. Shils praised its 'sobriety, liberal spirit, and toughness of mind'. Berlin called it 'disturbing, penetrating and serious'.[28]

Crick's thinking also bore the hallmarks of a contemporary preoccupation with 'consensus', which appeared to be an increasing feature of domestic party politics as Labour sought to adjust to the electoral hegemony of the Conservatives

---

[27] See Freeden, 'The Arrogance of Politics'.
[28] These quotations were taken from reviews authored by Edward Shils (in *The Guardian*) and Isaiah Berlin (in *Twentieth Century*), and were included on the back jacket of later editions of *In Defence*. This book was first published as Crick, *In Defence of Politics* (London: Weidenfeld & Nicolson, 1962).

after 1951. A good deal of political commentary in the 1950s observed a diminution of the ideological differences shaping the outlooks of both main parties during this period of Conservative rule. The idea that a growing ideological consensus represented not just a description of the political perspectives of the main parties, but might also be conceived as a valuable achievement of the British political system, was never far beneath the surface of Crick's thinking. Despite the universalistic tones in which he discussed the nature of politics, his dismissal of 'extremist' ideological positions and concern about the dangers of an excess of democratizing zeal, reveal clear traces of Britain's elite liberal-conservative culture in this period. *In Defence* was in key respects a work steeped in domestic assumptions about the political landscape and the factors likely to constitute the major threats to political stability. It reflected too the influence upon this political culture of a defining opposition to the totalitarian regimes of extreme right and left, a commitment rooted in the politics of the 1930s and 1940s.

Crick's thinking was somewhat more unusual for its confident attempt to re-engage with a much older tradition of thinking about politics and political structures—the Aristotelian quest to determine the ethical point of equilibrium underpinning a stable political order. The influence of neo-Aristotelianism upon him suggests the continuing impact of the early twentieth-century paradigm of philosophical idealism, mediated through such figures as Ernest Barker, and also points to the importance of his extended engagement with the thought of Hannah Arendt. Her complex and unusual ideas were shaped around her dissection and rejection of the political logics associated with totalitarianism, and a highly distinctive reinterpretation of Aristotelian ethics.[29] Based on these sources, and his own immersion with the traditions of American republicanism,[30] Crick developed a view of politics that gave priority to conciliation over conflict, consensus over violence, and the importance of procedures that resolve disagreements.

Crick structured his book around introductory and concluding chapters in which he asserted his ethical understanding of the rationale for politics. Each of the chapters that fell in–between identified ideas and forces that represented an assortment of different threats to politics. These comprised 'Ideology', 'Democracy',

---

[29] On the nature of Arendt's account of totalitarianism and neo-Aristotelianism, see Margaret Canovan, *Hannah Arendt: A Reinterpretation of Her Political Thought* (Cambridge: Cambridge University Press, 1992). And for indications of Arendt's influence upon Crick's thought, see Crick, 'The Political and the Democratic', *British Journal of Educational Studies*, 55 (2007), 235–48; and 'Hannah Arendt: The Burden of Our Times', *Political Studies*, 68 (1997), 77–84.

[30] Crick's doctoral thesis involved an ambitious and powerful critique of the ideological character of American political science. This was subsequently published as *The American Science of Politics: Its Origins and Conditions* (Berkeley: University of California Press, 1959). For an assessment of the republican themes in this text, see Michael Kenny, 'History and Dissent: Bernard Crick's *The American Science of Politics*', *American Political Science Review*, 100 (2006), 547–53.

'Nationalism', 'Technology', and three different 'False Friends', the latter being several anti-political variants of conservatism, socialism, and liberalism.

His presentation of politics as beset by a host of antithetical ideologies was closely connected to his abiding anxiety that contemporary society was in danger of forgetting the 'truth', first systematically elaborated by Aristotle, about the merits of political rule. Linking the disparate body of anti-political ideologies that he bundled together were the entwined notions that politics should: enable us to reach hold of some overarching ideal; be ordered around the triumph of one grouping over others; or become redundant following the supersession of existing forms of social conflict and differentiation.

Given the current popularity of his account of politics, it is something of a jolt to find that Crick was so confident (and undoubtedly deliberately provocative) in placing democracy and nationalism in the enemy camp. His theoretical concern was that they each represented systems of value that appeared to trump the ancient political virtues of wisdom, proportion, compromise, and balance. Both held out the dangerous and illusory promise of achieving an unmediated alignment between 'the people' and the state. This illusion could only be pursued, he believed, at the expense of the acceptance of social pluralism and a focus upon the procedures required to manage and promote diversity. He grouped under the heading 'Technology' the recent appearance of a host of different claims to scientific authority in the areas where politics, not expertise, ought to remain sovereign.

The many different kinds of perspective which he brigaded under the labels of 'democracy', 'nationalism', and 'technology' were united in one further feature. All had the potential to appeal to publics that had become rather jaded about, or simply complacent towards, politics and politicians. *In Defence* therefore opened with a warning about the unavoidable danger of the growth of 'boredom with established truths'. It was, above all, intended as a restatement of the 'virtues of politics as a great and civilizing human activity'.[31]

But this position was afflicted by two sources of strain. First, those ideologies that were assumed to promote the anti-political delusion that, in order to create the realm of freedom, politics needed to be suppressed or captured, were much more protean than Crick suggested. The many different varieties of Marxist thought spawned very different responses to politics, and so too did the various brands of nationalism which were apparent in the political world of the 1950s. In addition to the inadequacy of this categorization to capture many familiar forms of ideological thinking, his framework also included very familiar features of political discourse, branding them as forms of anti-political thought. These included the articulation of visions of the good society, attempts to theorize political issues in moralistic terms, and

---

[31] Crick, *In Defence*, 15.

even interpretations of political thought and intellectual practice that saw these as contingent upon social interests rather than freely made choices. These emphases were, however, by no means confined to 'extremist' ideologies. They were rife within the more moderate doctrines he favoured.

These strains are most apparent in the chapter of the book labelled 'False Friends'. In this he attempted the ambitious task of identifying and isolating those manifestations of 'anti-political' sentiment that had developed within the political doctrines of conservatism, liberalism, and socialism. Illustrating and criticizing each, he did not, however, proceed to consider what it was about these 'political' doctrines which meant that they could spawn the kinds of anti-politics he lamented. But without such an enquiry, his account remained haunted by the possibility that the enemies of politics did not lie solely outside its walls—but were in fact rooted within the bodies of political thinking which were supposed to nourish and sustain politics.

This rather curious chapter reveals the inadequacy of its author's attempt to make meaningful a stable distinction between suspect and legitimate forms of political thinking. This dualistic framework also stopped him from investigating the possibility that the ideological traditions he deemed 'anti-political' may have been more important and integral to the political than he allowed. Might the fact of the plurality of political doctrines, rather than the supposed stance each took towards politics, be a constitutive ingredient of a political society? Might it also be that even 'anti-political' arguments and dreams have fulfilled political functions and embedded political orientations among their adherents and consumers?

Crick proved unable to offer an explanation of the propensity of thinkers and currents operating within more 'mainstream' political traditions to generate arguments and ideas that were inimical to his conception of politics. Thus, his unease about political actors who tend to 'think in terms of the stark contrast between good and bad...',[32] and the tendency of some modern thinkers to adopt 'in the terms of Max Weber's distinction, an ethic of ultimate ends rather an ethic of responsibility',[33] reflected a doomed attempt to expurgate from contemporary political thinking some of its most significant and vibrant elements.

The contemporary recycling of Crick's ideas has been too uncritical of this problematic attempt to defend a normative distinction between legitimate political thinking and ideological dogma. This dualism served to reinforce his normative emphasis upon such values as compromise, moderation, conciliation, and tolerance, while implicitly de-legitimizing other political characteristics, such as rhetoric, persuasion, and populism. This dichotomy, in

---

[32] Crick, *In Defence*, 133.   [33] Crick, *In Defence*, 134.

combination with some of his other favourite tropes—for instance 'politics is civilizing'—reflected the dominant sense which the political culture he inhabited had of itself. What is often viewed as a universally applicable theory of 'politics' is in important ways a more parochial reflection of the British elite's assumptions in the 1950s and early 1960s about the strengths of its institutions and culture.

EVALUATING CRICK

The most significant interpretative casualty of this model is the possibility that the enunciation of distaste for, or impatience with, political processes and politicians may well be a recurrent, perhaps even endemic, facet of political discourse. Campaigns for reform, populist mobilizations, attempts to castigate existing governments, and efforts to secure electoral support, are all likely to dip into the deep rhetorical pool of sceptical sentiments about the characteristics of politics and its associated actors. A pronounced hostility towards politics and scepticism about political actors does appear in historical terms to have been an eternal accompaniment to politics, rather than a distinctively modern phenomenon, even if current forms of anti-politics have their own singular character. The mere expression of such sentiments may be, and typically is, entirely compatible with the construction of political arguments or appeals.

Crick and his later adherents are in danger of neglecting the contribution to politics made by the competitive interaction of diverse political perspectives. These may express frustration with, and sometimes contempt for, the limitations of politics. But a consequence of their coexistence, interaction, and competitive attempts to corral the meanings of key political concepts is that they make an integral contribution to political life. They do this both by actualizing the plurality of perspectives which political societies possess and by socializing citizens into an awareness of the multiplicity of political viewpoints that shape debate on policy issues. An account of the political, which renders the many visionary, redemptive, and forward-looking ideas that have inspired movements seeking progressive or regressive change as features that lie outside the realm of political thinking, is an enormously attenuated one. In this important regard, those keen to defend politics in the present would do well to steer away from the Manichean attempt to distinguish between political doctrine and ideological thought which structures much of the argument of *In Defence*.

The second normative feature of Crick's argument that merits critical reconsideration concerns his attempt to reanimate the classical republican conception of politics in the conditions of the mid to late twentieth century.

The neo-republican strain running throughout the book is undoubtedly an additional reason for its more recent appeal, as republicanism has re-emerged as a significant perspective among progressively minded theorists.[34] But the terms and implications of the republican position developed in his book merit careful assessment.

One important consequence of his republican commitments was his insistence upon the centrality of freedom as the moral core of truly political societies. This was the theme of the inaugural lecture he delivered at the University of Sheffield in 1966.[35] In an extensive meditation upon Isaiah Berlin's influential elaboration of the two key conceptions of 'liberty' in Western thought, Crick argued for the logical and empirical interdependence between freedom and politics, and attempted to supplant the idea of negative liberty: 'The very possibility of privacy depends upon some public action; and conversely public life is indeed all just "telegrams and anger" if it does not accommodate private happiness.'[36] Freedom is, contra Berlin, a concept that requires and promotes certain kinds of social relationships. It necessitates the stability and procedures associated with politics in order to flourish. But respect for the exercise of individual freedom is at the same time the normative premise for any established political regime.

Given that politics was practised in many countries where the liberty of the individual was not prized, this was an eye-catching, counter-intuitive claim. He proceeded to suggest that a significant homology existed between any society where political rule was practised and those states which the ancients characterized as 'republics'. It was not, in other words, merely modern democracies that approximated to the republican ideal but any community which committed itself to establishing the procedures and virtues required by a political system.[37] Both were linked by their reliance upon the levels of civic virtue manifest throughout their populations. Freedom itself is at risk if politically regulated societies begin to decay.

Characterizing contemporary polities in terms of the character and virtues of their citizens and the resilience of their political cultures, as opposed to the strength of their institutions, their commitment to the rule of law, or the acquisition of basic civil and political rights, is an important facet of the book's continuing appeal. Crick's critique of the normative attempt to ground the

---

[34] See for instance: Philip Pettit, *Republicanism: A Theory of Freedom and Government* (Oxford: Oxford University Press, 1999); Quentin Skinner, *Liberty Before Liberalism* (Cambridge: Cambridge University Press, 1998); Cecile Laborde and John Maynor (eds.), *Republicanism and Political Theory* (Oxford: Blackwell, 1998); and John Maynor, *Republicanism in the Modern World* (Cambridge: Polity Press, 2003).
[35] See Crick, 'Freedom as Politics', in Preston King (ed), *The Study of Politics: A Collection of Inaugural Lectures* (London: Frank Cass, 1977).
[36] Crick, 'Freedom as Politics', 301.
[37] Crick, 'Freedom as Politics', 310.

legitimacy of democratic polities upon abstract principles, which were elaborated prior to their instantiation within political systems and institutions, makes *In Defence* an important precursor of more recent republican trends in the political theorizing of democracy.[38]

But in some key respects the conflation of his views on politics with his advocacy of republicanism makes this a troubling work. Repeating Aristotle's commitment to the idea of the political as the 'master-science', he placed politics at the moral apex of social activities. At a time when modern societies were marked by increasing degrees of differentiation, consumerist forms of individualism were emerging as significant social pressures, and the neo-romantic ethos of personal fulfilment was becoming a major cultural motif, his attempt to privilege politics above numerous other social domains and practices ran significantly against the grain of contemporary life. And so too did the relatively austere set of public ethics he sought to champion. Crick's latter-day adherents have perhaps surprisingly been disinclined to pose critical questions about the basis upon which he reiterated 'the arrogance of politics', to borrow a term from Michael Freeden's recent writing.[39] Crick's thinking failed to engage either with the sociological realities of complex modern societies or the normative force of the leading liberal objections to the application of the republican model in modernity. This is not necessarily an argument against republicanism *tout court*, since some of its strands may well intertwine fruitfully with liberalism.[40] But the particular form of republican politics that Crick advocated may well deserve a more sceptical reception in current circumstances. His presumption that the compliance and participation which political republics require, necessarily override the many other identities and interests that free individuals possess, remains morally unappealing and sociologically improbable.

Crick's position did, however, represent an important departure from the republican heritage in one important, and rather overlooked, aspect. While republicans had long argued for the importance of civic instruction for inculcating the public-spiritedness which this form of state required, Crick advanced a rather different claim in relation to education. In addition to favouring the kinds of educational practice and institutional reform that would engender a more civically minded atmosphere, he argued that achieving a significant improvement in the quantum of political understanding was itself an important prerequisite for political stability.

---

[38] See for instance Barber, *Conquest of Politics*.
[39] See Freeden, 'The Arrogance of Politics'.
[40] Conceptualizing the relationship of republicanism to liberal political theory, in both historical and normative terms, represents one of the most contentious themes within this paradigm. For contrasting formulations of this relationship, see Pettit, *Republicanism*, and Skinner, *Liberty Before Liberalism*.

This was an ambitious and somewhat counter-intuitive claim, one that some earlier republicans would have regarded with suspicion. On what basis, we should ask, can we share his confidence that a more informed and educated citizenry is necessarily more inclined to appreciate the political qualities he favoured? The history of the last fifty years of Western states that have proved highly stable politically, but have arguably weakened in terms of their democratic cultures, suggests that higher rates of education do not necessarily point in the direction suggested by Crick. Indeed there are good reasons to believe that a more educated populace, in tandem with such trends as consumerism and social individualization, is less inclined to accept the injunction to appreciate the common good, and increasingly cynical about the capacity of politics and politicians to serve the public interest. Nor is this merely an empirical and historical question. The normative assumption at the heart of *In Defence* that greater realism about politics sits neatly within the value set implied by a modern account of civic virtue, requires much more extensive justification than Crick supplied. Why exactly will a more rounded understanding of the nature of political processes, and a better appreciation of the value and limits of political institutions, usher in an improved sense of political engagement and involvement? Might it be the case that better political understanding is as likely to undermine, not bolster, the civic disposition that he and others want to reanimate?

FREEDEN AND CRICK

Michael Freeden's scholarly analyses of the composition and nature of modern political ideologies, and his more recent work on the characteristics of political language, offer a very different vantage point upon these issues. Here I briefly consider their pertinence to the areas of weakness in Crick's argument identified above—the endeavour to maintain a conceptual distinction between more or less legitimate forms of political thinking, and the attempt to revive a republican form of political morality.

Freeden's argument for a 'morphological' understanding of the nature and conceptual dynamics of patterns of modern political thinking, in his analysis of political ideologies, is an important alternative to the attempt of Crick and others to identify and demarcate acceptable forms of political thinking, and to hive these off from anti-political ideologies. Freeden has focused upon the distinctive properties of ideological thinking, and how patterns of meaning established through the coalescence of fluid clusters of 'core' and peripheral concepts. His demonstration that ideologies are protean and intrinsically fluid in their composition, and are involved in an ongoing competition to frame the meanings of a lexicon of largely shared political concepts, undermines the purchase of the binary framework wielded by Crick.

Freeden's more persuasive position is that a key task for those seeking improved political understanding is to comprehend the logical and cultural force that ideological thinking exhibits. We should therefore expect characterizations of terms like 'politics' and a thicket of closely associated concepts, such as parliament, political system, politician, voting, and state, to be the object of considerable competitive efforts at 'decontestation'. In short, we should regard the nature, boundaries, and purposes of politics to be among the most recurrent and contestable themes in political thinking. Normative efforts to hive off a band of political theorizing that conforms to prior rules about their position in relation to liberal democratic values inhibit our understanding of how political discourse about politics shapes politics itself.

Freeden's conception of a more systematic and dispassionate assessment of the operation and composition of ideologies leads him to observe the integral character of the visionary, utopian/dystopian, and forward- and backward-looking dimensions of political thinking. These and other related genres contribute vitally to the performance of political functions—including the mobilization of citizens, attempts to jolt publics into alternative ways of viewing political phenomena, and the provision of new justifications for the 'natural' political and social orders. The moral, the utopian, and the diachronic, are all vital registers, in others words, of political thinking.

The contemporary inclination, following Crick, to frame these as potential threats to the kinds of balanced, modest, and 'realistic' conceptions of politics that we should be trying to inculcate, ought to be regarded as the manifestations of a particularly partisan form of thinking, not the basis for the renewal of democratic culture. Rather than seeking to rule out those forms of ideology, passion, and sentiment that are deemed to be a menace, today's defenders of politics would do better to take a more lateral and inclusive approach to the many different ideas that have over time engaged citizens with political structures and processes.

The second feature of Crick's arguments which, I suggested above, deserves more sceptical consideration, involves his republicanism. While the merits and weaknesses of republican political theory have been much debated, Freeden's reflections upon the nature and importance of concepts and language to the health and character of political life provide an important alternative vantage point upon some facets of republican thinking about politics. Thus, in a number of his most recent essays, Freeden has shifted his intellectual focus from the macro-level analysis of patterns of political ideas to the micro-level character and constitution of political language.[41] This is largely a virgin

---

[41] See for instance Freeden, 'Languages of Political Support'.

territory for political analysis, where he is joined by only a handful of his fellow political theorists. Among a variety of features of everyday political vernaculars to which he draws attention are: the establishment through political discourse of the manufacture of an apparent consensus around a particular programme of action or policy; the important efforts to demarcate boundaries between politics and other arenas, and the recurrent propensity of politics to display an 'arrogance' towards other social domains; and the ubiquity of power within the terminology, as well as relationships, through which power is conducted.[42]

There are some interesting indirect echoes here of Crick's stance towards politics. This is most apparent in their shared conviction that there are recurrent empirical functions and features of political thinking to which political analysis should pay greater attention. And, like Crick, Freeden is clearly animated by a desire to resist the colonial ambitions of theoretical paradigms associated with neighbouring disciplines, including philosophy and economics. But Freeden's position is far more sensitized to the different ideological and cultural traditions that inform the construction of the multitude of subjectivities in modern political society. On this count, Crick's understanding of the relationship between individual citizen and the public good is especially attenuated. His formulation of the ethical character of this relationship within *In Defence* was characterized by an abiding indifference to the class background and social identities of the citizens to whom the book's arguments are directed, a surprising absence perhaps given his own leftist political sympathies. Indeed, despite his empirical observation that preferences are shaped by individuals' interests and backgrounds, Crick insulated this recognition from the highly optimistic contention that citizens can be rationally persuaded to understand the need to subsume or sacrifice these for the common good. The overriding focus upon the relationship between individual citizen and the republic which infuses Crick's analysis, offers a uni-dimensional perspective, in both sociological and normative terms, upon the relationship between individual, citizen, community, and state in complex, modern societies.

CONCLUSIONS

A full discussion of the worth of Freeden's analytical claims and proposed methodology for decoding political language lies beyond the scope of this particular essay. I alight upon Freeden's work here in part to indicate the

---

[42] See Freeden, 'Political Thinking as Power'.

fertility of his thinking in relation to some of the questions animating contemporary political commentators, but also to highlight the perils associated with particular kinds of normative theoretical approaches to the political—in this case that developed by Bernard Crick.

Yet, despite the repeated declaration of his ambition to develop a non-partisan analytical framework for the study of ordinary political thinking, Freeden's own position is by no means devoid of normative imperatives and commitments. His recent writings put forward lists of empirically observable political characteristics that theorists are reprimanded for having neglected. But it is clear that a deep underlying commitment to the integrity and value of politics, a strong preference for democratic outcomes and contexts, and a clear affiliation with a set of liberal values animates his own thinking and shapes his choice of salient political features. This raises the key interpretative question of whether it is possible to pursue the framework he proposes, and his methodological account of the generation and interpretation of the meaning of concepts, without also subscribing to his own liberal preferences.

In this respect perhaps, Crick's work possesses an advantage in that the normative predilections shaping his arguments are laid out in a highly explicit fashion. He bequeathed a passionate and clear-sighted account of why exactly politics matters so much, and spent much of his subsequent career arguing for measures that would improve and promote political understanding. Freeden's recent call for political theorists to step away from the kinds of 'public intellectual' stance that Crick, and others, have played, in pursuit of a more analytical approach to everyday politics, might be seen as signalling a retreat from the sense of public responsibility which Crick urged upon the scholarly community.[43]

Several different questions need to be untangled and assessed afresh here. At what point of magnification, in analytical terms, is the character of political thinking best grasped? Is the micro-level focus proposed by Freeden an alternative, a complement, or an adjunct to the macro-level approach favoured by most academic theorizing about politics? Does the adoption of more robust and dispassionate analyses of political ideas necessitate the attempt to distance from their everyday formulation, which Freeden's call for the professionalization of political-theoretical analysis implies? Or is there, as Crick maintained throughout his career, a distinctive responsibility upon the academic political theorist to bring illumination, via engagement, to the processes and thinking that politics requires?

These important and open-ended questions are part of the pertinent and challenging legacy which Crick's arguments about politics bequeathed, but which have been somewhat obscured by the rush to sanctify his justification

---

[43] See Freeden, 'Thinking Politically and Thinking about Politics: Language, Interpretation, and Ideology'.

for politics. One rather perverse consequence of the contemporary return to *In Defence* is a tendency in today's commentary to blame the public for its shallow, venal, and simplistic expectations of politics.[44] Harnessing Crick's book to this kind of polemical purpose is problematic, given his own more nuanced conception of the reasons for inadequate levels of political understanding. Such an approach, and the more general tendency to cite Crick's emphasis upon civic virtue without further analysis of what he actually said, has left contemporary commentary unaware of the contextual character of his argument, and inattentive to some major weaknesses in Crick's position. Specifically, I have argued that the untenable distinction he defends between political doctrines and anti-political ideologies blights our understanding of the integral character of ideological competition to politics. And I have pointed to some of the difficulties associated with his advocacy of a republican approach to politics.

My recourse to some of the ideas associated with Michael Freeden is motivated in part by a desire to deploy his work as an illustration of the development and import of a more recent body of political theorizing which has reflected deeply and thoughtfully on exactly these issues. More specifically, I hope to have signalled a wider range of potential application for Freeden's ideas than is conventionally granted. No single political theorist has all the answers to the tangle of issues associated with current concerns about the intensification of political disenchantment and the malaise affecting the civic cultures of today's democracies. But it would be worth today's political commentators looking beyond Crick, as well as to him, for thoughtful and pertinent reflections on these themes. From Freeden they would gain an appreciation of the limitations of moralized accounts of politics and an improved understanding of the complex political character of thinking and argument, which is, on the face of it, anti-political.

---

[44] See Hay's perceptive analysis of this tendency in *Why We Hate Politics*.

12

Getting 'Real' About Political Ideas: Conceptual Morphology and the Realist Critique of Anglo-American Political Philosophy

Mathew Humphrey

INTRODUCTION

How should political theory be conducted? We are currently seeing something of an upsurge in 'realism' in political philosophy, which offers a distinctive way to think about this question. 'Realism' is a label that has been applied to the work of a number of authors with related but distinct concerns about what they see as the failings of political philosophy in its 'ideal' mode, and in particular as it is practised in the Anglo-American tradition by the likes of John Rawls, Ronald Dworkin, Robert Nozick, and their followers. Leading scholars associated with the realist trend, such as Raymond Geuss, Charles Mills, Colin Farrelly, and the late Bernard Williams, berate ideal theory for its severe abstraction, misguided idealizations, impracticality, acontextuality, utopian aspirations, and embodiment of a kind of ethical imperialism, as moral philosophy seeks to conquer the distinctive terrain of the political.[1] The central claim of this chapter is that this realist critique is clearly prefigured in the analysis of Anglo-American political philosophy offered over a number of years by Michael Freeden. His analysis is worthy of much wider attention, as it both offers a trenchant critique of what Freeden calls 'philosophical liberalism', and a distinctive answer to our opening question.

---

[1] See for example Raymond Geuss, *Philosophy and Real Politics* (Princeton: Princeton University Press, 2008); Bernard Williams, *In the Beginning was the Deed: Realism and Moralism in Political Argument* (Princeton: Princeton University Press, 2005); Charles W. Mills, '"Ideal Theory" as Ideology', *Hypatia*, 20 (2005), 165–84; Colin Farrelly, 'Justice in Ideal Theory: A Refutation', *Political Studies*, 55 (2007), 844–64.

From (at least) the publication of *Ideologies and Political Theory* in 1996,[2] Michael Freeden has been developing the approach he calls 'conceptual morphology' for the analysis of political thought. In the process he has developed a thoroughgoing critique of what he sees as the currently dominant modes of practising political philosophy, particularly in its Anglo-American form.[3] It is of interest that this critique has some striking similarities with the claims of the realist arguments referred to above, and it is something of a travesty that his work is not cited by realist scholars as a precursor to their own views. Freeden also expresses concern about the acontextuality and imagined timelessness of contemporary normative political philosophy, about the application of methods derived from philosophical ethics to the arena of political thought, and the ways in which, as a result, political philosophy condemns itself to political irrelevance. Although Freeden and the realists are writing for different purposes (more on this below), both offer reflections on the question of how political philosophy should or should not be done. What unites the two approaches is a conception of the political as a distinct field of enquiry, to which the application of methods developed for moral philosophy is, at best, far from straightforward, and at worst leads political philosophers badly astray. There are divergences too, however, and in particular on Freeden's own understanding the realists are engaged in 'thinking politically' whilst the application of conceptual morphology is an exercise in 'thinking about politics'. This places the two schools of thought on either side of an important methodological divide, by which realism is itself raw material for ideological decoding. We will question the sustainability of this divide in the process of assessing the relationship between Freeden's work and realist political philosophy.

The following sections will set out some of the key areas where both Freeden and the realists share fundamental concerns about the nature of Anglo-American political philosophy, comparing the arguments of both in each case. I will argue that many of realism's core objections to ideal political philosophy are prefigured in Freeden's work. The penultimate section will explore some of the divergences between the two approaches, and look at the reasons underlying these differences. Finally we will return to our opening question and ask what these two critiques may tell us about how political philosophy should be conducted.

---

[2] Oxford: Oxford University Press.
[3] A note on terminology is necessary. The realists tend to target 'ideal theory' or 'Anglo-American political philosophy'; Freeden to discuss 'philosophical liberalism' or also 'Anglo-American political philosophy'. I will use these terms interchangeably here, along with 'analytical political philosophy'. This allows for some terminological variety, although it is of course not necessarily the case that an argument deploying 'analytical' methods would also have to be 'ideal' in the sense that realists object to.

THE DIMENSIONS OF THE CRITIQUE OF IDEAL THEORY

There is no neatly defined school of political theorists who self-describe as 'realists' and engage in debate with another well-defined set of 'idealists'. What we see emerging in recent years is rather a set of debates about how political theory should be undertaken, what its purpose is, and what the most appropriate role of the political theorist consists in. In these debates those who are critical of what they see as unjustified levels of abstraction and idealization in much analytical political theory attract the label (or sometimes self-describe as) 'realist'. This does not necessarily entail an ontological or epistemological realism, so much as a commitment to some form of contextualism in political theory. Below I will focus on three important areas of the realist critique of ideal political theory. Firstly, the lack of awareness of historical and locational contingency; secondly, the failure to appreciate the autonomy of the political realm, and the resulting inapplicability of moral philosophy to questions of politics; and thirdly, the unacknowledged ways in which ideal theory operates as a form of ideology. I will show that these are exactly the concerns about the nature of Anglo-American political philosophy that emerge from the work of Michael Freeden, although for Freeden the 'form of ideology' refers to the articulation of a set of non-negotiable and often unexamined values via a structured arrangement of propositions and political concepts, rather than as a form of false consciousness. Indeed it is precisely its *failure* as an ideological vehicle that constitutes one of philosophical liberalism's major flaws on Freeden's view.

HISTORICAL CONTINGENCY

It would be odd to deny that our thoughts and writings are intimately connected with the historical epoch in which we live, and indeed the thought that they are so connected has spawned a subdiscipline of the 'sociology of knowledge'.[4] However, a common complaint against 'ideal' political theory is that it is written as a timeless and rootless philosophy, dispensing principles of justice or obligation with a startling lack of historical awareness. There are at least two elements to this objection which need to be kept distinct. Firstly, we have the degree to which political philosophers either wilfully or unreflectively ignore the historical and social context in which they have developed their own views and for which they write. This relates, obviously enough, to the

---

[4] Karl Mannheim, *Ideology and Utopia* (London: Routledge, 1960 [1936]).

degree of *abstraction* from context that their work manifests, and how that abstraction is justified. Another objection is to the *results* of this abstraction, the extent to which political philosophers take the principles they develop to be timeless and/or universal in their application. They are principles, that is, that are true for many times and many places,[5] even if they were not recognized as valid principles in the past, or are not recognized as valid principles now, by the wider society. Abstraction would seem to be a necessary condition for theorizing at all, but it is not the case that abstraction from current context *has* to lead to the development of universal principles. Wrapped up in this complaint about acontextuality is an observation about contingency in politics. For those theorists to whom history and context are crucially important factors in defining parameters of possibility, we must recognize the historical and locational contingency of any principles or institutions that we develop. The possibilities of politics are always subject to chance, and this does not just entail that there may be circumstances where we cannot apply certain principles (this would not necessarily motivate objections to the idealist approach), but more profoundly that contingent circumstance inflects what we are able to think and our very capacity to develop political principles in the first place. If we recognize the fragility and transient nature of the circumstances that *allow* us to think politically in the way we do, then we will appreciate the importance of maintaining these conditions. This in turn may bring us to the view that the maintenance of the very circumstances that allow us to both think and act politically is the prime question of politics.[6]

Let us try to understand the exact nature of the objection to abstraction. Geuss has this to say: 'The reasons why we have most of the political and moral concepts we have... are contingent, historical reasons, and *only* a historical account will give us the beginnings of understanding of them and allow us to reflect critically on them rather than simply taking them for granted.'[7] For Williams, philosophers cannot ignore history if they are to understand our concepts at all, and 'one reason for this is that in many cases the content of our concepts is a contingent historical phenomenon'.[8] This objection is taken to strike at the foundations of ideal theory, as on both views political philosophers will fail to understand the concepts that are the very building blocks of their theories if they are not sensitive to the contingent

---

[5] There are degrees of latitude between a severe parochialism and a strict universalism. There is, however, a strong sense in much Rawlsian and post-Rawlsian work that the principles being advocated apply outside of this time and place, and possibly to many times and places displaying varying degrees of similarity with this time and place.

[6] Williams, *In the Beginning*, 62, and Geuss, *Philosophy and Real Politics*, also suggest that this question is underestimated by ideal theorists.

[7] Geuss, *Philosophy and Real Politics*, 69. Emphasis added.

[8] Bernard Williams, *Philosophy as a Humanistic Discipline* (Princeton: Princeton University Press, 2006), 191.

history of their actual use. As Williams says, our conceptions of concepts, such as freedom, consist in a 'historical deposit'.[9] Failure to appreciate this leads political philosophers to ask the wrong questions, or to insist on the prioritization of a local and contextual understanding of a concept as if it were truly universal.[10] Thus, for Geuss, both Nozick and Rawls are engaged in the 'wrong' kind of analysis in investing the logical consequences of the assertion of the primacy of rights (in Nozick's case), or the assertion of the primacy of a conception of justice (in Rawls's). Rawls may have an 'intuitive conviction of the primacy of justice', but there 'is no account of where these intuitions come from, whether they may be in any way historically or sociologically variable, or what role they play in society'.[11] Such forms of enquiry into the intuitive predispositions of the political philosopher are designed to be 'disjoined from real politics'[12] and cannot tell us anything politically useful as they commence from the wrong starting point. There are however 'some historically more specific questions [that] are good starting points' for political philosophy.[13] If we want to understand the limits of the politically possible, we have to understand the meanings these concepts have in the actual political discourse of our society, and that entails understanding their history.

This concern about the acontextuality of Anglo-American political philosophy also comes through very clearly in the work of Michael Freeden, and in particular the way in which he sees ideal theorists as seeking to 'freeze' historical time such that their chosen principles will appear universally valid. Ideal theorists seek to 'depoliticize' their political theory, as politics provides a historically rooted and spatially located context from which they seek to set their theories free. Thus, Freeden quotes Rawls where the latter states in *Political Liberalism* that 'liberal principles meet the urgent political requirement to fix, once and for all, the content of certain political basic rights and liberties, and to assign them special priority. Doing this takes those guarantees off the political agenda and puts them beyond the calculus of social interests'.[14] Thus, philosophical liberalism embraces the 'ahistoricity of arrested time', 'depoliticization', and 'justice through individual rights' as specific ideological features[15]. The liberal projects of thinkers such as Rawls and Dworkin 'prioritize rules as stasis, equilibrium and consensus over rules of change', as they seek to see their preferred principles 'removed from the ravages of social

---

[9] Williams, *In the Beginning*, 75.
[10] Geuss, *Philosophy and Real Politics*, 91.
[11] Geuss, *Philosophy and Real Politics*, 71.
[12] Geuss, *Philosophy and Real Politics*, 73.
[13] Geuss, *Philosophy and Real Politics*, 69.
[14] John Rawls, *Political Liberalism*, quoted in Michael Freeden, *Liberal Languages: Ideological Imaginations and Twentieth Century Political Thought* (Princeton: Princeton University Press, 2005), 10.
[15] Freeden, *Liberal Languages*, 10.

time',[16] and 'exalted above all historical and empirical contingency'.[17] This view is shared by Bernard Williams, who argues that 'many liberals' proceed 'as though liberalism were timeless'. Such liberals are reproached for not asking 'why their most basic convictions should seem to be... simply there. It is part and parcel of a philosophical attitude that makes them equally uninterested in how those convictions got there'.[18] For Freeden, even if this is not an inherently misguided way of doing political philosophy, as Geuss suggests it is, we should at least recognize it as a particular manifestation of ideological liberalism, itself located in a particular social and historical context, even as it seeks itself to escape the limitations of that context. That said, there is no doubt that Freeden believes Anglo-American political philosophy drives itself towards political irrelevance when 'the disciplinary constraints that apply to producing good philosophy have all too often distanced its practitioners from that actual stuff of politics'.[19] When this occurs the result is a curiously apolitical form of liberal politics.

THE AUTONOMY OF THE POLITICAL

That observation regarding the 'apolitical' nature of contemporary political philosophy brings us to another common dimension of the two critiques we are considering here. Both see 'the political' as a sphere of human activity that requires modes of intellectual enquiry that are specific to it, rather than one that draws almost exclusively on the external discipline of philosophy.[20] Political philosophers are not directly 'students of *politics*', as Freeden puts it;[21] they are philosophers, who use the tools of one particular area of intellectual enquiry in order to illuminate another. But what if politics requires a light of its own? What is lost in the translation from philosophy, and in particular moral philosophy, to politics? In seeking to answer this question, both Freeden and the realists focus on what they take a moral-philosophical approach to politics to miss. That is, they delineate certain elements or questions which they take to be central to politics, and which they think that contemporary

---

[16] Freeden, *Liberal Languages*, 25.
[17] Guido de Ruggiero, *A History of European Liberalism*, quoted in Freeden, *Liberal Languages*, 28.
[18] Williams, *Humanistic Discipline*, 197.
[19] Michael Freeden, 'Ideology, Political Theory, and Political Philosophy', in Gerald F. Gaus and Chandran Kukathas (eds.), *Handbook of Political Theory* (London: Sage, 2004), 4.
[20] Freeden sees history as the other dominant discipline from which methods are borrowed, but not in a way that gives philosophical liberalism any historical awareness. Historical methods are applied rather to the separate subdiscipline of the history of political thought.
[21] Freeden, 'Ideology, Political Theory, and Political Philosophy', 4. Emphasis in the original.

political philosophers either ignore or at best treat superficially as a direct result of the application of moral philosophy to politics. In particular, the professional philosopher's drive to meet the standards of logic, consistency, and coherence required by her peers at best bears no relation to, and at worst positively divorces the philosopher from, an understanding of politics in its 'concrete' forms.

Of these thinkers it is Williams who offers a relatively well-specified account of what he takes the political to consist in. Whilst he will not be giving a 'general characterization' of the political, he does highlight the following. The political is 'to an important degree focused in the idea of political disagreement; and political disagreement is significantly different from moral disagreement'.[22] We have to recognize that *disagreement* is the norm for political life, it is something we have to learn to live with and accommodate, not something we should be seeking to expunge. Attempts to foster consensus (overlapping or otherwise) amongst groups of human beings are doomed to failure and always carry the risk of coercive imposition when they (inevitably) fail to materialize spontaneously. Political philosophy, when done adequately, will recognize the distinctive nature of its subject matter, and more importantly, the fact that this distinctive subject matter (to do with the exercise of power, the development of authoritative institutions, the need to reach a moment of collective rather than individual decision) may require a method or an approach to philosophical questions about politics, which is distinct from that applied to moral philosophy.

It is because Williams believes the political has these particular characteristics that he is able to characterize a certain conception of liberty as 'thoroughly political'[23] as it acknowledges in its construction (not definition) the ongoing inevitability of political disagreement. He contrasts this version with Ronald Dworkin's account of liberty, which Dworkin hives off to a constitutional realm, in an attempt to insulate it from inevitable disagreement. Williams thus shows a clear preference for the 'liberalism of fear' over what Freeden would call 'philosophical liberalism', because the liberalism of fear accepts certain realities of politics, as a distinct sphere of human activity, that the 'strongly moralized'[24] version of liberalism, dominant in contemporary political theory, fails to understand—precisely because it treats politics as merely a subject ripe for the application of moral philosophy. The liberalism of fear is sensitive to the 'first question' of politics, the Hobbesian requirement for order, and the avoidance of 'suffering and disaster', without which nothing else of political value can be achieved. Because the liberalism of fear takes such threats to order seriously, it is a 'more sceptical, historically alert, politically direct conception' of liberty that offers 'the best hope for humanly acceptable

---

[22] Williams, *In the Beginning*, 77. [23] Williams, *In the Beginning*, 126.
[24] Williams, *In the Beginning*, 138.

legitimate government'.[25] By contrast, philosophical liberalism appears a rather frivolous and trivial form of liberalism, taking for granted a whole series of substantive preconditions which in fact can only be provided by conscious human effort. In the language of an earlier set of critics of liberalism, it is a philosophy for an age of plenty, but would not withstand a politics for hard times.[26] For Williams ethical considerations form a part of political judgment, but only a part, and some of the wrong-headedness of philosophical liberalism is to mistake this part for the whole.

Geuss also suggests that philosophical liberalism lacks political relevance due to its transposition of moral philosophy to a realm sufficiently distinct to make that transposition highly problematic. Liberalism (what we might call 'really political liberalism', as opposed to the Rawlsian variety) has grown out of real political struggles, and is historically located. Questions of logical consistency are 'not the most relevant' ones to ask in politics, and it is 'highly unlikely that the analysis of a concept like "justice" . . . could give one any real grasp of the central phenomena of politics'.[27] Rawlsian deliberators have been idealized in such a way as to 'nullify any political relations that might be thought to exist between them'.[28] There is an Oakeshottian tone to Geuss's declaration that politics is more akin to an art of craft than the application of a theory or philosophy to a set of problems.[29] As for what characterizes politics, Geuss indicates a similar concern to Williams in thinking both that questions of security and order are important,[30] and that politics is first and foremost about power,[31] a concept with which philosophical liberalism is often said to be uncomfortable.

Freeden tends to contrast philosophical liberalism with what he calls 'concrete political thinking', although this is clearly related to politics more generally and the question of what may be practically possible. His concern is with the subject matter of political theory, and this is (or should be) political thought, in all of its various manifestations, rather than ethics or history. Political theory should be the study of 'actual political thinking',[32] but Anglo-American political philosophers have turned away from this realm, 'in a manner that few past political theorists had contemplated, thus condemning most of their efforts to sterility and to public invisibility'.[33] With Geuss, Freeden believes that analytical political

---

[25] Williams, *In the Beginning*, 138.
[26] William Ophuls, *Ecology and the Politics of Scarcity* (San Francisco: W. H. Freeman & Co., 1977).
[27] Raymond Geuss, *Outside Ethics* (Princeton, Princeton University Press, 2005), 15–16.
[28] Geuss, *Outside Ethics*, 32.
[29] Guess, *Philosophy and Real Politics*, 15.
[30] Guess, *Philosophy and Real Politics*, 22.
[31] Guess, *Philosophy and Real Politics*, 97.
[32] Michael Freeden, 'Thinking Politically and Thinking About Politics: Language, Interpretation, and Ideology', in David Leopold and Marc Stears (eds.), *Political Theory: Methods and Approaches* (Oxford: Oxford University Press), 197.
[33] Michael Freeden, 'Ideology and Political Theory', *Journal of Political Ideologies*, 11 (2006), 9.

philosophers have problems with the contingency and indeterminacy of politics, and so 'endorsed the retreat into the safety of modelling utopian worlds, or persevered in conducting philosophical laboratory experiments, or reassumed the mantle of ethicists (though, really, of ideologists) in fighting the good fight'[34] for moral certainty. This account of a retreat or withdrawal from the political realm in political philosophy is a theme to which Freeden frequently returns. Anglo-American political philosophers lose touch with the 'real-world arena of policy-making',[35] they 'removed themselves from the practice and language of politics and engaged in private discourses',[36] or engaged in a 'flight from the political'.[37] In so doing they exchange political influence for peer endorsement, as the 'specialized language of late-twentieth-century liberal philosophers [is] directed mainly at their colleagues rather than at the thinking public',[38] and intellectual ideological producers (post-Marxist as well as Rawlsian) have exchanged public meaning for 'professional acclaim'.[39] This means that there is overriding concern with logical validity and argumentative coherence, but, along with Geuss and Williams, Freeden is not convinced that these are the most important attributes of political thought. Normative theorists cannot escape contingency and indeterminacy through linguistic precision, although they appear to desire this. 'Normative theorists always operate under the general limitations of language and conceptual morphology, and should acknowledge the contestability of their normative positions. In addition, their ideal-type solutions should not stray too far from the plausible contexts in which they would be located, nor ignore the experience of the impact of various political theories that has built up over time'.[40] In this regard Freeden distinguishes two levels of political thought: 'thinking politically' as a first-order activity, and 'thinking about politics' as a second-order one. Normative theorists are 'thinking politically' in that they are making a contribution, albeit an idiosyncratic one, to political discourse (although they also dress monologue up as dialogue, suggesting a rather one-way conversation).[41] When engaging in the second-order activity of 'studying political thought', however (*including* political philosophy), there is 'no direct conversation between the researcher and the researched'.[42] What is contrasted with political philosophy here then, is not so much 'politics'

---

[34] Freeden, 'Ideology and Political Theory', 12.
[35] Freeden, *Liberal Languages*, 6.
[36] Michael Freeden, 'Political Ideologies in Substance and Method: Appraising a Transformation', in Michael Freeden (ed.), *Reassessing Political Ideologies: The Durability of Dissent* (London: Routledge, 2001), 8.
[37] Michael Freeden, 'What Should the "Political" in Political Theory Explore?', *Journal of Political Philosophy*, 13 (2005), 113.
[38] Freeden, *Liberal Languages*, 6.
[39] Freeden, 'Political Ideologies in Substance', 8.
[40] Freeden, 'Thinking Politically', 214–15.
[41] Freeden, 'Thinking Politically', 207.
[42] Freeden, 'Thinking Politically', 208.

per se, understood as an arena of disagreement in which a fragile order is always subject to potential breakdown (although it may be this as well), as 'ordinary' political thought, which is redolent with emotion, rhetorical appeals, faulty logic, cultural constraints, and dogmatic (if always temporary) closures of meaning. As we shall see in the next section, despite this contrast, and the real differences of method and content it refers to, for Freeden political philosophy does not escape the plane of 'ordinary' political thought (it merely becomes an idiosyncratic version of it). Both are forms of ideology, although philosophical liberalism is ideology of a particularly ineffectual sort.

POLITICAL PHILOSOPHY AS IDEOLOGY

For Michael Freeden it is important that we see contemporary Anglo-American political philosophy as neither a 'neutral' set of observations and judgements about politics, nor as a superior form of substantive political belief (due to its logical rigour, for example). In so far as it is 'liberal' in terms of its assumptions, methods, conceptual structures, and/or substantive propositions, it is an example of liberal ideology, albeit, as noted, a somewhat unusual version by comparison with earlier (not to mention earthier) forms of liberal political thought. Liberal political philosophy (in so far as it lacks methodological self-reflexivity) is a first-order contribution to 'thinking politically', rather than a second-order contribution to 'thinking about politics'. That many normative theorists are 'relatively disengaged from methodological reflections'[43] reinforces this view of the activity.

Some realists also see analytical political philosophy as a form of ideology, although for them this observation is suffused with a different meaning. Key here is the work of Charles Mills, who argues that contemporary normative theory is ideological, and that this ideological nature prevents normative theorists from engaging with the 'real' inequalities and forms of discrimination in society. Instead, philosophical liberals embark on the utopian projects that Freeden objected to above, but utopian projects that become inflected with the power differentials that already exist in Western societies. For him ideal theory is 'really an *ideology*, a distortional complex of ideas, values, norms, and beliefs that reflects the non-representative interests and experiences of a small minority of the national population—middle-to-upper-class white males—who are hugely *over-represented* in the professional philosophical population'.[44] Here a

---

[43] Freeden, 'Thinking Politically', 205.
[44] Mills, '"Ideal Theory" as Ideology', 172. Mills is perhaps best known for his work on domination and contractualism, and, in particular, *The Racial Contract* (Ithaca: Cornell University Press, 1997). See also Carole Pateman and Charles Mills, *Contract & Domination* (Cambridge: Polity Press, 2007).

'nonrepresentative phenomenological lifeworld [is] (mis)taken for *the* world', and although not as a result of a conscious, manipulative act, 'ideal theory can only serve the interests of the privileged'.[45] On this understanding of political philosophy as ideology, then, ideal theory has to be unmasked in order to reveal its true, if subconscious, motivations and make clear whose interests it serves. That ideal theory is ideological is in and of itself the problem.

Freeden also holds that philosophical liberalism is a form of ideology, but this does not entail that a process of unmasking the 'real' interests served by ideal theory is necessary. Rather, philosophical liberalism can be 'decoded' as an ideology in the same way that less sophisticated forms of political thought can also be. Although philosophical liberalism places huge emphasis on rationality, clarity of argument, logical coherence, and consistency, it still displays features common to other ideological forms—such as an appeal to unexamined value assumptions, and the investment of emotional attachment to particular points of view. Thus 'from the perspective of analysing ideologies, philosophical texts are selective decontestations of political concepts like any other'.[46] Rawlsian political liberalism is 'undoubtedly a reflection of American ideological conceptions of the constitution as a facilitator of a common, yet neutral, good that is within reach of a diverse society'.[47] If the implication of this ideological status is not, as it is for Mills, that contemporary analytical political philosophy allows the interests and perspective of a particular social group (middle-class white professional academics) to wear the mask of disinterested analysis, what does ride on the identification of philosophy with ideology for Freeden?

There are three implications that are important for our understanding of what kind of activity political philosophizing is. The first of these takes us back to our opening concern—it identifies philosophical liberalism as a time- and culture-bound political phenomenon. At one level this may seem trivially true, all political thought is produced somewhere, at some time. But of course this point is taken to tell, not against a view about where philosophical liberalism is produced, but rather against its universalistic and idealizing aspirations. One point of strong commonality between Freeden and the realist critics of ideal theory that we have looked at here lies in a refusal to accept any claim to ethical universalism, by which they mean a view such that, to take an apposite example, a conceptual analysis of the nature of 'justice' can define principles of justice that reveal a 'truth' about the concept or which have general applicability.[48] Such claims may well 'relate to myths concerning the rationality of foundational values such as . . . the neutrality of democratic constitutions'. Indeed Freeden appears to

---

[45] Mills, '"Ideal Theory" as Ideology', 205.
[46] Freeden, 'Ideology, Political Theory, and Political Philosophy', 10.
[47] Freeden, 'Ideology and Political Theory', 14.
[48] How 'general' is of course variable between theories. The John Rawls of *Political Liberalism* limits his theoretical scope to 'modern democratic society' (New York: Columbia University Press, 1996), p. xviii.

have philosophical liberalism in his sights when he claims that 'using universalist language unintentionally is to indicate a belief in the overriding validity of intuitions and to make assumptions about human similarity' that may not be warranted.[49] A more conscious awareness of the time- and culture-bound nature of their intellectual efforts would help political philosophers to avoid some of their more egregious errors. Ideology analysis can be a 'tool', and a welcoming 'limiting framework' for work in political philosophy, the potential value of the latter being somewhat undercut by this divorce from 'concrete' political thought. There are several points at which Freeden suggests that political philosophy would gain from closer engagement with less intellectualized forms of ideology and from more contextual awareness. Philosophers can learn form 'the techniques and political nous of ideologists, from what actually takes place when political ideas flow through a society',[50] although ethicists will find 'the inclusion of the ordinary as a focus of study difficult to digest'.[51] The effort should, however, be made, as a more contextually aware political philosophy would also be better political philosophy:

> The usefulness, efficiency, and relevance of normative prescription would be considerably enhanced if conducted within an understanding of the nature, and the limitations, of its subject matter—political thought itself. Normative theorists—political philosophers and ideologists—need to know what can and cannot be done with political thought, and consequently to what political theory can aspire.[52]

Freeden's position on this aspect of philosophical liberalism appears reasonably clear, then. Ideal theory may have its place, but only within a recognition of contextual boundaries and an awareness of the limits of the domain of the political itself, and what political thought can achieve. We can learn something about these limits through the study of ideology and methodological reflection, and in this regard ideology analysis can be a useful tool for normative political philosophy. All of this assumes, of course, that the political philosopher is (a) willing to recognize herself as an ideological producer, and (b) wishes to attain some sort of relevance in terms of the ongoing conversations about policy and political practice that take place in her society. If philosophical liberals have absolutely no desire to influence policy, then they might rest content with highly abstract discussion within a closed circle of like-minded souls, although clearly for Freeden this would be a very strange form of 'political' activity.

This relates to the second and third points, which to some extent overlap with the first and can be dealt with more briefly. Political philosophy *is* ideology,

---

[49] Freeden, *Ideologies and Political Theory*, 33. Note that Geuss makes exactly the same point in *Philosophy and Real Politics*, 91.
[50] Freeden, 'Ideology and Political Theory', 9.
[51] Freeden, 'Ideology and Political Theory', 15.
[52] Freeden, 'Thinking Politically', 205.

on this view, a structured arrangement of decontested political concepts that its protagonists hope will provide a frame through which people believe they can understand and criticize current political arrangements, and possibly also provide the vision of a better political future. The problem for political philosophy is that *as* an ideology it is pretty hopeless. This is because for Freeden the measures of success and failure that apply to ideology are different to those that apply to philosophy. Here Freeden is with Geuss in thinking that, as noted earlier, 'questions of definition and of purely theoretical consistency are often not the most relevant ones to ask in politics'.[53] A successful ideology will need some measure of theoretical consistency,[54] although, given both the availability of cultural and emotional cues with which to truncate the logical chain of argument, and the need to bring matters to a decision point, consistency and coherence are not of the same importance in ideological discourse as they are for philosophers. Instead ideologies need to reach out and mobilize elements of the population if they are to seize control of the public policy agenda—this being the measure of success on their own terms. One is reminded here of Gramsci's distinction between 'abstract' and 'organic' ideologies, in that an ideology with no active followers in society, concocted by 'traditional' intellectuals, is a rather pointless beast. Philosophical liberalism might be seen as an archetypical abstract ideology, circulated in complex texts around university departments, but never becoming consolidated in a 'historical bloc' even if certain individual philosophers have some influence, from time to time, over government policy. The measure of philosophical success is publication in *Ethics* or *Philosophy & Public Affairs*. In contrast, the 'ultimate success of an ideology is in its mobilization of significant groups who compete ideationally in order to impact on acts of collective decision-making',[55] and on this measure philosophical liberalism fails.

Finally, as an example of ideology political philosophy is itself amenable to ideology analysis, and whilst this was mentioned above it is worth contemplating the implications of this claim in a little more detail, as I believe it is here above all that strong disagreement lies between Freeden and analytical political philosophers. The main implication of the claim is that political philosophy and ideology analysis lie on different sides of the 'thinking politically/ thinking about politics' divide. For all that this divide is not 'hard and fast' and for all that practitioners of both arts will at times occupy the territory of the other,[56] philosophical liberalism is a form of liberal ideology, and so constitutes an example of thinking politically, whilst forms of ideology analysis such as conceptual morphology are examples of thinking about politics and lie on

---

[53] Geuss, *Outside Ethics*, 13. [54] Freeden, *Ideologies and Political Theory*, 29.
[55] Freeden, 'Ideology, Political Theory, and Political Philosophy', 12.
[56] Freeden, 'Ideology and Political Theory', 17.

the other. There is, remember, 'no direct conversation between the researcher and the researched'. Rather like the scientist contemplating natural phenomena, the ideologist (on an understanding of 'ideologist' not a million miles from de Tracy's original conception of ideologist-as-scientist, although here analysing patterns of ideas rather than the human brain) decodes the ideological texts, and the political philosopher, unwittingly or not, provides the raw material for analysis. This understanding of the relationship between ideology and philosophy breaks down the barriers constructed by thinkers such as Leo Strauss and Michael Oakeshott, for whom there was a 'distinction between opinion and knowledge' to which 'political thought' was indifferent but political philosophy was not,[57] and for whom philosophy had to maintain 'its independence from all extraneous interests, and in particular from practical interest'.[58] On Freeden's view, political philosophy may pursue the truth, but it also engages in the practical exercise of seeking to persuade others of *its* truth, up to the point of seeing its preferred principles enacted in the public domain, and this is a practical interest from which any genuinely 'political' philosophy cannot be separated.

DIVERGENCES

The above analysis should be sufficient to show that the work of Michael Freeden should be a reference point for realist political philosophers. Both think that Anglo-American political philosophy is overidealized and abstract, lays too much stress on the philosophical standards of coherence and consistency, and that philosophical liberalism can be seen as a form of ideology (although with substantially different understandings of ideology, the common point of reference here is that political philosophy cannot be a 'neutral' contribution to political discourse that somehow stands above the fray of rhetoric or interest-based politics). Before concluding, it is also worth noting those areas in which Freeden and the realists part company in their analysis of political philosophy, as the existence of substantive differences may undermine my claim that Freeden should be a point of reference for the realists. It may be that the distinctions overwhelm the import of the similarities already noted. There are of course linguistic differences, contrasts in the conceptual vocabulary of each approach (such as the contrasting conceptions of ideology), but the most substantive difference lies in this: that realism posits one form of political

---

[57] Leo Strauss, *What is Political Philosophy? And Other Studies* (Westport: Greenwood Press, 1959), 12.

[58] Michael Oakeshott, *Experience and Its Modes* (Cambridge: Cambridge University Press, 1933), 3.

philosophy against another, whilst Freeden seeks to develop a second-order analysis of ideology that would recuperate *both* ideal and realist forms of political philosophizing under its analytical gaze. The realist objection to ideal theory is not that it *is* first-order political philosophy, but that it is political philosophy *done in the wrong way*. And whilst that may show realist political philosophy to be methodologically aware, relatively speaking, it does not seek to separate itself from the articulation of first-order political values. Thus, thinkers like Geuss and Williams are quite comfortable in claiming that the view that the first virtue of social institutions is justice is just *wrong*—there are other virtues that political institutions might possess, which are as, or more, important than justice. At the core of the failure of analytical political philosophy is the inability to understand the realm of the political as distinct in terms of the appropriate mode of philosophical enquiry. It is not an arena to which we can straightforwardly apply the methods of moral philosophy, which results in the universalization of the very particular intuitions of the theorist.

It is also central to Freeden's view that 'the political' constitutes a distinct subject of enquiry which requires methods of its own, not merely the application of philosophy or history. He does not, however, seek to substitute one (realist) philosophical approach for the idealist one, but rather to understand political thought through a second-order analysis. Realist political philosophy is just as amenable to this second-order analysis as ideal theory. Whilst the realist critique of ideal theory is understandable, given realist beliefs, it may seem odd that Freeden's approach results in a critique of philosophical liberalism—why berate analytical philosophers for how they go about their business rather than just study the products of their thought processes? Part of the answer here is that Freeden's views on analytical political theory just are part of that second-order analysis. What he is reporting are developments in liberal political thought that see it retreat from direct engagement with its political context and evolve into the subject of a scholarly philosophical discussion amongst university professors. There may be more to it than this though, and the strongly condemnatory tone towards philosophical liberalism that he adopts seems to betray Freeden's *normative* commitment to a contextual form of liberal politics. As he himself notes, that divide between first- and second-order analyses is not hard and fast, and I would certainly claim that his approach, and his understanding of the nature of ideology (in which families of ideas can be seen to compete in an ideational marketplace) reflect a certain liberal ontology. This is not to criticize, but merely to observe that the putative split between a normative first-order discourse and an analytical second-order discourse is an unstable one, even if it has some purchase in reality. Whilst this commitment to 'thinking about politics' distances Freeden from the realist camp methodologically, it does nothing to undermine the very clear substantive commonalities outlined in the rest of this paper.

CONCLUSION

This chapter has sought to compare the critiques of analytical political philosophy as offered both by contemporary realists and by Michael Freeden, in order to gain a better understanding of how the latter's engagement with 'philosophical liberalism' relates to a prominent contemporary debate. My aims therefore have been distinctly limited and interpretative, and specifically I have not here sought to address whether ideal theory has the resources to defend itself against such attacks.[59] What this analysis has shown is that there are some important common elements in both Michael Freeden's and the realists' understanding of 'ideal theory' or 'philosophical liberalism'. Both think that contemporary liberalism denies its own time-bound and culturally specific context, and seeks instead to produce principles of justice, obligation, equality, etc. that are removed from the contingencies of time and place, and which should be protected behind the walls of constitutional convention. Both also believe that 'the political' is a sphere that is clearly distinct from moral philosophy, providing not only a different field of application (if this were all, then we could after all see political philosophy as 'a branch, or subset, of moral philosophy'),[60] but also with unique characteristics that entail the need for a *sui generis* form of theory. In this both Geuss and especially Williams seem to look back to an older realist tradition (and one thinks particularly of Machiavelli here, who believed that sometimes what is the right thing to do politically appears scandalous from the perspective of conventional morality. See also Geuss's references to Lenin). We get to understand what 'works' politically by studying the 'art or craft' of politics and its history, not through conceptual analysis of a philosophical nature. We learn little about justice merely by thinking about justice.

This notion of a distinct political sphere is found in Freeden as well, although it plays out rather differently. With Williams he is happy to allow that ethics forms part of politics, but not all of it, and one problem with contemporary political philosophy is that it often takes that part to be the whole. But Freeden's concern is not redolent of Machiavellian republicanism. He is not offering a rival political philosophy, with a different 'first question' of politics; rather, he wants us to reflect on what it means to understand and analyse political thought, and to understand that difference between 'thinking about politics' and 'thinking politically'. If our aim is to be political theorists, i.e. theorize about politics, then we have to understand the nature of the political and the role of political thought in it, and this is why we cannot treat political philosophy as all

---

[59] This task has been taken up by others, see for example Adam Swift, 'The Value of Philosophy in Nonideal Circumstances', *Social Theory and Practice*, 34 (2008), 363–87.

[60] Daniel McDermott, 'Analytical Political Philosophy', in David Leopold and Marc Stears (eds.), *Political Theory*, 11–28.

of political thought, as it represents only a relatively small part of that universe, and if we do take that part for the whole we will have a hugely distorted understanding of what 'political thought' actually is. Concrete political thought in its predominant form is the product of ideologists, as seen in political pamphlets, manifestos, newspapers, popular books, magazines, speeches, and other material that would be considered 'substandard' by the expectations for philosophical argument. But this is why Freeden is so keen to dispel the 'rubbish in, rubbish out' view that holds such material unworthy of scholarly study.[61] To understand political thought we have to engage in ideology analysis, alongside, not instead of, the more traditional subdisciplines of political philosophy and the history of political thought. The problem with pursuing a singularly philosophical path is that it may not only fail to tell us 'what to do' (the common complaint against ideal theory), it may also seriously misguide us on the question of 'what to think' or even 'how to think' about politics.

On this last point, we should come back now to Freeden's 'distinctive answer' to which I alluded in the very first paragraph. Freeden's work sets up a tripartite division between ideology, political theory, and political philosophy. Ideology encompasses all forms of 'concrete' political thought, and as should by now be clear normative political philosophy, making as it does first-order political claims, forms a relatively distinct subset of ideology (even if the boundaries around it are inevitably fuzzy). Because its measures of success are incompatible with those that apply to ideology, it turns out that normative political philosophy is a terrible way to do ideology. So if the objective is to have influence on public policy and mobilize opinion, analytical political philosophy fails. If the philosopher claims that the objective is only to think clearly about politics, or particular normative problems in politics, it is still not obvious that political philosophy modelled on moral philosophy is the answer if it fails (as Freeden claims) to grasp the nature of the political realm adequately. Instead, those seeking to make normative contributions to political life should dirty their hands and engage with the ideologists, seeking to understand how political ideas flow through the social order. This brings us to *political theory*, which for Freeden is the second-order scholarly exercise of decoding, mapping, and understanding concrete political thought. The analyst of ideology may make normative claims as a citizen, but as a professional student of political thought s/he seeks merely to understand and interpret the subject matter (porous boundaries between the normative and the interpretative permitting).

Given that Freeden has been writing about philosophical liberalism in this vein since at least 1996, he should be a reference point for those of a realist bent who are making very similar claims about 'ideal theory' without making

---

[61] Freeden, 'Thinking Politically', 208.

any apparent connection to Freeden's work as of yet. However, these commonalities are not sufficient for us to sign Freeden up to the realist camp. Indeed, on a morphological reading of realist political philosophy as ideology, the priority given to the problem of order (or, in some versions, power) could be viewed as just as ahistorical and lacking in context as anything that Rawlsians have to say about justice. Freeden stands in some ways connected to realism in political philosophy, but in so far as his logic commits him to viewing it as yet another ideological manifestation, he remains also divorced from it, behind the barrier of non-conversation that exists between ideologist and analyst.

13

The Professional Responsibilities of the Political Theorist

Michael Freeden

Responding to this academic gift of supreme generosity is a delight, an embarrassment, and a challenge. I have come to esteem all the contributors greatly, some over many years of discussion and collaborations; others through their writings long before we met personally. Not a few began distinguished careers when they were among the most rewarding of my own students, doctoral and undergraduate, and I feel that we have travelled a considerable way together, while I have accumulated knowledge and insights from every one of them. Through the chapters in this volume I have realized the importance of Schleiermacher's observation about understanding authors better than they understand themselves. That is at least partly true, both because of the surplus of meaning—Ricoeur's phrase—that we as authors transmit to our ever-interpretative readers, and because those readers will reassess any text in the light of their own cultural and intellectual frameworks. Nonetheless, it is not entirely true, because living authors may have the luxury of disagreeing with their interpreters as well, and may have their own sense of the intellectual trajectory they have followed. Self-definition and other-definition, as in the study of ideologies, go hand in hand.

In the space allotted to me, I shall say something about the responsibility of the political theorist, not necessarily towards the world, as ethicists and ideologists may demand, but with regard to our academic practices. We all are acquainted with Max Weber's 'Politics as a Vocation' in which he entreated politicians to respond to their duties towards their general audiences with passion, an ethic of responsibility, and a sense of proportion. While Weber talked about the ethic of responsibility of leaders, I focus on the responsibilities that we as political theorists have towards our discipline, vague as its boundaries may be. I highlight five areas of such responsibility: the responsibility of relevance; of understanding; of inclusiveness; of critical distance; and of tentativeness. My examination of those responsibilities will incorporate some of the issues discussed by the contributors to this book, aware of my limitations in capturing the richness of arguments laid out in its pages and of the constraints of space in doing them even curtailed justice. But prior to that, in order to clarify my position, I shall briefly muse on some stepping stones in the development of my own thinking.

In *Liberal Languages* I first set down my own sense of my journey, one that moved through the three circles of analysing a particular ideological family—liberalism; to exploring the family characteristics of the general phenomenon of which liberalisms are a part—ideologies; to most recently investigating the raw features of the actual thought-practice of thinking politically, as a step back from the thinking *about* politics that distinguishes ideologies. There was both a methodological and a substantive continuity to my research agenda. In the earlier stages of my work—the 1970s and 1980s—I had looked at the structure of a particular genre of progressive liberal thinking: the complex and fluid nature of British liberal thought between the 1880s and 1940s, put across in my first two books: *The New Liberalism* and *Liberalism Divided*. I still return to that theme, and have done so most recently in a comparative article on European liberalisms and in various essays on liberal theory and ideology, as well as in a continental project on European conceptual history in which I am currently closely involved. In the middle stage—the 1990s—I developed a general morphological theory of ideology, looking at the conceptual structures, combinations, and decontestations required in order to identify fluctuating fields of meaning that compete over the control of political language—fields that are always rooted in concrete temporal and spatial contexts. Their ostensible stability thus became a problem, not a feature. Currently, in my work on the political theory of political thinking, I attempt to theorize about what thinking *politically* means, to examine the diversity and elusiveness of political language itself, and to suggest ways of making sense of that very central human thought-practice. All along I have been concerned with what we are doing as political theorists in the broad sense. My focus is on the kinds of evidence we should consider when exploring our disciplinary sphere of interest; on the kinds of understandings we should be entrusted to form and develop when confronted with such evidence; and on the interdisciplinary inspirations of such understandings.

My interest in political theory began as an undergraduate and postgraduate when I discovered the history of political thought, which I was fortunate enough to study in great detail at the Hebrew University of Jerusalem, in a course that ranged over two years and contained over fifty lectures, not only on the classical canon, but on Marsilius of Padua and Dante, on the Diggers and Levellers, and on Joseph de Maistre and Herbert Spencer. I recall also a postgraduate class I took with Shlomo Avineri in which we read Hegel's *Philosophy of Right* for twenty-eight weeks, a level of intense exposure to a major philosophical text that must be an increasing rarity. Returning to the UK for a visiting fellowship at St Antony's College, Oxford—where I had previously studied for my D.Phil.—and then obtaining a permanent political theory post at Mansfield College and the University of Oxford, a far more analytical approach to political philosophy, dominating the 1970s and 1980s, confronted me. I was charged with teaching political theory at College and Departmental level and prepared myself by doing what I believed was the sensible thing: I consulted the sacred 'Grey Book', the examination regulations that listed the rubrics of all courses. The first line under 'theory of politics' read: 'The critical study of political values and of the concepts used in political analysis,' and then went on to list some of the basic concepts and ideologies.[1] Innocently, I took those instructions seriously and began to explore the constitution of political concepts, little realizing that my colleagues were concentrating instead on the arguments of the major philosophers who had addressed those concepts. Thus sprang into existence, somewhat idiosyncratically and accidentally, a focus on the nature, structure, and components of concepts. That eventually developed into my theory of conceptual decontestation and the triple dimensions of a concept, its micro-components, and the conceptual configurations in which a concept may be durably or fleetingly set and which—among others—are the key to the formation of ideological families.

Let me illustrate the impact of the study of concepts on my work. In 1990 I wrote a short book on *Rights*, for a series on concepts in the social sciences. My colleagues strongly advised me against tackling that subject, assuring me that it was an unrewarding and probably hopeless endeavour. Nonetheless, I wrote the book, preferring not to regard rights primarily as a legal or moral concept, but as a device with the specific task of prioritizing and protecting the valued ends of a society, or what I have since termed the distribution of significance— the right always being the containing capsule for the good attached to it: life, liberty, happiness, property, and the like. The book attained only modest success and was largely ignored by moral rights theorists. It has taken me twenty years to relocate that work in my wider search for the defining components of the political and to understand myself better than I had understood myself when writing it.

I have described myself as a conceptologist who descends among political concepts and observes them at work and play, deciphering their conduct and trying to identify the possible patterns of their conjunctions and to interpret the significance of the messages embodied in those patterns. But I am more observer than participant. As a scholar I am not primarily focused on changing the lives of human beings by improving the acuity and ethical content of

---

[1] *University of Oxford: Examination Decrees and Regulations 1978* (Oxford: Oxford University Press, 1978), 266.

those concepts, as I am interested in improving the range of comprehension at the disposal of students of society and politics. Although that range may ultimately be put to work in promoting the 'good life', it cannot be done effectively unless we have a complex grasp of the possibilities embedded in actual political thinking as a resource from which to fashion ethical positions. If one gazes reflectively at the interlinking areas through which to enrich our comprehension of the actual practising of political thought, they encompass the study of ideologies, the comparative study of political thought, intellectual history, conceptual history, discourse analysis (though not necessarily its critical mode), and a large number of post-structural approaches influenced by diverse perspectives such as psychoanalysis, post-Marxism, ethnography, the linguistic turn, or artistic performativity.

None of these is the key to interpreting political thought on its own, but each brings insights that enrich such interpretation in an accumulative manner. Above all, understanding political thought needs to come to terms with its disarray, its loose ends, and its resistance to categorization. The neatness that some philosophers (and most ideologists, too) seek to impose on the world will merely conceal its disjointedness and, in particular, the slipperiness and contingency of political thought and language, against which perennial decontestation is a futile—if inescapable—attempt to freeze time and anchor space. The study of ideologies and their complex and flexible morphology should be combined with an appreciation of the unpredictable historical paths of conceptual change. But that change is not only diachronic. Grafted onto the morphological analysis of conceptual constellations it may be possible to realize how concepts bump into and intersect with one another, how they shed components, how they emerge with the debris of other concepts stuck onto them, how they change shape and trajectory, how nailing them down can only be achieved in short bursts of time and insight, how they slither through our fingers—yet how their patterns can nonetheless be adumbrated, if only to be redrawn again and again.

The study of ideologies, with their central feature of competing over the control of political language, has occupied my interest for the past twenty years. In particular, the decontestation of essentially contested concepts and configurations underscores ideological ubiquity and diversity, as well as underlining the fleeting nature of ideological variants and families within some overall durabilities. One by-product of my fascination with ideologies, as the carriers of the substance of actual political thinking, was my founding of the *Journal of Political Ideologies*, now in its seventeenth year, and for me an intellectual mission and a labour of love.

My current interests—advanced further especially in the chapters by Mathew Humphrey and Michael Kenny, which also contain searching discussions of my more recent work—have broadened to address the nature of political thinking itself, in a move from what I have termed 'thinking about politics' (a practice of the producers and consumers of ideology) to 'thinking politically'.[2] I have become convinced that any serious political theory needs to engage centrally with the question: 'What has to occur in a person's mind for us to say that that person is thinking politically, rather than ethically, or sexually, or historically, or artistically?' I hold that the political, and thinking politically, cannot be summed up by one or two characteristics, such as power or conflict or sovereignty, or by fundamental dichotomies such as friend–enemy or public–private. Like any form of thinking, it is complex, multi-dimensional, partly fragmented, and in constant flux, with its various components appearing in different weightings. Thinking politically refers to collectivities and includes the attempted arrogation of the ultimate control over decisions that affect all social spheres; the distribution of significance by ranking social aims and demands; the channelling of support, critique, or rejection of collective entities and their procedures; the articulation of stabilizing or conflictual arrangements for groups; the construction of macro-political visions and detailed micro-plans involved in policymaking; and the expression of power through the linguistic and visual intensities and skills of persuasion, rhetoric, emotion, or menace. In this volume, Kenny has developed his own insights into different understandings of the political—within the concrete context of elite thinking in mid-twentieth-century Britain—through an examination of Bernard Crick's thinking.

THE RESPONSIBILITY OF RELEVANCE

Sheldon Wolin pre-empted me in picking a title for his 1969 article that I would have chosen for this chapter: 'Political Theory as a Vocation'. As do many others, Wolin called for a politically engaged political theory, but his idea of political theory centred on the intellectual curiosity and internal sources of a meditative culture of creativity of the political theorist—termed by him tacit political knowledge. Wolin berated political scientists for constructing 'unpolitical theories': they offered 'no significant choice or analysis of the quality, direction, or fate of public life'. His model was the 'epic political theorist', tackling issues such as historical understanding and caring for public things. In his words: 'political theory is, among many other things, a sum of judgments, shaped by the theorist's notion of what matters.' And also: 'It is too vague to leave it that theorists are stimulated by problems-in-the-world...

---

[2] Michael Freeden, 'Thinking Politically and Thinking about Politics: Language, Interpretation and Ideology', in D. Leopold and M. Stears (eds.), *Political Theory: Methods and Approaches* (Oxford: Oxford University Press, 2008), 196–215; and my forthcoming *The Political Theory of Political Thinking*.

what is all-important is that a problem be a truly theoretical one.'[3] Wolin's vocation is about the residually elitist responsibility of the theorist in making a difference to the society in which he or she resides, rather than about a sustained wrestling with actual political thinking. I have no quarrel with most of Wolin's points on their own, but it is only part of the story we need to tell.

The responsibility of relevance operates on three dimensions. The first concerns another kind of political engagement which passes quite a few philosophers by. It is our engagement as theorists with constructing theories that have a reasonable chance of relating to the thought-practices of the intricate, messy world which both political elites and ordinary people display. As David Weinstein has astutely observed about analytical political philosophy in his chapter, 'the more professional it has become, the less it has flourished ideologically', a point also made by Mathew Humphrey. Even a moderate success at relating to actual thought-practices will, I firmly believe, help to pave the way for the arguments of ethico-political philosophers to have a more reasonable chance of being implemented in that messy world.[4] Contrast that with Wolin's sense of vocation: 'although the vocabulary of the political theorist carries the trace of everyday language and experience, it is largely the product of the theorist's creative efforts.'[5] He was of course right that our professional vocabulary may be more technical and sophisticated than everyday language, but he aimed at sanctioning the gap between amateur and professional political thinking. Nowhere did he suggest that our professional skills should be directed at making sense of those everyday patterns of political thinking. The study of amateur thinking was for amateurs, as many philosophers would strongly argue. It may well be, as Humphrey has observed of the recent emergence of political realism in political theory, that 'the realist objection to ideal theory is not that it *is* first-order political philosophy, but that it is political philosophy *done in the wrong way*'.[6] But it is equally possible that political philosophy is being done in the 'right way', yet in so doing it does not satisfy additional demands political theorists need to make of the subject matter of political thinking. I am less concerned with what Humphrey terms leading political philosophers 'badly astray' because they should, in my view,

---

[3] Sheldon Wolin, 'Political Theory as a Vocation', *American Political Science Review*, 63 (1969), 1063.

[4] Some philosophers are attempting to achieve moderate success through what they term non-ideal theory, but they still have a long way to go. See A. Swift, 'The Value of Philosophy in Nonideal Circumstances', *Social Theory and Practice*, 34 (2008), 363–87; and 'Symposium: Contract and Domination by Carole Pateman and Charles W. Mills', *Journal of Political Ideologies*, 13 (2008), 227–62.

[5] Sheldon Wolin, *Politics and Vision* (Princeton: Princeton University Press, 2nd expanded edition, 2004), 15.

[6] Humphrey's chapter in this volume, p. 255.

stick to what they are good at while leaving political theorists to get on with their own job.

This links up to Jerry Gaus's spirited critique of my approach and his defence of philosophy. Some of the differences between us are genuine; others based on mutual misunderstandings. So while Gaus suspects me of claiming that Rawls is full of bad arguments (of which Rawls does indeed have a smattering, such as maintaining that the Supreme Court is the exemplar of public reason, or implying that the least advantaged member of a society could be located at the bottom of a single ranking order of disadvantage), I contend rather that the crucial question is one of relevance. Rawls addresses issues that are relevant to what Gaus terms philosophy's 'universalistic and rationalistic self-image, for it sees itself as rationally clarifying what at first seems murky and confused'. So far, so plausible from the viewpoint of political philosophy, but something goes askew when such clarifying tendencies and instructive philosophical exercises are applied to the world of politics, a world in which contestations, temporary decontestations, indeterminacy, and vagueness rule the roost. We need to develop approaches that can navigate through those actual features of political thinking, especially when philosophers are tempted to change the world. I don't think that I am uncharitable to Rawls's deep humanism, sense of justice, and imaginative power, but I am frustrated by his methodological optimism. And when Gaus admonishes me for apparently and misguidedly invoking a 'non-normative perspective from which one can dispute the normative soundness of American philosophical liberalism', my retort is that I am not disputing its normative soundness at all. To the contrary, philosophical liberals (for contemporary ethical political philosophy articulates positions tantamount to ideal-type liberal precepts) engage in the highest forms of ethical reflectiveness. As ethical thought experiments they have immense exploratory value, which operate significantly in the sphere of regulative ideals. But regulative ideals are far too fuzzy and inconclusive to offer concrete guidelines for policies and activities that collectivities can undertake. They eschew the constraints of the political world, constraints that cannot be removed through ratiocination or searching for optimal virtue.

There is even less allusion in contemporary political theory to the second domain of relevance, to our responsibility to make the practice of political thinking more accessible to ordinary people—that is, not only to theorize *about* their language but to theorize *in* language with which they can connect. And that is important because the realm of politics is a public, or collective, one that necessarily involves large numbers of individuals, whether actively or passively. The skill of connectivity is a skill that many—though not all—past social and political theorists possessed, as they lived parallel lives as subtle scholars and as reader-friendly commentators on the hustle and bustle of everyday politics, before the extreme specialization of academia began to take its toll. There is no demerit in fashioning one's language to the diverse expectations of disparate targeted audiences of readerships, in translating the same arguments into different, parallel voices. To the contrary, that prime rhetorical talent underpins the crucial importance of communicability both as an intellectual and a political resource.

The third domain of relevance is opened up both by Marc Stears and David Leopold, when they cross the divide between 'professional' and vernacular political thinking in their contributions (there are of course numerous professional languages, of academics, intellectuals, politicians, bureaucrats). I refer here not to understanding what *political* discourse is, nor to the employment of accessible language, but to our capacity to theorize about ordinary forms of political expression, in journalism, demonstrations, conversations in the piazza, constituency meetings, pageants, or reactions of immigration officers. Stears's fascinating account of American liberalism through popular stories, novels, and films, and through an exploration of the Freedom Train, alerts us to the kind of source material we need to assimilate into our broader analysis of political thought, visual and performative as well as textual. With probing originality he corrects Hartz's influential yet myth-making academic account of the dominance of American liberalism through an investigation of the actual multiple discourses and activities that sought to recreate a common liberalism believed, rather, to be imperilled.

Leopold's bold attempt to compare like with unlike is another such instance. He juxtaposes one of the most rigorous political philosophers of the mid and late twentieth century, Rawls, with one of the most creative, but occasionally inexact, liberal theorists and writers of the early twentieth century, J. A. Hobson. Hobson—in the company of whose writings I spent many years— was one of my early 'discoveries' as a major liberal theorist, rather than solely an economist and anti-imperialist. I am therefore delighted that Leopold has chosen to investigate a new Hobsonian angle with his usual meticulousness and freshness, namely, the role of utopianism in Hobson's (and Rawls's) liberal motivational inspiration. On the surface it may seem odd to attribute relevance to the theme of utopianism, but its evaluation is highly pertinent as a prevalent instance of actual political thinking.

My own work has grappled with the language of vernacular protest, in the case of the women camping outside the US nuclear base at Greenham Common for many years; and the language of civic pride and national mourning, in the case of the ceremonies honouring the British war-dead who are returned from Afghanistan.[7] The daunting problem here is that of translation into the languages that we use as professional political theorists. We need to shift from

---

[7] See Michael Freeden, 'Languages of Political Support: Engaging with the Public Realm', *Critical Review of International Social and Political Philosophy*, 12 (2009), 183–202; Freeden, 'Editorial: The Politics of Ceremony: The Wootton Bassett Phenomenon', *Journal of Political Ideologies*, 16 (2011), 1–10.

vernacular to academic languages out of respect to our professional training, yet transplanting a vernacular term such as 'commitment' into the more technical 'political obligation' may involve a considerable additional degree of indeterminacy and fail to impress our professional colleagues. Alternatively, reformulating vernacular idioms in new elite registers may result not simply in losing in translation but in the opposite problem: adding complexity where less existed originally. Whatever our difficulties in tackling those issues, we need to be attuned to accept the 'vulgarization' of complex political discourses and texts as part of the usual subject matter of political theory. Difficulties of cultural transmission occur inside societies as well as across them. The professional thinking produced by philosophers, ideologues, academics, and even politicians is atypical of the political thinking in a society; and as political theorists embedded in the social sciences we ought to be acquainted with its actual, 'normal', as well as 'abnormal', manifestations.

THE RESPONSIBILITY OF UNDERSTANDING

The Weberian aim of *Verstehen* requires us to become acquainted with the fundamental features of political speech and writing that we may then process in our different ways. There is no end to understanding, yet understanding is an end in itself; it is not merely instrumental to justifying, or recommending, or predicting. It is intimately associated with interpretation, which offers not the correct view of the world of political thought, but as plausible a view as the scholar can conjure up. Interpretation is always in the eyes of the beholder, but the beholder as political theorist is entrusted with making an effort to understand the practices she or he is investigating, their context, their meaning both to their producers and to some of their various consumers (however elusive that might be to determine), and the possibility both of conscious and unconscious messages being imparted in a given discourse. Above all, understanding thinking politically and ideologies necessitates striking a balance between restoring manageable interpretative complexity to what frequently are simplifying discourses and detecting general regularities that can be transmitted as provisional scholarly findings.

The significance of symbols and of meaning is well known in many disciplines, especially in linguistics and semiotics, but political theory was not among those in the forefront of that recognition. Anthropologists such as Clifford Geertz served as conduits for that realization due to the fortuitous link (in terms of the development of the study of ideology) he forged between culture and ideology as systems of signification. As Andrew Vincent has observed in his illuminating dissection of the fourfold relationship between political theory and ideology, the fourth possibility—their positive segregation—has emphasized the mapping function of political thinking, which I, too, profoundly defend. Interpretation, however, as Vincent rightly comments, may involve distortion. Here also the responsibility of the political theorist is vital. If we subscribe to Marxisant theories of ideology, distortion is what ideologies peddle, deliberately or otherwise, in their role of obfuscating truth. But if social truths are unknowable (as Slavoj Žižek[8] would have it) or illusory, or partial, or temporary—as we flit from one 'truth' to another—or even irrelevant to some heuristic purposes, then the question of distortion recedes considerably. Moreover, searching for the rational intentionality ascribed to truth will blind us to the roles of emotion and passion in shaping and conveying political messages. Crucially, there is no fixed ratio between reason and emotion in political thinking; no minimal threshold for either of them beneath which we should either disregard such thinking or consider it beyond interpretation.

That said, we need to distinguish between the potentially distorted ideas that we study and the compounded distortions that we may pile onto those ideas in our own interpretative endeavours. Political theorists should foster curiosity about 'distortions', some of which are obvious when they fly against all reasonable evidence. But that should not trouble a discipline with an already strong pedigree of exposing historical relativism. In addition, the essential contestability of concepts approach is bound to question the appropriateness of persistent distortion.[9] Though, say, some forms of 'democracy' are so far from accepted definitions that they may be labelled distortions (the former German Democratic Republic is one such candidate), the more recent question of democratic deficits in the EU (another form of distortion) is unanswerable when components of democracy such as self-determination, equality, participation, and accountability pull in different and sometimes zero-sum directions and disable the envisaging of a perfect, *sans*-deficit, democracy. There are other 'distortions', too, to which Rochana Bajpai has drawn attention in her excellent account of Indian liberalism: patterns of thinking that are misidentified or underrated in their societies, yet nonetheless possess considerable salience and subtlety. Good scholarship should also challenge culturally prevalent self-understandings and try to detect some of the blind spots that political thought-practices will always exhibit. But we must always take on board the possible weaknesses of our own interpretations—we may simply get things wrong, say, by failing to allocate the proper weighting to the components of the story we are trying to tell. Understanding also requires comprehension of what cannot be answered.

---

[8] S. Žižek, 'The Spectre of Ideology', in S. Žižek (ed.), *Mapping Ideology* (London: Verso, 1994), 1–33.

[9] For an overarching discussion, see D. Collier, F. D. Hidalgo, and A. O. Maciuceanu, 'Essentially Contested Concepts: Debates and Applications', *Journal of Political Ideologies*, 11 (2006), 211–46.

Furthermore, we should not forget that ideology doesn't entirely populate the realm of the political and its investigation should not marginalize other kinds of understanding. Ideology is typical of, and pervades all, political thinking, but it is not sufficient to describe political thinking. One can equally engage in critical thinking, with tools borrowed from philosophy or, for that matter, literary criticism. However such critique may wish to be transformative, it is nonetheless centrally interpretative too. That is something that Vincent understands well. As he reminds us, invoking Gadamer and others, 'There is no conceptual clarity, empirical reference, moral truth or logical self-consistency, which magically exceeds language'. Interpretation needs to be reassessed continuously, both by the original interpreter and by later textual consumers.

Kenny and Humphrey note the link between method and understanding. They are right, broadly speaking, that my methodology comes from a liberal stable, which is only to underline that methodology is never neutral and that the divide between first- and second-order analysis may be contestable in principle. My methodology is liberal, I suppose, because it is pluralist, because I endorse the openness, mutability, and flexibility of interpretation that is also endemic to a liberal mindset (though not a sufficient characterization of that mindset), and because I do not believe in the form of perfectionism that some liberal philosophers appropriated in the 1980s, but in the possibility of achieving (and even choosing to achieve) less than one's best, as a true liberal would maintain.[10] My approach to the analysis of political thinking is not, I trust, too substantively liberal. There is a crucial distinction between aiming to understand through decoding—to which I subscribe—and aiming to prescribe substantive values and improve the nature of political thinking, to which I do not purport as a scholar, though of course I do as a political participant, an amateur ethicist, and an inevitable holder of ideological viewpoints.

Hence Gaus's claim that my conceptual morphology is normative fails to distinguish between substantive norms and heuristic preferences. To prefer certain methods of analysis, or value certain ways of extracting information is not tantamount to the normative competition over the control of public political languages or collective aims and goals, which ideologies pursue, but an attempt to employ ontological and epistemological choices in the service of recommending productive or insightful ways of interpreting political thought. Normative analysis aims at improving the quality of social life; a useful methodology aims at improving the quality of scholarship. Many years ago, following a lecture I delivered in North Carolina, two staff members rose and said: 'We teach our students the values of the American Constitution. What values do you teach yours?' I sheepishly responded that I did not deliberately

---

[10] H. H. Asquith, 18 April 1907, *Parl. Deb.*, 4th ser., vol. 172, col. 1189.

teach my students any ideological values, though I conceded that some might sneak out in unguarded moments. More recently I was asked at an Ivy League university what was the urgency of my message, and responded more measuredly—to the consternation of much of my audience, who expected a rousing call to greater democratic transparency or some such thing—that its urgency was in pleading with political theorists to ask themselves what they were doing in practising their discipline. If that is being a methodological liberal, then I am indeed one.

THE RESPONSIBILITY OF INCLUSIVENESS

The responsibility of inclusiveness operates on two levels. First, it requires us to acknowledge, if not to study, all available forms of political thinking—the latter clearly being a task for a multitude of scholars. Second, it requires a specific attitude towards the accumulation and processing of knowledge, and it is that aspect that I shall stress in this section: the responsibility to acquire whatever knowledge—given our current resources and capabilities—may be extracted from the disciplinary field and from neighbouring ones. If that means leaving no stones unturned, it also means that we cannot turn all stones on our own. And because no one person can cover the field, no one has the right to exclude any serious approach and to compel it to lie fallow, nor can we risk the loss that might entail. That 'episteme-diversity' does not, obviously, require fluency in all relevant approaches, but it demands an inquisitiveness that does not rule out any approach that may offer illumination—however partial—and a willingness to converse with others with the aim of optimizing understanding and insight. In particular, whether we are historians, ethicists, analytical philosophers, cultural anthropologists, sociologists, discourse analysts, or plain students of politics, we need to know two things. First, what are the unavoidable constraints on, as well as the possibilities of, the raw material called political thinking, in relation to which we need to work? Second, which boundaries between the disciplines and subdisciplines may be abolished with a particular job in mind—that is to say, what work can be done through importing a particular disciplinary outlook; which boundaries need to be retained or even constructed anew, when being submerged in another perspective or interpretative horizon may conceal more than it reveals; and which perspectives sit happily across the formal organization of disciplines in universities? With the exclusion of much analytical philosophy (though non-ideal theory is doing its best), the focus of every one of the above-mentioned disciplines—when directed at political thought—is ultimately on actual political thinking. If that is the case, diachronic and comparative investigations provide the inseparable arenas in which our knowledge is accrued and tested.

Time and space are not optional methods here; they are the given parameters in which human activity takes place.

Traversing boundaries entails the search for cross-fertilization and inspiration. We often plunder other disciplines in order to gain insights into our own, and do so in ways that in their original field may be misconceived and even wrong; but that can still open up a vista useful for our purposes. When I draw an analogy between a concept and an atom, adding that it is now time for us to look at subatomic particles, at the components of a concept, I have no idea whether that kind of physics is still acceptable, but it has provided me with a lever through which to make sense of my world. We can recognize that other disciplines, neighbouring or not, ask different questions, or they may assign different weights to the same phenomena, but it is precisely in appreciation of what those different tweakings can bring to our understanding that we can stray outside the disciplinary boundaries within which we are most comfortable.

But I want to talk mainly about disciplines close to political theory. Take history for instance. History offers the elements of genesis, intentionality, and context—by which I mean here not simply time and space but the perceived order of the environment in which our selected focus makes sense. In my own work I refer to the conceptual setting within which a particular concept is located. And we can be selective about the uses of, say, historical approaches: we can, for example, remind ourselves that our recognition of unintentionality should play as important a role as our reconstruction of intentionality, because in that case we are superimposing certain perspectives from discourse analysis, post-structuralism, and continental philosophy onto historical understanding, taking those pickings with us to the realm of political theory. Nor is that simple eclecticism; it is rather an attempt at a responsible and careful layering of insights in order to broaden and deepen our analytical potential.

Paolo Pombeni's erudite comparative analysis of the problematic relationship between liberal ideologies and parties incisively probes the tension between liberalism's individualist and constitutional impulses. The development of European mass parties offers alternative and parallel readings of the potentials and pitfalls of a liberalism navigating uneasily among the undisciplined forces of history. Such historical investigation underscores importantly that ideologies are group phenomena, and their variable legitimizations depend on the structures that sustain them. In the world of politics, ideas do not float in the ether; they are reified and conducted through collective institutions. Gayil Talshir, looking at contemporary developments, sees a weakening of party democracy, and the rise of alternative, non-mainstream, and radical ideological carriers. But rather than institutions cementing an ideology, she sees the process as potentially reversed: ideologies cementing party cohesion. At any rate, the study of comparative politics aids us in reasserting that ideologies are always with us, always adopting new shapes:

they are no epiphenomenon, nor incidental to political thinking. Her plea for greater convergence between political theorists and political scientists should rank high on the agenda of our increasingly fractured university departments.

Jerry Gaus contends that I have adopted an unmasking approach to political ideologies that assumes a superior perspective, which cannot of course then be inclusive. I profoundly hope that I am not guilty of that—I would be mortified to be seen as that arrogant and overconfident! To begin with, the enterprise of unmasking assumes that there is an authentic face behind the mask—the equivalent of a correct or true view of the world—about which I am highly sceptical. Correct political views are exclusive, not inclusive. The responsibility of inclusiveness demands not a superior perspective (which would also gainsay the responsibility of tentativeness, discussed below) but a readiness to balance view against view in an effort to determine what explanatory, justificatory, or interpretative power each is capable of discharging, and what each cannot discharge. I, too, want to make sense of what others think, but not just on their conscious and deliberate terms. Disciplines and subdisciplines need to assess and evaluate each other in order to gain greater inclusiveness—as Gaus is rightly doing with my approach—though some inclusions may also be legitimately resisted by the assessed scholars. That is indeed the process of give and take that enhances *Verstehen*. And it is not a question of seeing things more clearly, further, or deeper, and certainly not from a lofty standpoint. In this case, the challenge of inclusiveness lies in the possibility of seeing things *differently* and pointing out what we as political theorists may take from political philosophy, while explaining in which respect certain philosophical positions do not work well as *political* theory, though they may be outstanding as *philosophical* theory.[11] To understand is also to accept the variable distribution of the significance of observations and findings.

Bo Stråth's chapter is another example of inclusiveness, in his highly deft admixture of the history of political thought and its comparative analysis. The attention paid to the dual diachronic and synchronic dimensions of political thought and its conceptual configurations enables conceptual historians to invigorate the development of political theory, as well as to reclaim alternative narratives, as David Weinstein has done. Here interpretation relates not to a theory or argument, but to the validity of mapping. While Stråth teases out a conflation of different liberal ideational trends that can be traced back to Adam Smith and contextualized, Weinstein insists on adding Sidgwick to the central repository of liberal narratives. Indeed, we still need to assert that there is no canonical tradition of political thought, other than in the minds of certain educators, but parallel and interleaving traditions, or thought streams. Through broadening his sources, Marc Stears convincingly argues

---

[11] See Michael Freeden, 'Ideology, Political Theory and Political Philosophy', in Gerald Gaus and Chandran Kukathas (eds.), *Handbook of Political Theory* (London: Sage, 2004), 3–17.

that the American liberal tradition is far more open than it is usually assumed to be (and distinct from European liberalisms, themselves also—as I have contended—a melange of different varieties).[12] And Ben Jackson has impressively explored the overflow of certain ideas associated with socialism into liberal discourse and has raised the testing question whether a key ideological feature such as public ownership can survive outside its progenitor ideology or, indeed, develop simultaneously within other ideological families without 'contaminating' them with the epithet 'socialist'. Jackson persuasively reminds us that reassessments of ideological traditions—reflecting horizons of scholarly understanding that are formed by their own particular intellectual and ideological fashions—must themselves necessarily succumb to further revision in which the re-exclusion of an interpretation is quite possible. Theorists, too, need to learn to cope with loss! In sum, the arrogance of disciplinary insularity and complacency must be tackled.

But here then is the problem with much American-inspired political philosophy: it has comprehensively rejected the path of inclusion. That is a serious matter at stake for the future of the discipline of political theory and of theorizing about political thought. It is emphasized even more by small breakaway groups of political philosophers, notably those of the so-called realist school, who have begun to discover very belatedly what should in fact be a default position of political theory—that good political theory should be contextual and relate to concrete issues, and that thinking about the political is a complex set of ubiquitous thought-practices that have characterized both professional and amateur thinking from their inception (Humphrey generously notes that I have been arguing for that long before the 'realists' emerged on the scene). Even then, that school pursues a prescriptive realism in advocating the implementation of certain values, rather than an interpretative realism that seeks to explore the nature of thinking politically itself.

The time has come to regard the colonization of political theory (by which I mean what should be theory about the political) by analytical and ethical philosophers over the past forty years—and its consequent crowding out of disciplinary pluralism—not as a mainstream occurrence, but as a rearguard intellectual diversion from what we should be investigating in our role as students of society and of the thought that societies host. If I have devoted much space to those philosophers in this chapter, it is because they have become the main threat to the flourishing of an inclusive political theory. Analytical philosophers and ethicists inhabit a very different discipline, but they fail in their ethical responsibility by using their concerted academic power to wrest the subject matter of politics away from its closest and most dedicated practitioners. That power is aided to a large extent by the muscle of American

---

[12] See Michael Freeden, 'European Liberalisms: An Essay in Comparative Political Thought', *European Journal of Political Theory*, 7 (2008), 9–30.

publishing, the propensity of universities there to adopt a few basic texts as the focus of their studies, and the sense of public mission to shore up democratic republican constitutionalism to which many American teachers of politics are committed.

The deployment of that power shows, at the very least, disrespect for ideational diversity and, at worst, an anti-egalitarianism that demonstrates intolerance for other views and a monism that conspires, consciously or unconsciously, to endanger the field of politics as a discipline. There can only be losers in such an endeavour. The point is not to rescue political philosophers from their methods—to which they are of course entitled within the confines of their own discipline and in which, as I have repeatedly stated, they are doing excellent work as evaluators, improvers, and critics of philosophical thinking—but rather to protect political theory from what has been a highly harmful invasion. That invasion has stunted the kind of development of political theory one could have been led to expect since the 1970s, had so many philosophers not attempted—through a combination of lack of interest and insistence on the primacy of their approaches—to insulate political theory from beneficial contacts with the innovations pursued in other disciplines: hermeneutics, literary criticism, psychoanalysis, or discourse analysis. Fortunately, the more insubordinate among the political theorists continued to engage in undercover activities, always risking the wrath of analytical and ethical philosophers and, in the now past days of Rawlsian predominance, sometimes risking their academic careers as well. I am of course not arguing that contacts between political philosophers and political theorists have not been immensely fruitful. The latter are and should be heavily in the formers' debt and, as with other neighbouring disciplines, the borders should be open, but not for occupying armies. Nor am I arguing that political philosophers do not engage in political thinking, such as the constructing of social visions, the ranking of collective goods, and the exercise of persuasive power, let alone their clear ideological points of embarkation. But when they do all those, they too think politically, and think about politics, and are categorically the subject matter of students of politics.

THE RESPONSIBILITY OF CRITICAL DISTANCE

The plea here is to maintain a critical distance from our own work, not only from that of others! I refer here not to the changing horizons of interpretation, so central to the approaches of hermeneuticists and conceptual historians, nor to the reflective appraisal of substantive scholarly arguments. Rather, I wish to emphasize two issues. The one concerns alertness to the characteristics of method and perspective, including our own, and knowing their limitations and potential. There are no methodless or perspectiveless approaches to the study of political thought. They are inextricably wrapped up in the ontological and epistemological assumptions that we carry with us as researchers, deliberately or unwittingly. Moreover, the questions that interest us may require varied methods in order to get the raw material to reveal its secrets. To take one major distinction in the various branches of our profession: the difference between unmasking and decoding, to which I have frequently alluded. Decoding purports to extract significant messages from polysemic texts; unmasking purports to reveal the hitherto obscured, real and sole meaning of a text. By opting for the one or the other we are nailing our methodological colours to the mast. But those colours cannot be nailed down in perpetuity: a readiness to discard paradigms found wanting is part of one's academic resocialization. We need to distance ourselves, from time to time, from our own education.

It is hence crucially important for scholars to examine their arguments from a series of alternative standpoints, moving around a table on which their intellectual wares have been laid out, so to speak, and viewing them from angle after angle. That is what makes an academic an intellectual rather than a technician. Liberal philosophers talk of constantly revising one's conception of the good. Scholars should strive constantly to revise their perception of their own work and be ready to reshuffle their cards, when the original hand they have been dealt is inadequate. That imperative for reflectiveness may require some courage and it may involve juggling with a number of methodologies in parallel.

The other feature of distance is to choose the level of magnification we want to use in illuminating a particular issue. Those who swear by regulative ideals are looking at their subject matter from a great distance with a small degree of magnification: that lacks conclusiveness. If they zoom in on the particulars of each case they are bound to be confounded in their aim: alighting on a few pixels is hardly going to do the generalizing work they require. Those who prefer micro-analysis will have to choose a smaller distance and a larger level of magnification but forsake the chimera of effective regulative principles. The point is, as with good photographers, that you have to keep changing lenses for any project. Micro-analysis has to be checked against macro-structures. Macro-analysis has to offer sufficient detail to keep individual cases in play. Foreground and background change places, but both are necessary in either case. And then, as Bo Stråth reminds us in his comparative project, distance is also attained through ascertaining how political languages form different conceptual fields using similar notions, as well as discovering that they employ quite different political concepts, or that they radically reorder existing ones. The comparative study of political thought project launched by the Oxford Centre for Political Ideologies in 2008 has focused on similar issues and those must become far more central to political theory. One result of such centrality will be to explore further common ground with comparative political scientists, for which the impetus has receded badly in recent years. Most importantly, the decentring of political thought from its 'Western' anchoring will serve to remind us that political thinking takes place across the planet, and that it may do so in forms we have not been trained to recognize, and for which we require disciplinary innovation and receptiveness.

THE RESPONSIBILITY OF TENTATIVENESS

Rawls's exhortation to fix liberal principles once and for all[13] is not only contextually absurd; it is frightening. Ahistoricity? Wishful thinking? There is something unsettling about that avowed certainty, with its implicit quasi-religious faith in absolutes. Even the natural sciences have long incorporated indeterminacy into their theories. Former communists who became political philosophers have also carried with them the confident power of their own convictions. My plea for tentativeness is not a matter of faith, but a rational reaction to the plethora of information, to the existence of multiple paths of interpretation, and to the laboriousness of knowledge construction, which is more likely to be threadbare than solidly accumulative. Political theorizing requires its own kind of creativity—the excitement of exploring, of uncovering, of reassembling, of interpreting—together with the acceptance of human fragility and of professional inadequacy in confronting the untidiness of social thought.

Tentativeness may appear as false modesty, as intellectual insecurity, as cynicism. It may well have elements of all these. But above all it is an appeal to flexibility, to avoid the seductiveness of argumentative neatness. Making sense doesn't mean getting it right. It means offering a plausible set of insights, always awaiting contrary interpretation, as I have often contended. And yes, once again there are value preferences tucked into that responsibility which, broadly speaking, may derive from the liberal tradition: the openness and inconclusiveness of the human imagination; the normality of error; and the diversity of *reasonable* paths of thought and action. But for students of politics, constantly facing the vocabulary of the spurious finality always present in the political thought-practices of our societies—the urge to produce decisions, to control and order, to legitimize, and to settle disputes authoritatively—and constantly confronting the archetypal feature of ideologizing in the doomed yet ineluctable act of decontestation, there is an additional incentive to tread with caution in their own theories. In the academic world, too many false expectations are made to rely on the power of theory.

---

[13] John Rawls, *Political Liberalism* (New York: Columbia University Press, 1996), 161.

More recently, I have related tentativeness to the further possibility of the failure of political theories, in cases when they cannot deliver—for reasons clearly beyond the control of their articulators—what they have undertaken to deliver. The incapacity to control future trajectories (temporal contingency), the indeterminacy of concepts and of meaning, and the inconclusiveness of regulatory principles in managing the unavoidable details of political life hamper the potential success of a theory.[14] That has not gone down well with some political philosophers, who are loath to admit that their arguments may fail. The acknowledgement that theories are bound to be flawed does not come easily to philosophers and empirical political scientists nourished on precision or a belief in their analytical prowess. But tentativeness suggests that the distance between partial failure and partial success may be minuscule and hence meaningless. A theory that claims complete success or is deemed to have failed abjectly should worry us. Tentativeness, too, can be extracted from the depository of a liberal methodology. If the political world contains so many contingencies, the theories designed to fit it must remain accommodating, incomplete, and provisional.

Political theory has been abandoned for too long to the logicians, the harmonizers, the splitters and parsers. But it is a craft—a series of suggestions for understanding. It is itself an artistic practice: a way of rendering and interpreting the world as well as of challenging it. Theorizing should vitally be about the pleasure of extracting and shaping our comprehension of central discursive phenomena. We should bring our theories as a gift for the delectation of others, and eventually surpassed by others, not as a semi-private and often emaciated pontification about good or correct thinking. We need to appreciate the organics of political thinking above its mechanics. In that respect, the contributors to this volume have breathed life into our shared and largely enjoyable practice.

---

[14] Michael Freeden, 'Failures of Political Thinking', *Political Studies*, 57 (2009), 141–64.

Michael Freeden: A Bibliography

Books and Edited Books

J. A. Hobson, *Confessions of an Economic Heretic* [edited with an Introduction] (Hassocks: Harvester Press, 1976).

The New Liberalism: An Ideology of Social Reform (Oxford: Oxford University Press, 1978), 302 pp. (Reprinted in paperback edition 1986).

Liberalism Divided: A Study in British Political Thought 1914–1939 (Oxford: Oxford University Press, 1986), 409 pp.

J. A. Hobson: A Reader (London: Unwin Hyman, 1988), 212 pp. (hardback and paperback).

Minutes of the Rainbow Circle, 1894–1924 [edited and annotated with an Introduction] (London: Royal Historical Society, Camden Fourth Series, vol. 38, 1989), 370 pp.

Reappraising J. A. Hobson: Humanism and Welfare [editor and contributor] (London: Unwin Hyman, 1990), 196 pp. (Reprinted in hardback, 2009; in paperback 2010).

Rights (Milton Keynes: Open University Press, 1991), 134 pp. (hardback and paperback).

(Japanese translation, Showado, 1992).

(Romanian translation, Editura du Style, Bucharest, 1998).

(Chinese translation, GuiGuan Press, Taipei, 1998).

Green Ideology: Concepts and Structures (Oxford: OCEES Research Papers, 1995), 29 pp.

Ideologies and Political Theory: A Conceptual Approach (Oxford: Oxford University Press, 1996), 602 pp. (Reprinted in paperback edition 1998, 2001, 2003, 2008).

(Italian translation: *Ideologie e Teoria Politica* (Bologna: Il Mulino, 2000)).

Reassessing Political Ideologies: The Durability of Dissent [editor and contributor] (London: Routledge, 2001), 216 pp. (hardback and paperback).

(Croatian translation: *Političke Ideologije* (Zagreb: Algoritam, 2006)).

Ideology: A Very Short Introduction (Oxford: Oxford University Press, 2003), 142 pp.

(Italian translation: *Ideologia* (Torino: Codice Edizione, 2008).

Liberal Languages: Ideological Imaginations and Twentieth-Century Progressive Thought (Princeton: Princeton University Press, 2005), 271 pp. (hardback and paperback).

Taking Ideology Seriously [co-editor and contributor, with Gayil Talshir and Mathew Humphrey] (London: Routledge, 2006).

The Meaning of Ideology: Cross-disciplinary Perspectives [editor and contributor] (London: Routledge, 2007).

In preparation: *The Political Theory of Political Thinking* (Oxford: Oxford University Press, forthcoming).

Journal Articles

'J. A. Hobson as a New Liberal Theorist: Some Aspects of his Social Thought Until 1914', *Journal of the History of Ideas*, 34 (1973), 421–43.
(Reprinted in Jerrold Seigel (ed.), *Figures on the Horizon* (Rochester: University of Rochester Press, 1993), 91–113).
'Biological and Evolutionary Roots of the New Liberalism in England', *Political Theory*, 4 (1976), 471–90.
'The Liberal Tradition' (Review article), *Journal of Modern History*, 48 (1976), 547–52.
'Political Thought and Political Science: Towards Reintegration', *Social Research Review*, 12–19 (1977), 93–108 (in Hebrew).
'Eugenics and Progressive Thought: A Study in Ideological Affinity', *Historical Journal*, 22 (1979), 645–71.
'Eugenics and Ideology', *Historical Journal*, 26 (1983), 959–62.
'Human Rights and Welfare: A Communitarian View', *Ethics*, 100 (1990), 489–502.
'The Stranger at the Feast: Ideology and Public Policy in Twentieth-Century Britain', *Twentieth Century British History*, 1 (1990), 9–34.
'Liberalismo, Potere ed élites in Gran Bretagna 1890–1930' ('Liberalism, Power and Elites in Britain 1890–1930'), *Ricerche di Storia Politica*, 7 (1992), 7–21.
'Political Concepts and Ideological Morphology', *Journal of Political Philosophy*, 2 (1994), 140–64.
'Editorial', *Journal of Political Ideologies*, 1 (1996), 5–13.
'Editorial: Ideologies and Conceptual History', *Journal of Political Ideologies*, 2 (1997), 3–11.
'La Liberté entre libéralisme et socialisme', *Pouvoirs*, 84 (1998), 45–59.
'Editorial: Stormy Relationships: Ideology and Politics', *Journal of Political Ideologies*, 3 (1998), 5–11.
'Is Nationalism a Distinct Ideology?', *Political Studies*, 46 (1998), 748–65.
'Reputations: J. A. Hobson and Welfare Liberalism', *Political Quarterly*, 69 (1998), 441–50.
'The Ideology of New Labour', *Political Quarterly*, 70 (1999), 42–51.
(Abbreviated version reprinted in Andrew Chadwick and Richard Heffernan (eds.), *The New Labour Reader* (Cambridge: Polity Press, 2003), 43–8).
'Editorial: The "Beginning of Ideology" Thesis', *Journal of Political Ideologies*, 4 (1999), 5–11.
'Quale Socialismo dopo le Ideologie?', *Ideazione*, 6 (March–April 1999), 38–52.
'Communication', *Political Studies*, 47 (1999), 380.
'Ideologies as Communal Resources', *Journal of Political Ideologies*, 4 (1999), 411–17.
'Editorial: Political Ideologies at Century's End', *Journal of Political Ideologies*, 5 (2000), 5–15.
'Practising Ideology and Ideological Practices', *Political Studies*, 48 (2000), Special Issue (Rodney Barker (ed.), *Political Ideas and Political Action*), 302–22.
'Editorial: What is Special about Ideologies?', *Journal of Political Ideologies*, 6 (2001), 5–12.
'Editorial: On Pluralism through the Prism of Ideology', *Journal of Political Ideologies*, 7 (2002), 5–14.

'Dynamics and Sentiment: The Evolution of British Liberalism', *Mélanges de l'Ecole Française de Rome. Italie et Méditerranée*, 114 (2002), 657–71.
'Editorial: Ideological Boundaries and Ideological Systems', *Journal of Political Ideologies*, 8 (2003), 3–12.
'Livelli de Legittimità: Linguaggi Politici Inglesi de Consenso e Dissenso', *Scienza & Politica*, 29 (2003), 9–24.
'Editorial: Essential Contestability and Effective Contestability', *Journal of Political Ideologies*, 9 (2004), 3–11.
'Editorial: Fundaments and Foundations in Ideology', *Journal of Political Ideologies*, 10 (2005), 1–9.
'What Should the "Political" in Political Theory Explore?', *Journal of Political Philosophy*, 13 (2005), 113–34.
'Confronting the Chimera of a "Post-Ideological" Age', *Critical Review of International Social and Political Philosophy*, 8 (2005), 247–62.
'What Makes a Political Concept Political?', *Qualitative Methods*, 3 (2005), 20–4.
'Ideology and Political Theory', *Journal of Political Ideologies*, 11 (2006), 3–22.
'Editorial: The Comparative Study of Political Thinking', *Journal of Political Ideologies*, 12 (2007), 1–9.
'European Liberalisms: An Essay in Comparative Political Thought', *European Journal of Political Theory*, 7 (2008), 9–30 (and guest editor of issue).
'Editorial: Thinking Politically and Thinking Ideologically', *Journal of Political Ideologies*, 13 (2008), 1–10.
'Comment' in 'Symposium: *Contract and Domination*', *Journal of Political Ideologies*, 13 (2008), 239–43.
'Szabadság és Identitás' ('Liberty and Identity'), *Magyar Tudomány*, January 2008, 12–16.
'Editorial: What Fails in Ideologies?', *Journal of Political Ideologies*, 14 (2009), 1–9.
'Failures of Political Thinking', *Political Studies*, 57 (2009), 141–64.
'Languages of Political Support: Engaging with the Public Realm', *Critical Review of International Social and Political Philosophy*, 12 (2009), 183–202.
'Liberalism in the Twilight Zone', *Public Policy Research*, 16 (2009), 110–13.
'David Weinstein's Hobson', *Collingwood and British Idealism Studies*, 15 (2009), 76–87.
'Editorial: Liberalism in the Limelight', *Journal of Political Ideologies*, 15 (2010), 1–9.
'The Liberal Party and the New Liberalism', *Journal of Liberal History*, 67 (Summer 2010), Special Issue (*Liberals and the Left*), 14–20.
'Editorial: The Politics of Ceremony: The Wootton Bassett Phenomenon', *Journal of Political Ideologies*, 16 (2011), 1–10.

Chapters in Edited Books

'L. T. Hobhouse', in *The Blackwell Encyclopaedia of Political Thought* (Oxford: Basil Blackwell, 1987), 213–14.
'Hobbes' and 'Locke', in *The Blackwell Encyclopaedia of Political Institutions* (Oxford: Basil Blackwell, 1987), 272–3, 345.

'The New Liberalism Revisited', in Karl Rohe (ed.), *Englischer Liberalismus im 19. und Frühen 20. Jahrhundert* (Bochum: Brockmeyer, 1987), 133–54.

'The New Liberalism and its Aftermath', in Richard Bellamy (ed.), *Victorian Liberalism* (London: Routledge, 1990), 175–92.

'Rights, Needs and Community: The Emergence of British Welfare Thought', in Alan Ware and Robert Goodin (eds.), *Needs and Welfare* (London: Sage Publications, 1990), 54–72.

'Liberal Communitarianism and Basic Income', in Philippe Van Parijs (ed.), *Arguing for Basic Income* (London: Verso, 1992), 185–91.

'J. A. Hobson as a Political Theorist', in John Pheby (ed.), *J. A. Hobson after Fifty Years: Freethinker of the Social Sciences* (Basingstoke: Macmillan, 1994), 19–33.

'Le concept de la pauvreté et le libéralisme progressiste au tournant de siècle en Grande Bretagne', in F.-X. Merrien (ed.), *Face à la Pauvreté* (Paris: Les Éditions de l'Atelier, 1994), 71–98.

'J. A. Hobson', in F. Leventhal (ed.), *Twentieth-Century Britain: An Encyclopedia* (New York: Garland, 1995), 365–7.

'The Family of Liberalisms: A Morphological Analysis', in James Meadowcroft (ed.), *The Liberal Political Tradition: Contemporary Reappraisals* (Aldershot: Edward Elgar, 1996), 14–39.

'Partiti ed Ideologie nella Gran Bretagna Postbellica' ('Political Parties and Ideologies in Post-War Britain'), in F. G. Orsini and G. Quagliariello (eds.), *Il Partito Politico dalla Grande Guerra al Fascismo* (Bologna: Il Mulino, 1996), 147–56.

'Ideology', in *Routledge Encyclopedia of Philosophy*, vol. 4 (London: Routledge, 1998), 681–5.

'True Blood or False Genealogy: New Labour and British Social Democratic Thought', in Andrew Gamble and Tony Wright (eds.), *The New Social Democracy* (Oxford: Blackwell, 1999), 151–65.

'Health, Welfare and Community: The Extension of Liberal Rights in Britain', in O. N. Haberl and T. Korenke (eds.), *Politische Deutungskulturen: Festschrift für Karl Rohe* (Baden-Baden: Nomos Verlagsgesellschaft, 1999), 527–39.

Mini-essays on 'anarchism', 'liberalism', 'politics', in *New Penguin English Dictionary* (London: Penguin Books, 2000).

'Ideological Indeterminacy: Political Families and Family Resemblances', in S. Berstein (ed.), *Les Familles politiques en Europe Occidentale au XXéme siécle* (Rome: École Française de Rome, 2000), 381–96.

'Élie Halévy e il liberalismo inglese di fino secolo' ('Élie Halévy and Fin-de-Siècle English Liberalism'), in M. Griffo and G. Quagliariello (eds.), *Élie Halévy e l'era delle Tirannie* (Rome: Rubbettino, 2001), 263–77.

'Twentieth Century Liberal Thought: Development or Transformation?', in Mark Evans (ed.), *The Edinburgh Companion to Contemporary Liberalism* (Edinburgh: Edinburgh University Press, 2001), 21–32.

'Liberal Community: An Essay in Retrieval', in Avital Simhony and David Weinstein (eds.), *The New Liberalism: Reconciling Liberty and Community* (Cambridge: Cambridge University Press, 2001), 26–48.

'Ideology, Political Aspects of', *International Encyclopedia of Social and Behavioral Sciences* (Oxford: Pergamon, 2001), 7174–7.

'Political Theory and the Environment: Nurturing a Sustainable Relationship', in Andrew Light and Avner de-Shalit (eds.), *Moral and Political Reasoning in Environmental Practice* (Cambridge, MA: MIT Press, 2003), 31-44.

'Concepts, Ideology and Political Theory', in C. Dutt (ed.), *Herausforderungen der Begriffsgeschichte* (Heidelberg: Universitätsverlag Winter, 2003), 51-63.

'The Coming of the Welfare State', in Terence Ball and Richard Bellamy (eds.), *The Cambridge History of Twentieth-Century Political Thought* (Cambridge: Cambridge University Press, 2003), 7-44.

'Competing Conceptions of Citizenship in Twentieth Century Britain', in Jose Harris (ed.), *Civil Society in British History* (Oxford: Oxford University Press, 2003), 275-91.

'Ideology, Political Theory and Political Philosophy', in Gerald Gaus and Chandran Kukathas (eds.), *Handbook of Political Theory* (London: Sage, 2004), 3-17.

'J. M. Robertson', in *Oxford Dictionary of National Biography* (Oxford: Oxford University Press, 2004).

'J. A. Hobson', in *Oxford Dictionary of National Biography* (Oxford: Oxford University Press, 2004).

'L. T. Hobhouse', in *Oxford Dictionary of National Biography* (Oxford: Oxford University Press, 2004).

'L. T. Hobhouse', in M. Borlandi, R. Boudon, M. Cherkaoui, and B. Valade (eds.), *Dictionnaire de la Pensée Sociologique* (Paris: Presses Universitaires de France, 2005), 326-7.

'The Rainbow Circle', in *Oxford Dictionary of National Biography* (online), 2005.

'Foreword' to I. Z. Denes (ed.), *Liberty and the Search for Identity* (Budapest: CEU Press, 2006), pp. ix-xi.

'Liberal Passions: Reason and Emotion in Late and Post-Victorian Liberal Thought', in Peter Ghosh and Lawrence Goldman (eds.), *Politics and Culture in Victorian Britain: Essays in Memory of Colin Matthew* (Oxford: Oxford University Press, 2006), 136-49.

'Liberalism', in *Encyclopedia of British Philosophy* (Bristol: Thoemmes Press, 2006).

'Henry Colin Gray Matthew 1941-1999', *Proceedings of the British Academy*, 138 (Oxford: Oxford University Press, 2006), 209-28.

'More than Freedom: The Ideology of Liberalism', in Julia Margo (ed.), *Beyond Liberty: Is the Future of Liberalism Progressive?* (London: IPPR, 2007), 27-37.

'Recent Developments in Socialism', in Robert Goodin, Philip Pettit, and Thomas Pogge (eds.), *A Companion to Contemporary Political Philosophy*, 2nd edition (Cambridge: Blackwell, 2007), 435-8.

'Thinking Politically and Thinking about Politics: Language, Interpretation, and Ideology', in David Leopold and Marc Stears (eds.), *Political Theory: Methods and Approaches* (Oxford: Oxford University Press, 2008), 196-215.

'Democracy and Paternalism: The Struggle over Shaping British Liberal Welfare Thinking', in Alice Kessler-Harris and Maurizio Vaudagna (eds.), *Democracy and Social Rights in the 'Two Wests'* (Torino: Otto, 2009), 107-22.

'On European and Other Intellectuals', in Justine Lacroix and Kalypso Nicolaïdis (eds.), *European Stories: Intellectual Debates on Europe in National Contexts* (Oxford: Oxford University Press, 2010), 77-84.

'Political Thinking as Power', in Keith Dowding (ed.), *Encyclopedia of Power* (London: Sage, 2011) 492-6.

'Perceptual Symbols of Power', in Keith Dowding (ed.), *Encyclopedia of Power* (London: Sage, 2011) 477-8.

'Ideology and Conceptual History: The Interrelationship between Method and Meaning', in Javier Fernández Sebastián (ed.), *Political Concepts and Time: New Approaches to Conceptual History* (Santander: McGraw Hill/Cantabria University Press, 2011), 73-101.

'Introduction' to R. Ingham and D. Brack (eds.), *Peace, Reform and Liberation: A History of Liberal Politics in Britian 1679-2011* (London: Biteback Publishing and the Robson Press, 2011), 1-6.

'Europäische Liberalismen', *Merkur*, vol. 65, issue 750 (November 2011), 1028-1031.

'Un Mondo a Misura delle Ideologie?', in Maurizio Cau (ed.), *L'Europe di De Gasperi e Adenauer: La sfida della ricostruzione (1945-1951)* (Bologna: Il Mulino, 2011), 1-12.

'The Professional Responsibilities of the Political Theorist', in Ben Jackson and Marc Stears (eds.), *Liberalism as Ideology: Essays in Honour of Michael Freeden* (Oxford: Oxford University Press, 2012) 259-77.

'Ideology', in Gregory Claeys and Lyman Tower Sargent (eds.), *Encyclopedia of Modern Political Thought* (Washington, DC: CQ Press, forthcoming, 2012).

'Liberalism', in Fred D'Agostino and Gerald Gaus (eds.), *The Routledge Companion to Social and Political Philosophy* (London: Routledge, forthcoming, 2012).

'The Concept of Ideology: From Temporal Contingency to Political Ubiquity', in A. Linklater (ed.), *Politics and Ideology: Engelsberg Seminar 2011* (Stockholm: Ax:son Johnson Foundation, forthcoming, 2012).

Index

abstraction 23, 170, 243–4, 110–11
Adivasis 74
Adorno, Theodor 13
Advertising Council of America 80, 81
Agamben, Giorgio 91
Ali, Syed Ameer 67
Almond, Gabriel 202
Ambedkar, B. R. 70–5
America *see* United States of America
American Heritage Foundation 80, 84, 90
Anscombe, G. E. M. 147–9
anthropology 172–3, 190–5, 267, 270
Anti-Corn Law League 96
Arendt, Hannah 168, 230
Aristotle 144, 148–9, 152, 230–1, 235
  Ethics 148
Aron, Raymond 14, 102
aryan theory of race 71
Ashcroft, Richard 166
associations 57, 110, 206–19, 213, 215, 219; *see also* civil society
Ayer, A. J. 142, 164; *see also* logical positivism

Bagehot, Walter 126–7
Bajpai, Rochana 2, 268
Banerjea, Surendranath 64
Barker, Ernest 230
Barry, Brian 142, 170
  Political Argument 142
Bayly, Christopher 57, 63, 70, 72
Beard, Charles A. 17
behaviouralism 162–4
Bellamy, Edward 15–21
  Looking Backwards 2000–1887 15–21
Benhabib, Seyla 203, 209
Bentham, Jeremy 60, 150, 152, 156
  Benthamites 59, 63; *see also* utilitarianism
Berlin, Irving 80
Berlin, Isaiah 14, 74, 112–13, 142, 145, 149, 155–6, 229, 234
  'Two Concepts of Liberty' 142, 234
Bernard Shaw, George 30–1
Beveridge, William 36, 38, 49–52
  Beveridge Report, the (1942) 10, 50, 135
  Full Employment in a Free Society 50–1
Bhargava, Rajeev 57
Big Society, the 206–8, 219; *see also* Conservative Party

Birmingham 'caucus' 127
Blair, Tony 36, 213–15; *see also* New Labour
Blunkett, David 226
Bluntschli, Johan Kasper 121–4
  Charakter und Geist der Politischen Parteien 121
  Politik als Wissenschaft 121
Bosanquet, Bernard 186, 192
Bourdieu, Pierre 167
Bradley, F. H. 151, 157
brahmin 66, 71, 74
Brandt, Richard 150
Britain, politics of 34–52, 58, 115–16, 124–32, 206–8, 213–16, 223–33
Brophy, Thomas D'Arcy 80
Brown, Gordon 215–16
Bryce, James 127, 131, 136
  Modern Democracies 131
  American Commonwealth, The 127
Burke, Edmund 120, 126, 131
Burnett, Leo 80
  Good Citizen, The 80

Cambridge School, the 143
Cameron, David 206–8
capabilities 113
Carnap, Rudolf 164; *see also* logical positivism
Cassirer, Ernst 171
  Philosophy of Symbolic Forms, The 171
caste 68–73
catch-all party *see* Kirchheimer, Otto
Catholicism 26
Cecil, Robert *see* Salisbury, Lord
Chamberlain, Joseph 125–6, 127–8
Chapman, John 193
  'Political Theory: Logical Structure and Enduring Types' 193
Charter Act (1883) 60
Chase, Stuart 85
  Roads to Agreement 85
Chiozza Money, Leo 44–5
  Triumph of Nationalization, The 44
circumstances of justice 25–8, 33
citizenship (school subject) 225–6
civic engagement 209–10, 213
civic rights 105, 108
civic virtue 92, 224, 225, 226, 234, 236, 240
civic society *see* civil society

civil rights movement (USA) 90-1
civil society 200-20, 240
Civil War, American 90
Christian Democratic Union (Germany) 135
Clark, Tom 79-80, 89, 92
Clarke, William 41
coal industry, British 39-47, 49
Colbert, Jean-Baptiste 101
Cold War 80-1, 84-5, 88, 89-93, 229
Cold War realists 85-94; see also realism
Cole, G. D. H. 45, 50
Collingwood, R. G. 146
communism 74, 78, 84, 201, 113
Communist Party (USA) 90
community 206-8, 210, 213-14, 217, 226
comparative politics 5, 199-202, 218-20, 271-2
conceptual history 260, 262, 274
conceptual morphology 11, 173, 179, 188, 258, 260-2
Congress Party (India) 56, 64, 67, 69
  Karachi resolution on fundamental rights (1931) 69
  Moderates faction 64
consensus, British post-war 52, 229, 230
conservatism 206, 207, 216
Conservative Party (Britain) 129-31, 205-8, 214, 229-30
consumerism 227, 235, 236
contextualism 95, 96, 143, 144, 146, 150, 152, 154, 155, 243, 244, 252, 258, 273
contingency 243, 244, 245, 249, 256, 262, 276
Cornwallis, Charles 59, 61
Crick, Bernard 5, 223-40, 263
  In Defence of Politics 223-4, 227, 229-36, 238, 240
Critchley, Simon 140
critical theory 167, 201
culture wars (USA) 93

dalits 74; see also Untouchables
Dalton, Dennis 56
Dalton, Russell 203
  Parties Without Partisans 203
Darwin, Charles 108
Davidson, Donald 190-1, 193
Deigh, John 153
Democratic Party (USA) 89
Depression (economic, USA, 1929-41) 80, 82, 84, 86
Dewey, John 17, 73, 157-8
discourse analysis 167, 201, 262, 270, 271, 274
Disraeli, Benjamin 96, 125
Downs, Anthony 201
Dreben, Burton 146
Durkheim, Émile 162

Duverger, Maurice 135
Dworkin, Ronald 11, 180, 188, 197, 241, 245, 247

Eagleton, Terry 167
Eastern Europe 76
East India Company 60-3
Easton, David 162-3
  'The Decline of Political Theory' 163
economics (academic discipline) 162
education 66, 67
  liberal 9
elections 81, 93, 129, 130, 209
Ellison, Ralph 85, 86, 88, 92
  Invisible Man 85
Emancipation Declaration 91
emotions 87, 88, 90, 92-4, 169, 183, 185, 250, 251, 253, 268
emotivism 142, 145
empirical theory 163-4
employer combinations 99-100
Engels, Friedrich 160-1; see also Marx, Karl
Enlightenment, the 86, 99, 106-9, 116, 118, 131, 147, 160, 175, 215, 216; see also Scottish Enlightenment
equality 98, 109, 110, 115
  equal citizenship 68, 70, 71, 73
Essays on Reform 125
ethical universalism 251
Ethics 253
ethnography 262
Eucken, Walter 103
eugenics 72
Europe, politics within 3, 65, 77-78, 86, 95-117, 118-20, 127, 132, 135, 158, 260
evolution, theory of 66, 72; see also Darwin, Charles

Fabianism 17, 40, 41, 43, 50
Fabian Society 17, 39-44, 227, 228
Farrelly, Colin 241
Farr, James 163
fascism 78, 86, 116, 192-3, 201
Feigel, Herbert 164; see also logical positivism
feudalism 83
Fichte, Johann Gottlieb 109
financial crisis (2008) 117
First World War 43, 49, 85, 102, 109
Flurscheim, Michael 20
  Real History of Money Island, The 20
Folkrörelserna 114; see also people's movements
Foucault, Michel 167
France, politics of 125, 211-13; see also French Revolution
Frankfurt School 201; see also critical theory

Index

Freeden, Michael 1–5, 9–10, 10–14, 34–37, 52, 54, 57, 76, 77–8, 94, 95, 105, 108, 119, 131, 139, 142, 145, 156, 157, 172–4, 178–198, 202, 221–3, 229, 235, 236–40, 241–3, 245–58
  'distinctive basement office' of 10
  Ideologies and Political Theory 1, 179–81, 193, 197, 211, 242
  Liberalism Divided 1, 36, 260
  Liberal Languages 260
  New Liberalism, The 1, 36–7, 54, 260
  Rights 261
  teacher and supervisor 2, 9–10, 34, 78
freedom 12, 22, 26, 38, 47, 51, 54–6, 62, 65–6, 68–9, 72, 73, 74, 76, 77–94, 106, 109–13, 114, 118, 119, 142, 145, 150, 155, 189, 200, 206, 210, 229, 234, 247
Freedom Train 3, 78–84, 85–6, 88, 89–93, 266
free trade 101, 102, 105, 107, 108
French Revolution 69, 102, 107, 109–10, 115
Freud, Sigmund 191–3

Gadamer, Hans-Georg 143–4, 175–6, 269
Gamble, Andrew 228
Gandhi, Mohandas 55, 57, 66, 68–9, 73, 76
Gaus, Gerald 4, 265, 269, 272
  Political Theories and Political Concepts 180, 193
Geertz, Clifford 171–4, 175, 267
  'Ideology as a Cultural System' 171
General Will, the 186; *see also* Rousseau, Jean-Jacques
Germany, politics of 44, 116, 121–4, 128, 132–6, 208–10, 268
  political system 132, 133, 134
  socialism 96
  Volkspartei 132
Germino, Dante 168
Geuss, Raymond 5, 241, 244–6, 248–9, 253, 256
Giddens, Anthony 213, 215–16
Gladstone, William 39, 125, 126, 128–9
  Bulgarian Agitations 126, 129
  Midlothian Campaign 128–9
globalization 101, 102, 104, 117–18, 109
Glorious Revolution, the 128
Gokhale, G. K. 64
Goodman, Nelson 171
  Ways of World Making, The 171
governance 104, 203
Gramsci, Antonio 166–7, 253
  Prison Notebooks 167
Gray, John 150–1
Green Party (German) 205, 208–10, 216, 218
Green, T. H. 11, 145, 154, 157–8

Greenwood, Arthur 45
Grey, Annie 91
guild socialism 40, 43, 45–9; *see also* syndicalism
Gutmann, Amy 203

Habermas, Jürgen 174–6, 203
Hall, Stuart 167
Hardie, Keir 38
Harding College of Arkansas 81
Harris, José 49, 50
Harrison, Frederic 126
Hart, H. L. A. 142
  Concept of Law, The 142
Hartz, Louis 3, 78, 82–6, 89, 92, 266
  Liberal Tradition in America, The 3, 78, 82
Hay, Colin 228
Hayek, Friedrich 102, 103, 112–13, 117
Hebrew University of Jerusalem 260
Hegel 142, 157, 158, 179, 260
  Philosophy of Right 179, 260
Heidegger, Martin 141
Herder, Johann Gottfried 109
hermeneutics 143–4, 274
Hertzka, Theodor 19
  Ein sociales Zukunftsbild 19
historicism 141, 148
historicity 140, 143
history of political thought 257, 272
Hobbes, Thomas 97, 144, 148, 189–91, 247
Hobhouse, L. T. 11, 36, 38–41, 43–6, 48–9, 51, 158
  Elements of Social Justice 48
  Labour Movement, The 40–1
Hobson, J. A. 2, 11, 13, 14–21, 28–33, 36, 38–43, 45–6, 48–9, 51, 158, 266
  Incentives in the New Industrial Order, 48–9
  Social Problem, The 42
Hodges, Frank 45
Hooker, Brad 150, 152, 156, 157
Hoover, J. Edgar 89
Hughes, Langston 90
Humanitarian 15
Human Rights Act (Britain) 215
Hume, David 25, 185
Humphrey, Mathew 5, 262, 264, 269, 273

Ibarra, Pedro 203
  Social Movements and Democracy 203
idealism 142, 145, 162
ideal theory 24–33, 241–5, 250–8, 264
ideology 2, 4, 159–92, 197, 199, 201–2, 220–1, 257
  'core and peripheral' concepts 236
  'end of' 162

ideology (cont.)
  Marxist theories of 196, 268
  relationship with political philosophy/theory 159, 161, 165–73, 179–193, 197, 199, 201, 220, 257
Ilbert Bill controversy 61
immigration 211, 219
Independent Labour Party (ILP) 38
India 53–76, 268
  constitution of 55, 71, 72, 73, 75
  Hindu social reform 62, 65, 66
  limitations of Indian nationalism 56, 57
  middle classes in 62, 66
  testing ground for reform 59
individual, the 20, 55, 56, 57, 65, 68, 72, 96, 97, 101, 110, 186, 206, 210, 211, 214, 215, 217
industrial democracy 40, 44–9
Industrial Democracy for the Miners 45
Institut International de Coopération 102
intellectual history 147; see also history of political thought
intuitionism 156
irony 167; see also satire
Italy, politics of 116, 165

Jackson, Ben 2, 273
Jinnah, Mohammed Ali 67, 68
Journal of Political Ideologies 202, 221, 222, 262

Kahneman, Daniel 184, 195
Kant, Immanuel 12, 26, 97, 140, 144, 148, 157–8
Katwala, Sunder 228
Kenny, Michael 5, 262, 263, 269
Keynesianism see Keynes, J. M.
Keynes, J. M. 14–15, 36, 49, 50, 102, 103, 104, 117
  General Theory of Employment, Interest, and Money, The 14–15
Khan, Sayyid Ahmad 67
Khilani, Sunil 69
Kirchheimer, Otto 132–5
Kjellén, Rudolf 108
Korsch, Karl 161

labour 98, 99, 100, 114
Labour Party (Britain) 35–6, 229–30; see also New Labour
Laclau, Ernesto 167
laissez-faire 23, 64, 65, 82, 96, 97, 101
language 175–6
Laslett, Peter 142
Lassalle, Ferdinand 96
Lenin, V. I. 14, 161, 256
Imperialism, the Highest Stage of Capitalism 14
Leopold, David 2, 266
Le Pen, Jean-Marie 211, 213
Liberal Democrats (political party, Britain) 35
liberalism
  adaptability of 94
  American liberalism 3, 77–94, 266
  American philosophical liberalism 139, 141, 179, 180, 181, 188, 197, 265; see also Rawls, John
  classical liberalism 53; see also nineteenth-century liberalism
  German liberalism 116, 122–4
  Indian liberalism 53–76
  Italian liberalism 116
  Manchester liberalism 96–102
  new liberalism, the 2, 11, 12, 13, 34–52, 142, 145, 193, 221, 266
  nineteenth-century liberalism 11, 12, 38, 53
  'philosophical liberalism' 11, 12, 13, 241, 247, 248, 251, 252, 253, 256, 265; see also American philosophical liberalism
  postcolonial critiques of 56
  Whig liberalism 59, 74
Liberal Party (Britain) 125
liberty see freedom
linguistic turn 201, 262
Lippmann, Walter 104
  Good Society, The 104
literary criticism 269, 274
literature 15, 16
Lloyd George, David 47
Locke, John 53, 59, 82, 84, 97, 112, 144, 189
logical positivism 142, 144, 164, 169
London Dock Strike (1889) 40
London Ethical Society 41
London Society for the Extension of University Teaching 15
Lukács, György 166
  History and Class Consciousness 166
Luxemburg, Rosa 161
Lyons, David 151

Macaulay, Thomas 58, 60, 61, 74
McCarthy, Eugene 84
MacDonald, Ramsay 41–3
Machiavelli 256
MacIntyre, Alasdair 141, 144, 147–9, 152
Malthusianism 64
Mannheim, Karl 178, 179
Manor, James 58
Marcuse, Herbert 13
Marshall, T. H. 213
Marx, Karl 17, 42, 99, 105, 107, 110–11, 160–2, 178–9, 187–8, 196, 201

Capital 17, 42, 107
Communist Manifesto, The 107, 160
Critique of the Gotha Programme 111
German Ideology, The 179
Preface to the Critique of Political Economy 161
Marxism 56, 15, 134, 161-2, 167, 196, 231, 268
  heterodox Marxism 70
  Neo-Marxism 166-7, 201
  Post-Marxism 201, 225, 249, 262
  Structuralist Marxism 167
  Western Marxism 13
Mehta, Pherozeshah 64
Mehta, Uday Singh 60
Metcalf, Thomas 58
Mickey Mouse 92
middle class 62, 66, 12, 134, 162, 251
Mill, James 48, 59
  History of British India 59
Mill, John Stuart 10, 11-12, 26, 38, 41, 53, 58-60, 96, 140, 141, 146-153, 154-8
  On Liberty 146, 155, 156
  Utilitarianism 146, 156, 158
Mills, Charles 241, 250-1
Miners Federation of Great Britain (MFGB) 44-6
Miners' Next Step, The 45
Mises, Ludwig von 102, 104
Mitchell, William C. 163
Mohl, Robert von 122
Montagu, Edwin 61
Montesquieu, Charles Louis de Secondat 97
Mont Pèlerin Society 104
Moore, G. E. 142, 145
More, Thomas 17
Morgan, Kenneth 38
Morgan, Kevin 40
Morley, Henry 126
Morris, William 17, 20-1
Mukherjee, Arun 73
multiculturalism 204, 205, 206, 215, 217
Myrdal, Gunnar 90

Naoroji, Dadabhai 64
National Archives, American 79-80
National Front (France) 205, 211-13
national identity 107, 77-94, 211, 212, 217
nationalism 105, 106, 108, 109, 211, 231
  Muslim 67, 68
nationalization *see* public ownership
National Socialism 87, 108, 192
Nation, The 48
Nazism *see* National Socialism
Nehru, Jawaharla 66, 68, 69, 73, 74, 75

Glimpses of World History 68, 69
Neibhur, Reinhold 85, 86, 87
  Children of Light and the Children of Darkness, The 85
neo-capitalism 102
neo-liberalism 98, 101-5, 117-18, 214, 217
New Deal, the (USA) 82, 83
new historicism 143; *see also* historicism
New Labour 36, 205, 213-16
New Left 212, 214, 216, 217, 218
New Republic, The 90
new unionism 40
New York Times 79
Nicholson, Peter 150
Nietzche, Friedrich 95, 144
non-foundationalism 167
non-ideal theory 24-33
Nozick, Robert 241, 245
Nuffield College Social Reconstruction Survey 50

Oakeshott, Michael 168, 170, 229, 248, 254
O'Hanlon, Rosalind 70
Old Labour 213; *see also* Labour Party
Omvedt, Gail 71
organicism 15, 19, 66, 108
Ostrogorski, Moisei 127, 131
Oxford Committee for University Extension 15
Oxford University 9-10, 125
  Centre for Political Ideologies 222, 275
  Department of Politics and International Relations 10
  Mansfield College 10, 261
  St Antony's College 261

Paine, Tom 70
  Rights of Man 70
Pakistan Constituent Assembly 68
Pantham, Thomas 63
Parel, Antony 68
Parliament, Westminster 63
Parsons, Talcott 162
paternalism 58-60, 66
people's movements 114-15
Permanent Settlement of Bengal 59
philosophy; *see also* political philosophy
  continental philosophy 140-1, 144
  moral philosophy 149, 153-8, 187-8, 241-58
  ordinary-language philosophy 169
  rationalism of 265
Philosophy & Public Affairs 253
Phule, Mhatma Jotira 70-2
Physiocrats 101
Plamenatz, John 178

planning, economic 49–51
Plato 144, 188
pluralism 26, 229, 231, 232, 233
Pocock, J. G. A. 143–4, 146
political moralism 215, 216
political parties 3, 4, 119–36, 201, 218, 233, 271
  British approaches to 124–8
  German approaches to 121–4
political philosophy/theory 4, 21, 139–58, 159–77, 225, 241, 243, 245, 246, 248, 249, 250, 251, 254, 255, 257, 261; *see also* ideal theory
  relationship with ideology 159, 161, 165–73, 179–93, 197, 199, 201, 220, 257
political science 13, 104, 124, 164, 197, 200, 218–20, 224–6
Political Theory 156
'political thinking' 266–9
politicians 223, 224, 233
Pombeni, Paolo 3, 271
Popeye 92
Popper, Karl 14, 147
post-structuralism 262, 271
psychoanalysis 167, 191, 192, 193, 262, 274
psychology 13, 20, 21, 25, 29, 32, 149, 184
  psychological theory of politics 121, 122, 123
public ownership 37–52, 101–5, 112; *see also* socialism
public sphere 97
Punchayat 64

Quarterly Review 130, 131
Quesnay, François 96, 101
Qur'an, the 67

race 71, 73, 75, 109
Rainbow Circle 11, 41
Rammohan Roy, Raja 63, 64, 71, 75
Ranade, M. G. 64, 65, 66, 71, 74, 75
  Essays on Indian Economics 64, 65
Raphael, David 169
rationality 121, 190, 193
  irrationalism 120, 172
Rawls, John 2, 4, 11, 13, 14, 21–33, 53, 54, 145–7, 149, 170, 180–2, 183, 184, 186, 188–9, 197–8, 241, 245, 248, 258, 265, 266, 274, 276
  A Theory of Justice 21–8, 145, 152, 156, 158
  'Justice as Fairness' 142
  Political Liberalism 170, 245
Reader's Digest 80
realism 2, 3, 18, 24, 32, 33, 134, 227, 241, 242, 243, 254, 255, 256, 257, 258, 264, 273
'Red Scare' 84

Reform Act (1832) 125
Reform Act (1867) 120, 130
republicanism 224, 227, 230, 233, 234, 235, 236, 237, 240, 256
Republican Party (USA) 89
Riddell, Peter 228
Riesman, David 93
Riley, Jonathan 150
Ripon, Lord 61
Ritchie, D. G. 11, 43
Robinson, Joan 50
Röhmer, Theodor 121, 122
Roosevelt, F. D. 83
Röpke, Wilhelm 102, 103
Rorty, Richard 140–1, 157–8, 167–8
Ross, W. D. 153
  Foundations of Ethics, The 153
Rougier, Louis 102
Rousseau, Jean-Jacques 24, 31, 97
Royal Commission on the Coal Industry (1919) 44–8
Roy, M. N. 70
Rueff, Jacques 102
Russell, Bertrand 142, 145
Russell, Meg 226–7
Russian Revolution (1917) 69; *see also* Soviet communism
Rüstow, Alexander 102, 103

Said, Edward 167
Salisbury, Lord 129–31
Sankey Commission *see* Royal Commission on the Coal Industry (1919)
Sankey, Sir John 44
Sartori, Giovanni 201
satire 91, 92
Scandinavia, politics of 114–16
Scheffler, Samuel 152
Schelsky, Helmut 133
Schlesinger, Arthur 85, 88, 92
  Vital Center 85
Schmitt, Carl 132
Schneewind, J. B. 145, 153–4, 186
  Sidgwick's Ethics and Victorian Moral Philosophy 153, 186
Schultz, Bart 145, 153
Schumpeter, Joseph 201, 218
Scottish Enlightenment, the 215–16
Second World War 80, 85, 87, 102, 103
self-interest 97–9, 110
semiotics 167, 267
Sen, Amartya 113, 152
Shils, Edward 163, 229
Shklar, Judith 54, 55, 56, 57
Sidgwick, Henry 140, 145, 149, 152–8
  The Methods of Ethics 152–4, 158

Index

Simon, Herbert 163
Skinner, Quentin 143, 146, 165; *see also* Cambridge School, the
  Foundations of Modern Political Thought, The 165
Smith, Adam 65, 96–101, 105, 107, 109, 112, 115
  Theory of Moral Sentiments, The 101
  Wealth of Nations, The 97, 99, 101, 107
social Darwinism 108
Social Democratic Party (Germany) 102, 111, 132–4
socialism 2, 17, 23, 34–52, 273
social science 162–4; *see also* political science; sociology
social Spencerianism 108
sociology 13, 162, 270
Soviet communism 78
Soviet Union 49, 92
soziale Marktwirtschaft 103
Spencer, Herbert 66, 108, 109, 154
Stahl, Julius von 122
state ownership *see* public ownership
Stears, Marc 3, 266, 272–3
Stephen, James Fitzjames 48
Stoker, Gerry 228
  Why Politics Matters 228
Stokes, Eric 59, 60
Strath, Bö 3–4, 272, 273
Strauss, Leo 141, 144, 147–8, 152, 168–9, 170, 254
student protests (1968) 120, 136, 211–12
sudras 71, 72
Sumner, Wayne 152
syndicalism 40, 43, 44, 45, 46, 47, 48, 49
swaraj 68
Sweden, politics of 114–15

Tagore, Rabindranath 55
Talshir, Gayil 4–5, 271
Tawney, R. H. 44, 47
Taylor, Charles 145
Thatcher, Margaret 206–8, 213
Third Way, the 214–15, 217
Thompson, Dennis 203
Tocqueville, Alexis de 53, 97, 110–11, 118
  Democracy in America Vol. II 110
totalitarianism 78, 113, 135–6, 201, 229–30

trade unions 99, 100; *see also* Miners Federation of Great Britain
Truman, Harry 79–80
Tully, James 165
Tversky, Amos 184, 195

United States of America, politics of 2, 72, 77–94, 110–11, 115–16, 127–8, 170, 230
  African Americans 90, 91
  American national identity 88
  communism 90, 111
  civil rights 90, 91
Untouchables 72, 73
utilitarianism 59, 144–8, 150–2, 154–8
utopia/utopianism 13–33, 98, 118, 160

Vedic tradition 66, 71
Vincent, Andrew 4, 267–9
virtue 110, 148, 149, 150
Vivekananda, Swami 55, 62
Voeglin, Eric 168
Voltaire 180
Vora, Rajendra 66, 71

Wagner Act (1935) 89
Wallas, Graham 41, 45
Wall, Wendy 85
Webb, Beatrice 40, 50
Webb, Sidney 40, 41–4, 45, 50
Webbs, Beatrice & Sidney 40–1, 50
  Soviet Communism 50
Weber, Max 232, 259, 267
Weeks, Edward 17
Weinstein, David 4, 264, 272
welfare state 23, 37, 104, 133, 134, 135, 136, 213, 215
Whig history 11, 61
Williams, Bernard 149, 241, 244–9, 256
Wittgenstein, Ludwig 141, 169, 188
  Philosophical Investigations 169, 188
  Tractatus Logico-Philosophicus 188
Wolin, Sheldon 263–4
Wright, Tony 228

Yack, Bernard 186
Young, Iris Marion 203

zamindars 59
Žižek, Slavoj 268